W9-ARM-434

Ryan Stephens
Ron Plew
Arie D. Jones

Sams **Teach Yourself**

SQL

in **24** **Hours**

FIFTH EDITION

SAMS   800 East 96th Street, Indianapolis, Indiana, 46240 USA

Sams Teach Yourself SQL in 24 Hours, Fifth Edition

Copyright © 2011 by Pearson Education, Inc.

Oracle and Java are registered trademarks of Oracle and/or its affiliates. Other names may be trademarks of their respective owners.

ISBN-13: 978-0-672-33541-9
ISBN-10: 0-672-33541-7
The Library of Congress cataloging-in-publication data is on file.

Printed in the United States of America
First Printing May 2011

Trademarks

All terms mentioned in this book that are known to be trademarks or service marks have been appropriately capitalized. Sams Publishing cannot attest to the accuracy of this information. Use of a term in this book should not be regarded as affecting the validity of any trademark or service mark.

Warning and Disclaimer

Every effort has been made to make this book as complete and as accurate as possible, but no warranty or fitness is implied. The information provided is on an "as is" basis. The authors and the publisher shall have neither liability nor responsibility to any person or entity with respect to any loss or damages arising from the information contained in this book or from the programs accompanying it.

Bulk Sales

Sams Publishing offers excellent discounts on this book when ordered in quantity for bulk purchases or special sales. For more information, please contact

U.S. Corporate and Government Sales
1-800-382-3419
corpsales@pearsontechgroup.com

For sales outside of the U.S., please contact

International Sales
international@pearson.com

Associate Publisher
Mark Taub

Acquisitions Editor
Trina MacDonald

Development Editor
Michael Thurston

Managing Editor
Kristy Hart

Project Editor
Jovana San Nicolas-Shirley

Copy Editor
The Wordsmithery LLC

Indexer
Lisa Stumpf

Proofreader
Gill Editorial Services

Technical Editor
Benjamin Schupak

Publishing Coordinator
Olivia Basegio

Book Designer
Gary Adair

Composition
Gloria Schurick

Contents at a Glance

Table of Contents

About the Author

For more than 10 years, the authors have studied, applied, and documented the SQL standard and its application to critical database systems in this book.

Ryan Stephens and **Ron Plew** are entrepreneurs, speakers, and cofounders of Perpetual Technologies, Inc. (PTI), a fast-growing IT management and consulting firm. PTI specializes in database technologies, primarily Oracle and SQL servers running on all UNIX, Linux, and Microsoft platforms. Starting out as data analysts and database administrators, Ryan and Ron now lead a team of impressive technical subject matter experts who manage databases for clients worldwide. They authored and taught database courses for Indiana University-Purdue University in Indianapolis for five years and have authored more than a dozen books on Oracle, SQL, database design, and high availability of critical systems.

Arie D. Jones is the principal technology manager for Perpetual Technologies, Inc. (PTI) in Indianapolis, Indiana. Arie leads PTI's team of experts in planning, design, development, deployment, and management of database environments and applications to achieve the best combination of tools and services for each client. He is a regular speaker at technical events and has authored several books and articles pertaining to database-related topics.

Dedication

This book is dedicated to my parents, Thomas and Karlyn Stephens, who always taught me that I can achieve anything if determined. This book is also dedicated to my brilliant son, Daniel, and to my beautiful daughters, Autumn and Alivia; don't ever settle for anything less than your dreams.

—Ryan

This book is dedicated to my family: my wife, Linda; my mother, Betty; my children, Leslie, Nancy, Angela, and Wendy; my grandchildren, Andy, Ryan, Holly, Morgan, Schyler, Heather, Gavin, Regan, Caleigh, and Cameron; and my sons-in-law, Jason and Dallas. Thanks for being patient with me during this busy time. Love all of you.

—Poppy

I would like to dedicate this book to my wife, Jackie, for being understanding and supportive during the long hours that it took to complete this book.

—Arie

Acknowledgments

Thanks to all the people in our lives who have been patient during all editions of this book—mostly to our wives, Tina and Linda. Thanks to Arie Jones for stepping up to the plate and helping so much with this edition. Thanks also to the editorial staff at Sams for all of their hard work to make this edition better than the last. It has been a pleasure to work with each of you.

—Ryan and Ron

We Want to Hear from You!

As the reader of this book, you are our most important critic and commentator. We value your opinion and want to know what we're doing right, what we could do better, what areas you'd like to see us publish in, and any other words of wisdom you're willing to pass our way.

You can email or write me directly to let me know what you did or didn't like about this book—as well as what we can do to make our books stronger.

Please note that I cannot help you with technical problems related to the topic of this book, and that due to the high volume of mail I receive, I might not be able to reply to every message.

When you write, please be sure to include this book's title and author as well as your name and phone or email address. I will carefully review your comments and share them with the author and editors who worked on the book.

Email: opensource@samspublishing.com

Mail: Mark Taub
          Associate Publisher
          Sams Publishing
          800 East 96th Street
          Indianapolis, IN 46240 USA

Reader Services

Visit our website and register this book at informit.com/register for convenient access to any updates, downloads, or errata that might be available for this book.

HOUR 1

Welcome to the World of SQL

What You'll Learn in This Hour:

- ▶ An introduction to and brief history of SQL
- ▶ An introduction to database management systems
- ▶ An overview of some basic terms and concepts
- ▶ An introduction to the database used in this book

Welcome to the world of SQL and the vast, growing database technologies of today's businesses all over the world. By reading this book, you have begun accepting the knowledge that will soon be required for survival in today's world of relational databases and data management. Unfortunately, because it is first necessary to provide the background of SQL and cover some preliminary concepts that you need to know, the majority of this hour is overview before we jump into actual coding. Bear with this hour of the book; this will be exciting, and the "boring stuff" in this hour definitely pays off.

SQL Definition and History

Every modern-day business has data, which requires some organized method or mechanism for maintaining and retrieving the data. When the data is kept within a database, this mechanism is referred to as a *database management system (DBMS)*. Database management systems have been around for years, many of which started out as flat-file systems on a main-frame. With today's technologies, the accepted use of database management systems has begun to flow in other directions, driven by the demands of growing businesses, increased volumes of corporate data, and of course, Internet technologies.

The modern wave of information management is primarily carried out through the use of a *relational database management system (RDBMS)*, derived from the traditional DBMS. Modern databases combined with client/server and web technologies are typical combinations used by current businesses to successfully manage their data and stay competitive in their appropriate markets. The trend for many businesses is to move from a client/server environment to the Web, where location is not a restriction when users need access to important data. The next few sections discuss SQL and the relational database, the most common DBMS implemented today. A good fundamental understanding of the relational database and how to apply SQL to managing data in today's information technology world is important to your understanding of the SQL language.

What Is SQL?

Structured Query Language (SQL) is the standard language used to communicate with a relational database. The prototype was originally developed by IBM using Dr. E.F. Codd's paper ("A Relational Model of Data for Large Shared Data Banks") as a model. In 1979, not long after IBM's prototype, the first SQL product, ORACLE, was released by Relational Software, Incorporated (which was later renamed Oracle Corporation). Today it is one of the distinguished leaders in relational database technologies.

If you travel to a foreign country, you might be required to know that country's language to get around. For example, you might have trouble ordering from a menu via your native tongue if the waiter speaks only his country's language. Look at a database as a foreign land in which you seek information. SQL is the language you use to express your needs to the database. Just as you would order a meal from a menu in another country, you can request specific information from within a database in the form of a query using SQL.

What Is ANSI SQL?

The *American National Standards Institute (ANSI)* is an organization that approves certain standards in many different industries. SQL has been deemed the standard language in relational database communication, originally approved in 1986 based on IBM's implementation. In 1987, the ANSI SQL standard was accepted as the international standard by the *International Standards Organization (ISO)*. The standard was revised again in 1992 (SQL-92) and once again in 1999 (SQL-99). The newest standard is now called SQL-2008, which was officially adopted in July of 2008.

The New Standard: SQL-2008

SQL-2008 has nine interrelated documents, and other documents might be added in the near future as the standard is expanded to encompass newly emerging technology needs. The nine interrelated parts are as follows:

▶ **Part 1: SQL/Framework**—Specifies the general requirements for conformance and defines the fundamental concepts of SQL.

▶ **Part 2: SQL/Foundation**—Defines the syntax and operations of SQL.

▶ **Part 3: SQL/Call-Level Interface**—Defines the interface for application programming to SQL.

▶ **Part 4: SQL/Persistent Stored Modules**—Defines the control structures that then define SQL routines. Part 4 also defines the modules that contain SQL routines.

▶ **Part 9: Management of External Data (SQL/MED)**—Defines extensions to SQL to support the management of external data through the use of data-wrappers and datalink types.

▶ **Part 10: Object Language Bindings**—Defines extensions to the SQL language to support the embedding of SQL statements into programs written in Java.

▶ **Part 11: Information and Definition Schemas**—Defines specifications for the Information Schema and Definition Schema, which provide structural and security information related to SQL data.

▶ **Part 13: Routines and Types Using the Java Programming Language**—Defines the capability to call Java static routines and classes as SQL-invoked routines.

▶ **Part 14: XML-Related Specifications**—Defines ways in which SQL can be used with XML.

The new ANSI standard (SQL-2008) has two levels of minimal compliance that a DBMS may claim: Core SQL Support and Enhanced SQL Support. You can find a link to the ANSI SQL standard on this book's web page, www.informit.com/title/9780672335419.

With any standard comes numerous, obvious advantages, as well as some disadvantages. Foremost, a standard steers vendors in the appropriate industry direction for development. In the case of SQL, a standard provides a basic skeleton of necessary fundamentals, which, as an end result, enables consistency between various implementations and better serves increased portability (not only for database programs, but databases in general and individuals who manage databases).

Some might argue that a standard is not so good, limiting the flexibility and possible capabilities of a particular implementation. However, most vendors who comply with the standard have added product-specific enhancements to standard SQL to fill in these gaps.

A standard is good, considering the advantages and disadvantages. The expected standard demands features that should be available in any complete SQL implementation and outlines basic concepts that not only force consistency between all competitive SQL implementations, but also increase the value of an SQL programmer.

An *SQL implementation* is a particular vendor's SQL product, or RDBMS. It is important to note, as you will hear numerous times in this book, that implementations of SQL vary widely. There is no one implementation that follows the standard completely, although some are mostly ANSI-compliant. It is also important to note that in recent years the list of functionality within the ANSI standard that must be adhered to in order to be considered complaint has not changed dramatically. Hence, when new versions of RDBMS are released, they will most likely claim ANSI SQL compliance.

What Is a Database?

In simple terms, a *database* is a collection of data. Some like to think of a database as an organized mechanism that has the capability of storing information, through which a user can retrieve stored information in an effective and efficient manner.

People use databases every day without realizing it. A phone book is a database. The data contained consists of individuals' names, addresses, and telephone numbers. The listings are alphabetized or indexed, which enables the user to reference a particular local resident with ease. Ultimately, this data is stored in a database somewhere on a computer. After all, each page of a phone book is not manually typed each year a new edition is released.

The database has to be maintained. As people move to different cities or states, entries might have to be added or removed from the phone book. Likewise, entries have to be modified for people changing names, addresses, telephone numbers, and so on. Figure 1.1 illustrates a simple database.

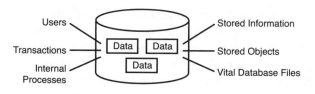

FIGURE 1.1
The database.

The Relational Database

A *relational database* is a database divided into logical units called *tables*, where tables are related to one another within the database. A relational database allows data to be broken down into logical, smaller, manageable units, enabling easier maintenance and providing more optimal database performance according to the level of organization. In Figure 1.2, you can see that tables are related to one another through a common key (data value) in a relational database.

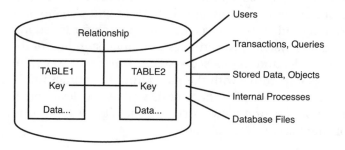

FIGURE 1.2
The relational database.

Again, tables are related in a relational database, allowing adequate data to be retrieved in a single query (although the desired data may exist in more than one table). By having common *keys*, or *fields*, among relational database tables, data from multiple tables can be joined to form one large set of data. As you venture deeper into this book, you see more of a relational database's advantages, including overall performance and easy data access.

Client/Server Technology

In the past, the computer industry was predominately ruled by mainframe computers—large, powerful systems capable of high storage capacity and high data processing capabilities. Users communicated with the mainframe through dumb terminals—terminals that did not think on their own but relied solely on the mainframe's CPU, storage, and memory. Each terminal had a data line attached to the mainframe. The mainframe environment definitely served its purpose and does today in many businesses, but a greater technology was soon to be introduced: the client/server model.

In the *client/server system*, the main computer, called the *server*, is accessible from a network—typically a *local area network (LAN)* or a *wide area network (WAN)*. The server is normally accessed by personal computers (PCs) or by other servers, instead of dumb terminals. Each PC, called a *client*, is provided access to the network, allowing communication between the client and the server, thus explaining the name client/server. The main difference between client/server and mainframe environments is that the user's PC in a client/server environment is capable of thinking on its own, capable of running its own processes using its own CPU and memory, but readily accessible to a server computer through a network. In most cases, a client/server system is much more flexible for today's overall business needs and is much preferred.

Modern database systems reside on various types of computer systems with various operating systems. The most common types of operating systems are Windows-based systems, Linux, and command-line systems such as UNIX. Databases reside mainly in client/server and web environments. A lack of training and experience is the main reason for failed implementations of database systems. Nevertheless, an understanding of the client/server model and web-based systems, which will be explained in the next section, is imperative with the rising (and sometimes unreasonable) demands placed on today's businesses as well as the development of Internet technologies and network computing. Figure 1.3 illustrates the concept of client/server technology.

FIGURE 1.3
The client/
server model.

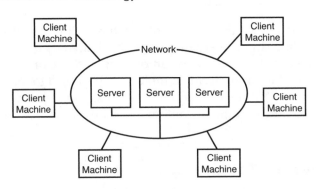

Web-Based Database Systems

Business information systems are moving toward web integration. Databases are now accessible through the Internet, meaning that customers' access to an organization's information is enabled through an Internet browser such as Internet Explorer or Firefox. Customers (users of data) are able to order merchandise, check on inventories, check on the status of orders, make administrative changes to accounts, transfer money from one account to another, and so forth.

A customer simply invokes an Internet browser, goes to the organization's website, logs in (if required by the organization), and uses an application built into the organization's web page to access data. Most organizations require users to register with them and issue a login and password to the customer.

Of course, many things occur behind the scenes when a database is being accessed via a web browser. SQL, for instance, can be executed by the web application. This executed SQL is used to access the organization's database, return data to the web server, and then return that data to the customer's Internet browser.

The basic structure of a web-based database system is similar to that of a client-server system from a user's standpoint (refer to Figure 1.3). Each user has a client machine, which has a connection to the Internet and contains a web browser. The network in Figure 1.3 (in the case of a web-based database) just happens to be the Internet, as opposed to a local network. For the most part, a client is still accessing a server for information. It doesn't matter that the server might exist in another state or even another country. The main point of web-based database systems is to expand the potential customer base of a database system that knows no physical location bounds, thus increasing data availability and an organization's customer base.

Popular Database Vendors

Some of the most predominant database vendors include Oracle, Microsoft, Informix, Sybase, and IBM. These vendors distribute various versions of the relational database for a base license fee and are normally referred to as *closed source*. Many other vendors supply an open-source version of an SQL database (relational database). Some of these vendors include MySQL, PostgresSQL, and SAP. Although many more vendors exist than those mentioned, this list includes names that you might have recognized on the bookshelf, in the newspaper, in magazines, on the stock market, or on the World Wide Web.

Each vendor-specific implementation of SQL is unique in both features and nature. A database server is a product—like any other product on the market—manufactured by a widespread number of vendors. It is to the benefit of the vendor to ensure that its implementation is compliant with the current ANSI standard for portability and user convenience. For instance, if a company is migrating from one database server to another, it would be rather discouraging for the database users to have to learn another language to maintain functionality with the new system.

With each vendor's SQL implementation, however, you find that there are enhancements that serve the purpose for each database server. These enhancements, or *extensions*, are additional commands and options that are simply a bonus to the standard SQL package and available with a specific implementation.

SQL Sessions

An *SQL session* is an occurrence of a user interacting with a relational database through the use of SQL commands. When a user initially connects to the database, a session is established. Within the scope of an SQL session, valid SQL commands can be entered to query the database, manipulate data in the database, and define database structures, such as tables. A session may be invoked by either direct connection to the database or through a front-end application. In both cases, sessions are normally established by a user at a terminal or workstation that communicates through a network with the computer that hosts the database.

CONNECT

When a user connects to a database, the SQL session is initialized. The CONNECT command is used to establish a database connection. With the CONNECT command, you can either invoke a connection or change connections to the database. For example, if you are connected as USER1, you can use the CONNECT command to connect to the database as USER2. When this happens, the SQL session for USER1 is implicitly disconnected. You would normally use the following:

```
CONNECT user@database
```

When you attempt to connect to a database, you are automatically prompted for a password that is associated with your current username. The username is used to authenticate you to the database, and the password is the key that allows entrance.

DISCONNECT and EXIT

When a user disconnects from a database, the SQL session is terminated. The DISCONNECT command is used to disconnect a user from the database. When you disconnect from the database, the software you are using might still appear to be communicating with the database, but you have lost your connection. When you use EXIT to leave the database, your SQL session is terminated, and the software that you are using to access the database is normally closed.

```
DISCONNECT
```

Types of SQL Commands

The following sections discuss the basic categories of commands used in SQL to perform various functions. These functions include building database objects, manipulating objects, populating database tables with data, updating existing data in tables, deleting data, performing database queries, controlling database access, and overall database administration.

The main categories are

- ▶ Data Definition Language (DDL)
- ▶ Data Manipulation Language (DML)
- ▶ Data Query Language (DQL)
- ▶ Data Control Language (DCL)
- ▶ Data administration commands
- ▶ Transactional control commands

Defining Database Structures

Data Definition Language (DDL) is the part of SQL that enables a database user to create and restructure database objects, such as the creation or the deletion of a table.

Some of the most fundamental DDL commands discussed during the following hours include

- ▶ CREATE TABLE
- ▶ ALTER TABLE
- ▶ DROP TABLE
- ▶ CREATE INDEX
- ▶ ALTER INDEX
- ▶ DROP INDEX

▶ CREATE VIEW

▶ DROP VIEW

These commands are discussed in detail during Hour 3, "Managing Database Objects," Hour 17, "Improving Database Performance," and Hour 20, "Creating and Using Views and Synonyms."

Manipulating Data

Data Manipulation Language (DML) is the part of SQL used to manipulate data within objects of a relational database.

The three basic DML commands are

▶ INSERT

▶ UPDATE

▶ DELETE

These commands are discussed in detail during Hour 5, "Manipulating Data."

Selecting Data

Though comprised of only one command, *Data Query Language (DQL)* is the most concentrated focus of SQL for modern relational database users. The base command is SELECT.

This command, accompanied by many options and clauses, is used to compose queries against a relational database. A *query* is an inquiry to the database for information. A query is usually issued to the database through an application interface or via a command-line prompt. You can easily create queries, from simple to complex, from vague to specific.

The SELECT command is discussed in exhilarating detail during Hours 7 through 16.

Data Control Language

Data control commands in SQL enable you to control access to data within the database. These *Data Control Language (DCL)* commands are normally used to create objects related to user access and also control the distribution of privileges among users. Some data control commands are as follows:

- ▶ ALTER PASSWORD

- ▶ GRANT

- ▶ REVOKE

- ▶ CREATE SYNONYM

You will find that these commands are often grouped with other commands and might appear in a number of lessons throughout this book.

Data Administration Commands

Data administration commands enable the user to perform audits and perform analyses on operations within the database. They can also be used to help analyze system performance. Two general data administration commands are as follows:

- ▶ START AUDIT

- ▶ STOP AUDIT

Do not get data administration confused with database administration. *Database administration* is the overall administration of a database, which envelops the use of all levels of commands. *Data administration* is much more specific to each SQL implementation than are those core commands of the SQL language.

Transactional Control Commands

In addition to the previously introduced categories of commands, there are commands that enable the user to manage database transactions:

- ▶ **COMMIT**—Saves database transactions

- ▶ **ROLLBACK**—Undoes database transactions

- ▶ **SAVEPOINT**—Creates points within groups of transactions in which to ROLLBACK

- ▶ **SET TRANSACTION**—Places a name on a transaction

Transactional commands are discussed extensively during Hour 6, "Managing Database Transactions."

The Database Used in This Book

Before continuing with your journey through SQL fundamentals, the next step is introducing the tables and data that you use throughout the course of instruction for the next 23 one-hour lessons. The following sections provide an overview of the specific tables (the database) being used, their relationship to one another, their structure, and examples of the data contained.

Figure 1.4 reveals the relationship between the tables that you use for examples, quiz questions, and exercises in this book. Each table is identified by the table name as well as each residing field in the table. Follow the mapping lines to compare the specific tables' relationship through a common field, in most cases referred to as the *primary key* (discussed in Hour 3).

FIGURE 1.4
Table relationships for this book.

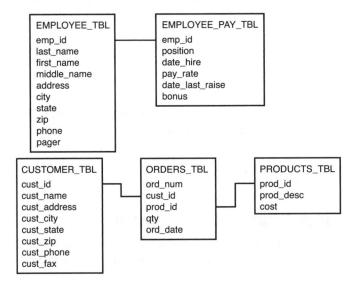

Table-Naming Standards

> **Naming Standards**
>
> You should not only adhere to the object-naming syntax of any SQL implementation, but also follow local business rules and create names that are descriptive and related to the data groupings for the business.

Table-naming standards, as well as any standard within a business, are critical to maintaining control. After studying the tables and data in the previous sections, you probably noticed that each table's suffix is _TBL. This is a naming standard selected for use, such as what's been used at various client sites. The _TBL suffix simply tells you that the object is a table; there are many different types of objects in a relational database. For example, in later hours you see that the suffix _INX is used to identify indexes on tables. Naming standards exist almost exclusively for overall organization and assist immensely in the administration of any relational database. Remember, the use of a suffix is not mandatory when naming database objects. A naming convention is merely used to provide some order when creating objects. You may choose to utilize whatever standard you wish.

A Look at the Data

This section offers a picture of the data contained in each one of the tables used in this book. Take a few minutes to study the data, the variations, and the relationships between the tables and the data. Notice that some fields might not require data, which is specified when each table is created in the database.

EMPLOYEE_TBL

EMP_ID	LAST_NAM	FIRST_NA	M	ADDRESS	CITY	ST	ZIP	PHONE
311549902	STEPHENS	TINA	D	RR 3 BOX 17A	GREENWOOD	IN	47890	3178784465
442346889	PLEW	LINDA	C	3301 BEACON	INDIANAPOLIS	IN	46224	3172978990
213764555	GLASS	BRANDON	S	1710 MAIN ST	WHITELAND	IN	47885	3178984321
313782439	GLASS	JACOB		3789 RIVER BLVD	INDIANAPOLIS	IN	45734	3175457676
220984332	WALLACE	MARIAH		7889 KEYSTONE	INDIANAPOLIS	IN	46741	3173325986
443679012	SPURGEON	TIFFANY		5 GEORGE COURT	INDIANAPOLIS	IN	46234	3175679007

EMPLOYEE_PAY_TBL

EMP_ID	POSITION	DATE_HIRE	PAY_RATE	DATE_LAST	SALARY	BONUS
311549902	MARKETING	23-MAY-1999		01-MAY-2009	4000	
442346889	TEAM LEADER	17-JUN-2000	14.75	01-JUN-2009		
213764555	SALES MANAGER	14-AUG-2004		01-AUG-2009	3000	2000
313782439	SALESMAN	28-JUN-2007			2000	1000

```
220984332 SHIPPER         22-JUL-2006      11 01-JUL-2009
443679012 SHIPPER         14-JAN-2001      15 01-JAN-2009

CUSTOMER_TBL

CUST_ID CUST_NAME        ADDRESS       CUST_CITY    ST ZIP    CUST_PHONE
CUST_FAX
---------------------------------------------------------------------
----
232     LESLIE GLEASON   798 HARDAWAY DR INDIANAPOLIS IN 47856 3175457690

109     NANCY BUNKER     APT A 4556 WATERWAY BROAD RIPPLE IN 47950
3174262323

345     ANGELA DOBKO     RR3 BOX 76 LEBANON       IN 49967 7658970090

090     WENDY WOLF       3345 GATEWAY DR  INDIANAPOLIS IN 46224 3172913421

12      MARYS GIFT SHOP 435 MAIN ST DANVILLE     IL 47978 3178567221
3178523434

432     SCOTTYS MARKET  RR2 BOX 173 BROWNSBURG    IN 45687 3178529835
3178529836

333     JASONS AND DALLAS GOODIES  LAFAYETTE SQ MALL INDIANAPOLIS IN 46222
3172978886 3172978887

21      MORGANS CANDIES AND TREATS 5657 W TENTH ST   INDIANAPOLIS IN 46234
3172714398

43      SCHYLERS NOVELTIES 17 MAPLE ST   LEBANON      IN 48990 3174346758

287     GAVINS PLACE     9880 ROCKVILLE RD  INDIANAPOLIS IN 46244 3172719991
3172719992

288     HOLLYS GAMEARAMA 567 US 31  WHITELAND      IN 49980 3178879023

590     HEATHERS FEATHERS AND THINGS   4090 N SHADELAND AVE INDIANAPOLIS IN
43278 3175456768

610     REGANS HOBBIES  451 GREEN  PLAINFIELD    IN 46818 3178393441
3178399090

560     ANDYS CANDIES   RR 1  BOX 34     NASHVILLE    IN 48756 8123239871

221     RYANS STUFF     2337 S SHELBY ST    INDIANAPOLIS IN 47834
3175634402

175     CAMERON'S PIES   178 N TIBBS AVON IN 46234 3174543390

290     CALEIGH'S KITTENS 244 WEST ST LEBANON IN 47890 3174867754

56      DANIELS SPANIELS 17 MAIN ST GREENWOOD IN 46578 3172319908
```

```
978     AUTUMN'S BASKETS 5648 CENTER ST SOUTHPORT IN 45631 3178887565
```

ORDERS_TBL

ORD_NUM	CUST_ID	PROD_ID	QTY	ORD_DATE
56A901	232	11235	1	22-OCT-2009
56A917	12	907	100	30-SEP-2009
32A132	43	222	25	10-OCT-2009
16C17	090	222	2	17-OCT-2009
18D778	287	90	10	17-OCT-2009
23E934	432	13	20	15-OCT-2009

PRODUCTS_TBL

PROD_ID	PROD_DESC	COST
11235	WITCH COSTUME	29.99
222	PLASTIC PUMPKIN 18 INCH	7.75
13	FALSE PARAFFIN TEETH	1.10
90	LIGHTED LANTERNS	14.50
15	ASSORTED COSTUMES	10.00
9	CANDY CORN	1.35
6	PUMPKIN CANDY	1.45
87	PLASTIC SPIDERS	1.05
119	ASSORTED MASKS	4.95

A Closer Look at What Comprises a Table

The storage and maintenance of valuable data is the reason for any database's existence. You have just viewed the data that is used to explain SQL concepts in this book. The following sections take a closer look at the elements within a table. Remember, a table is the most common and simple form of data storage.

Fields

Every table is broken into smaller entities called fields. A *field* is a column in a table that is designed to maintain specific information about every record in the table. The fields in the PRODUCTS_TBL table consist of PROD_ID, PROD_DESC, and COST. These fields categorize the specific information that is maintained in a given table.

Records, or Rows of Data

A *record*, also called a *row* of data, is each horizontal entry that exists in a table. Looking at the last table, PRODUCTS_TBL, consider the following first record in that table:

```
11235    WITCH COSTUME          29.99
```

The record is obviously composed of a product identification, product description, and unit cost. For every distinct product, there should be a corresponding record in the PRODUCTS_TBL table.

A *row of data* is an entire record in a relational database table.

Columns

A *column* is a vertical entity in a table that contains all information associated with a specific field in a table. For example, a column in the PRODUCTS_TBL having to do with the product description consists of the following:

```
WITCH COSTUME
PLASTIC PUMPKIN 18 INCH
FALSE PARAFFIN TEETH
LIGHTED LANTERNS
ASSORTED COSTUMES
CANDY CORN
PUMPKIN CANDY
PLASTIC SPIDERS
ASSORTED MASKS
```

This column is based on the field PROD_DESC, the product description. A column pulls information about a certain field from every record within a table.

Primary Keys

A *primary key* is a column that makes each row of data in the table unique in a relational database. The primary key in the PRODUCTS_TBL table is PROD_ID, which is typically initialized during the table creation process. The nature of the primary key is to ensure that all product identifications are unique, so that each record in the PRODUCTS_TBL table has its own PROD_ID. Primary keys alleviate the possibility of a duplicate record in a table and are used in other ways, which you will read about in Hour 3.

NULL Values

NULL is the term used to represent a missing value. A *NULL value* in a table is a value in a field that appears to be blank. A field with a NULL value is a field with no value. It is important to understand that a NULL value is different from a zero value or a field that contains spaces. A field with a NULL value is one that has been left blank during record creation. Notice that in the EMPLOYEE_TBL table, not every employee has a middle initial. Those records for employees who do not have an entry for middle initial signify a NULL value.

Additional table elements are discussed in detail during the next two hours.

Examples and Exercises

Many exercises in this book use the MySQL, Microsoft SQL Server, and Oracle databases to generate the examples. We decided to concentrate on these three database implementations because they allow freely distributed versions of their database to be available. This enables you to select an implementation of your choice, install it, and follow along with the exercises in the book. Note that because these databases are not 100% compliant to SQL-2008, the exercises might present slight variations or nonadoption of the ANSI standard. However, by learning the basics of the ANSI standard, you will be able in most cases to easily translate your skills between different database implementations.

Summary

You have been introduced to the standard language of SQL and have been given a brief history and thumbnail of how the standard has evolved over the past several years. Database systems and current technologies were also discussed, including the relational database, client/server systems, and web-based database systems, all of which are vital to your understanding of SQL. The main SQL language components and the fact that there are numerous players in the relational database market, and likewise, many different flavors of SQL, were discussed. Despite ANSI SQL variations, most vendors do comply to some extent with the current standard (SQL-2008), rendering consistency across the board and forcing the development of portable SQL applications.

The database that is used during your course of study was also introduced. The database, as you have seen it so far, has consisted of a few tables (which are related to one another) and the data that each table contains at this point (at the end of Hour 1). You should have acquired some overall background knowledge of the fundamentals of SQL and should understand the concept of a modern database. After a few refreshers in the Workshop for this hour, you should feel confident about continuing to the next hour.

Q&A

Q. *If I learn SQL, will I be able to use any of the implementations that use SQL?*

A. Yes, you will be able to communicate with a database whose implementation is ANSI SQL compliant. If an implementation is not completely compliant, you should be able to pick it up quickly with some adjustments.

Q. *In a client/server environment, is the personal computer the client or the server?*

A. The personal computer is known as the client, although a server can also serve as a client.

Q. *Do I have to use _TBL for each table I create?*

A. Certainly not. The use of _TBL is a standard chosen for use to name and easily identify the tables in your database. You could spell out TBL as TABLE, or you might want to avoid using a suffix. For example, EMPLOYEE TBL could simply be EMPLOYEE.

Workshop

The following workshop is composed of a series of quiz questions and practical exercises. The quiz questions are designed to test your overall understanding of the current material. The practical exercises are intended to afford you the opportunity to apply the concepts discussed during the current hour, as well as build upon the knowledge acquired in previous hours of study. Please take time to complete the quiz questions and exercises before continuing. Refer to Appendix C, "Answers to Quizzes and Exercises," for answers.

Quiz

1. What does the acronym SQL stand for?
2. What are the six main categories of SQL commands?
3. What are the four transactional control commands?
4. What is the main difference between client/server and web technologies as they relate to database access?
5. If a field is defined as NULL, does something have to be entered into that field?

Exercises

1. Identify the categories in which the following SQL commands fall:

```
CREATE TABLE
DELETE
SELECT
```

```
INSERT
ALTER TABLE
UPDATE
```

2. Study the following tables, and pick out the column that would be a good candidate for the primary key:

EMPLOYEE_TBL	INVENTORY_TBL	EQUIPMENT_TBL
name	item	model
phone	description	year
start date	quantity	serial number
address	item number	equipment number
employee number	location	assigned to

3. Refer to Appendix B, "Using the Databases for Exercises." Download and install one of the three database implementations on your computer to prepare for hands-on exercises in the following hours of instruction.

HOUR 2

Defining Data Structures

What You'll Learn in This Hour:

▶ A look at the underlying data of a table
▶ An introduction to the basic data types
▶ Instruction on the use of various data types
▶ Examples depicting differences between data types

In this second hour, you learn more about the data you viewed at the end of Hour 1, "Welcome to the World of SQL." You learn the characteristics of the data and how such data is stored in a relational database. There are several data types, as you'll soon discover.

What Is Data?

Data is a collection of information stored in a database as one of several different data types. Data includes names, numbers, dollar amounts, text, graphics, decimals, figures, calculations, summarization, and just about anything else you can possibly imagine. Data can be stored in uppercase, lowercase, or mixed case. Data can be manipulated or changed; most data does not remain static for its lifetime.

Data types are used to provide rules for data for particular columns. A data type deals with the way values are stored in a column as far as the length allocated for a column and whether values such as alphanumeric, numeric, and date and time data are allowed. There is a data type for every possible bit or combination of data that can be stored in a particular database. These data types are used to store data such as characters, numbers, date and time, images, and other binary data. More specifically, the data might consist of names, descriptions, numbers, calculations, images, image descriptions, documents, and so forth.

The data is the purpose of any database and must be protected. The protector of the data is normally the *database administrator (DBA)*, although it is every database user's responsibility to ensure that measures are taken to protect data. Data security is discussed in depth in Hour 18, "Managing Database Users," and Hour 19, "Managing Database Security."

Basic Data Types

The following sections discuss the basic data types supported by ANSI SQL. Data types are characteristics of the data itself, whose attributes are placed on fields within a table. For example, you can specify that a field must contain numeric values, disallowing the entering of alphanumeric strings. After all, you would not want to enter alphabetic characters in a field for a dollar amount. Defining each field in the database with a data type eliminates much of the incorrect data found in a database due to data entry errors. *Field definition* (data type definition) is a form of data validation that controls the type of data that may be entered into each given field.

Depending on your implementation of *relational database management system (RDBMS)*, certain data types can be converted automatically to other data types depending upon their format. This type of conversion in known as an *implicit conversion*, which means that the database handles the conversion for you. An example of this is taking a numeric value of 1000.92 from a numeric field and inputting it into a string field. Other data types cannot be converted implicitly by the host RDBMS and therefore must undergo an explicit conversion. This usually involves the use of an SQL function, such as CAST or CONVERT. For example

```
SELECT CAST('12/27/1974' AS DATETIME) AS MYDATE
```

The very basic data types, as with most other languages, are

- ▶ String types
- ▶ Numeric types
- ▶ Date and time types

SQL Data Types

Every implementation of SQL seems to have its own specific set of data types. The use of implementation-specific data types is necessary to support the philosophy of each implementation on how to handle the storage of data. However, the basics are the same among all implementations.

Fixed-Length Strings

Constant characters, those strings that always have the same length, are stored using a fixed-length data type. The following is the standard for an SQL fixed-length character:

```
CHARACTER(n)
```

n represents a number identifying the allocated or maximum length of the particular field with this definition.

Some implementations of SQL use the CHAR data type to store fixed-length data. You can store alphanumeric data in this data type. An example of a constant length data type would be for a state abbreviation because all state abbreviations are two characters.

Spaces are normally used to fill extra spots when using a fixed-length data type; if a field's length was set to 10 and data entered filled only 5 places, the remaining 5 spaces would be recorded as spaces. The padding of spaces ensures that each value in a field is a fixed length.

Fixed-Length Data Types

Be careful not to use a fixed-length data type for fields that might contain varying-length values, such as an individual's name. If you use the fixed-length data type inappropriately, you eventually encounter problems such as the waste of available space and the inability to make accurate comparisons between data.

Always use the varying-length data type for nonconstant character strings to save database space.

Watch Out!

Varying-Length Strings

SQL supports the use of *varying-length strings*, strings whose length is not constant for all data. The following is the standard for an SQL varying-length character:

```
CHARACTER VARYING(n)
```

n represents a number identifying the allocated or maximum length of the particular field with this definition.

Common data types for variable-length character values are the VARCHAR, VARBINARY, and VARCHAR2 data types. VARCHAR is the ANSI standard, which Microsoft SQL Server and MySQL use; Oracle uses both VARCHAR and VARCHAR2. The data stored in a character-defined column can be alphanumeric, which means that the data value may contain numeric characters. VARBINARY is similar to VARCHAR and VARCHAR2 except that it contains a variable length of bytes. Normally, you would use a type such as this to store some kind of digital data such as possibly an image file.

Remember that fixed-length data types typically pad spaces to fill in allocated places not used by the field. The varying-length data type does not work this way. For instance, if the allocated length of a varying-length field is 10, and a string of 5 characters is entered, the total length of that particular value would be only 5. Spaces are not used to fill unused places in a column.

Large Object Types

Some variable-length data types need to hold longer lengths of data than what is traditionally reserved for a VARCHAR field. The BLOB and TEXT data types are two examples of such data types in modern database implementations. These data types are specifically made to hold large sets of data. The BLOB is a binary large object, so its data is treated as a large binary string (a byte string). A BLOB is especially useful in an implementation that needs to store binary media files in the database, such as images or MP3s.

The TEXT data type is a large character string data type that can be treated as a large VARCHAR field. It is often used when an implementation needs to store large sets of character data in the database. An example of this would be storing HTML input from the entries of a blog site. Storing this type of data in the database enables the site to be dynamically updated.

Numeric Types

Numeric values are stored in fields that are defined as some type of number, typically referred to as NUMBER, INTEGER, REAL, DECIMAL, and so on.

The following are the standards for SQL numeric values:

- ▶ BIT(n)
- ▶ BIT VARYING(n)
- ▶ DECIMAL(p,s)
- ▶ INTEGER
- ▶ SMALLINT
- ▶ BIGINT
- ▶ FLOAT(p,s)
- ▶ DOUBLE PRECISION(p,s)
- ▶ REAL(s)

p represents a number identifying the allocated or maximum length of the particular field for each appropriate definition.

s is a number to the right of the decimal point, such as 34.*ss*.

A common numeric data type in SQL implementations is NUMERIC, which accommodates the direction for numeric values provided by ANSI. Numeric values can be stored as zero, positive, negative, fixed, and floating-point numbers. The following is an example using NUMERIC:

```
NUMERIC(5)
```

This example restricts the maximum value entered in a particular field to 99999. Note that all the database implementations that we use for the examples support the NUMERIC type but implement it as a DECIMAL.

Decimal Types

Decimal values are numeric values that include the use of a decimal point. The standard for a decimal in SQL follows, where *p* is the precision and *s* is the decimal's scale:

```
DECIMAL(p,s)
```

The *precision* is the total length of the numeric value. In a numeric defined DECIMAL(4,2), the precision is 4, which is the total length allocated for a numeric value. The *scale* is the number of digits to the right of the decimal point. The scale is 2 in the previous DECIMAL(4,2) example. If a value has more places to the right side of the decimal point than the scale allows, the value is rounded; for instance, 34.33 inserted into a DECIMAL(3,1) is typically rounded to 34.3.

If a numeric value was defined as the following data type, the maximum value allowed would be 99.99:

```
DECIMAL(4,2)
```

The precision is 4, which represents the total length allocated for an associated value. The scale is 2, which represents the number of *places*, or *bytes*, reserved to the right side of the decimal point. The decimal point does not count as a character.

Allowed values for a column defined as DECIMAL(4,2) include the following:

- 12

- 12.4

▶ 12.44

▶ 12.449

The last numeric value, 12.449, is rounded off to 12.45 upon input into the column. In this case, any numbers between 12.445 and 12.449 would be rounded to 12.45.

Integers

An *integer* is a numeric value that does not contain a decimal, only whole numbers (both positive and negative).

Valid integers include the following:

▶ 1

▶ 0

▶ −1

▶ 99

▶ −99

▶ 199

Floating-Point Decimals

Floating-point decimals are decimal values whose precision and scale are variable lengths and virtually without limit. Any precision and scale is acceptable. The REAL data type designates a column with single-precision, floating-point numbers. The DOUBLE PRECISION data type designates a column that contains double-precision, floating-point numbers. To be considered a single-precision floating point, the precision must be between 1 and 21 inclusive. To be considered a double-precision floating point, the precision must be between 22 and 53 inclusive. The following are examples of the FLOAT data type:

▶ FLOAT

▶ FLOAT(15)

▶ FLOAT(50)

Date and Time Types

Date and time data types are quite obviously used to keep track of information concerning dates and time. Standard SQL supports what are called DATETIME data types, which include the following specific data types:

▶ DATE

▶ TIME

▶ DATETIME

▶ TIMESTAMP

The elements of a DATETIME data type consist of the following:

▶ YEAR

▶ MONTH

▶ DAY

▶ HOUR

▶ MINUTE

▶ SECOND

Date and Time Types

The SECOND element can also be broken down to fractions of a second. The range is from 00.000 to 61.999, although some implementations of SQL might not support this range. The extra 1.999 seconds is used for leap seconds.

Be aware that each implementation of SQL might have its own customized data type for dates and times. The previous data types and elements are standards to which each SQL vendor should adhere, but be advised that most implementations have their own data type for date values, varying in both appearance and the way date information is actually stored internally.

A length is not normally specified for a date data type. Later in this hour, you learn more about dates, how date information is stored in some implementations, and how to manipulate dates and times using conversion functions. You also study practical examples of how dates and times are used in the real world.

Literal Strings

A *literal string* is a series of characters, such as a name or a phone number, that is explicitly specified by a user or program. Literal strings consist of data with the same attributes as the previously discussed data types, but the value of the string is known. The value of a column is usually unknown because a column typically has a different value associated with each row of data in a table.

You do not actually specify data types with literal strings—you simply specify the string. Some examples of literal strings follow:

► 'Hello'

► 45000

► "45000"

► 3.14

► 'November 1, 1997'

The alphanumeric strings are enclosed by single quotation marks, whereas the number value 45000 is not. Also notice that the second numeric value of 45000 is enclosed by quotation marks. Generally speaking, character strings require quotation marks, whereas numeric strings don't.

The process that converts a number into a numeric type is known as an *implicit conversion*. This means that the database attempts to figure out what type it needs to create for the object. So if you do not have a number enclosed with single quotation marks, the SQL compiler assumes that you want a numeric type. You need to be careful when working with data to ensure that the data is being represented as you want it to be. Otherwise, it might skew your results or result in an unexpected error. You see later how literal strings are used with database queries.

NULL Data Types

As you should know from Hour 1, a NULL value is a missing value or a column in a row of data that has not been assigned a value. NULL values are used in nearly all parts of SQL, including the creation of tables, search conditions for queries, and even in literal strings.

The following are two methods for referencing a NULL value:

► NULL (the keyword NULL itself)

The following does not represent a NULL value, but a literal string containing the characters N-U-L-L:

```
'NULL'
```

When using the NULL data type, it is important to realize that data is not required in a particular field. If data is always required for a given field, always use NOT NULL with a data type. If there is a chance that there might not always be data for a field, it is better to use NULL.

BOOLEAN Values

A BOOLEAN value is a value of TRUE, FALSE, or NULL. BOOLEAN values are used to make data comparisons. For example, when criteria are specified for a query, each condition evaluates to a TRUE, FALSE, or NULL. If the BOOLEAN value of TRUE is returned by all conditions in a query, data is returned. If a BOOLEAN value of FALSE or NULL is returned, data might not be returned.

Consider the following example:

```
WHERE NAME = 'SMITH'
```

This line might be a condition found in a query. The condition is evaluated for every row of data in the table that is being queried. If the value of NAME is SMITH for a row of data in the table, the condition returns the value TRUE, thereby returning the data associated with that record.

Most database implementations do not implement a strict BOOLEAN type and instead opt to use their own methodology. MySQL contains the BOOLEAN type but it is merely a synonym for their existing TINYINT type. Oracle prefers to direct its users to use a CHAR(1) value to denote a BOOLEAN, and Microsoft SQL Server uses a value known as BIT.

By the Way

Differences in Data Type Implementations

Some of the data types mentioned during this hour might not be available by name in the implementation of SQL that you are using. Data types are often named differently among implementations of SQL, but the concept behind each data type remains. Most, if not all, data types are supported by relational databases.

User-Defined Types

A *user-defined type* is a data type that the user defines. User-defined types allow users to customize their own data types to meet data storage needs and are based on existing data types. User-defined data types can assist the developer by providing greater flexibility during database application development because they maximize the number of possibilities for data storage. The CREATE TYPE statement is used to create a user-defined type.

For example, you can create a type as follows in both MySQL and Oracle:

```
CREATE TYPE PERSON AS OBJECT
(NAME       VARCHAR (30),
 SSN        VARCHAR (9));
```

You can reference your user-defined type as follows:

```
CREATE TABLE EMP_PAY
(EMPLOYEE   PERSON,
 SALARY     DECIMAL(10,2),
 HIRE_DATE  DATE);
```

Notice that the data type referenced for the first column EMPLOYEE is PERSON. PERSON is the user-defined type you created in the first example.

Domains

A *domain* is a set of valid data types that can be used. A domain is associated with a data type, so only certain data is accepted. After you create a domain, you can add constraints to the domain. Constraints work in conjunction with data types, allowing you to further specify acceptable data for a field. The domain is used like the user-defined type.

You can create a domain as follows:

```
CREATE DOMAIN MONEY_D AS NUMBER(8,2);
```

You can add constraints to your domain as follows:

```
ALTER DOMAIN MONEY_D
ADD CONSTRAINT MONEY_CON1
CHECK (VALUE > 5);
```

You can reference the domain as follows:

```
CREATE TABLE EMP_PAY
(EMP_ID      NUMBER(9),
 EMP_NAME    VARCHAR2(30),
 PAY_RATE    MONEY_D);
```

Summary

Several data types are available with SQL. If you have programmed in other languages, you probably recognize many of the data types mentioned. Data types allow different types of data to be stored in the database, ranging from simple characters to decimal points to date and time. The concept of data types is the same in all languages, whether programming in a third-generation language such as C and passing variables or using a relational database implementation and coding in SQL. Of course, each implementation has its own names for standard data types, but they basically work the same. Also remember that an RDBMS does not have to implement all of the data types in the ANSI standard to be considered ANSI compliant. Therefore, it is prudent to check with the documentation of your specific RDBMS implementation to see what options you have available.

You must take care in planning for both the near and distant future when deciding on data types, lengths, scales, and precisions in which to store your data. Business rules and how you want the end user to access the data are other factors in deciding on specific data types. You should know the nature of the data and how data in the database is related to assign proper data types.

Q&A

Q. *How is it that I can enter numbers such as a person's Social Security number in fields defined as character fields?*

A. Numeric values are still alphanumeric, which are allowed in string data types. The process is called an implicit conversion because the database system handles it automatically. Typically, the only data stored as numeric values are values used in computations. However, it might be helpful for some to define all numeric fields with a numeric data type to help control the data entered in that field.

Q. *I still do not understand the difference between constant-length and varying-length data types. Can you explain?*

A. Say you have an individual's last name defined as a constant-length data type with a length of 20 bytes. Suppose the individual's name is Smith. When the data is inserted into the table, 20 bytes are taken: 5 for the name, and 15 for the extra spaces. (Remember that this is a constant-length data type.) If you use a varying-length data type with a length of 20 and insert `Smith`, only 5 bytes of space are taken. If you then imagine that you are inserting 100,000 rows of data into this system, you could possibly save 1.5 million bytes of data.

Q. *Are there limits on the lengths of data types?*

A. Yes, there are limits on the lengths of data types, and they do vary among the various implementations.

Workshop

The following workshop is composed of a series of quiz questions and practical exercises. The quiz questions are designed to test your overall understanding of the current material. The practical exercises are intended to afford you the opportunity to apply the concepts discussed during the current hour, as well as build upon the knowledge acquired in previous hours of study. Please take time to complete the quiz questions and exercises before continuing. Refer to Appendix C, "Answers to Quizzes and Exercises," for answers.

Quiz

1. True or false: An individual's Social Security number, entered in the format '111111111', can be any of the following data types: constant-length character, varying-length character, or numeric.

2. True or false: The scale of a numeric value is the total length allowed for values.

3. Do all implementations use the same data types?

4. What are the precision and scale of the following?

   ```
   DECIMAL(4,2)
   DECIMAL(10,2)
   DECIMAL(14,1)
   ```

5. Which numbers could be inserted into a column whose data type is `DECIMAL(4,1)`?

   A. `16.2`

   B. `116.2`

   C. `16.21`

   D. `1116.2`

   E. `1116.21`

6. What is data?

Exercises

1. Take the following column titles, assign them to a data type, decide on the proper length, and give an example of the data you would enter into that column.

    A. ssn

    B. state

    C. city

    D. phone_number

    E. zip

    F. last_name

    G. first_name

    H. middle_name

    I. salary

    J. hourly_pay_rate

    K. date_hired

2. Take the same column titles and decide whether they should be NULL or NOT NULL, realizing that in some cases where a column would normally be NOT NULL, the column could be NULL or vice versa, depending on the application.

    A. ssn

    B. state

    C. city

    D. phone_number

    E. zip

    F. last_name

    G. first_name

    H. middle_name

    I. salary

    J. hourly_pay_rate

    K. date_hired

3. We are going to set up a database to use for the subsequent hours in this book. Remember that you have to have installed one of the three database implementations—MySQL, Oracle, or Microsoft SQL Server—before continuing:

MySQL

From Windows Explorer, go to the folder where you installed MySQL on your computer. Double-click on the `bin` folder, and then double-click on the executable file called `mysql.exe`. If you receive an error stating that `the server could not be found`, first execute `winmysqladmin.exe` from the `bin` folder, and then enter a username and password. After the server is started, execute `mysql.exe` from the `bin` folder.

At the `mysql>` command prompt, enter the following command to create a database to use for this book's exercises:

```
create database learnsql;
```

Be sure to press the Enter key on your keyboard after entering the command.

For all subsequent hands-on exercises in this book, you double-click on the `mysql.exe` executable and then enter the following command to use the database you just created:

```
use learnsql;
```

Oracle

Open your web browser and navigate to the administration home page, which is typically located at http://127.0.0.1:8080/apex. At the login prompt, if this is the first time that you are logging into the system, use `system` as the username and the password that you set up during the installation. From the administration screen you can select SQL, SQL Commands, Enter Command. Now in the command window, input the following command and click the Run button:

```
create user learnsql identified by learnsql_2010;
```

In Oracle, when you create a user, the RDMS automatically creates a schema. So with this command you not only created a user for querying the data but a schema named `learnsql`. Oracle treats the schema in much the same way that MySQL and Microsoft SQL Server treat a database. You can view your schema by simply logging out and then logging back in as the newly created user.

Microsoft

From the Start menu, type SSMS.exe into the Run box and press Enter. This brings up SQL Server Management Studio. The first dialog box to open is for your database connection. If it is not already filled in with localhost as the server name, type localhost into the box. Leave the other values such as Windows Authentication as they are, and click the Connect button. On the left side of the screen is an area called Object Explorer showing your localhost database instance. Right-click on localhost and select New Query. This opens a query window in the right pane. Now type the following command and press F5:

```
Create database learnsql;
```

Then right-click the folder underneath localhost that's labeled Databases and select Refresh. Now if you expand the folder tree by clicking on the + symbol, you should see your learnsql database.

Managing Database Objects

What You'll Learn in This Hour:

- ▶ An introduction to database objects
- ▶ An introduction to the schema
- ▶ An introduction to the table
- ▶ A discussion of the nature and attributes of tables
- ▶ Examples for the creation and manipulation of tables
- ▶ A discussion of table storage options
- ▶ Concepts on referential integrity and data consistency

In this hour, you learn about database objects: what they are, how they act, how they are stored, and how they relate to one another. Database objects are the logical units that compose the building blocks of the database. The majority of the instruction during this hour revolves around the table, but keep in mind that there are other database objects, many of which are discussed in later hours of study.

What Are Database Objects?

A *database object* is any defined object in a database that is used to store or reference data. Some examples of database objects include tables, views, clusters, sequences, indexes, and synonyms. The table is this hour's focus because it is the primary and simplest form of data storage in a relational database.

What Is a Schema?

A *schema* is a collection of database objects normally associated with one particular database username. This username is called the *schema owner*, or the owner of the related group of objects. You may have one or multiple schemas in a database. The user is only associated with the schema of the same name, and often the terms are used interchangeably. Basically, any user who creates an object has just created it in her own schema unless she specifically instructs it to be created in another one. So, based on a user's privileges within the database, the user has control over objects that are created, manipulated, and deleted. A schema can consist of a single table and has no limits to the number of objects that it may contain, unless restricted by a specific database implementation.

Say you have been issued a database username and password by the database administrator. Your username is USER1. Suppose you log on to the database and then create a table called EMPLOYEE_TBL. According to the database, your table's actual name is USER1.EMPLOYEE_TBL. The schema name for that table is USER1, which is also the owner of that table. You have just created the first table of a schema.

The good thing about schemas is that when you access a table that you own (in your own schema), you do not have to refer to the schema name. For instance, you could refer to your table as either one of the following:

```
EMPLOYEE_TBL
USER1.EMPLOYEE_TBL
```

The first option is preferred because it requires fewer keystrokes. If another user were to query one of your tables, the user would have to specify the schema as follows:

```
USER1.EMPLOYEE_TBL
```

In Hour 20, "Creating and Using Views and Synonyms," you learn about the distribution of permissions so that other users can access your tables. You also learn about synonyms, which enable you to give a table another name so you do not have to specify the schema name when accessing a table. Figure 3.1 illustrates two schemas in a relational database.

There are, in Figure 3.1, two user accounts in the database that own tables: USER1 and USER2. Each user account has its own schema. Some examples for how the two users can access their own tables and tables owned by the other user follow:

```
USER1 accesses own TABLE1:            TABLE1

USER1 accesses own TEST:              TEST

USER1 accesses USER2's TABLE10:       USER2.TABLE10

USER1 accesses USER2's TEST:          USER2.TEST
```

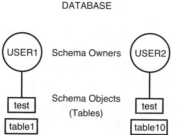

FIGURE 3.1
Schemas in a
database.

In this example, both users have a table called TEST. Tables can have the same names in a database as long as they belong to different schemas. If you look at it this way, table names are always unique in a database because the schema owner is actually part of the table name. For instance, USER1.TEST is a different table than USER2.TEST. If you do not specify a schema with the table name when accessing tables in a database, the database server looks for a table that you own by default. That is, if USER1 tries to access TEST, the database server looks for a USER1-owned table named TEST before it looks for other objects owned by USER1, such as synonyms to tables in another schema. Hour 21, "Working with the System Catalog," helps you fully understand how synonyms work.

You must be careful to understand the distinction between objects in your own schema and those objects in another schema. If you do not provide a schema when performing operations that alter the table, such as a DROP command, the database assumes that you mean a table in your own schema. This could possibly lead to your unintentionally dropping the wrong object. So you must always pay careful attention as to which user you are currently logged into the database with.

Object Naming Rules Differ Between Systems

Every database server has rules concerning how you can name objects and elements of objects, such as field names. You must check your particular implementation for the exact naming conventions or rules.

Watch
Out!

Tables: The Primary Storage for Data

The table is the primary storage object for data in a relational database. In its simplest form, a table consists of row(s) and column(s), both of which hold the data. A table takes up physical space in a database and can be permanent or temporary.

Columns

A *field*, also called a *column* in a relational database, is part of a table that is assigned a specific data type. The data type determines what kind of data the column is allowed to hold. This enables the designer of the table to help maintain the integrity of the data.

Every database table must consist of at least one column. Columns are those elements within a table that hold specific types of data, such as a person's name or address. For example, a valid column in a customer table might be the customer's name. Figure 3.2 illustrates a column in a table.

FIGURE 3.2
An example of a column.

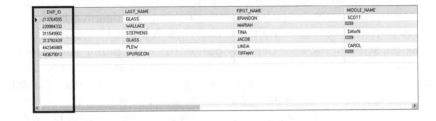

Generally, a column name must be one continuous string and can be limited to the number of characters used according to each implementation of SQL. It is typical to use underscores with names to provide separation between characters. For example, a column for the customer's name can be named CUSTOMER_NAME instead of CUSTOMERNAME. This is normally done to increase the readability of database objects. There are other naming conventions that you can utilize, such as Camel Case, to fit your specific preferences. As such, it is important for a database development team to agree upon a standard naming convention and stick to it so that order is maintained within the development process.

The most common form of data stored within a column is string data. This data can be stored as either uppercase or lowercase for character-defined fields. The case that you use for data is simply a matter of preference, which should be based on how the data will be used. In many cases, data is stored in uppercase for simplicity and consistency. However, if data is stored in different case types throughout the database (uppercase, lowercase, and mixed case), functions can be applied to convert the data to either uppercase or lowercase if needed. These functions are covered in Hour 11, "Restructuring the Appearance of Data."

Columns also can be specified as NULL or NOT NULL, meaning that if a column is NOT NULL, something must be entered. If a column is specified as NULL, nothing has to be entered. NULL is different from an empty set, such as an empty string, and holds a special place in database design. As such, you can relate a NULL value to a lack of any data in the field.

Rows

A *row* is a record of data in a database table. For example, a row of data in a customer table might consist of a particular customer's identification number, name, address, phone number, and fax number. A row is composed of fields that contain data from one record in a table. A table can contain as little as one row of data and up to as many as millions of rows of data or records. Figure 3.3 illustrates a row within a table.

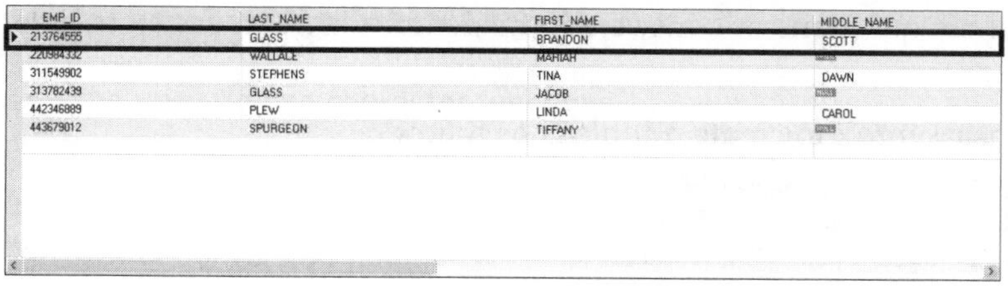

FIGURE 3.3
Example of a table row.

The CREATE TABLE Statement

The CREATE TABLE statement in SQL is used to create a table. Although the very act of creating a table is quite simple, much time and effort should be put into planning table structures before the actual execution of the CREATE TABLE statement. Carefully planning your table structure before implementation saves you from having to reconfigure things after they are in production.

> **Types We Use in This Hour**
>
> In this hour's examples, we use the popular data types CHAR (constant-length character), VARCHAR (variable-length character), NUMBER (numeric values, decimal, and nondecimal), and DATE (date and time values).

By the Way

Some elementary questions need to be answered when creating a table:

- ▶ What type of data will be entered into the table?
- ▶ What will be the table's name?
- ▶ What column(s) will compose the primary key?
- ▶ What names shall be given to the columns (fields)?

▶ What data type will be assigned to each column?

▶ What will be the allocated length for each column?

▶ Which columns in a table can be left as a null value?

By the Way

> **Existing Systems Often Have Existing Naming Rules**
>
> Be sure to check your implementation for rules when naming objects and other database elements. Often database administrators adopt a *naming convention* that explains how to name the objects within the database so you can easily discern how they are used.

After these questions are answered, the actual CREATE TABLE statement is simple.

The basic syntax to create a table is as follows:

```
CREATE TABLE table_name
( field1   data_type  [ not null ],
  field2   data_type  [ not null ],
  field3   data_type  [ not null ],
  field4   data_type  [ not null ],
  field5   data_type  [ not null ] );
```

Note that a semicolon is the last character in the previous statement. Also, brackets indicate portions that are optional. Most SQL implementations have some character that terminates a statement or submits a statement to the database server. Oracle, Microsoft SQL Server, and MySQL use the semicolon. Although Transact-SQL, Microsoft SQL Server's ANSI SQL version, has no such requirement, it is considered best practice to use it. This book uses the semicolon.

Create a table called EMPLOYEE_TBL in the following example using the syntax for MySQL:

```
CREATE TABLE EMPLOYEE_TBL
(EMP_ID        CHAR(9)       NOT NULL,
 EMP_NAME      VARCHAR (40)  NOT NULL,
 EMP_ST_ADDR   VARCHAR (20)  NOT NULL,
 EMP_CITY      VARCHAR (15)  NOT NULL,
 EMP_ST        CHAR(2)       NOT NULL,
 EMP_ZIP       INTEGER(5)    NOT NULL,
 EMP_PHONE     INTEGER(10)   NULL,
 EMP_PAGER     INTEGER(10)   NULL);
```

The following code would be the compatible code for both Microsoft SQL Server and Oracle:

```
CREATE TABLE EMPLOYEE_TBL
(EMP_ID          CHAR(9)       NOT NULL,
 EMP_NAME        VARCHAR (40)  NOT NULL,
 EMP_ST_ADDR     VARCHAR (20)  NOT NULL,
 EMP_CITY        VARCHAR (15)  NOT NULL,
 EMP_ST          CHAR(2)       NOT NULL,
 EMP_ZIP         INTEGER       NOT NULL,
 EMP_PHONE       INTEGER       NULL,
 EMP_PAGER       INTEGER       NULL);
```

Eight different columns make up this table. Notice the use of the underscore character to break the column names up into what appears to be separate words (EMPLOYEE ID is stored as EMP_ID). This is a technique that is used to make table or column name more readable. Each column has been assigned a specific data type and length, and by using the NULL/NOT NULL constraint, you have specified which columns require values for every row of data in the table. The EMP_PHONE is defined as NULL, meaning that NULL values are allowed in this column because there might be individuals without a telephone number. The information concerning each column is separated by a comma, with parentheses surrounding all columns (a left parenthesis before the first column and a right parenthesis following the information on the last column).

Limitations on Data Types Vary

Check your particular implementation for name length limits and characters that are allowed; they could differ from implementation to implementation.

Watch Out!

Each record, or row of data, in this table consists of the following:

EMP_ID, EMP_NAME, EMP_ST_ADDR, EMP_CITY, EMP_ST, EMP_ZIP, EMP_PHONE, EMP_PAGER

In this table, each field is a column. The column EMP_ID could consist of one employee's identification number or many employees' identification numbers, depending on the requirements of a database query or transaction.

Naming Conventions

When selecting names for objects, specifically tables and columns, make sure the name reflects the data that is to be stored. For example, the name for a table pertaining to employee information could be named EMPLOYEE_TBL. Names for columns should follow the same logic. When storing an employee's phone number, an obvious name for that column would be PHONE_NUMBER.

The ALTER TABLE Command

You can modify a table after the table has been created by using the ALTER TABLE command. You can add column(s), drop column(s), change column definitions, add and drop constraints, and, in some implementations, modify table STORAGE values. The standard syntax for the ALTER TABLE command follows:

```
alter table table_name [modify] [column column_name][datatype|null not
null]
[restrict|cascade]
[drop]    [constraint constraint_name]
[add]     [column] column definition
```

Modifying Elements of a Table

The *attributes* of a column refer to the rules and behavior of data in a column. You can modify the attributes of a column with the ALTER TABLE command. The word *attributes* here refers to the following:

▶ The data type of a column

▶ The length, precision, or scale of a column

▶ Whether the column can contain NULL values

The following example uses the ALTER TABLE command on EMPLOYEE_TBL to modify the attributes of the column EMP_ID:

```
ALTER TABLE EMPLOYEE_TBL MODIFY
EMP_ID VARCHAR(10);
Table altered.
```

The column was already defined as data type VARCHAR (a varying-length character), but you increased the maximum length from 9 to 10.

Adding Mandatory Columns to a Table

One of the basic rules for adding columns to an existing table is that the column you are adding cannot be defined as NOT NULL if data currently exists in the table. NOT NULL means that a column must contain some value for every row of data in the table. So, if you are adding a column defined as NOT NULL, you are contradicting the NOT NULL constraint right off the bat if the preexisting rows of data in the table do not have values for the new column.

There is, however, a way to add a mandatory column to a table:

1. Add the column and define it as NULL. (The column does not have to contain a value.)

2. Insert a value into the new column for every row of data in the table.

3. Alter the table to change the column's attribute to NOT NULL.

Adding Auto-Incrementing Columns to a Table

Sometimes it is necessary to create a column that auto-increments itself to give a unique sequence number for a particular row. You could do this for many reasons, such as not having a natural key for the data, or wanting to use a unique sequence number to sort the data. Creating an auto-incrementing column is generally quite easy. In MySQL, the implementation provides the SERIAL method to produce a truly unique value for the table. Following is an example:

```
CREATE TABLE TEST_INCREMENT(
        ID           SERIAL,
        TEST_NAME    VARCHAR(20));
```

Using NULL for Table Creation

NULL is a default attribute for a column; therefore, it does not have to be entered in the CREATE TABLE statement. NOT NULL must always be specified.

By the Way

In Microsoft SQL Server, we are provided with an IDENTITY column type. The following is an example for the SQL Server implementation:

```
CREATE TABLE TEST_INCREMENT(
        ID      INT IDENTITY(1,1) NOT NULL,
        TEST_NAME    VARCHAR(20));
```

Oracle does not provide a direct method for an auto-incrementing column. However, there is one method using an object called a SEQUENCE and a TRIGGER that simulates the effect in Oracle. This technique is discussed when we talk about TRIGGERs in Hour 22, "Advanced SQL Topics."

Now we can insert values into the newly created table without specifying a value for our auto-incrementing column:

```
INSERT INTO TEST_INCREMENT(TEST_NAME)
VALUES ('FRED'),('JOE'),('MIKE'),('TED');

SELECT * FROM TEST_INCREMENT;
```

```
| ID |    TEST_NAME |
|  1 |    FRED      |
|  2 |    JOE       |
|  3 |    MIKE      |
|  4 |    TED       |
```

Modifying Columns

You need to consider many things when modifying existing columns of a table. Following are some common rules for modifying columns:

▸ The length of a column can be increased to the maximum length of the given data type.

▸ The length of a column can be decreased only if the largest value for that column in the table is less than or equal to the new length of the column.

▸ The number of digits for a number data type can always be increased.

▸ The number of digits for a number data type can be decreased only if the value with the most number of digits for that column is less than or equal to the new number of digits specified for the column.

▸ The number of decimal places for a number data type can either be increased or decreased.

▸ The data type of a column can normally be changed.

Some implementations might actually restrict you from using certain ALTER TABLE options. For example, you might not be allowed to drop columns from a table. To do this, you have to drop the table itself and then rebuild the table with the desired columns. You could run into problems by dropping a column in one table that is dependent on a column in another table or dropping a column that is referenced by a column in another table. Be sure to refer to your specific implementation documentation.

By the Way

> **Creating Tables for Exercises**
>
> You will create the tables that you see in these examples at the end of this hour in the "Exercises" section. In Hour 5, "Manipulating Data," you will populate the tables you create in this hour with data.

Creating a Table from an Existing Table

Watch Out!

> **Altering or Dropping Tables Can Be Dangerous**
>
> Take heed when altering and dropping tables. If you make logical or typing mistakes when issuing these statements, you can lose important data.

You can create a copy of an existing table using a combination of the CREATE TABLE statement and the SELECT statement. The new table has the same column definitions. You can select any or all columns. New columns that you create via functions or a combination of columns automatically assume the size necessary to hold the data. The basic syntax for creating a table from another table is as follows:

```
create table new_table_name as
select [ * | column1, column2 ]
from table_name
[ where ]
```

Notice some new keywords in the syntax, particularly the SELECT keyword. SELECT is a database query and is discussed in more detail in Chapter 7, "Introduction to the Database Query." However, it is important to know that you can create a table based on the results from a query.

Both MySQL and Oracle support the CREATE TABLE AS SELECT method of creating a table based on another table. Microsoft SQL Server, however, uses a different statement. For that database implementation, you use a SELECT ... INTO statement. This statement is used like this:

```
select [ * | column1, columnn2]
into new_table_name
from table_name
[ where ]
```

Here you'll examine some examples of using this method.

First, do a simple query to view the data in the PRODUCTS_TBL table:

select * from products_tbl;

PROD_ID	PROD_DESC	COST
11235	WITCH COSTUME	29.99
222	PLASTIC PUMPKIN 18 INCH	7.75
13	FALSE PARAFFIN TEETH	1.1
90	LIGHTED LANTERNS	14.5
15	ASSORTED COSTUMES	10
9	CANDY CORN	1.35
6	PUMPKIN CANDY	1.45
87	PLASTIC SPIDERS	1.05
119	ASSORTED MASKS	4.95

Next, create a table called PRODUCTS_TMP based on the previous query:

```
create table products_tmp as
select * from products_tbl;

Table created.
```

In SQL Server, the same statement would be written as such:

```
select *
into products_tmp
 from products_tbl;

Table created.
```

Now if you run a query on the PRODUCTS_TMP table, your results appear the same as if you had selected data from the original table.

```
select *
from products_tmp;
PROD_ID    PROD_DESC                      COST
------------------------------------------------
11235      WITCH COSTUME                  29.99
222        PLASTIC PUMPKIN 18 INCH         7.75
13         FALSE PARAFFIN TEETH            1.1
90         LIGHTED LANTERNS               14.5
15         ASSORTED COSTUMES              10
9          CANDY CORN                      1.35
6          PUMPKIN CANDY                   1.45
87         PLASTIC SPIDERS                 1.05
119        ASSORTED MASKS                  4.95
```

Did You Know?

What the * Means

SELECT * selects data from all fields in the given table. The * represents a complete row of data, or record, in the table.

Did You Know?

Default STORAGE Attributes for Tables

When creating a table from an existing table, the new table takes on the same STORAGE attributes as the original table.

Dropping Tables

Dropping a table is actually one of the easiest things to do. When the RESTRICT option is used and the table is referenced by a view or constraint, the DROP statement returns an error. When the CASCADE option is used, the drop succeeds and all referencing views and constraints are dropped. The syntax to drop a table follows:

```
drop table table_name [ restrict|cascade ]
```

SQL Server does not allow for the use of the CASCADE option. So for that particular implementation, you must ensure that you drop all objects that reference the table you are removing to ensure that you are not leaving an invalid object in your system.

In the following example, you drop the table that you just created:

```
drop table products_tmp;

Table dropped.
```

Be Specific When Dropping a Table

Whenever you're dropping a table, be sure to specify the schema name or owner of the table before submitting your command. You could drop the incorrect table. If you have access to multiple user accounts, ensure that you are connected to the database through the correct user account before dropping tables.

Watch Out!

Integrity Constraints

Integrity constraints ensure accuracy and consistency of data in a relational database. Data integrity is handled in a relational database through the concept of referential integrity. Many types of integrity constraints play a role in *referential integrity (RI)*.

Primary Key Constraints

Primary key is the term that identifies one or more columns in a table that make a row of data unique. Although the primary key typically consists of one column in a table, more than one column can comprise the primary key. For example, either the employee's Social Security number or an assigned employee identification number is the logical primary key for an employee table. The objective is for every record to have a unique primary key or value for the employee's identification number. Because there is probably no need to have more than one record for each employee in an employee table, the employee identification number makes a logical primary key. The primary key is assigned at table creation.

The following example identifies the EMP_ID column as the PRIMARY KEY for the EMPLOYEES table:

```
CREATE TABLE EMPLOYEE_TBL
(EMP_ID          CHAR(9)        NOT NULL PRIMARY KEY,
```

```
EMP_NAME        VARCHAR (40)     NOT NULL,
EMP_ST_ADDR     VARCHAR (20)     NOT NULL,
EMP_CITY        VARCHAR (15)     NOT NULL,
EMP_ST          CHAR(2)          NOT NULL,
EMP_ZIP         INTEGER(5)       NOT NULL,
EMP_PHONE       INTEGER(10)      NULL,
EMP_PAGER       INTEGER(10)      NULL);
```

This method of defining a primary key is accomplished during table creation. The primary key in this case is an implied constraint. You can also specify a primary key explicitly as a constraint when setting up a table, as follows:

```
CREATE TABLE EMPLOYEE_TBL
(EMP_ID          CHAR(9)          NOT NULL,
EMP_NAME        VARCHAR (40)     NOT NULL,
EMP_ST_ADDR     VARCHAR (20)     NOT NULL,
EMP_CITY        VARCHAR (15)     NOT NULL,
EMP_ST          CHAR(2)          NOT NULL,
EMP_ZIP         INTEGER(5)       NOT NULL,
EMP_PHONE       INTEGER(10)      NULL,
EMP_PAGER       INTEGER(10)      NULL,
PRIMARY KEY (EMP_ID));
```

The primary key constraint in this example is defined after the column comma list in the CREATE TABLE statement.

You can define a primary key that consists of more than one column by either of the following methods, which demonstrate creating a primary key in an Oracle table:

```
CREATE TABLE PRODUCT_TST
(PROD_ID         VARCHAR2(10)      NOT NULL,
 VEND_ID         VARCHAR2(10)      NOT NULL,
 PRODUCT         VARCHAR2(30)      NOT NULL,
 COST            NUMBER(8,2)       NOT NULL,
PRIMARY KEY (PROD_ID, VEND_ID));

ALTER TABLE PRODUCTS_TST
ADD CONSTRAINT PRODUCTS_PK PRIMARY KEY (PROD_ID, VEND_ID);
```

Unique Constraints

A *unique column constraint* in a table is similar to a primary key in that the value in that column for every row of data in the table must have a unique value. Although a primary key constraint is placed on one column, you can place a unique constraint on another column even though it is not actually for use as the primary key.

Study the following example:

```
CREATE TABLE EMPLOYEE_TBL
(EMP_ID          CHAR(9)         NOT NULL      PRIMARY KEY,
 EMP_NAME        VARCHAR (40)    NOT NULL,
 EMP_ST_ADDR     VARCHAR (20)    NOT NULL,
 EMP_CITY        VARCHAR (15)    NOT NULL,
 EMP_ST          CHAR(2)         NOT NULL,
 EMP_ZIP         INTEGER(5)      NOT NULL,
 EMP_PHONE       INTEGER(10)     NULL          UNIQUE,
 EMP_PAGER       INTEGER(10)     NULL);
```

The primary key in this example is EMP_ID, meaning that the employee identification number is the column ensuring that every record in the table is unique. The primary key is a column that is normally referenced in queries, particularly to join tables. The column EMP_PHONE has been designated as a UNIQUE value, meaning that no two employees can have the same telephone number. There is not a lot of difference between the two, except that the primary key provides an order to data in a table and, in the same respect, joins related tables.

Foreign Key Constraints

A *foreign key* is a column in a child table that references a primary key in the parent table. A *foreign key constraint* is the main mechanism that enforces referential integrity between tables in a relational database. A column defined as a foreign key references a column defined as a primary key in another table.

Study the creation of the foreign key in the following example:

```
CREATE TABLE EMPLOYEE_PAY_TST
(EMP_ID           CHAR(9)        NOT NULL,
 POSITION         VARCHAR2(15)   NOT NULL,
 DATE_HIRE        DATE           NULL,
 PAY_RATE         NUMBER(4,2)    NOT NULL,
 DATE_LAST_RAISE  DATE           NULL,
 CONSTRAINT EMP_ID_FK FOREIGN KEY (EMP_ID) REFERENCES EMPLOYEE_TBL
 (EMP_ID));
```

The EMP_ID column in this example has been designated as the foreign key for the EMPLOYEE_PAY_TBL table. This foreign key, as you can see, references the EMP_ID column in the EMPLOYEE_TBL table. This foreign key ensures that for every EMP_ID in the EMPLOYEE_PAY_TBL, there is a corresponding EMP_ID in the EMPLOYEE_TBL. This is called a *parent/child relationship*. The parent table is the EMPLOYEE_TBL table, and the child table is the EMPLOYEE_PAY_TBL table. Study Figure 3.4 for a better understanding of the parent table/child table relationship.

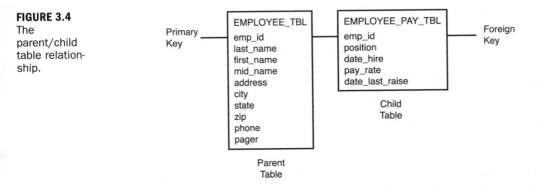

In this figure, the EMP_ID column in the child table references the EMP_ID
column in the parent table. For a value to be inserted for EMP_ID in the
child table, a value for EMP_ID in the parent table must exist. Likewise, for a
value to be removed for EMP_ID in the parent table, all corresponding first
values for EMP_ID must be removed from the child table. This is how referential integrity works.

You can add a foreign key to a table using the ALTER TABLE command, as
shown in the following example:

```
alter table employee_pay_tbl
add constraint id_fk foreign key (emp_id)
references employee_tbl (emp_id);
```

> **ALTER TABLE Variations**
>
> The options available with the ALTER TABLE command differ among implementa-
> tions of SQL, particularly when dealing with constraints. In addition, the actual
> use and definitions of constraints vary, but the concept of referential integrity
> should be the same with all relational databases.

NOT NULL Constraints

Previous examples use the keywords NULL and NOT NULL listed on the same
line as each column and after the data type. NOT NULL is a constraint that
you can place on a table's column. This constraint disallows the entrance of
NULL values into a column; in other words, data is required in a NOT NULL
column for each row of data in the table. NULL is generally the default for a
column if NOT NULL is not specified, allowing NULL values in a column.

Check Constraints

You can utilize check (CHK) constraints to check the validity of data entered into particular table columns. Check constraints provide back-end database edits, although edits are commonly found in the front-end application as well. General edits restrict values that can be entered into columns or objects, whether within the database or on a front-end application. The check constraint is a way of providing another protective layer for the data.

The following example illustrates the use of a check constraint in Oracle:

```
CREATE TABLE EMPLOYEE_CHECK_TST
(EMP_ID          CHAR(9)          NOT NULL,
 EMP_NAME        VARCHAR2(40)     NOT NULL,
 EMP_ST_ADDR     VARCHAR2(20)     NOT NULL,
 EMP_CITY        VARCHAR2(15)     NOT NULL,
 EMP_ST          CHAR(2)          NOT NULL,
 EMP_ZIP         NUMBER(5)        NOT NULL,
 EMP_PHONE       NUMBER(10)       NULL,
 EMP_PAGER       NUMBER(10)       NULL,
PRIMARY KEY (EMP_ID),
CONSTRAINT CHK_EMP_ZIP CHECK ( EMP_ZIP = '46234'));
```

The check constraint in this table has been placed on the EMP_ZIP column, ensuring that all employees entered into this table have a ZIP Code of '46234'. Perhaps that is a little restricting. Nevertheless, you can see how it works.

If you wanted to use a check constraint to verify that the ZIP Code is within a list of values, your constraint definition could look like the following:

```
CONSTRAINT CHK_EMP_ZIP CHECK ( EMP_ZIP in ('46234','46227','46745') );
```

If there is a minimum pay rate that can be designated for an employee, you could have a constraint that looks like the following:

```
CREATE TABLE EMPLOYEE_PAY_TBL
(EMP_ID            CHAR(9)         NOT NULL,
 POSITION          VARCHAR2(15)    NOT NULL,
 DATE_HIRE         DATE            NULL,
 PAY_RATE          NUMBER(4,2)     NOT NULL,
 DATE_LAST_RAISE   DATE            NULL,
CONSTRAINT  EMP_ID_FK FOREIGN KEY (EMP_ID) REFERENCES EMPLOYEE_TBL
(EMP_ID),
CONSTRAINT CHK_PAY CHECK ( PAY_RATE > 12.50 ) );
```

In this example, any employee entered into this table must be paid more than $12.50 an hour. You can use just about any condition in a check constraint, as you can with an SQL query. You learn more about these conditions in Hours 5 and 7.

Dropping Constraints

Using the ALTER TABLE command with the DROP CONSTRAINT option, you can drop any constraint that you have defined. For example, to drop the primary key constraint in the EMPLOYEES table, you can use the following command:

```
ALTER TABLE EMPLOYEES DROP CONSTRAINT EMPLOYEES_PK;
```

```
Table altered.
```

Some implementations provide shortcuts for dropping certain constraints. For example, to drop the primary key constraint for a table in MySQL, you can use the following command:

```
ALTER TABLE EMPLOYEES DROP PRIMARY KEY;
```

```
Table altered.
```

> **Other Ways of Dealing with Constraints**
>
> Instead of permanently dropping a constraint from the database, some implementations allow you to temporarily disable constraints and then enable them later.

Summary

You have learned a little about database objects in general, but you have specifically learned about the table. The table is the simplest form of data storage in a relational database. Tables contain groups of logical information, such as employee, customer, or product information. A table is composed of various columns, with each column having attributes; those attributes mainly consist of data types and constraints, such as NOT NULL values, primary keys, foreign keys, and unique values.

You learned the CREATE TABLE command and options, such as storage parameters, that might be available with this command. You also learned how to modify the structure of existing tables using the ALTER TABLE command. Although the process of managing database tables might not be the most basic process in SQL, if you first learn the structure and nature of tables, you will more easily grasp the concept of accessing the tables, whether through data manipulation operations or database queries. In later hours, you learn about the management of other objects in SQL, such as indexes on tables and views.

Q&A

Q. *When I name a table that I am creating, is it necessary to use a suffix such as _TBL?*

A. Absolutely not. You do not have to use anything. For example, a table to hold employee information could be named something similar to the following, or anything else that would refer to what type of data is to be stored in that particular table:

```
EMPLOYEE
EMP_TBL
EMPLOYEE_TBL
EMPLOYEE_TABLE
WORKER
```

Q. *Why is it so important to use the schema name when dropping a table?*

A. Here's a true story about a new DBA who dropped a table. A programmer had created a table under his schema with the same name as a production table. That particular programmer left the company. His database account was being deleted from the database, but the DROP USER statement returned an error because he owned outstanding objects. After some investigation, it was determined that his table was not needed, so a DROP TABLE statement was issued.

It worked like a charm, but the problem was that the DBA was logged in as the production schema when the DROP TABLE statement was issued. The DBA should have specified a schema name, or owner, for the table to be dropped. Yes, the wrong table in the wrong schema was dropped. It took approximately eight hours to restore the production database.

Workshop

The following workshop is composed of a series of quiz questions and practical exercises. The quiz questions are designed to test your overall understanding of the current material. The practical exercises are intended to afford you the opportunity to apply the concepts discussed during the current hour, as well as build upon the knowledge acquired in previous hours of study. Please take time to complete the quiz questions and exercises before continuing. Refer to Appendix C, "Answers to Quizzes and Exercises," for answers.

Quiz

1. Does the following CREATE TABLE statement work? If not, what needs to be done to correct the problem(s)? Are there limitations as to what database implementation it works in (MySQL, Oracle, SQL Server)?

```
Create table EMPLOYEE_TABLE as:
  ( ssn              number(9)        not null,
    last_name        varchar2(20)     not null,
    first_name       varchar2(20)     not null,
    middle_name      varchar2(20)     not null,
    st address       varchar2(30)     not null,
    city             char(20)         not null,
    state            char(2)          not null,
    zip              number(4)        not null,
    date hired       date);
```

2. Can you drop a column from a table?

3. What statement would you issue to create a primary key constraint on the preceding EMPLOYEE_TABLE?

4. What statement would you issue on the preceding EMPLOYEE_TABLE to allow the MIDDLE_NAME column to accept NULL values?

5. What statement would you use to restrict the people added into the preceding EMPLOYEE_TABLE to only reside in the state of New York ('NY')?

6. What statement would you use to add an auto-incrementing column called EMPID to the preceding EMPLOYEE_TABLE using both the MySQL and SQL Server syntax?

Exercises

In the following exercise, you will be creating all the tables in the database to set up the environment for later. Additionally, you will be executing several commands that will allow you to investigate the table structure in an existing database. For thoroughness we have provided instructions for each of the three implementations (MySQL, Microsoft SQL Server, and Oracle) because each is slightly different in its approach.

MySQL

Bring up a command prompt and use the following syntax to log onto your local MySQL instance, replacing *username* with your username and *password* with your password. Ensure that you do not leave a space between -p and your password.

```
Mysql  -h localhost -u username  -ppassword
```

At the `mysql>` command prompt, enter the following command to tell MySQL that you want to use the database you created previously:

```
use learnsql;
```

Now go to Appendix D, "CREATE TABLE Statements for Book Examples," to get the DDL for the tables used in this book. At the `mysql>` prompt, enter each CREATE TABLE statement. Be sure to include a semicolon at the end of each CREATE TABLE statement. The tables that you create are used throughout the book.

At the `mysql>` prompt, enter the following command to get a list of your tables:

```
show tables;
```

At the `mysql>` prompt, use the DESCRIBE command (desc for short) to list the columns and their attributes for each one of the tables you created. For
example:

```
describe employee_tbl;
describe employee_pay_tbl;
```

If you have errors or typos, simply re-create the appropriate table(s). If the table was successfully created but has typos (perhaps you did not properly define a column or forgot a column), drop the table, and issue the CREATE TABLE command again. The syntax of the DROP TABLE command is as follows:

```
drop table orders_tbl;
```

Microsoft SQL Server

Bring up a command prompt and use the following syntax to log onto your local SQL Server instance, replacing username with your username and password with your password. Ensure that you do not leave a space between -p and your password.

```
SQLCMD  -S localhost -U username   -Ppassword
```

At the 1> command prompt, enter the following command to tell SQL Server that you want to use the database you created previously. Remember that with SQLCMD you must use the keyword GO to tell the command tool that you want the previous lines to execute.

```
1>use learnsql;
2>GO
```

Now go to Appendix D to get the DDL for the tables used in this book. At the 1> prompt, enter each CREATE TABLE statement. Be sure to include a semicolon at the end of each CREATE TABLE statement and follow up with the keyword GO to have your statement execute. The tables that you create are used throughout the book.

At the 1> prompt, enter the following command to get a list of your tables. Follow this command with the keyword GO:

```
Select name from sys.tables;
```

At the 1> prompt, use the sp_help stored procedure to list the columns and their attributes for each one of the tables you created. For example:

```
Sp_help_ employee_tbl;
Sp_help employee_pay_tbl;
```

If you have errors or typos, simply re-create the appropriate table(s). If the table was successfully created but has typos (perhaps you did not properly define a column or forgot a column), drop the table and issue the CREATE TABLE command again. The syntax of the DROP TABLE command is as follows:

```
drop table orders_tbl;
```

Oracle

Bring up a command prompt, and use the following syntax to log onto your local Oracle instance. You are prompted to enter your username and password.

```
sqlplus
```

Now go to Appendix D to get the DDL for the tables used in this book. At the SQL> prompt, enter each CREATE TABLE statement. Be sure to include a semicolon at the end of each CREATE TABLE statement. The tables that you create are used throughout the book.

At the SQL> prompt, enter the following command to get a list of your tables:

```
Select * from cat;
```

At the SQL> prompt, use the DESCRIBE command (desc for short) to list the columns and their attributes for each one of the tables you created. For example:

```
describe employee_tbl;
describe employee_pay_tbl;
```

If you have errors or typos, simply re-create the appropriate table(s). If the table was successfully created but has typos (perhaps you did not properly define a column or forgot a column), drop the table, and issue the CREATE TABLE command again. The syntax of the DROP TABLE command is as follows:

```
drop table orders_tbl;
```

HOUR 4

The Normalization Process

In this hour, you learn the process of taking a raw database and breaking it into logical units called *tables*. This process is referred to as *normalization*. The normalization process is used by database developers to design databases in which it is easy to organize and manage data while ensuring the accuracy of data throughout the database. The great thing is that the process is the same regardless of which *relational database management system (RDBMS)* you are using.

The advantages and disadvantages of both normalization and denormalization of a database are discussed in this hour, as well as data integrity versus performance issues that pertain to normalization.

Normalizing a Database

Normalization is a process of reducing redundancies of data in a database. A technique that is used when designing and redesigning a database, normalization optimally designs a database to reduce redundant data. The actual guidelines of normalization, called *normal forms*, are discussed later in this hour. It was a difficult decision to cover normalization in this book because of the complexity involved. Understanding the rules of the normal forms can be difficult this early in your SQL journey. However, normalization is an important process that, if understood, increases your understanding of SQL. We have attempted to simplify the process of nor-malization as much as possible in this hour. At this point, don't be overly concerned with all the specifics of normalization; it is most important to understand the basic concepts.

The Raw Database

A database that is not normalized might include data that is contained in one or more tables for no apparent reason. This could be bad for security reasons, disk space usage, speed of queries, efficiency of database updates, and, maybe most importantly, data integrity. A database before normaliza-tion is one that has not been broken down logically into smaller, more manageable tables. Figure 4.1 illustrates the database used for this book before it was normalized.

FIGURE 4.1
The raw data-base.

COMPANY_DATABASE	
emp_id	cust_id
last_name	cust_name
first_name	cust_address
middle_name	cust_city
address	cust_state
city	cust_zip
state	cust_phone
zip	cust_fax
phone	ord_num
pager	qty
position	ord_date
date_hire	prod_id
pay_rate	prod_desc
bonus	cost
date_last_raise	

Determining the set of information that the raw database consists of is one of the first and most important steps in logical database design. You must know all the data elements that comprise your database to effectively apply the techniques discussed in this chapter. Taking the time to perform the due diligence of gathering the set of required data keeps you from having to backtrack your database design scheme because of missing data elements.

Logical Database Design

Any database should be designed with the end user in mind. Logical data-base design, also referred to as the *logical model*, is the process of arranging data into logical, organized groups of objects that can easily be maintained. The logical design of a database should reduce data repetition or go so far as to completely eliminate it. After all, why store the same data twice? Additionally, the logical database design should strive to make the database easy to maintain and update. Naming conventions used in a database should also be standard and logical to aid in this endeavor.

What Are the End User's Needs?

The needs of the end user should be one of the top considerations when designing a database. Remember that the end user is the person who ultimately uses the database. There should be ease of use through the user's *front-end tool* (a client program that enables a user access to a database), but this, along with optimal performance, cannot be achieved if the user's needs are not considered.

Some user-related design considerations include the following:

- ▶ What data should be stored in the database?
- ▶ How does the user access the database?
- ▶ What privileges does the user require?
- ▶ How should the data be grouped in the database?
- ▶ What data is the most commonly accessed?
- ▶ How is all data related in the database?
- ▶ What measures should be taken to ensure accurate data?
- ▶ What measures can be taken to reduce redundancy of data?
- ▶ What measures can be taken to ensure ease of use for the end user who is maintaining the data?

Data Redundancy

Data should not be redundant; the duplication of data should be kept to a minimum for several reasons. For example, it is unnecessary to store an employee's home address in more than one table. With duplicate data, unnecessary space is used. Confusion is always a threat when, for instance, an address for an employee in one table does not match the address of the same employee in another table. Which table is correct? Do you have documentation to verify the employee's current address? As if data management were not difficult enough, redundancy of data could prove to be a disaster.

Reducing redundancy also ensures that updating the data within the database is relatively simple. If you have a single table for the employees' addresses and you update that table with new addresses, you can rest assured that it is updated for everyone who is viewing the data.

The Normal Forms

The next sections discuss the normal forms, an integral concept involved in the process of database normalization.

Normal form is a way of measuring the levels, or depth, to which a database has been normalized. A database's level of normalization is determined by the normal form.

The following are the three most common normal forms in the normalization process:

▶ The first normal form

▶ The second normal form

▶ The third normal form

There are normal forms beyond these, but they are used far less often than the three major ones noted here. Of the three major normal forms, each subsequent normal form depends on normalization steps taken in the previous normal form. For example, to normalize a database using the second normal form, the database must be in the first normal form.

The First Normal Form

The objective of the first normal form is to divide the base data into tables. When each table has been designed, a primary key is assigned to most or all tables. Remember from Hour 3, "Managing Database Objects," that your primary key must be a unique value, so try to select a data element for the primary key that naturally uniquely identifies a specific piece of data. Examine Figure 4.2, which illustrates how the raw database shown in Figure 4.1 has been redeveloped using the first normal form.

You can see that to achieve the first normal form, data had to be broken into logical units of related information, each having a primary key and ensuring that there are no repeated groups in any of the tables. Instead of one large table, there are now smaller, more manageable tables: EMPLOYEE_TBL, CUSTOMER_TBL, and PRODUCTS_TBL. The primary keys are normally the first columns listed in a table, in this case, EMP_ID, CUST_ID, and PROD_ID. This is a normal convention that you should use when diagramming your database to ensure that it is easily readable.

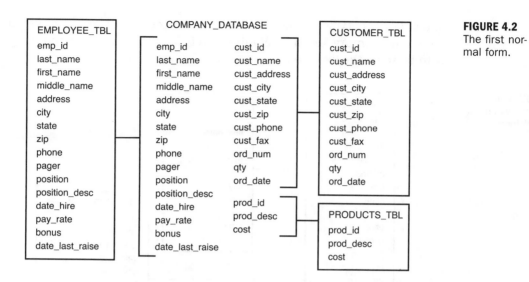

FIGURE 4.2
The first normal form.

However, your primary key could also be made up of more than one of the columns in the data set. Often times, these values are not simple database-generated numbers but logical points of data such as a product's name or a book's ISBN number. These are commonly referred to as *natural keys* because they would uniquely define a specific object regardless of whether it was in a database. The main thing that you need to remember in picking out your primary key for a table is that it must uniquely identify a single row. Without this, you introduce the possibility of adding duplication into your results of queries and prevent yourself from doing even simple things such as removing a particular row of data based solely on the key.

The Second Normal Form

The objective of the second normal form is to take data that is only partly dependent on the primary key and enter that data into another table. Figure 4.3 illustrates the second normal form.

According to the figure, the second normal form is derived from the first normal form by further breaking two tables into more specific units.

EMPLOYEE_TBL is split into two tables called EMPLOYEE_TBL and EMPLOYEE_PAY_TBL. Personal employee information is dependent on the primary key (EMP_ID), so that information remained in the EMPLOYEE_TBL (EMP_ID, LAST_NAME, FIRST_NAME, MIDDLE_NAME, ADDRESS, CITY, STATE, ZIP, PHONE, and PAGER). On the other hand, the information that is only partly dependent on the EMP_ID (each individual employee) populates EMPLOYEE_PAY_TBL (EMP_ID, POSITION, POSITION_DESC, DATE_HIRE, PAY_RATE, and DATE_LAST_RAISE). Notice that both tables contain the column EMP_ID. This is the primary key of each table and is used to match corresponding data between the two tables.

FIGURE 4.3
The second nor-
mal form.

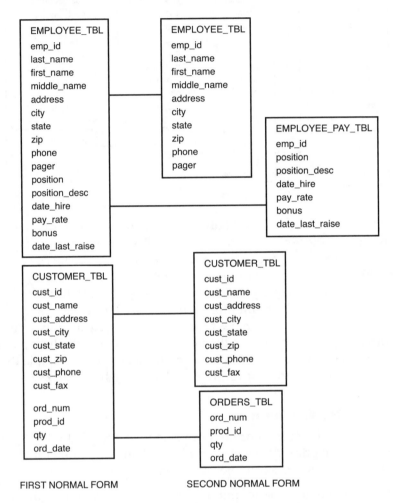

FIRST NORMAL FORM   SECOND NORMAL FORM

CUSTOMER_TBL is split into two tables called CUSTOMER_TBL and ORDERS_TBL. What took place is similar to what occurred in the EMPLOYEE_TBL. Columns that were partly dependent on the primary key were directed to another table. The order information for a customer depends on each CUST_ID but does not directly depend on the general customer information in the original table.

The Third Normal Form

The third normal form's objective is to remove data in a table that is not dependent on the primary key. Figure 4.4 illustrates the third normal form.

Another table was created to display the use of the third normal form. EMPLOYEE_PAY_TBL is split into two tables: one table containing the actual employee pay information and the other containing the position descriptions, which really do not need to reside in EMPLOYEE_PAY_TBL. The POSITION_DESC column is totally independent of the primary key, EMP_ID. As you can see, the normalization process is a series of steps that breaks down the data from your raw database into discrete tables of related data.

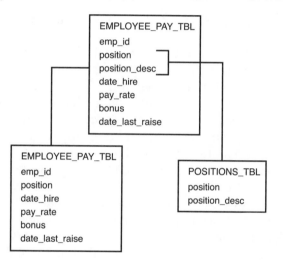

FIGURE 4.4
The third normal form.

Naming Conventions

Naming conventions are one of the foremost considerations when you're normalizing a database. Names are how you refer to objects in the database. You want to give your tables names that are descriptive of the type of information they contain so that the data you are looking for is easy to find. Descriptive table names are especially important for users who had no part in the database design but who need to query the database.

Companies should have a company-wide naming convention to provide guidance in the naming of not only tables within the database, but users, filenames, and other related objects. Naming conventions also help in database administration by making it easier to discern the purpose of tables and locations of files within a database system. Designing and enforcing naming conventions is one of a company's first steps toward a successful database implementation.

Benefits of Normalization

Normalization provides numerous benefits to a database. Some of the major benefits include the following:

- ▸ Greater overall database organization

- ▸ Reduction of redundant data

- ▸ Data consistency within the database

- ▸ A much more flexible database design

- ▸ A better handle on database security

- ▸ Reinforcement of the concept of referential integrity

Organization is brought about by the normalization process, making everyone's job easier, from the user who accesses tables to the *database administrator (DBA)* who is responsible for the overall management of every object in the database. Data redundancy is reduced, which simplifies data structures and conserves disk space. Because duplicate data is minimized, the possibility of inconsistent data is greatly reduced. For example, in one table an individual's name could read STEVE SMITH, whereas the name of the same individual might read STEPHEN R. SMITH in another table. Reducing duplicate data increases *data integrity*, or the assurance of consistent and accurate data within a database. Because the database has been normalized and broken into smaller tables, you have more flexibility in modifying existing structures. It is much easier to modify a small table with little data than to modify one big table that holds all the vital data in the database. Lastly, security is provided in the sense that the DBA can grant access to limited tables to certain users. Security is easier to control when normalization has occurred.

Referential integrity simply means that the values of one column in a table depend on the values of a column in another table. For instance, for a customer to have a record in the ORDERS_TBL table, there must first be a record for that customer in the CUSTOMER_TBL table. Integrity constraints can also control values by restricting a range of values for a column. The integrity constraint should be created at the table's creation. Referential integrity is typically controlled through the use of primary and foreign keys.

In a table, a foreign key, normally a *single field*, directly references a primary key in another table to enforce referential integrity. In the preceding paragraph, the CUST_ID in ORDERS_TBL is a foreign key that references CUST_ID in CUSTOMER_TBL. Normalization helps to enhance and enforce these constraints by logically breaking down data into subsets that are referenced by a primary key.

Drawbacks of Normalization

Although most successful databases are normalized to some degree, there is one substantial drawback of a normalized database: reduced database performance. The acceptance of reduced performance requires the knowledge that when a query or transaction request is sent to the database, there are factors involved, such as CPU usage, memory usage, and *input/output (I/O)*. To make a long story short, a normalized database requires much more CPU, memory, and I/O to process transactions and database queries than does a denormalized database. A normalized database must locate the requested tables and then join the data from the tables to either get the requested information or to process the desired data. A more in-depth discussion concerning database performance occurs in Hour 18, "Managing Database Users."

Denormalizing a Database

Denormalization is the process of taking a normalized database and modifying table structures to allow controlled redundancy for increased database performance. Attempting to improve performance is the only reason to denormalize a database. A denormalized database is not the same as a database that has not been normalized. Denormalizing a database is the process of taking the level of normalization within the database down a notch or two. Remember, normalization can actually slow performance with its frequently occurring table join operations. (Table joins are discussed during Hour 13, "Joining Tables in Queries.")

Denormalization might involve recombining separate tables or creating duplicate data within tables to reduce the number of tables that need to be joined to retrieve the requested data, which results in less I/O and CPU time. This is normally advantageous in larger data warehousing applications in which aggregate calculations are being made across millions of rows of data within tables.

There are costs to denormalization, however. Data redundancy is increased in a denormalized database, which can improve performance but requires more extraneous efforts to keep track of related data. Application coding renders more complications because the data has been spread across various tables and might be more difficult to locate. In addition, referential integrity is more of a chore; related data has been divided among a number of tables.

There is a happy medium in both normalization and denormalization, but both require a thorough knowledge of the actual data and the specific business requirements of the pertinent company. If you do look at denormalizing parts of your database structure, carefully document the process so you can see exactly how you are handling issues such as redundancy to maintain data integrity within your systems.

Summary

A difficult decision has to be made concerning database design—to normalize or not to normalize, that is the question. You always want to normalize a database to some degree. How much do you normalize a database without destroying performance? The real decision relies on the application. How large is the database? What is its purpose? What types of users are going to access the data? This hour covered the three most common normal forms, the concepts behind the normalization process, and the integrity of data. The normalization process involves many steps, most of which are optional but vital to the functionality and performance of your database. Regardless of how deep you decide to normalize, there is almost always a trade-off, either between simple maintenance and questionable performance or complicated maintenance and better performance. In the end, the individual (or team of individuals) designing the database must decide, and that person or team is responsible.

Q&A

Q. *Why should I be so concerned with the end user's needs when designing the database?*

A. The end users are the real data experts who use the database, and, in that respect, they should be the focus of any database design effort. The database designer only helps organize the data.

Q. *Is normalization more advantageous than denormalization?*

A. It can be more advantageous. However, denormalization, to a point, could be more advantageous. Remember, many factors help determine which way to go. You will probably normalize your database to reduce repetition in the database, but you might turn around and denormalize to a certain extent to improve performance.

Workshop

The following workshop is composed of a series of quiz questions and practical exercises. The quiz questions are designed to test your overall understanding of the current material. The practical exercises are intended to afford you the opportunity to apply the concepts discussed during the current hour, as well as build upon the knowledge acquired in previous hours of study. Please take time to complete the quiz questions and exercises before continuing. Refer to Appendix C, "Answers to Quizzes and Exercises," for answers.

Quiz

1. True or false: Normalization is the process of grouping data into logical related groups.

2. True or false: Having no duplicate or redundant data in a database, and having everything in the database normalized, is always the best way to go.

3. True or false: If data is in the third normal form, it is automatically in the first and second normal forms.

4. What is a major advantage of a denormalized database versus a normalized database?

5. What are some major disadvantages of denormalization?

6. How do you determine if data needs to be moved to a separate table when normalizing your database?

7. What are the disadvantages of overnormalizing your database design?

Exercises

1. You are developing a new database for a small company. Take the following data and normalize it. Keep in mind that there would be many more items for a small company than you are given here.

   Employees:

   Angela Smith, secretary, 317-545-6789, RR 1 Box 73, Greensburg, Indiana, 47890, $9.50 per hour, date started January 22, 2006, SSN is 323149669.

Jack Lee Nelson, salesman, 3334 N. Main St., Brownsburg, IN, 45687, 317-852-9901, salary of $35,000.00 per year, SSN is 312567342, date started 10/28/2005.

Customers:

Robert's Games and Things, 5612 Lafayette Rd., Indianapolis, IN, 46224, 317-291-7888, customer ID is 432A.

Reed's Dairy Bar, 4556 W 10th St., Indianapolis, IN, 46245, 317-271-9823, customer ID is 117A.

Customer Orders:

Customer ID is 117A, date of last order is December 20, 2009, the product ordered was napkins, and the product ID is 661.

2. Log in to your new database instance just as you did in Hour 3. Ensure that you are in the `learnsql` database by using the following statement:

Use learnsql;

In Oracle this is known as a schema; by default you create items in your user schema.

Now that you are in the database, open a command window and enter some CREATE TABLE statements based on the tables you defined in Exercise 1.

HOUR 5

Manipulating Data

What You'll Learn in This Hour:

▶ An overview of DML

▶ Instruction on how to manipulate data in tables

▶ Concepts behind table population of data

▶ How to delete data from tables

▶ How to change or modify data in tables

In this hour, you learn the part of SQL known as *Data Manipulation Language (DML)*. DML is the part of SQL that you use to change data and tables in a relational database.

Overview of Data Manipulation

DML is the part of SQL that enables a database user to actually propagate changes among data in a relational database. With DML, the user can populate tables with new data, update existing data in tables, and delete data from tables. Simple database queries can also be performed within a DML command.

The three basic DML commands in SQL are

▶ INSERT

▶ UPDATE

▶ DELETE

The SELECT command, which can be used with DML commands, is discussed in more detail in Hour 7, "Introduction to the Database Query." The SELECT command is the basic query command that you can use after you have entered data into the database with the INSERT command. So in this hour we concentrate on getting the data into our tables so that we have something interesting to use the SELECT command on.

Populating Tables with New Data

Populating a table with data is simply the process of entering new data into a table, whether through a manual process using individual commands or through batch processes using programs or other related software. *Manual population of data* refers to data entry via a keyboard. *Automated population* normally deals with obtaining data from an external data source (such as another database or possibly a flat file) and loading the obtained data into the database.

Many factors can affect what data and how much data can be put into a table when populating tables with data. Some major factors include existing table constraints, the physical table size, column data types, the length of columns, and other integrity constraints, such as primary and foreign keys. The following sections help you learn the basics of inserting new data into a table, in addition to offering some Do's and Don'ts.

Inserting Data into a Table

Use the INSERT statement to insert new data into a table. There are a few options with the INSERT statement; look at the following basic syntax to begin:

```
INSERT INTO TABLE_NAME
VALUES ('value1', 'value2', [ NULL ] );
```

Watch Out!

> **Data Is Case Sensitive**
>
> Do not forget that SQL statements can be in uppercase or lowercase. However, data is always case-sensitive. For example, if you enter data into the database as uppercase, it must be referenced in uppercase. These examples use both lower-case and uppercase statements just to show that it does not affect the outcome.

Using this INSERT statement syntax, you must include every column in the specified table in the VALUES list. Notice that each value in this list is separated by a comma. Enclose the values inserted into the table by single quotation marks for character and date/time data types. Single quotation marks are not required for numeric data types or NULL values using the NULL keyword. A value should be present for each column in the table, and those values must be in the same order as the columns are listed in the table. In later sections, you learn how to specify the column ordering, but for now just know that the SQL engine you are working with assumes that you want to enter the data in the same order in which the columns were created.

In the following example, you insert a new record into the PRODUCTS_TBL table.

Here is the table structure:

```
products_tbl

COLUMN Name                    Null?    DATA Type
- - - - - - - - - - - - - - - - - - - - - - - - - - - - - - - - - - - - - - - - -
PROD_ID                        NOT NULL VARCHAR(10)
PROD_DESC                      NOT NULL VARCHAR(25)
COST                           NOT NULL NUMBER(6,2)
```

Here is the sample INSERT statement:

```
INSERT INTO PRODUCTS_TBL
VALUES ('7725','LEATHER GLOVES',24.99);

1 row created.
```

In this example, three values were inserted into a table with three columns. The inserted values are in the same order as the columns listed in the table. The first two values are inserted using single quotation marks because the data types of the corresponding columns are of character type. The third value's associated column, COST, is a numeric data type and does not require quotation marks, although you can use them without fear of affecting the outcome of the statement.

By the Way

When to Use Quotation Marks

Although single quotation marks are not required around numeric data that is being inserted, they may be used with any data type. Said another way, single quotation marks are optional when referring to numeric data values in the database, but they are required for all other data values (data types). Although usually a matter of preference, most SQL users choose not to use quotation marks with numeric values because it makes their queries more readable.

Inserting Data into Limited Columns of a Table

There is a way you can insert data into specified columns. For instance, suppose you want to insert all values for an employee except a pager number. You must, in this case, specify a column list as well as a VALUES list in your INSERT statement.

```
INSERT INTO EMPLOYEE_TBL
(EMP_ID, LAST_NAME, FIRST_NAME, MIDDLE_NAME, ADDRESS, CITY, STATE, ZIP,
PHONE)
VALUES
('123456789', 'SMITH', 'JOHN', 'JAY', '12 BEACON CT',
'INDIANAPOLIS', 'IN', '46222', '3172996868');

1 row created.
```

The syntax for inserting values into a limited number of columns in a table is as follows:

```
INSERT INTO TABLE_NAME ('COLUMN1', 'COLUMN2')
VALUES ('VALUE1', 'VALUE2');
```

You use ORDERS_TBL and insert values into only specified columns in the following example.

Here is the table structure:

```
ORDERS_TBL

COLUMN NAME                          Null?    DATA TYPE
-------------------------------------------------------
ORD_NUM                              NOT NULL VARCHAR2(10)
CUST_ID                              NOT NULL VARCHAR2(10)
PROD_ID                              NOT NULL VARCHAR2(10)
QTY                                  NOT NULL NUMBER(4)
ORD_DATE                                      NULL  DATE
```

Here is the sample INSERT statement:

```
insert into orders_tbl (ord_num,cust_id,prod_id,qty)
values ('23A16','109','7725',2);

1 row created.
```

You have specified a column list enclosed by parentheses after the table name in the INSERT statement. You have listed all columns into which you want to insert data. ORD_DATE is the only excluded column. If you look at the table definition, you can see that ORD_DATE does not require data for every record in the table. You know that ORD_DATE does not require data because NOT NULL is not specified in the table definition. NOT NULL tells us that NULL values are not allowed in the column. Furthermore, the list of values must appear in the same order as the column list.

Did You Know?

Column List Ordering Can Differ

The column list in the INSERT statement does not have to reflect the same order of columns as in the definition of the associated table, but the list of values must be in the order of the associated columns in the column list. Additionally, you can leave off the NULL syntax for a column because the defaults for most RDBMS specify that columns allow NULL values.

Inserting Data from Another Table

You can insert data into a table based on the results of a query from another table using a combination of the INSERT statement and the

SELECT statement. Briefly, a *query* is an inquiry to the database that either expects or does not expect data to be returned. See Hour 7 for more information on queries. A query is a question that the user asks the database, and the data returned is the answer. In the case of combining the INSERT statement with the SELECT statement, you are able to insert the data retrieved from a query into a table.

The syntax for inserting data from another table is

```
insert into table_name [('column1', 'column2')]
select [*|('column1', 'column2')]
from table_name
[where condition(s)];
```

You see three new keywords in this syntax, which are covered here briefly. These keywords are SELECT, FROM, and WHERE. SELECT is the main command used to initiate a query in SQL. FROM is a clause in the query that specifies the names of tables in which the target data should be found. The WHERE clause, also part of the query, is places conditions on the query. A *condition* is a way of placing criteria on data affected by an SQL statement. A sample condition might state this: WHERE NAME = 'SMITH'. These three keywords are covered extensively during Hour 7 and Hour 8, "Using Operators to Categorize Data."

The following example uses a simple query to view all data in the PRODUCTS_TBL table. SELECT * tells the database server that you want information on all columns of the table. Because no WHERE clause is used, you see all records in the table as well.

```
select * from products_tbl;
PROD_ID    PROD_DESC                         COST
- - - - - - - - - - - - - - - - - - - - - - - - - - - - - - - - -
11235      WITCH COSTUME                     29.99
222        PLASTIC PUMPKIN 18 INCH            7.75
13         FALSE PARAFFIN TEETH               1.1
90         LIGHTED LANTERNS                  14.5
15         ASSORTED COSTUMES                 10
9          CANDY CORN                         1.35
6          PUMPKIN CANDY                      1.45
87         PLASTIC SPIDERS                    1.05
119        ASSORTED MASKS                     4.95
1234       KEY CHAIN                          5.95
2345       OAK BOOKSHELF                     59.99

11 rows selected.
```

Now insert values into the PRODUCTS_TMP table based on the preceding query. You can see that 11 rows are created in the temporary table.

```
insert into products_tmp
select * from products_tbl;

11 rows created.
```

You must ensure that the columns returned from the SELECT query are in the same order as the columns that you have in your table or INSERT statement. Additionally, double-check that the data from the SELECT query is compatible with the data type of the column that it is inserting into the table. For example, trying to insert a VARCHAR field with 'ABC' into a numeric column would cause your statement to fail.

The following query shows all data in the PRODUCTS_TMP table that you just inserted:

```
select * from products_tmp;
PROD_ID    PROD_DESC                            COST
-------------------------------------------------
11235      WITCH COSTUME                        29.99
222        PLASTIC PUMPKIN 18 INCH              7.75
13         FALSE PARAFFIN TEETH                 1.1
90         LIGHTED LANTERNS                     14.5
15         ASSORTED COSTUMES                    10
9          CANDY CORN                           1.35
6          PUMPKIN CANDY                        1.45
87         PLASTIC SPIDERS                      1.05
119        ASSORTED MASKS                       4.95
1234       KEY CHAIN                            5.95
2345       OAK BOOKSHELF                        59.99

11 rows selected.
```

Inserting NULL Values

Inserting a NULL value into a column of a table is a simple matter. You might want to insert a NULL value into a column if the value of the column in question is unknown. For instance, not every person carries a pager, so it would be inaccurate to enter an erroneous pager number—not to mention, you would not be budgeting space. You can insert a NULL value into a column of a table using the keyword NULL.

The syntax for inserting a NULL value follows:

```
insert into schema.table_name values
('column1', NULL, 'column3');
```

Use the NULL keyword in the proper sequence of the associated column that exists in the table. That column does not have data in it for that row if you

enter NULL. In the syntax, a NULL value is being entered in the place of
COLUMN2.

Study the two following examples:

```
insert into orders_tbl (ord_num,cust_id,prod_id,qty,ORD_DATE)
values ('23A16','109','7725',2,NULL);

1 row created.
```

In this example, all columns in which to insert values are listed, which also
happen to be every column in the ORDERS_TBL table. You insert a NULL value
for the ORD_DATE column, meaning that you either do not know the order
date, or there is no order date at this time. Now look at the second example:

```
insert into orders_tbl
values ('23A16','109','7725',2);

1 row created.
```

The second example contains two differences from the first statement, but
the results are the same. First, there is not a column list. Remember that a
column list is not required if you are inserting data into all columns of a
table. Second, instead of inserting the value NULL into the ORD_DATE column,
you simply leave off the last value, which signifies that a NULL value should
be added. Remember that a NULL value signifies an absence of value from a
field and is different from an empty string.

Lastly, consider an example where our PRODUCTS_TBL table allowed NULL values and you wanted to insert values into the PRODUCTS_TMP table using it:

```
select * from products_tb;l
PROD_ID    PROD_DESC                        COST
------------------------------------------------
11235      WITCH COSTUME                    29.99
222        PLASTIC PUMPKIN 18 INCH          7.75
13         FALSE PARAFFIN TEETH             1.1
90         LIGHTED LANTERNS                 14.5
15         ASSORTED COSTUMES                10
9          CANDY CORN                       1.35
6          PUMPKIN CANDY                    1.45
87         PLASTIC SPIDERS                  1.05
119        ASSORTED MASKS                   4.95
1234       NULL                             5.95
2345       OAK BOOKSHELF                    59.99
11 rows selected.

insert into products_tmp
select * from products_tbl;

11 rows created.
```

In this case the NULL values would be inserted without intervention needed on your part as long as the column that the data is being inserted into allowed NULL values. Later this book addresses the need to specify a DEFAULT value for a column that allows you to automatically substitute a value for any NULLs that are inserted.

Updating Existing Data

You can modify pre-existing data in a table using the UPDATE command. This command does not add new records to a table, nor does it remove records—UPDATE simply updates existing data. The update is generally used to update one table at a time in a database, but you can use it to update multiple columns of a table at the same time. An individual row of data in a table can be updated, or numerous rows of data can be updated in a single statement, depending on what's needed.

Updating the Value of a Single Column

The most simple form of the UPDATE statement is its use to update a single column in a table. Either a single row of data or numerous records can be updated when updating a single column in a table.

The syntax for updating a single column follows:

```
update table_name
set column_name = 'value'
[where condition];
```

The following example updates the QTY column in the ORDERS_TBL table to the new value 1 for the ORD_NUM 23A16, which you have specified using the WHERE clause:

```
update orders_tbl
set qty = 1
where ord_num = '23A16';
```

```
1 row updated.
```

The following example is identical to the previous example, except for the absence of the WHERE clause:

```
update orders_tbl
set qty = 1;
```

```
11 rows updated.
```

Notice that in this example, 11 rows of data were updated. You set the QTY to 1, which updated the quantity column in the ORDERS_TBL table for all rows of data. Is this really what you wanted to do? Perhaps in some cases, but rarely do you issue an UPDATE statement without a WHERE clause. An easy way to check to see whether you are going to be updating the correct dataset is to write a SELECT statement for the same table with your WHERE clause that you are using in the INSERT statement. Then you can physically verify that these are the rows you want to update.

Test Your UPDATE and DELETE Statements

Use extreme caution when using the UPDATE statement without a WHERE clause. The target column is updated for all rows of data in the table if conditions are not designated using the WHERE clause. In most situations, the use of the WHERE clause with a DML command is appropriate.

Updating Multiple Columns in One or More Records

Next, you see how to update multiple columns with a single UPDATE statement. Study the following syntax:

```
update table_name
set column1 = 'value',
   [column2 = 'value',]
   [column3 = 'value']
[where condition];
```

Notice the use of the SET in this syntax—there is only one SET, but multiple columns. Each column is separated by a comma. You should start to see a trend in SQL. The comma usually separates different types of arguments in SQL statements. In the following code, a comma separates the two columns being updated. Again, the WHERE clause is optional, but it's usually necessary.

```
update orders_tbl
set qty = 1,
   cust_id = '221'
where ord_num = '23A16';

1 row updated.
```

When to Use the SET Keyword

The SET keyword is used only once for each UPDATE statement. If more than one column is to be updated, use a comma to separate the columns to be updated.

Later in this book you learn how to write more complex statements so you can update values in one table using values from one or more outside tables through a construct known as a JOIN.

Deleting Data from Tables

The DELETE command removes entire rows of data from a table. It does not remove values from specific columns; a full record, including all columns, is removed. Use the DELETE statement with caution—because it works all too well.

Don't Omit the WHERE Clause

If the WHERE clause is omitted from the DELETE statement, all rows of data are deleted from the table. As a general rule, always use a WHERE clause with the DELETE statement. Additionally, test your WHERE clause with a SELECT statement first.

Also, remember that the DELETE command might have a permanent effect on the database. Ideally, it should be possible to recover erroneously deleted data via a backup, but in some cases, it might be difficult or even impossible to recover data. If you cannot recover data, you must re-enter it into the database—trivial if dealing with only one row of data, but not so trivial if dealing with thousands of rows of data. Hence, the importance of the WHERE clause.

To delete a single record or selected records from a table, use the DELETE statement with the following syntax:

```
delete from table_name
[where condition];

delete from orders_tbl
where ord_num = '23A16';

1 row deleted.
```

Notice the use of the WHERE clause. It is an essential part of the DELETE statement if you are attempting to remove selected rows of data from a table. You rarely issue a DELETE statement without the use of the WHERE clause. If you do, your results are similar to the following example:

```
delete from orders_tbl;

11 rows deleted.
```

The temporary table that was populated from the original table earlier in this hour can be useful for testing the DELETE and UPDATE commands before issuing them against the original table. Also, remember the technique discussed earlier when we talked about the UPDATE command. Write a SELECT statement using the same WHERE clause that you are attempting to use for the DELETE statement. That way you can verify that the data being deleted is actually the data you want.

Summary

You have learned the three basic commands in DML: the INSERT, UPDATE, and DELETE statements. As you have seen, data manipulation is a powerful part of SQL, allowing the database user to populate tables with new data, update existing data, and delete data.

An important lesson when updating or deleting data from tables in a database is sometimes learned when neglecting the use of the WHERE clause. Remember that the WHERE clause places conditions on an SQL statement—particularly in the case of UDPATE and DELETE operations, when you are specifying specific rows of data that are affected during a transaction. All target table data rows are affected if the WHERE clause is not used, which could be disastrous to the database. Protect your data, and be cautious during data manipulation operations.

Q&A

Q. *With all the warnings about DELETE and UPDATE, I'm a little afraid to use them. If I accidentally update all the records in a table because I didn't use the WHERE clause, can I reverse the changes?*

A. There is no reason to be afraid, because there is not much you can do to the database that cannot be corrected, although considerable time and work might be involved. Hour 6, "Managing Database Transactions," discusses the concepts of transactional control, which allows data manipulation operations to be finalized or undone.

Q. *Is the INSERT statement the only way to enter data into a table?*

A. No, but remember that the INSERT statement is ANSI standard. The various implementations have their tools to enter data into tables. For example, Oracle has a utility called SQL*Loader. Also, many of the various implementations have utilities called IMPORT that can insert data. There are many good books on the market that expand on these utilities.

Workshop

The following workshop is composed of a series of quiz questions and practical exercises. The quiz questions are designed to test your overall understanding of the current material. The practical exercises are intended to afford you the opportunity to apply the concepts discussed during the current hour, as well as build upon the knowledge acquired in previous hours of study. Please take time to complete the quiz questions and exercises before continuing. Refer to Appendix C, "Answers to Quizzes and Exercises," for answers.

Quiz

1. Use the EMPLOYEE_TBL with the following structure:

```
Column         data type      (not)null
last_name      varchar2(20)   not null
first_name     varchar2(20)   not null
ssn            char(9)        not null
phone          number(10)     null
```

LAST_NAME	FIRST_NAME	SSN	PHONE
SMITH	JOHN	312456788	3174549923
ROBERTS	LISA	232118857	3175452321
SMITH	SUE	443221989	3178398712
PIERCE	BILLY	310239856	3176763990

What would happen if the following statements were run?

a.
```
insert into employee_tbl
('JACKSON', 'STEVE', '313546078', '3178523443');
```

b.
```
insert into employee_tbl values
('JACKSON', 'STEVE', '313546078', '3178523443');
```

c.
```
insert into employee_tbl values
('MILLER', 'DANIEL', '230980012', NULL);
```

d.
```
insert into employee_tbl values
('TAYLOR', NULL, '445761212', '3179221331');
```

e.
```
delete from employee_tbl;
```

f.
```
delete from employee_tbl
where last_name = 'SMITH';
```

g.
```
delete from employee_tbl
where last_name = 'SMITH'
and first_name = 'JOHN';
```

h.
```
update employee_tbl
set last_name = 'CONRAD';
```

i.
```
update employee_tbl
set last_name = 'CONRAD'
where last_name = 'SMITH';
```

j.
```
update employee_tbl
set last_name = 'CONRAD',
first_name = 'LARRY';
```

k.
```
update employee_tbl
set last_name = 'CONRAD'
first_name = 'LARRY'
where ssn = '313546078';
```

Exercises

1. Go to Appendix E, "INSERT Statements for Data in Book Examples." Invoke your RDBMS query editor as you have done in previous exercises.

   Now you need to insert the data into the tables that you created in Hour 3, "Managing Database Objects." Carefully type and execute each of the INSERT statements in Appendix E to populate your tables. After you have executed all the commands for this hour in Appendix E, your tables will be populated with data, and you can proceed with the exercises in the rest of this book.

2. Use the PRODUCTS_TBL for this exercise.

   Add the following products to the product table:

PROD_ID	PROD_DESC	COST
301	FIREMAN COSTUME	24.99
302	POLICEMAN COSTUME	24.99
303	KIDDIE GRAB BAG	4.99

Write DML to correct the cost of the two costumes added. The cost should be the same as the witch costume.

Now we have decided to cut our product line, starting with the new products. Remove the three products you just added.

Before you executed the statements to remove the products you added, what should you have done to ensure that you only delete the desired rows?

HOUR 6

Managing Database Transactions

What You'll Learn in This Hour:

▶ The definition of a transaction

▶ The commands used to control transactions

▶ The syntax and examples of transaction commands

▶ When to use transactional commands

▶ The consequences of poor transactional control

In this hour, you learn the concepts behind the management of database transactions.

What Is a Transaction?

A *transaction* is a unit of work that is performed against a database. Transactions are units or sequences of work accomplished in a logical order, whether in a manual fashion by a user or automatically by some sort of a database program. In a relational database using SQL, transactions are accomplished using the *Data Manipulation Language (DML)* commands that were discussed during Hour 5, "Manipulating Data," (INSERT, UPDATE, and DELETE). A transaction is the propagation of one or more changes to the database. For instance, you are performing a transaction if you perform an UPDATE statement on a table to change an individual's name.

A transaction can either be one DML statement or a group of statements. When managing transactions, each designated transaction (group of DML statements) must be successful as one entity, or none of them will be successful.

The following list describes the nature of transactions:

▶ All transactions have a beginning and an end.

▶ A transaction can be saved or undone.

▶ If a transaction fails in the middle, no part of the transaction can be saved to the database.

Controlling Transactions

By the
Way

> **Transactions Are Implementation Specific**
>
> Starting or executing transactions is implementation specific. You must check your particular implementation for how to begin transactions.

Transactional control is the capability to manage various transactions that might occur within a *relational database management system (RDBMS)*. When you speak of transactions, you are referring to the INSERT, UPDATE, and DELETE commands, which were covered during the previous hour.

When a transaction is executed and completes successfully, the target table is not immediately changed, although it might appear so according to the output. When a transaction successfully completes, transactional control commands are used to finalize the transaction, either saving the changes made by the transaction to the database or reversing the changes made by the transaction.

Three commands are used to control transactions:

▶ COMMIT

▶ ROLLBACK

▶ SAVEPOINT

Each of these is discussed in detail in the following sections.

By the
Way

When Can You Use Transactions

Transactional control commands are only used with the DML commands INSERT, UPDATE, and DELETE. For example, you do not issue a COMMIT statement after creating a table. When the table is created, it is automatically committed to the database. Likewise, you cannot issue a ROLLBACK statement to replenish a table that was just dropped. Also, there are other commands such as TRUNCATE that are not logged and cannot be recovered from. So please make sure you check your RDBMS's documentation before executing new commands to ensure you understand how they implement their transaction support.

When a transaction has completed, the transactional information is stored either in an allocated area or in a temporary rollback area in the database. All changes are held in this temporary rollback area until a transactional control command is issued. When a transactional control command is issued, changes are either made to the database or discarded; then the temporary rollback area is emptied. Figure 6.1 illustrates how changes are applied to a relational database.

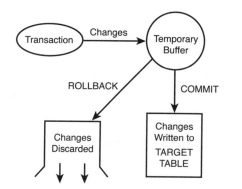

FIGURE 6.1
Rollback area.

The COMMIT Command

The COMMIT command is the transactional command used to save changes invoked by a transaction to the database. The COMMIT command saves all transactions to the database since the last COMMIT or ROLLBACK command. The syntax for this command is

```
commit [ work ];
```

The keyword COMMIT is the only mandatory part of the syntax, along with the character or command that terminates a statement according to each implementation. WORK is a keyword that is completely optional; its only purpose is to make the command more user-friendly.

In the following example, you begin by selecting all data from the
PRODUCT_TMP table:

```
SELECT * FROM PRODUCTS_TMP;
```

```
PROD_ID    PROD_DESC                      COST
---------------------------------------------
11235      WITCH COSTUME                 29.99
222        PLASTIC PUMPKIN 18 INCH        7.75
13         FALSE PARAFFIN TEETH           1.1
90         LIGHTED LANTERNS              14.5
15         ASSORTED COSTUMES             10
9          CANDY CORN                     1.35
6          PUMPKIN CANDY                  1.45
87         PLASTIC SPIDERS                1.05
119        ASSORTED MASKS                 4.95
1234       KEY CHAIN                      5.95
2345       OAK BOOKSHELF                 59.99

11 rows selected.
```

Next, you delete all records from the table where the product cost is less
than $14.00.

```
DELETE FROM PRODUCTS_TMP
WHERE COST < 14;

8 rows deleted.
```

A COMMIT statement is issued to save the changes to the database, complet-
ing the transaction.

```
COMMIT;

Commit complete.
```

Frequent COMMIT statements in large loads or unloads of the database are
highly recommended; however, too many COMMIT statements cause the job to
take a lot of extra time to complete. Remember that all changes are sent to
the temporary rollback area first. If this temporary rollback area runs out of
space and cannot store information about changes made to the database,
the database will probably halt, disallowing further transactional activity.

You should realize that when an UPDATE, INSERT, or DELETE is issued, most
RDBMSs are using a form of transaction in the background so that if the
query is cancelled or runs into an error, changes are not committed. So issuing a transaction is more of an action to ensure that a set of transactions
are run as what is commonly referred to as a *unit of work*. So in a real-world
example, you might be processing a bank transaction at an ATM with a

client wanting to withdraw money. In such a situation, you need to both insert a transaction for the money being withdrawn as well as update the client's balance to reflect the new total. Obviously, we would want either both of these statements to be successful or both of them to fail. Otherwise, our system's data integrity is compromised. So in this instance, you would wrap your unit of work in a transaction to ensure that you could control the outcome of both statements.

Some Implementations Treat the COMMIT Differently

Watch Out!

In some implementations, transactions are committed without issuing the COMMIT command—instead, merely signing out of the database causes a commit to occur. However, in some implementations, such as MySQL, after you perform a SET TRANSACTION command, the auto-commit functionality does not resume until it has received a COMMIT or ROLLBACK statement. Additionally, in other implementations such as Microsoft SQL Server, statements are auto-committed unless a transaction is specifically used. So ensure that you check the documentation of your particular RDBMS to understand exactly how transactions and committing of statements are handled.

The ROLLBACK Command

The ROLLBACK command is the transactional control command that undoes transactions that have not already been saved to the database. You can only use the ROLLBACK command to undo transactions since the last COMMIT or ROLLBACK command was issued.

The syntax for the ROLLBACK command is as follows:

```
rollback [ work ];
```

Once again, as in the COMMIT statement, the WORK keyword is an optional part of the ROLLBACK syntax.

In the following example, you begin by selecting all records from the PRODUCTS_TMP table since the previous deletion of 14 records:

```
SELECT * FROM PRODUCTS_TMP;
```

PROD_ID	PROD_DESC	COST
11235	WITCH COSTUME	29.99
90	LIGHTED LANTERNS	14.5
2345	OAK BOOKSHELF	59.99

```
3 rows selected.
```

Next, you update the table, changing the product cost to $39.99 for the product identification number 11235:

```
update products_tmp
set cost = 39.99
where prod_id = '11235';
```

```
1 row updated.
```

If you perform a quick query on the table, the change appears to have occurred:

select * from products_tmp;

```
PROD_ID    PROD_DESC                             COST
- - - - - - - - - - - - - - - - - - - - - - - - - - - - - - - - - - - - - -
11235      WITCH COSTUME                         39.99
90         LIGHTED LANTERNS                      14.5
2345       OAK BOOKSHELF                         59.99
```

```
3 rows selected.
```

Now issue the ROLLBACK statement to undo the last change:

rollback;

```
Rollback complete.
```

Finally, verify that the change was not committed to the database:

select * from products_tmp;

```
PROD_ID    PROD_DESC                             COST
- - - - - - - - - - - - - - - - - - - - - - - - - - - - - - - - - - - - - -
11235      WITCH COSTUME                         29.99
90         LIGHTED LANTERNS                      14.5
2345       OAK BOOKSHELF                         59.99
```

```
3 rows selected
```

The SAVEPOINT Command

A *savepoint* is a point in a transaction where you can roll the transaction back to this point without rolling back the entire transaction.

The syntax for the SAVEPOINT command is

```
savepoint savepoint_name
```

This command serves only to create a savepoint among transactional statements. The ROLLBACK command undoes a group of transactions. The savepoint is a way of managing transactions by breaking large numbers of transactions into smaller, more manageable groups.

Microsoft SQL Server uses a slightly different syntax. In SQL Server, you would use the statement SAVE TRANSACTION instead of SAVEPOINT, as is shown in the statement that follows:

```
save transaction savepoint_name
```

Otherwise, the procedure works exactly as the other implementations.

The ROLLBACK TO SAVEPOINT Command

The syntax for rolling back to a savepoint is as follows:

```
ROLLBACK TO SAVEPOINT_NAME;
```

In this example, you are going to delete the remaining three records from the PRODUCTS_TMP table. You want to issue a SAVEPOINT command before each delete, so you can issue a ROLLBACK command to any savepoint at any time to return the appropriate data to its original state:

```
savepoint sp1;
```

Savepoint created.

```
delete from products_tmp where prod_id = '11235';
```

1 row deleted.

```
savepoint sp2;
```

Savepoint created.

```
delete from products_tmp where prod_id = '90';
```

1 row deleted.

```
savepoint sp3;
```

Savepoint created.

```
delete from products_tmp where prod_id = '2345';
```

1 row deleted.

SAVEPOINT Names Need to Be Unique

The SAVEPOINT name must be unique to the associated group of transactions. However, it can have the same name as a table or other object. Refer to specific implementation documentation for more details on naming conventions. Otherwise, savepoint names are a matter of personal preference and are used only by the database application developer to manage groups of transactions.

Now that the three deletions have taken place, let's say you have changed
your mind and decided to issue a ROLLBACK command to the savepoint that
you identified as SP2. Because SP2 was created after the first deletion, the
last two deletions are undone:

```
rollback to sp2;
```

Rollback complete.

Notice that only the first deletion took place because you rolled back to SP2:

```
select * from products_tmp;
```

PROD_ID	PROD_DESC	COST
90	LIGHTED LANTERNS	14.5
2345	OAK BOOKSHELF	59.99

2 rows selected.

Remember, the ROLLBACK command by itself rolls back to the last COMMIT or
ROLLBACK statement. You have not yet issued a COMMIT, so all deletions are
undone, as in the following example:

```
rollback;
```

Rollback complete.

```
select * from products_tmp;
```

PROD_ID	PROD_DESC	COST
11235	WITCH COSTUME	29.99
90	LIGHTED LANTERNS	14.5
2345	OAK BOOKSHELF	59.99

3 rows selected.

The RELEASE SAVEPOINT Command

The RELEASE SAVEPOINT command removes a savepoint that you have created. After a savepoint has been released, you can no longer use the ROLLBACK
command to undo transactions performed since the savepoint. You might
want to issue a RELEASE SAVEPOINT command to avoid the accidental rollback to a savepoint that is no longer needed.

```
RELEASE SAVEPOINT savepoint_name;
```

Microsoft SQL Server does not support the RELEASE SAVEPOINT syntax; instead, all SAVEPOINTs are released when the transaction is completed. This is either by the COMMIT or the ROLLBACK of the transaction. Remember this point when you are structuring your transactions within your environment.

The SET TRANSACTION Command

You can use the SET TRANSACTION command to initiate a database transaction. This command specifies characteristics for the transaction that follows. For example, you can specify a transaction to be read-only or read/write:

```
SET TRANSACTION READ WRITE;
SET TRANSACTION READ ONLY;
```

READ WRITE is used for transactions that are allowed to query and manipulate data in the database. READ ONLY is used for transactions that require query-only access. READ ONLY is useful for report generation and for increasing the speed at which transactions are accomplished. If a transaction is READ WRITE, the database must create locks on database objects to maintain data integrity if multiple transactions are happening concurrently. If a transaction is READ ONLY, no locks are established by the database, thereby improving transaction performance.

Other characteristics can be set for a transaction, but these are out of the scope of this book. MySQL supports this syntax for setting an isolation level for the transaction but in slightly different syntax. For more information, see the documentation for your implementation of SQL.

Transactional Control and Database Performance

Poor transactional control can hurt database performance and even bring the database to a halt. Repeated poor database performance might be due to a lack of transactional control during large inserts, updates, or deletes. Large batch processes also cause temporary storage for rollback information to grow until either a COMMIT or a ROLLBACK command is issued.

When a COMMIT is issued, rollback transactional information is written to the target table, and the rollback information in temporary storage is cleared. When a ROLLBACK is issued, no changes are made to the database and the rollback information in the temporary storage is cleared. If neither a COMMIT nor ROLLBACK is issued, the temporary storage for rollback information continues to grow until there is no more space left, thus forcing the database to stop all processes until space is freed. Although space usage is ultimately controlled by the *database administrator (DBA)*, a lack of transactional control can still cause database processing to stop, sometimes forcing the DBA to take action that might consist of killing running user processes.

Summary

During this hour, you learned the preliminary concepts of transactional management through the use of three transactional control commands: COMMIT, ROLLBACK, and SAVEPOINT. You use COMMIT to save a transaction to the database. You use ROLLBACK to undo a transaction you performed. You use SAVEPOINT to break a transaction or transactions into groups, which allows you to roll back to specific logical points in transaction processing.

Remember that you should frequently use the COMMIT and ROLLBACK commands when running large transactional jobs to keep space free in the database. Also, keep in mind that these transactional commands are used only with the three DML commands (INSERT, UPDATE, and DELETE).

Q&A

Q. *Is it necessary to issue a commit after every INSERT statement?*

A. No, absolutely not. If you were inserting a few hundred thousand rows into a table, a COMMIT would be recommended every 5,000–10,000 rows, depending on the size of the temporary rollback area. (Seek the advice of your database administrator.) Remember that the database might freeze up or not function properly when the rollback area fills up.

Q. *How does the ROLLBACK command undo a transaction?*

A. The ROLLBACK command clears all changes from the rollback area.

Q. *If I issue a transaction and 99% of the transaction completes but the other 1% errs, will I be able to redo only the error part?*

A. No, the entire transaction must succeed; otherwise, data integrity is compromised.

Q. *A transaction is permanent after I issue a COMMIT, but can't I change data with an UPDATE command?*

A. The word *permanent* used in this matter means that it is now a part of the database. You can always use the UPDATE statement to make modifications or corrections to the data.

Workshop

The following workshop is composed of a series of quiz questions and practical exercises. The quiz questions are designed to test your overall understanding of the current material. The practical exercises are intended to afford you the opportunity to apply the concepts discussed during the current hour, as well as build upon the knowledge acquired in previous hours of study. Please take time to complete the quiz questions and exercises before continuing. Refer to Appendix C, "Answers to Quizzes and Exercises," for answers.

Quiz

1. True or false: If you have committed several transactions, have several more transactions that have not been committed, and issue a ROLLBACK command, all your transactions for the same session are undone.

2. True or false: A SAVEPOINT command actually saves transactions after a specified number of transactions have executed.

3. Briefly describe the purpose of each one of the following commands: COMMIT, ROLLBACK, and SAVEPOINT.

4. What are some differences in the implementation of transactions in Microsoft SQL Server?

5. What are some performance implications when using transactions?

Exercises

1. Take the following transactions and create a SAVEPOINT or a SAVE TRANSACTION command after the first three transactions. Then create a ROLLBACK statement for your savepoint at the end. Try to determine what the CUSTOMER_TBL will look like after you are done.

```
INSERT INTO CUSTOMER_TBL VALUES(615,'FRED WOLF','109 MEMORY
LANE','PLAINFIELD','IN',46113,'3175555555',NULL);
INSERT INTO CUSTOMER_TBL VALUES(559,'RITA THOMPSON','125
PEACHTREE','INDIANAPOLIS','IN',46248,'3171111111',NULL);
INSERT INTO CUSTOMER_TBL VALUES(715,'BOB DIGGLER','1102 HUNTINGTON
ST','SHELBY','IN',41234,'3172222222',NULL);
UPDATE CUSTOMER_TBL SET CUST_NAME='FRED WOLF' WHERE CUST_ID='559';
UPDATE CUSTOMER_TBL SET CUST_ADDRESS='APT C 4556 WATERWAY' WHERE
CUST_ID='615';
UPDATE CUSTOMER_TBL SET CUST_CITY='CHICAGO' WHERE CUST_ID='715';
```

2. Take the following group of transactions and create a savepoinpt after the first three transactions.

   Then place a COMMIT statement at the end, followed by a ROLLBACK statement to your savepoint. What do you think should happen?

```
UPDATE CUSTOMER_TBL SET CUST_NAME='FRED WOLF' WHERE CUST_ID='559';
UPDATE CUSTOMER_TBL SET CUST_ADDRESS='APT C 4556 WATERWAY' WHERE
CUST_ID='615';
UPDATE CUSTOMER_TBL SET CUST_CITY='CHICAGO' WHERE CUST_ID='715';
DELETE FROM CUSTOMER_TBL WHERE CUST_ID='615';
DELETE FROM CUSTOMER_TBL WHERE CUST_ID='559';
DELETE FROM CUSTOMER_TBL WHERE CUST_ID='615';
```

Introduction to the Database Query

What You'll Learn in This Hour:

- ▶ What a database query is
- ▶ How to use the SELECT statement
- ▶ Adding conditions to queries using the WHERE clause
- ▶ Using column aliases
- ▶ Selecting data from another user's table

In this seventh hour, you learn about database queries, which involve the use of the SELECT statement. The SELECT statement is the most frequently used of all SQL commands after a database's establishment. The SELECT statement enables you to view data that is stored in the database.

What Is a Query?

A *query* is an inquiry into the database using the SELECT statement. A query is used to extract data from the database in a readable format according to the user's request. For instance, if you have an employee table, you might issue an SQL statement that returns the employee who is paid the most. This request to the database for usable employee information is a typical query that can be performed in a relational database.

Introduction to the SELECT Statement

The SELECT statement, the command that represents *Data Query Language (DQL)* in SQL, is the basic statement used to construct database queries. The SELECT statement is not a standalone statement, which means that one or more additional clauses (elements) are required for a syntactically correct query. In addition to the required clauses, there are optional clauses that increase the overall functionality of the SELECT statement. The SELECT statement is by far one of the most powerful statements in SQL. The FROM clause is a mandatory clause and must always be used in conjunction with the SELECT statement.

There are four keywords, or *clauses*, that are valuable parts of a SELECT statement. These keywords are as follows:

- ▶ SELECT
- ▶ FROM
- ▶ WHERE
- ▶ ORDER BY

Each of these keywords is covered in detail during the following sections.

The SELECT Statement

The SELECT statement is used in conjunction with the FROM clause to extract data from the database in an organized, readable format. The SELECT part of the query is for selecting the data you want to see according to the columns in which they are stored in a table.

The syntax for a simple SELECT statement is as follows:

```
SELECT [ * | ALL | DISTINCT COLUMN1, COLUMN2 ]
FROM TABLE1 [ , TABLE2 ];
```

The SELECT keyword in a query is followed by a list of columns that you want displayed as part of the query output. The asterisk (*) denotes that all columns in a table should be displayed as part of the output. Check your particular implementation for its usage. The ALL option displays all values for a column, including duplicates. The DISTINCT option suppresses duplicate rows from being displayed in the output. The ALL option is considered an inferred option. It is thought of as the default; therefore, it does not necessarily need to be used in the SELECT statement. The FROM keyword is followed by a list of one or more tables from which you want to select data. Notice that the columns following the SELECT clause are separated by commas, as is the table list following the FROM clause.

Use Commas to Separate List Items

Commas separate arguments in a list in SQL statements. *Arguments* are values that are either required or optional to the syntax of a SQL statement or command. Some common lists include lists of columns in a query, lists of tables to be selected from in a query, values to be inserted into a table, and values grouped as a condition in a query's WHERE clause.

Explore the basic capabilities of the SELECT statement by studying the following examples. First, perform a simple query from the PRODUCTS_TBL table:

```
SELECT * FROM PRODUCTS_TBL;
```

```
PROD_ID    PROD_DESC                      COST
- - - - - - - - - - - - - - - - - - - - - - - - - - - - - - - - - - - -
11235      WITCH COSTUME                  29.99
222        PLASTIC PUMPKIN 18 INCH         7.75
13         FALSE PARAFFIN TEETH            1.1
90         LIGHTED LANTERNS               14.5
15         ASSORTED COSTUMES              10
9          CANDY CORN                      1.35
6          PUMPKIN CANDY                   1.45
87         PLASTIC SPIDERS                 1.05
119        ASSORTED MASKS                  4.95
1234       KEY CHAIN                       5.95
2345       OAK BOOKSHELF                  59.99

11 rows selected.
```

The asterisk represents all columns in the table, which, as you can see, are displayed in the form PROD_ID, PROD_DESC, and COST. Each column in the output is displayed in the order that it appears in the table. There are 11 records in this table, identified by the feedback 11 rows selected. This feedback differs among implementations; for example, another feedback for the same query would be 11 rows affected. Although the asterisk is a helpful piece of shorthand when writing SQL queries, it is considered best practice to explicitly name your columns that you are returning.

Now select data from another table, CANDY_TBL. Create this table in the image of the PRODUCTS_TBL table for the following examples. List the column name after the SELECT keyword to display only one column in the table:

```
SELECT PROD_DESC FROM CANDY_TBL;
```

```
PROD_DESC
- - - - - - - - - - - - - - - -
CANDY CORN
CANDY CORN
HERSHEYS KISS
SMARTIES

4 rows selected.
```

Four records exist in the CANDY_TBL table. The next statement uses the ALL option to show you that the ALL is optional and redundant. There is never a need to specify ALL; it is a default option.

```
SELECT ALL PROD_DESC
FROM CANDY_TBL;
```

```
PROD_DESC
-----------------
CANDY CORN
CANDY CORN
HERSHEYS KISS
SMARTIES
```

```
4 rows selected.
```

The DISTINCT option is used in the following statement to suppress the display of duplicate records. Notice that the value CANDY CORN is printed only once in this example.

```
SELECT DISTINCT PROD_DESC
FROM CANDY_TBL;
```

```
PROD_DESC
-----------------
CANDY CORN
HERSHEYS KISS
SMARTIES
```

```
3 rows selected.
```

You can also use DISTINCT and ALL with parentheses enclosing the associated column. Parentheses are often used in SQL—as well as many other languages—to improve readability.

```
SELECT DISTINCT(PROD_DESC)
FROM CANDY_TBL;
```

```
PROD_DESC
-----------------
CANDY CORN
HERSHEYS KISS
SMARTIES
```

```
3 rows selected.
```

The FROM Clause

The FROM clause must be used in conjunction with the SELECT statement. It is a required element for any query. The FROM clause's purpose is to tell the database what table(s) to access to retrieve the desired data for the query. The FROM clause may contain one or more tables. The FROM clause must always list at least one table.

The syntax for the FROM clause is as follows:

```
from table1 [ , table2 ]
```

The WHERE Clause

A *condition* is part of a query that displays selective information as specified by the user. The value of a condition is either TRUE or FALSE, thereby limiting the data received from the query. The WHERE clause places conditions on a query by eliminating rows that would normally be returned by a query without conditions.

There can be more than one condition in the WHERE clause. If there is more than one condition, the conditions are connected by the AND and OR operators, which are discussed during Hour 8, "Using Operators to Categorize Data." As you also learn during the next hour, several conditional operators exist that can be used to specify conditions in a query. This hour deals with only a single condition for each query.

An *operator* is a character or keyword in SQL that combines elements in an SQL statement.

The syntax for the WHERE clause is as follows:

```
select [ all | * | distinct column1, column2 ]
from table1 [ , table2 ]
where [ condition1 | expression1 ]
[ and|OR condition2 | expression2 ]
```

The following is a simple SELECT statement without conditions specified by the WHERE clause:

```
SELECT *
FROM PRODUCTS_TBL;
```

PROD_ID	PROD_DESC	COST
11235	WITCH COSTUME	29.99
222	PLASTIC PUMPKIN 18 INCH	7.75
13	FALSE PARAFFIN TEETH	1.1
90	LIGHTED LANTERNS	14.5
15	ASSORTED COSTUMES	10
9	CANDY CORN	1.35
6	PUMPKIN CANDY	1.45
87	PLASTIC SPIDERS	1.05
119	ASSORTED MASKS	4.95
1234	KEY CHAIN	5.95
2345	OAK BOOKSHELF	59.99

```
11 rows selected.
```

Now add a condition for the same query:

```
SELECT * FROM PRODUCTS_TBL
WHERE COST < 5;
```

```
PROD_ID     PROD_DESC                           COST
--------------------------------------------------
13          FALSE PARAFFIN TEETH                1.1
9           CANDY CORN                          1.35
6           PUMPKIN CANDY                       1.45
87          PLASTIC SPIDERS                     1.05
119         ASSORTED MASKS                      4.95

5 rows selected.
```

The only records displayed are those that cost less than $5.

In the following query, you want to display the product description and cost that matches product identification 119:

```
SELECT PROD_DESC, COST
FROM PRODUCTS_TBL
WHERE PROD_ID = '119';

PROD_DESC                       COST
------------------------------------
ASSORTED MASKS                  4.95

1 row selected.
```

The ORDER BY Clause

You usually want your output to have some kind of order. Data can be sorted by using the ORDER BY clause. The ORDER BY clause arranges the results of a query in a listing format you specify. The default ordering of the ORDER BY clause is an *ascending order*; the sort displays in the order A–Z if it's sorting output names alphabetically. A *descending order* for alphabetical output would be displayed in the order Z–A. Ascending order for output for numeric values between 1 and 9 would be displayed 1–9; descending order would be displayed as 9–1.

The syntax for the ORDER BY clause is as follows:

```
select [ all | * | distinct column1, column2 ]
from table1 [ , table2 ]
where [ condition1 | expression1 ]
[ and|OR condition2 | expression2 ]
ORDER BY column1|integer [ ASC|DESC ]
```

Begin your exploration of the ORDER BY clause with an extension of one of the previous statements. You order the product description in ascending order, or alphabetical order. Note the use of the ASC option. You can specify ASC after any column in the ORDER BY clause.

```
SELECT PROD_DESC, PROD_ID, COST
FROM PRODUCTS_TBL
WHERE COST < 20
ORDER BY PROD_DESC ASC;
```

```
PROD_DESC                  PROD_ID        COST
----------------------------------------------
ASSORTED COSTUMES          15             10
ASSORTED MASKS             119            4.95
CANDY CORN                 9              1.35
FALSE PARAFFIN TEETH       13             1.1
LIGHTED LANTERNS           90             14.5
PLASTIC PUMPKIN 18 INCH    222            7.75
PLASTIC SPIDERS            87             1.05
PUMPKIN CANDY              6              1.45
```

8 rows selected.

By the Way

Rules for Sorting

SQL sorts are ASCII, character-based sorts. The numeric values 0–9 would be sorted as character values and sorted before the characters A–Z. Because numeric values are treated like characters during a sort, the following list of numeric values would be sorted in the following order: 1, 12, 2, 255, 3.

You can use DESC, as in the following statement, if you want the same output to be sorted in reverse alphabetical order:

```
SELECT PROD_DESC, PROD_ID, COST
FROM PRODUCTS_TBL
WHERE COST < 20
ORDER BY PROD_DESC DESC;
```

```
PROD_DESC                  PROD_ID        COST
----------------------------------------------
PUMPKIN CANDY              6              1.45
PLASTIC SPIDERS            87             1.05
PLASTIC PUMPKIN 18 INCH    222            7.75
LIGHTED LANTERNS           90             14.5
FALSE PARAFFIN TEETH       13             1.1
CANDY CORN                 9              1.35
ASSORTED MASKS             119            4.95
ASSORTED COSTUMES          15             10
```

8 rows selected.

There Is a Default for Ordering

Because ascending order for output is the default, you do not have to specify ASC.

Did You Know?

Shortcuts do exist in SQL. A column listed in the ORDER BY clause can be abbreviated with an integer. The *integer* is a substitution for the actual column name (an alias for the purpose of the sort operation), identifying the position of the column after the SELECT keyword.

An example of using an integer as an identifier in the ORDER BY clause follows:

```
SELECT PROD_DESC, PROD_ID, COST
FROM PRODUCTS_TBL
WHERE COST < 20
ORDER BY 1;
```

```
PROD_DESC                 PROD_ID        COST
-------------------------------------------------
ASSORTED COSTUMES         15             10
ASSORTED MASKS            119            4.95
CANDY CORN                9              1.35
FALSE PARAFFIN TEETH      13             1.1
LIGHTED LANTERNS          90             14.5
PLASTIC PUMPKIN 18 INCH   222            7.75
PLASTIC SPIDERS           87             1.05
PUMPKIN CANDY             6              1.45

8 rows selected.
```

In this query, the integer 1 represents the column PROD_DESC. The integer 2 represents the PROD_ID column, 3 represents the COST column, and so on.

You can order by multiple columns in a query, using either the column name or the associated number of the column in the SELECT:

```
ORDER BY 1,2,3
```

Columns in an ORDER BY clause are not required to appear in the same order as the associated columns following the SELECT, as shown by the following example:

```
ORDER BY 1,3,2
```

The order in which the columns are specified within the ORDER BY clause is the manner in which the ordering process is done. So the statement that follows first orders by the PROD_DESC column and then by the COST column:

```
ORDER BY PROD_DESC,COST
```

Case Sensitivity

Case sensitivity is an important concept to understand when coding with SQL. Typically, SQL commands and keywords are not case sensitive, which enables you to enter your commands and keywords in either uppercase or lowercase—whatever you prefer. The case may also be mixed (both uppercase and lowercase for a single word or statement), which is often referred to as *camel case*. See Hour 5, "Manipulating Data," on case sensitivity.

Collation is the mechanism that determines how the *relational database management system (RDBMS)* interprets data. This includes methods of ordering the data as well as case sensitivity. Case sensitivity in relation to your data is important because it determines how your WHERE clauses, among other things, interpret matches. You need to check with your specific RDBMS implementation to determine what the default collation is on your system. Some systems, such as MySQL and Microsoft SQL Server, have a default collation that is case insensitive. This means that it matches strings without considering their case. Other systems, such as Oracle, have a default collation that is case sensitive. This means that strings are matched with case taken into account, as described next. Because case sensitivity is a factor at the database level, its importance as a factor in your queries varies.

Use a Standard Case in Your Queries

It is a good practice to use the same case in your query as the data that is stored in your database. Moreover, it is good to implement a corporate policy to ensure that data entry is handled in the same manner across an enterprise.

Watch Out!

Case sensitivity is, however, a factor in maintaining data consistency within your RDBMS. For instance, your data would not be consistent if you arbitrarily entered your data using random case:

SMITH

Smith

smith

If the last name was stored as smith and you issued a query as follows in an RDBMS such as Oracle, which is case sensitive, no rows would be returned:

```
SELECT *
FROM EMPLOYEE_TBL
WHERE LAST_NAME = 'SMITH';

SELECT *
FROM EMPLOYEE_TBL
WHERE UPPER(LAST_NAME) = UPPER('Smith');
```

Examples of Simple Queries

This section provides several examples of queries based on the concepts that have been discussed. The hour begins with the simplest query you can issue and builds upon the initial query progressively. You use the EMPLOYEE_TBL table.

Select all records from a table and display all columns:

```
SELECT * FROM EMPLOYEE_TBL;
```

Select all records from a table and display a specified column:

```
SELECT EMP_ID
FROM EMPLOYEE_TBL;
```

Overcoming Case-Sensitive Issues

In systems that are case sensitive, once again like Oracle, you can overcome the case sensitivity by either ensuring that your data is entered in the same case every time or using SQL functions, which are discussed in later lessons, to modify the case. Following is an example of using the UPPER function to change the cases of the data used in the WHERE clause:

Select all records from a table and display a specified column. You can enter code on one line or use a carriage return as desired:

```
SELECT EMP_ID FROM EMPLOYEE_TBL;
```

Select all records from a table and display multiple columns separated by commas:

```
SELECT EMP_ID, LAST_NAME
FROM EMPLOYEE_TBL;
```

Display data for a given condition:

```
SELECT EMP_ID, LAST_NAME
FROM EMPLOYEE_TBL
WHERE EMP_ID = '333333333';
```

Ensure That Your Queries Are Constrained

When selecting all rows of data from a large table, the results could return a substantial amount of data.

Display data for a given condition and sort the output:

```
SELECT EMP_ID, LAST_NAME
FROM EMPLOYEE_TBL
```

```
WHERE CITY = 'INDIANAPOLIS'
ORDER BY EMP_ID;
```

Display data for a given condition and sort the output on multiple columns, one column sorted in reverse order. In the instance that follows, the EMP_ID column is sorted in ascending order, whereas the LAST_NAME column is sorted in descending order:

```
SELECT EMP_ID, LAST_NAME
FROM EMPLOYEE_TBL
WHERE CITY = 'INDIANAPOLIS'
ORDER BY EMP_ID, LAST_NAME DESC;
```

Display data for a given condition and sort the output using an integer in the place of the spelled-out column name:

```
SELECT EMP_ID, LAST_NAME
FROM EMPLOYEE_TBL
WHERE CITY = 'INDIANAPOLIS'
ORDER BY 1;
```

Display data for a given condition and sort the output by multiple columns using integers. The order of the columns in the sort is different from their corresponding order after the SELECT keyword:

```
SELECT EMP_ID, LAST_NAME
FROM EMPLOYEE_TBL
WHERE CITY = 'INDIANAPOLIS'
ORDER BY 2, 1;
```

Counting the Records in a Table

You can issue a simple query on a table to get a quick count of the number of records in the table or the number of values for a column in the table. A count is accomplished by the function COUNT. Although functions are not discussed until later in this book, this function should be introduced here because it is often a part of one of the simplest queries that you can create.

The syntax of the COUNT function is as follows:

```
SELECT COUNT(*)
FROM TABLE_NAME;
```

The COUNT function is used with parentheses, which enclose the target column to count or the asterisk to count all rows of data in the table.

Counting Basics

Counting the number of values for a column is the same as counting the number of records in a table if the column being counted is NOT NULL (a required column). However, COUNT(*) is typically used for counting the number of rows for a table.

Counting the number of records in the PRODUCTS_TBL table:

```
SELECT COUNT(*) FROM PRODUCTS_TBL;

COUNT(*)
----------
         9

1 row selected.
```

Counting the number of values for PROD_ID in the PRODUCTS_TBL table:

```
SELECT COUNT(PROD_ID) FROM PRODUCTS_TBL;

COUNT(PROD_ID)
--------------
             9

1 row selected.
```

If you want to count only the unique values that show up within a table, you would use the DISTINCT syntax within the COUNT function. For example, if you want to get the distinct states represented in the STATE column of the EMPLOYEE_TBL, use a query such as the one that follows:

```
SELECT COUNT(DISTINCT PROD_ID) FROM PRODUCTS_TBL;

COUNT(DISTINCT PROD_ID)
---------------------------------------
             1
```

Selecting Data from Another User's Table

Permission must be granted to a user to access another user's table. If no permission has been granted, access is not allowed. You can select data from another user's table after access has been granted (the GRANT command is discussed in Hour 20, "Creating and Using Views and Synonyms"). To access another user's table in a SELECT statement, precede the table name with the schema name or the username that owns (created) the table, as in the following example:

```
SELECT EMP_ID
FROM SCHEMA.EMPLOYEE_TBL;
```

Using Column Aliases

Column aliases are used to temporarily rename a table's columns for the purpose of a particular query. The following syntax illustrates the use of column aliases:

```
SELECT COLUMN_NAME ALIAS_NAME
FROM TABLE_NAME;
```

The following example displays the product description twice, giving the second column an alias named PRODUCT. Notice the column headers in the output.

```
select prod_desc,
       prod_desc product
from products_tbl;
```

```
PROD_DESC                  PRODUCT
------------------------------------------------
WITCH COSTUME              WITCH COSTUME
PLASTIC PUMPKIN 18 INCH    PLASTIC PUMPKIN 18 INCH
FALSE PARAFFIN TEETH       FALSE PARAFFIN TEETH
LIGHTED LANTERNS           LIGHTED LANTERNS
ASSORTED COSTUMES          ASSORTED COSTUMES
CANDY CORN                 CANDY CORN
PUMPKIN CANDY              PUMPKIN CANDY
PLASTIC SPIDERS            PLASTIC SPIDERS
ASSORTED MASKS             ASSORTED MASKS
KEY CHAIN                  KEY CHAIN
OAK BOOKSHELF              OAK BOOKSHELF

11 rows selected.
```

Using Synonyms in Queries

If a synonym exists in the database for the table to which you desire access, you do not have to specify the schema name for the table. *Synonyms* are alternate names for tables, which are discussed in Hour 21, "Working with the System Catalog."

Column aliases can be used to customize names for column headers and reference a column with a shorter name in some SQL implementations.

Aliasing a Column in a Query

When a column is renamed in a SELECT statement, the name is not a permanent change. The change is only for that particular SELECT statement.

Summary

You have been introduced to the database query, a means for obtaining useful information from a relational database. The SELECT statement, which is known as the Data Query Language (DQL) command, creates queries in SQL. You must include the FROM clause with every SELECT statement. You have learned how to place a condition on a query using the WHERE clause and how to sort data using the ORDER BY clause. You have also learned the fundamentals of writing queries. After a few exercises, you should be prepared to learn more about queries during the next hour.

Q&A

Q. *Why won't the SELECT clause work without the FROM clause?*

A. The SELECT clause merely tells the database what data you want to see. The FROM clause tells the database where to get the data.

Q. *When I use the ORDER BY clause and choose the option descending, what does that really do to the data?*

A. Say that you use the ORDER BY clause and have selected last_name from the EMPLOYEE_TBL. If you use the descending option, the order starts with the letter Z and finishes with the letter A. Now, let's say that you have used the ORDER BY clause and have selected the salary from the EMPLOYEE_PAY_TBL. If you use the descending option, the order starts with the largest salary and goes down to the lowest salary.

Q. *What advantage is there to renaming columns?*

A. The new column name could fit the description of the returned data more closely for a particular report.

Q. *What would be the ordering of the following statement:*
```
SELECT PROD_DESC,PROD_ID,COST FROM PRODUCTS_TBL
ORDER BY 3,1
```

A. The query would be ordered by the COST column, and then by the PROD_DESC column. Because no ordering preference was specified, they would both be in ascending order.

Workshop

The following workshop is composed of a series of quiz questions and practical exercises. The quiz questions are designed to test your overall understanding of the current material. The practical exercises are intended to afford you the opportunity to apply the concepts discussed during the current hour, as well as build upon the knowledge acquired in previous hours of study. Please take time to complete the quiz questions and exercises before continuing. Refer to Appendix C, "Answers to Quizzes and Exercises," for answers.

Quiz

1. Name the required parts for any SELECT statement.

2. In the WHERE clause, are single quotation marks required for all the data?

3. Under what part of the SQL language does the SELECT statement (database query) fall?

4. Can multiple conditions be used in the WHERE clause?

5. What is the purpose of the DISTINCT option?

6. Is the ALL option required?

7. How are numeric characters treated when ordering based upon a character field?

8. How does Oracle handle its default case sensitivity different from MySQL and Microsoft SQL Server?

Exercises

1. Invoke your RDBMS query editor on your computer. Using your learn-sql database, enter the following SELECT statements. Determine whether the syntax is correct. If the syntax is incorrect, make corrections to the code as necessary. We are using the EMPLOYEE_TBL here.

   a.
   ```
   SELECT EMP_ID, LAST_NAME, FIRST_NAME,
   FROM EMPLOYEE_TBL;
   ```
   b.
   ```
   SELECT EMP_ID, LAST_NAME
   ORDER BY EMPLOYEE_TBL
   FROM EMPLOYEE_TBL;
   ```

c.
```
SELECT EMP_ID, LAST_NAME, FIRST_NAME
FROM EMPLOYEE_TBL
WHERE EMP_ID = '213764555'
ORDER BY EMP_ID;
```

d.
```
SELECT EMP_ID SSN, LAST_NAME
FROM EMPLOYEE_TBL
WHERE EMP_ID = '213764555'
ORDER BY 1;
```

e.
```
SELECT EMP_ID, LAST_NAME, FIRST_NAME
FROM EMPLOYEE_TBL
WHERE EMP_ID = '213764555'
ORDER BY 3, 1, 2;
```

2. Does the following SELECT statement work?

```
SELECT LAST_NAME, FIRST_NAME, PHONE
FROM EMPLOYEE_TBL
WHERE EMP_ID = '333333333';
```

3. Write a SELECT statement that returns the name and cost of each product from the PRODUCTS_TBL. Which product is the most expensive?

4. Write a query that generates a list of all customers and their telephone numbers.

5. Write a simple query to return a list of customers with a particular last name. Try using a WHERE clause with the name in mixed case and uppercase. What case sensitivity is your RDBMS set to?

HOUR 8

Using Operators to Categorize Data

What You'll Learn in This Hour:

▶ What is an operator?

▶ An overview of operators in SQL

▶ How are operators used singularly?

▶ How are operators used in combinations?

Operators are used in conjunction with the SELECT command's WHERE clause to place extended constraints on data that a query returns. Various operators are available to the SQL user that support all data querying needs. In this hour we will show you what operators are available for you to use as well as how to utilize them properly within the WHERE clause.

What Is an Operator in SQL?

An operator is a reserved word or a character used primarily in an SQL statement's WHERE clause to perform operation(s), such as comparisons and arithmetic operations. *Operators* are used to specify conditions in an SQL statement and to serve as conjunctions for multiple conditions in a statement.

The operators discussed during this hour are

▶ Comparison operators

▶ Logical operators

▶ Operators used to negate conditions

▶ Arithmetic operators

Comparison Operators

Comparison operators test single values in an SQL statement. The comparison operators discussed consist of =, <>, <, and >.

These operators are used to test

- Equality
- Non-equality
- Less-than values
- Greater-than values

Examples and the meanings of comparison operators are covered in the following sections.

Equality

The *equal operator* compares single values to one another in an SQL statement. The equal sign (=) symbolizes equality. When testing for equality, the compared values must match exactly, or no data is returned. If two values are equal during a comparison for equality, the returned value for the comparison is TRUE; the returned value is FALSE if equality is not found. This Boolean value (TRUE/FALSE) is used to determine whether data is returned according to the condition.

You can use the = operator by itself or combine it with other operators. Remember from the previous chapter that character data comparisons can either be case sensitive or case insensitive depending on how your *relational database management system (RDBMS)* is set up. So remember to check to ensure that you understand how exactly your values are compared by the query engine.

The following example shows that salary is equal to 20000:

```
WHERE SALARY = '20000'
```

The following query returns all rows of data where the PROD_ID is equal to 2345:

```
SELECT *
FROM PRODUCTS_TBL
WHERE PROD_ID = '2345';

PROD_ID    PROD_DESC                     COST
-------------------------------------------------
2345       OAK BOOKSHELF                 59.99

1 row selected.
```

Non-Equality

For every equality, there are multiple non-equalities. In SQL, the operator used to measure non-equality is <> (the less than sign combined with the greater than sign). The condition returns TRUE if the condition finds non-equality; FALSE is returned if equality is found.

The following example shows that salary is not equal to 20000:

```
WHERE SALARY <> '20000'
```

Did You Know?

Options for Non-Equality

Another option comparable to <> is !=. Many of the major implementations have adopted != to represent not-equal. Microsoft SQL Server, MySQL, and Oracle support both versions of the operator. Oracle actually supports a third, ^= , as another version, but it is rarely used because most people are accustomed to using the earlier two versions.

The following example shows all the product information from the PRODUCTS table that do not have the product ID of 2345:

```
SELECT *
FROM PRODUCTS_TBL
WHERE PROD_ID <> '2345';
```

PROD_ID	PROD_DESC	COST
11235	WITCH COSTUME	29.99
222	PLASTIC PUMPKIN 18 INCH	7.75
13	FALSE PARAFFIN TEETH	1.1
90	LIGHTED LANTERNS	14.5
15	ASSORTED COSTUMES	10
9	CANDY CORN	1.35
6	PUMPKIN CANDY	1.45
87	PLASTIC SPIDERS	1.05
119	ASSORTED MASKS	4.95
1234	KEY CHAIN	5.95
2345	OAK BOOKSHELF	59.99

```
11 rows selected.
```

Once again, remember that your collation and specifically whether your system is set up as case sensitive or case insensitive plays a critical role in these comparisons. If your system is case sensitive, then KEY CHAIN, Key Chain, and key chain would be considered different values, which might or might not be your intention.

Less Than, Greater Than

You can use the symbols < (less than) and > (greater than) by themselves or in combination with each other or other operators.

The following examples show that salary is less than or greater than 20000:

```
WHERE SALARY < '20000'
WHERE SALARY > '20000'
```

In the first example, anything less than and not equal to 20000 returns TRUE. Any value of 20000 or more returns FALSE. Greater than works the opposite of less than.

```
SELECT *
FROM PRODUCTS_TBL
WHERE COST > 20;
```

PROD_ID	PROD_DESC	COST
11235	WITCH COSTUME	29.99
2345	OAK BOOKSHELF	59.99

2 rows selected.

In the next example, notice that the value 29.99 was not included in the query's result set. The less than operator is not inclusive.

```
SELECT *
FROM PRODUCTS_TBL
WHERE COST < 29.99;
```

PROD_ID	PROD_DESC	COST
222	PLASTIC PUMPKIN 18 INCH	7.75
13	FALSE PARAFFIN TEETH	1.1
90	LIGHTED LANTERNS	14.5
15	ASSORTED COSTUMES	10
9	CANDY CORN	1.35
6	PUMPKIN CANDY	1.45
87	PLASTIC SPIDERS	1.05
119	ASSORTED MASKS	4.95
1234	KEY CHAIN	5.95

9 rows selected.

Combinations of Comparison Operators

The equal operator can be combined with the less than and greater than operators.

The following example shows that salary is less than or equal to 20000:

```
WHERE SALARY <= '20000'
```

The next example shows that salary is greater than or equal to 20000:

```
WHERE SALARY >= '20000'
```

Less than or equal to 20000 includes 20000 and all values less than 20000. Any value in that range returns TRUE; any value greater than 20000 returns FALSE. Greater than or equal to also includes the value 20000 in this case and works the same as the <= operator.

```
SELECT *
FROM PRODUCTS_TBL
WHERE COST <= 29.99;
```

PROD_ID	PROD_DESC	COST
222	PLASTIC PUMPKIN 18 INCH	7.75
13	FALSE PARAFFIN TEETH	1.1
90	LIGHTED LANTERNS	14.5
15	ASSORTED COSTUMES	10
9	CANDY CORN	1.35
6	PUMPKIN CANDY	1.45
87	PLASTIC SPIDERS	1.05
119	ASSORTED MASKS	4.95
1234	KEY CHAIN	5.95
11235	WITCH COSTUME	29.99

```
10 rows selected.
```

Logical Operators

Logical operators are those operators that use SQL keywords to make comparisons instead of symbols. The logical operators covered in the following subsections are

- ▶ IS NULL
- ▶ BETWEEN
- ▶ IN
- ▶ LIKE
- ▶ EXISTS

▶ UNIQUE

▶ ALL and ANY

IS NULL

The NULL operator is used to compare a value with a NULL value. For example, you might look for employees who do not have a pager by searching for NULL values in the PAGER column of the EMPLOYEE_TBL table.

The following example compares a value to a NULL value; here, salary has no value:

```
WHERE SALARY IS NULL
```

The following example demonstrates finding all the employees from the EMPLOYEE table who do not have a pager:

```
SELECT EMP_ID, LAST_NAME, FIRST_NAME, PAGER
FROM EMPLOYEE_TBL
WHERE PAGER IS NULL;
```

```
EMP_ID     LAST_NAM FIRST_NA PAGER
---------------------------------
311549902 STEPHENS TINA
442346889 PLEW     LINDA
220984332 WALLACE  MARIAH
443679012 SPURGEON TIFFANY

4 rows selected.
```

Understand that the literal word *null* is different from a NULL value. Examine the following example:

```
SELECT EMP_ID, LAST_NAME, FIRST_NAME, PAGER
FROM EMPLOYEE_TBL
WHERE PAGER = 'NULL';
```

```
no rows selected.
```

BETWEEN

The BETWEEN operator is used to search for values that are within a set of values, given the minimum value and the maximum value. The minimum and maximum values are included as part of the conditional set.

The following example shows that salary must fall between 20000 and 30000, including the values 20000 and 30000:

```
WHERE SALARY BETWEEN '20000' AND '30000'
```

Proper Use of Between

BETWEEN is inclusive and therefore includes the minimum and maximum values in the query results.

The following example shows all the products that cost between $5.95 and $14.50:

```
SELECT *
FROM PRODUCTS_TBL
WHERE COST BETWEEN 5.95 AND 14.5;
```

```
PROD_ID    PROD_DESC                      COST
- - - - - - - - - - - - - - - - - - - - - - - - - - - - - - - - - - -
222        PLASTIC PUMPKIN 18 INCH        7.75
90         LIGHTED LANTERNS               14.5
15         ASSORTED COSTUMES              10
1234       KEY CHAIN                      5.95
```

4 rows selected.

Notice that the values 5.95 and 14.5 are included in the output.

IN

The IN operator compares a value to a list of literal values that have been specified. For TRUE to be returned, the compared value must match at least one of the values in the list.

The following example shows that salary must match one of the values 20000, 30000, or 40000:

```
WHERE SALARY IN('20000', '30000', '40000')
```

The following example shows using the IN operator to match all the products that have a product ID within a certain range of values:

```
SELECT *
FROM PRODUCTS_TBL
WHERE PROD_ID IN ('13','9','87','119');
```

```
PROD_ID    PROD_DESC                      COST
- - - - - - - - - - - - - - - - - - - - - - - - - - - - - - - - - - -
119        ASSORTED MASKS                 4.95
87         PLASTIC SPIDERS                1.05
9          CANDY CORN                     1.35
13         FALSE PARAFFIN TEETH           1.1
```

4 rows selected.

Using the IN operator can achieve the same results as using the OR operator and can return the results more quickly.

LIKE

The LIKE operator is used to compare a value to similar values using wild-card operators. There are two wildcards used in conjunction with the LIKE operator:

▸ The percent sign (%)

▸ The underscore (_)

The percent sign represents zero, one, or multiple characters. The under-score represents a single number or character. The symbols can be used in combinations.

To find any values that start with 200:

```
WHERE SALARY LIKE '200%
```

To find any values that have 200 in any position:

```
WHERE SALARY LIKE '%200%'
```

To find any values that have 00 in the second and third positions:

```
WHERE SALARY LIKE '_00%'
```

To find any values that start with 2 and are at least three characters in length:

```
WHERE SALARY LIKE '2_%_%'
```

To find any values that end with 2:

```
WHERE SALARY LIKE '%2'
```

To find any values that have a 2 in the second position and end with a 3:

```
WHERE SALARY LIKE '_2%3'
```

To find any values in a five-digit number that start with 2 and end with 3:

```
WHERE SALARY LIKE '2___3'
```

The following example shows all product descriptions that end with the let-ter *S* in uppercase:

```
SELECT PROD_DESC
FROM PRODUCTS_TBL
WHERE PROD_DESC LIKE '%S';

PROD_DESC
-----------------
LIGHTED LANTERNS
ASSORTED COSTUMES
PLASTIC SPIDERS
ASSORTED MASKS

4 rows selected.
```

The following example shows all product descriptions whose second character is the letter S in uppercase:

```
SELECT PROD_DESC
FROM PRODUCTS_TBL
WHERE PROD_DESC LIKE '_S%';

PROD_DESC
-----------------
ASSORTED COSTUMES
ASSORTED MASKS

2 rows selected.
```

EXISTS

The EXISTS operator is used to search for the presence of a row in a specified table that meets certain criteria.

The following example searches to see whether the EMP_ID 3333333333 is in EMPLOYEE_TBL:

```
WHERE EXISTS (SELECT EMP_ID FROM EMPLOYEE_TBL WHERE EMPLOYEE_ID
='333333333')
```

The following example is a form of a subquery, which is further discussed during Hour 14, "Using Subqueries to Define Unknown Data":

```
SELECT COST
FROM PRODUCTS_TBL
WHERE EXISTS ( SELECT COST
               FROM PRODUCTS_TBL
               WHERE COST > 100 );

No rows selected.

----------
```

There were no rows selected because no records existed where the cost was greater than 100.

Consider the following example:

```
SELECT COST
FROM PRODUCTS_TBL
WHERE EXISTS ( SELECT COST
               FROM PRODUCTS_TBL
               WHERE COST < 100 );
```

```
COST
-----------
     29.99
      7.75
       1.1
      14.5
      10
       1.35
       1.45
       1.05
       4.95
       5.95
     59.99

11 rows selected.
```

The cost was displayed for records in the table because records existed where the product cost was less than 100.

ALL, SOME, and ANY Operators

The ALL operator is used to compare a value to all values in another value set.

The following example tests salary to see whether it is greater than all salaries of the employees living in Indianapolis:

```
WHERE SALARY > ALL SALARY (SELECT FROM EMPLOYEE_TBL WHERE CITY =
'INDIANAPOLIS')
```

The following example shows how the ALL operator is used in conjunction with subquery:

```
SELECT *
FROM PRODUCTS_TBL
WHERE COST > ALL ( SELECT COST
                   FROM PRODUCTS_TBL
                   WHERE COST < 10 );
```

```
PROD_ID    PROD_DESC                    COST
- - - - - - - - - - - - - - - - - - - - - - - - - - - - - - - - - - - - - - - -
11235      WITCH COSTUME                29.99
90         LIGHTED LANTERNS             14.5
15         ASSORTED COSTUMES            10
2345       OAK BOOKSHELF                59.99

4 rows selected.
```

In this output, five records had a cost greater than the cost of all records having a cost less than 10.

The ANY operator compares a value to any applicable value in the list according to the condition. SOME is an alias for ANY, so you can use them interchangeably.

The following example tests salary to see whether it is greater than any of the salaries of employees living in Indianapolis:

```
WHERE SALARY > ANY (SELECT SALARY FROM EMPLOYEE_TBL WHERE CITY =
'INDIANAPOLIS')
```

The following example shows the use of the ANY operator used in conjunction with a subquery:

```
SELECT *
FROM PRODUCTS_TBL
WHERE COST > ANY ( SELECT COST
                   FROM PRODUCTS_TBL
                   WHERE COST < 10 );
```

```
PROD_ID    PROD_DESC                    COST
- - - - - - - - - - - - - - - - - - - - - - - - - - - - - - - - - - - - - - - -
11235      WITCH COSTUME                29.99
222        PLASTIC PUMPKIN 18 INCH      7.75
13         FALSE PARAFFIN TEETH         1.1
90         LIGHTED LANTERNS             14.5
15         ASSORTED COSTUMES            10
9          CANDY CORN                   1.35
6          PUMPKIN CANDY                1.45
119        ASSORTED MASKS               4.95
1234       KEY CHAIN                    5.95
2345       OAK BOOKSHELF                59.99

10 rows selected.
```

In this output, more records were returned than when using ALL because the cost only had to be greater than any of the costs that were less than 10. The one record that was not displayed had a cost of 1.05, which was not greater than any of the values less than 10 (which was, in fact, 1.05). It should also be noted that ANY is not a synonym for IN because the IN operator can take an expression list of the form shown below, while ANY cannot:

```
IN (<Item#1>,<Item#2>,<Item#3>)
```

Additionally, the negation of IN, discussed in the section "Negative Operators," would be NOT IN, and its alias would be <>ALL instead of <>ANY.

Conjunctive Operators

What if you want to use multiple conditions to narrow data in an SQL statement? You must be able to combine the conditions, and you would do this with conjunctive operators. These operators are

- ▶ AND

- ▶ OR

Conjunctive operators provide a means to make multiple comparisons with different operators in the same SQL statement. The following sections describe each operator's behavior.

AND

The AND operator allows the existence of multiple conditions in an SQL statement's WHERE clause. For an action to be taken by the SQL statement, whether it be a transaction or query, all conditions separated by the AND must be TRUE.

The following example shows that the EMPLOYEE_ID must match 333333333 and the salary must equal 20000:

```
WHERE EMPLOYEE_ID = '333333333' AND SALARY = '20000'
```

The following example shows the use of the AND operator to find the products with a cost between two limiting values:

```
SELECT *
FROM PRODUCTS_TBL
WHERE COST > 10
  AND COST < 30;
```

```
PROD_ID    PROD_DESC                          COST
-----------------------------------------------------
11235      WITCH COSTUME                      29.99
90         LIGHTED LANTERNS                   14.5

2 rows selected.
```

In this output, the value for cost had to be both greater than 10 and less than 30 for data to be retrieved.

This statement retrieves no data because each row of data has only one product identification:

```
SELECT *
FROM PRODUCTS_TBL
WHERE PROD_ID = '7725'
  AND PROD_ID = '2345';
```

```
no rows selected
```

OR

The OR operator combines multiple conditions in an SQL statement's WHERE clause. For an action to be taken by the SQL statement, whether it is a transaction or query, at least one of the conditions that are separated by OR must be TRUE.

The following example shows that salary must match either 20000 or 30000:

```
WHERE SALARY = '20000' OR SALARY = '30000'
```

The following example shows the use of the OR operator to limit a query on the PRODUCTS table:

```
SELECT *
FROM PRODUCTS_TBL
WHERE PROD_ID = '90'
   OR PROD_ID = '2345';
```

```
PROD_ID    PROD_DESC                     COST
---------------------------------------------------
2345       OAK BOOKSHELF                 59.99
90         LIGHTED LANTERNS              14.5
2 rows selected.
```

In this output, either one of the conditions had to be TRUE for data to be retrieved.

Comparison Operators Can Be Stacked

Each of the comparison and logical operators can be used singularly or in combination with each other.

By the Way

Two records that met either one or the other condition were found.

In the next example, notice the use of the AND and two OR operators. In addition, notice the logical placement of the parentheses to make the statement more readable.

```
SELECT *
FROM PRODUCTS_TBL
WHERE COST > 10
  AND ( PROD_ID = '222'
   OR    PROD_ID = '90'
   OR    PROD_ID = '11235' );
PROD_ID    PROD_DESC                       COST
--------------------------------------------------
11235      WITCH COSTUME                   29.99
90         LIGHTED LANTERNS                14.5

2 rows selected.
```

Did You Know?

> **Group Your Queries to Make Them Easily Understandable**
>
> When using multiple conditions and operators in an SQL statement, you might find that using parentheses to separate statements into logical groups improves overall readability. However, be aware that the misuse of parentheses could adversely affect your output results.

The cost in this output had to be greater than 10, and the product identification had to be any one of the three listed. A row was not returned for PROD_ID 222 because the cost for this identification was not greater than 10. Parentheses are not used just to make your code more readable but to ensure that logical grouping of conjunctive operators is evaluated properly. By default, operators are parsed from left to right in the order that they are listed. For example, you want to return all the products in a table whose cost is greater than 5 and whose PRODUCT_ID is in the range of values 222, 90, 11235, and 13. Try the following query to see the result set it returns:

```
SELECT *
FROM PRODUCTS_TBL
WHERE COST > 5
   AND   (PROD_ID = '222'
   OR    PROD_ID = '90'
   OR    PROD_ID = '11235'
   OR    PROD_ID = '13');


PROD_ID        PROD_DESC                   COST
11235          WITCH COSTUME               29.99
222            PLASTIC PUMPKIN 18 INCH      7.75
90             LIGHTED LANTERNS            14.50

3 rows in set
```

If you remove the parentheses, you can see how the result is much different:

```
SELECT *
FROM PRODUCTS_TBL
WHERE COST > 5
    AND   PROD_ID = '222'
    OR    PROD_ID = '90'
    OR    PROD_ID = '11235'
    OR    PROD_ID = '13';
```

```
PROD_ID        PROD_DESC                  COST
11235          WITCH COSTUME              29.99
13             FALSE PARAFFIN TEETH        1.10
222            PLASTIC PUMPKIN 18 INCH     7.75
90             LIGHTED LANTERNS           14.50

3 rows in set
```

FALSE PARAFFIN TEETH gets returned now because this SQL query asks to return a PROD_ID equal to 222 and COST greater than 5 or any rows with PROD_ID equal to 90, 11235, or 13. Use parentheses properly within your WHERE clause to ensure that you are returning the correct logical result set. Otherwise, remember that your operators are evaluated in a certain order, which is normally from left to right.

Negative Operators

Of all the conditions tested by the logical operators discussed here, there is a way to negate each one of these operators to change the condition's viewpoint.

The NOT operator reverses the meaning of the logical operator with which it is used. The NOT can be used with other operators to form the following methods:

- ▶ <>, != (NOT EQUAL)

- ▶ NOT BETWEEN

- ▶ NOT IN

- ▶ NOT LIKE

- ▶ IS NOT NULL

- ▶ NOT EXISTS

- ▶ NOT UNIQUE

Each method is discussed in the following sections. First, let's look at how to test for inequality.

NOT EQUAL

You have learned how to test for inequality using the <> operator. Inequality is worth mentioning in this section because to test for it, you are actually negating the equality operator. Here we cover a second method for testing inequality available in some SQL implementations.

The following examples show that salary is not equal to 20000:

```
WHERE SALARY <> '20000'
WHERE SALARY != '20000'
```

In the second example, you can see that the exclamation mark negates the equality comparison. The use of the exclamation mark is allowed in addition to the standard operator for inequality <> in some implementations.

> **Check Your Implementation**
>
> Check your particular implementation for the use of the exclamation mark to negate the inequality operator. The other operators mentioned are almost always the same if compared between different SQL implementations.

NOT BETWEEN

> **Remember How BETWEEN Works**
>
> Remember that BETWEEN is inclusive; therefore, in the previous example, any rows that equal 5.95 or 14.50 are not included in the query results.

The BETWEEN operator is negated as follows:

```
WHERE Salary NOT BETWEEN '20000' AND '30000'
```

The value for salary cannot fall between 20000 and 30000 or include the values 20000 and 30000. Let's see how this works on PRODUCTS_TBL:

```
SELECT *
FROM PRODUCTS_TBL
WHERE COST NOT BETWEEN 5.95 AND 14.5;
```

```
PROD_ID     PROD_DESC                    COST
- - - - - - - - - - - - - - - - - - - - - - - - - - - - - - - - - - -
11235       WITCH COSTUME                29.99
13          FALSE PARAFFIN TEETH         1.1
9           CANDY CORN                   1.35
6           PUMPKIN CANDY                1.45
87          PLASTIC SPIDERS              1.05
119         ASSORTED MASKS               4.95
2345        OAK BOOKSHELF                59.99

7 rows selected.
```

NOT IN

The IN operator is negated as NOT IN. All salaries in the following example that are not in the listed values, if any, are returned:

```
WHERE SALARY NOT IN ('20000', '30000', '40000')
```

The following example demonstrates using the negation of the IN operator:

```
SELECT *
FROM PRODUCTS_TBL
WHERE PROD_ID NOT IN (119,13,87,9);
```

```
PROD_ID     PROD_DESC                    COST
- - - - - - - - - - - - - - - - - - - - - - - - - - - - - - - - - - -
11235       WITCH COSTUME                29.99
222         PLASTIC PUMPKIN 18 INCH      7.75
90          LIGHTED LANTERNS             14.5
15          ASSORTED COSTUMES            10
6           PUMPKIN CANDY                1.45
1234        KEY CHAIN                    5.95
2345        OAK BOOKSHELF                59.99

7 rows selected.
```

In this output, records were not displayed for the listed identifications after the NOT IN operator.

NOT LIKE

The LIKE, or wildcard, operator is negated as NOT LIKE. When NOT LIKE is used, only values that are not similar are returned.

To find values that do not start with 200:

```
WHERE SALARY NOT LIKE '200%'
```

To find values that do not have 200 in any position:

```
WHERE SALARY NOT LIKE '%200%'
```

To find values that do not have 00 starting in the second position:

```
WHERE SALARY NOT LIKE '_00%'
```

To find values that do not start with 2 and have a length of 3 or greater:

```
WHERE SALARY NOT LIKE '2_%_%'
```

The following example demonstrates using the NOT LIKE operator to display a list of values:

```
SELECT PROD_DESC
FROM PRODUCTS_TBL
WHERE PROD_DESC NOT LIKE 'L%';

PROD_DESC
----------------------
WITCH COSTUME
PLASTIC PUMPKIN 18 INCH
FALSE PARAFFIN TEETH
ASSORTED COSTUMES
CANDY CORN
PUMPKIN CANDY
PLASTIC SPIDERS
ASSORTED MASKS
KEY CHAIN
OAK BOOKSHELF

10 rows selected.
```

In this output, the product descriptions starting with the letter *L* were not displayed.

IS NOT NULL

The IS NULL operator is negated as IS NOT NULL to test for values that are not NULL. The following example only returns NOT NULL rows:

```
WHERE SALARY IS NOT NULL
```

The following example demonstrates using the IS NOT NULL operator to retrieve a list of employees whose page number is NOT NULL:

```
SELECT EMP_ID, LAST_NAME, FIRST_NAME, PAGER
FROM EMPLOYEE_TBL
WHERE PAGER IS NOT NULL;

EMP_ID     LAST_NAM FIRST_NA PAGER
-------------------------------------
213764555 GLASS     BRANDON  3175709980
313782439 GLASS     JACOB    8887345678

2 rows selected.
```

NOT EXISTS

EXISTS is negated as NOT EXISTS.

The following example searches to see whether the EMP_ID 3333333333 is not in EMPLOYEE_TBL:

```
WHERE NOT EXISTS (SELECT EMP_ID FROM EMPLOYEE_TBL WHERE EMP_ID =
'3333333333')
```

The following example demonstrates the use of the NOT EXISTS operator in conjunction with a subquery:

```
SELECT MAX(COST)
FROM PRODUCTS_TBL
WHERE NOT EXISTS ( SELECT COST
                   FROM PRODUCTS_TBL
                   WHERE COST > 100 );
```

```
MAX(COST)
----------
    59.99
```

The maximum cost for the table is displayed in this output because no records contained a cost greater than 100.

Arithmetic Operators

Arithmetic operators perform mathematical functions in SQL—the same as in most other languages. The four conventional operators for mathematical functions are

- ▶ + (addition)
- ▶ - (subtraction)
- ▶ * (multiplication)
- ▶ / (division)

Addition

Addition is performed through the use of the plus (+) symbol.

The following example adds the SALARY column with the BONUS column for a total for each row of data:

```
SELECT SALARY + BONUS FROM EMPLOYEE_PAY_TBL;
```

This example returns all rows where the total of the SALARY and BONUS columns together is greater than 40000:

```
SELECT SALARY FROM EMPLOYEE_PAY_TBL WHERE SALARY + BONUS > '40000';
```

Subtraction

Subtraction is performed using the minus (-) symbol.

The following example subtracts the BONUS column from the SALARY column for the difference:

```
SELECT SALARY - BONUS FROM EMPLOYEE_PAY_TBL;
```

This example returns all rows where the SALARY minus the BONUS is greater than 40000:

```
SELECT SALARY FROM EMPLOYEE_PAY_TBL WHERE SALARY - BONUS > '40000';
```

Multiplication

Multiplication is performed by using the asterisk (*) symbol.

The following example multiplies the SALARY column by 10:

```
SELECT SALARY * 10 FROM EMPLOYEE_PAY_TBL;
```

The next example returns all rows where the product of the SALARY multiplied by 10 is greater than 40000:

```
SELECT SALARY FROM EMPLOYEE_PAY_TBL WHERE SALARY * 10 > '40000';
```

The pay rate in the following example is multiplied by 1.1, which increases the current pay rate by 10%:

```
SELECT EMP_ID, PAY_RATE, PAY_RATE * 1.1
FROM EMPLOYEE_PAY_TBL
WHERE PAY_RATE IS NOT NULL;

EMP_ID      PAY_RATE PAY_RATE*1.1
--------------------------------
442346889     14.75      16.225
220984332        11        12.1
443679012        15        16.5

3 rows selected.
```

Division

Division is performed through the use of the slash (/) symbol.

The following example divides the SALARY column by 10:

```
SELECT SALARY / 10 FROM EMPLOYEE_PAY_TBL;
```

This example returns all rows that are greater than 40000:

```
SELECT SALARY FROM EMPLOYEE_PAY_TBL WHERE SALARY > '40000';
```

This example returns all rows where the salary divided by 10 is greater than 40000:

```
SELECT SALARY FROM EMPLOYEE_PAY_TBL WHERE (SALARY / 10) > '40000';
```

Arithmetic Operator Combinations

You can use the arithmetic operators in combination with one another. Remember the rules of precedence in basic mathematics. Multiplication and division operations are performed first, and then addition and subtraction operations. The only way the user has control over the order of the mathematical operations is through the use of parentheses. Parentheses surrounding an expression cause that expression to be evaluated as a block.

Precedence is the order in which expressions are resolved in a mathematical expression or with embedded functions in SQL. The table that follows shows some simple examples of how operator precedence can affect the outcome of a calculation:

Expression	Result
1 + 1 * 5	6
(1 + 1) * 5	10
10 − 4 / 2 + 1	9
(10 − 4) / (2 + 1)	2

In the following examples, notice that the placement of parentheses in an expression does not affect the outcome if only multiplication and division are involved. Precedence is not a factor in these cases. Although it might not appear to make sense, it is possible that some implementations of SQL do not follow the ANSI standard in cases like this; however, this is unlikely.

Expression	Result
4 * 6 / 2	12
(4 * 6) / 2	12
4 * (6 / 3)	12

Ensure That Your Math Is Correct

When combining arithmetic operators, remember to consider the rules of precedence. The absence of parentheses in a statement could render inaccurate results. Although the syntax of an SQL statement is correct, a logical error might result.

The following are some more examples:

```
SELECT SALARY * 10 + 1000
FROM EMPLOYEE_PAY_TBL
WHERE SALARY > 20000;

SELECT SALARY / 52 + BONUS
FROM EMPLOYEE_PAY_TBL;

SELECT (SALARY - 1000 + BONUS) / 52 * 1.1
FROM EMPLOYEE_PAY_TBL;
```

And here's a rather wild example:

```
SELECT SALARY
FROM EMPLOYEE_PAY_TBL
WHERE SALARY < BONUS * 3 + 10 / 2 - 50;
```

Because parentheses are not used, mathematical precedence takes effect, altering the value for BONUS tremendously for the condition.

Summary

You have been introduced to various operators available in SQL. You have learned the hows and whys of operators. You have also seen examples of operators being used by themselves and in various combinations with one another, using the conjunctive-type operators AND and OR. You have learned the basic arithmetic functions: addition, subtraction, multiplication, and division. Comparison operators test equality, inequality, less than values, and greater than values. Logical operators include BETWEEN, IN, LIKE,

EXISTS, ANY, and ALL. You are already experiencing how elements are added to SQL statements to further specify conditions and better control the processing and retrieving capabilities provided with SQL.

Q&A

Q. *Can I have more than one AND in the WHERE clause?*

A. Yes. In fact, you can use all the operators multiple times. An example would be

```
SELECT SALARY
FROM EMPLOYEE_PAY_TBL
WHERE SALARY > 20000
AND BONUS BETWEEN 1000 AND 3000
AND POSITION = 'VICE PRESIDENT'
```

Q. *What happens if I use single quotation marks around a NUMBER data type in a WHERE clause?*

A. Your query still processes. Quotation marks are not necessary for NUMBER fields.

Workshop

The following workshop is composed of a series of quiz questions and practical exercises. The quiz questions are designed to test your overall understanding of the current material. The practical exercises are intended to afford you the opportunity to apply the concepts discussed during the current hour, as well as build upon the knowledge acquired in previous hours of study. Please take time to complete the quiz questions and exercises before continuing. Refer to Appendix C, "Answers to Quizzes and Exercises," for answers.

Quiz

1. True or false: Both conditions when using the OR operator must be TRUE.

2. True or false: All specified values must match when using the IN operator.

3. True or false: The AND operator can be used in the SELECT and the WHERE clauses.

4. True or false: The ANY operator can accept an expression list.

5. What is the logical negation of the IN operator?

6. What is the logical negation of the ANY and ALL operators?

7. What, if anything, is wrong with the following SELECT statements?

   a.
   ```
   SELECT SALARY
   FROM EMPLOYEE_PAY_TBL
   WHERE SALARY BETWEEN 20000, 30000
   ```

   b.
   ```
   SELECT SALARY + DATE_HIRE
   FROM EMPLOYEE_PAY_TBL
   ```

   c.
   ```
   SELECT SALARY, BONUS
   FROM EMPLOYEE_PAY_TBL
   WHERE DATE_HIRE BETWEEN 2009-09-22
   AND 2009-11-23
   AND POSITION = 'SALES'
   OR POSITION = 'MARKETING'
   AND EMPLOYEE_ID LIKE '%55%'
   ```

Exercises

1. Using the following CUSTOMER_TBL, write a SELECT statement that returns customer IDs and customer names (alpha order) for customers who live in Indiana, Ohio, Michigan, or Illinois and whose names begin with the letters *A* or *B*:

   ```
   DESCRIBE CUSTOMER_TBL;
   ```

Name	Null?	Type
CUST_ID	NOT NULL	VARCHAR (10)
CUST_NAME	NOT NULL	VARCHAR (30)
CUST_ADDRESS	NOT NULL	VARCHAR (20)
CUST_CITY	NOT NULL	VARCHAR (12)
CUST_STATE	NOT NULL	VARCHAR (2)
CUST_ZIP	NOT NULL	VARCHAR (5)
CUST_PHONE		VARCHAR (10)
CUST_FAX		VARCHAR (10)

2. Using the following PRODUCTS_TBL, write a SELECT statement that returns the product ID, product description, and product cost. Limit the product cost to between $1.00 and $12.50:

```
DESCRIBE PRODUCTS_TBL
```

```
Name                            Null?   Type
- - - - - - - - - - - - - - - - - - - - - - - - - - - - - - - - - - - - - -
PROD_ID                         NOT NULL VARCHAR (10)
PROD_DESC                       NOT NULL VARCHAR (25)
COST                            NOT NULL DECIMAL(6,2)
```

3. Assuming that you used the BETWEEN operator in Exercise 2, rewrite your SQL statement to achieve the same results using different operators. If you did not use the BETWEEN operator, do so now.

4. Write a SELECT statement that returns products that are either less than 1.00 or greater than 12.50. There are two ways to achieve the same results.

5. Write a SELECT statement that returns the following information from PRODUCTS_TBL: product description, product cost, and 5% sales tax for each product. List the products in order from most to least expensive.

6. Write a SELECT statement that returns the following information from PRODUCTS_TBL: product description, product cost, 5% sales tax for each product, and total cost with sales tax. List the products in order from most to least expensive. There are two ways to achieve the same results. Try both.

7. Pick three items from the PRODUCTS_TBL. Now write a query to return the rows of data from the table associated with those three items. Now rewrite the query to return everything but those three items. For your query use combinations of equality operators and conjunctive operators.

8. Rewrite the queries you wrote in Exercise 7 using the IN operator. Which statement is more efficient? Which one is more readable?

9. Write a query to return all the products that start with the letter P. Now write a query to return all products that do not start with the letter P.

HOUR 9

Summarizing Data Results from a Query

What You'll Learn in This Hour:

- ▶ What functions are
- ▶ How functions are used
- ▶ When to use functions
- ▶ Using aggregate functions
- ▶ Summarizing data with aggregate functions
- ▶ Results from using functions

In this hour, you learn about SQL's aggregate functions. You can perform a variety of useful functions with aggregate functions, such as getting the highest total of a sale or counting the number of orders processed on a given day. The real power of aggregate functions will be discussed in the next hour when we tackle the GROUP BY clause.

What Are Aggregate Functions?

Functions are keywords in SQL used to manipulate values within columns for output purposes. A *function* is a command normally used in conjunction with a column name or expression that processes the incoming data to produce a result. SQL contains several types of functions. This hour covers aggregate functions. An *aggregate function* provides summarization information for an SQL statement, such as counts, totals, and averages.

The basic set of aggregate functions discussed in this hour are

- ▶ COUNT
- ▶ SUM
- ▶ MAX

▶ MIN

▶ AVG

The following queries show the data used for most of this hour's examples:

```
SELECT * FROM PRODUCTS_TBL;
```

PROD_ID	PROD_DESC	COST
11235	WITCH COSTUME	29.99
222	PLASTIC PUMPKIN 18 INCH	7.75
13	FALSE PARAFFIN TEETH	1.1
90	LIGHTED LANTERNS	14.5
15	ASSORTED COSTUMES	10
9	CANDY CORN	1.35
6	PUMPKIN CANDY	1.45
87	PLASTIC SPIDERS	1.05
119	ASSORTED MASKS	4.95
1234	KEY CHAIN	5.95
2345	OAK BOOKSHELF	59.99

11 rows selected.

The following query lists the employee information from the EMPLOYEE_TBL table. Note that some of the employees do not have pager numbers assigned.

```
SELECT EMP_ID, LAST_NAME, FIRST_NAME, PAGER
FROM EMPLOYEE_TBL;
```

EMP_ID	LAST_NAM	FIRST_NA	PAGER
311549902	STEPHENS	TINA	
442346889	PLEW	LINDA	
213764555	GLASS	BRANDON	3175709980
313782439	GLASS	JACOB	8887345678
220984332	WALLACE	MARIAH	
443679012	SPURGEON	TIFFANY	

6 rows selected.

COUNT

You use the COUNT function to count rows or values of a column that do not contain a NULL value. When used within a query, the COUNT function returns a numeric value. You can also use the COUNT function with the DISTINCT command to only count the distinct rows of a dataset. ALL (opposite of DISTINCT) is the default; it is not necessary to include ALL in the syntax.

Duplicate rows are counted if DISTINCT is not specified. One other option with the COUNT function is to use it with an asterisk. COUNT(*) counts all the rows of a table including duplicates, whether a NULL value is contained in a column or not.

DISTINCT Can Only Be Used in Certain Circumstances

You cannot use the DISTINCT command with COUNT(*), only with COUNT (*column_name*).

By the Way

The syntax for the COUNT function is as follows:

```
COUNT [ (*) | (DISTINCT | ALL) ] (COLUMN NAME)
```

This example counts all employee IDs:

```
SELECT COUNT(EMPLOYEE_ID) FROM EMPLOYEE_PAY_ID
```

This example counts only the distinct rows:

```
SELECT COUNT(DISTINCT SALARY)FROM EMPLOYEE_PAY_TBL
```

This example counts all rows for SALARY:

```
SELECT COUNT(ALL SALARY)FROM EMPLOYEE_PAY_TBL
```

This final example counts all rows of the EMPLOYEE table:

```
SELECT COUNT(*) FROM EMPLOYEE_TBL
```

COUNT(*) is used in the following example to get a count of all records in the EMPLOYEE_TBL table. There are six employees.

```
SELECT COUNT(*)
FROM EMPLOYEE_TBL;

COUNT(*)
---------
6
```

COUNT(*) Is Different from Other Versions

COUNT(*) produces slightly different calculations than other count variations. This is because when the COUNT function is used with the asterisk, it counts the rows in the returned result set without regard to duplicates and NULL values. This is an important distinction. If you need your query to return a count of a particular field and include NULLs, you need to use a function such as ISNULL to replace the NULL values.

Watch Out!

COUNT(EMP_ID) is used in the next example to get a count of all the employee identification IDs that exist in the table. The returned count is the same as the last query because all employees have an identification number.

```
SELECT COUNT(EMP_ID)
FROM EMPLOYEE_TBL;

COUNT(EMP_ID)
- - - - - - - - - - - - -
6
```

COUNT(PAGER) is used in the following example to get a count of all the employee records that have a pager number. Only two employees had pager numbers.

```
SELECT COUNT(PAGER)
FROM EMPLOYEE_TBL;

COUNT(PAGER)
- - - - - - - - - - - -
2
```

The ORDERS_TBL table is shown next:

```
SELECT *
FROM ORDERS_TBL;

ORD_NUM    CUST_ID    PROD_ID        QTY ORD_DATE_
- - - - - - - - - - - - - - - - - - - - - - - - - - - - - - - - - - - - - - - - - -
56A901     232        11235            1 22-OCT-99
56A917     12         907            100 30-SEP-99
32A132     43         222             25 10-OCT-99
16C17      090        222              2 17-OCT-99
18D778     287        90              10 17-OCT-99
23E934     432        13              20 15-OCT-99
90C461     560        1234             2

7 rows selected.
```

This example obtains a count of all distinct product identifications in the ORDERS_TBL table.

```
SELECT COUNT(DISTINCT PROD_ID )
FROM ORDERS_TBL;

COUNT(DISTINCT PROD_ID )
- - - - - - - - - - - - - - - - - - - - - - -
                       6
```

The PROD_ID 222 has two entries in the table, thus reducing the distinct values from 7 to 6.

> **Data Types Do Not COUNT**
>
> Because the COUNT function counts the rows, data types do not play a part. The rows can contain columns with any data type.

SUM

The SUM function returns a total on the values of a column for a group of rows. You can also use the SUM function in conjunction with DISTINCT.

When you use SUM with DISTINCT, only the distinct rows are totaled, which might not have much purpose. Your total is not accurate in that case because rows of data are omitted.

The syntax for the SUM function is as follows:

```
SUM ([ DISTINCT ] COLUMN NAME)
```

> **SUM Must Be Numeric**
>
> The value of an argument must be numeric to use the SUM function. You cannot use the SUM function on columns having a data type other than numeric, such as character or date.

This example totals the salaries:

```
SELECT SUM(SALARY) FROM EMPLOYEE_PAY_TBL
```

This example totals the distinct salaries:

```
SELECT SUM(DISTINCT SALARY) FROM EMPLOYEE_PAY_TBL
```

In the following query, the *sum*, or total amount, of all cost values is being retrieved from the PRODUCTS_TBL table:

```
SELECT SUM(COST)
FROM PRODUCTS_TBL;

 SUM(COST)
-----------
163.07
```

Observe the way the DISTINCT command in the following example skews the previous results. This is why it is rarely useful:

```
SELECT SUM(DISTINCT COST)
FROM PRODUCTS_TBL;
```

```
SUM(COST)
----------
72.14
```

The following query demonstrates that, although some aggregate functions require numeric data, this is only limited to the type of data. Here the PAGER column of the EMPLOYEE_TBL table shows that the implicit conversion of the CHAR data to a numeric type is supported:

```
SELECT SUM(PAGER)
FROM EMPLOYEE_TBL;
```

```
SUM(PAGER)
----------
12063055658
```

When you use a type of data that cannot be implicitly converted to a numeric type, such as the LAST_NAME column, it returns a result of 0.

```
SELECT SUM(LAST_NAME)
FROM EMPLOYEE_TBL;
```

```
SUM(LAST_NAME)
----------
0
```

AVG

The AVG function finds the average value for a given group of rows. When used with the DISTINCT command, the AVG function returns the average of the distinct rows. The syntax for the AVG function is as follows:

```
AVG ([ DISTINCT ] COLUMN NAME)
```

By the Way

> **AVG Must Be Numeric**
> The value of the argument must be numeric for the AVG function to work.

This example returns the average salary:

```
SELECT AVG(SALARY) FROM EMPLOYEE_PAY_TBL
```

This example returns the distinct average salary:

```
SELECT AVG(DISTINCT SALARY) EMPLOYEE_PAY_TBL
```

The average value for all values in the PRODUCTS_TBL table's COST column is being retrieved in the following example:

```
SELECT AVG(COST)
FROM PRODUCTS_TBL;

 AVG(COST)
----------
13.5891667
```

Sometimes Your Data Is Truncated

In some implementations, the results of your query might be truncated to the precision of the data type.

The next example uses two aggregate functions in the same query. Because some employees are paid hourly and others are on salary, you want to retrieve the average value for both PAY_RATE and SALARY.

```
SELECT AVG(PAY_RATE), AVG(SALARY)
FROM EMPLOYEE_PAY_TBL;

AVG(PAY_RATE)       AVG(SALARY)
-------------       ----------
  13.5833333        30000
```

MAX

The MAX function returns the maximum value from the values of a column in a group of rows. NULL values are ignored when using the MAX function. The DISTINCT command is an option. However, because the maximum value for all the rows is the same as the distinct maximum value, DISTINCT is useless.

The syntax for the MAX function is

```
MAX([ DISTINCT ] COLUMN NAME)
```

This example returns the highest salary:

```
SELECT MAX(SALARY) FROM EMPLOYEE_PAY_TBL
```

This example returns the highest distinct salary:

```
SELECT MAX(DISTINCT SALARY) FROM EMPLOYEE_PAY_TBL
```

The following example returns the maximum value for the COST column in the PRODUCTS_TBL table:

```
SELECT MAX(COST)
FROM PRODUCTS_TBL;
```

```
 MAX(COST)
----------29.99

SELECT MAX(DISTICNT COST)
FROM PRODUCTS_TBL;

 MAX(COST)
29.99
```

You can also use aggregate functions such as MAX and MIN on character data. In the case of these values, collation of your database comes into play again. Most commonly your database collation is set to a dictionary order, so the results are ranked according to that. For example, say we performed a MAX on the PRODUCT_DESC column of the products table:

```
SELECT MAX(PRODUCT_DESC)
FROM PRODUCTS_TBL;

MAX(PRODUCT_DESC)
-------------------
WITCH COSTUME
```

In this instance, the function returned the largest value according to a dictionary ordering of the data in the column.

MIN

The MIN function returns the minimum value of a column for a group of rows. NULL values are ignored when using the MIN function. The DISTINCT command is an option. However, because the minimum value for all rows is the same as the minimum value for distinct rows, DISTINCT is useless.

The syntax for the MIN function is

```
MIN([ DISTINCT ] COLUMN NAME)
```

This example returns the lowest salary:

```
SELECT MIN(SALARY) FROM EMPLOYEE_PAY_TBL
```

This example returns the lowest distinct salary:

```
SELECT MIN(DISTINCT SALARY) FROM EMPLOYEE_PAY_TBL
```

The following example returns the minimum value for the COST column in the PRODUCTS_TBL table:

```
SELECT MIN(COST)
FROM PRODUCTS_TBL;
```

```
MIN(COST)
----------
      1.05
SELECT MIN(DISTINCT COST)
FROM PRODUCTS_TBL;

MIN(COST)
----------
1.05
```

DISTINCT and Aggregate Functions Don't Always Mix

By the Way

One important thing to keep in mind when using aggregate functions with the DISTINCT command is that your query might not return the desired results. The purpose of aggregate functions is to return summarized data based on all rows of data in a table.

As with the MAX function, the MIN function can work against character data and returns the minimum value according to the dictionary ordering of the data.

```
SELECT MINPRODUCT_DESC)
FROM PRODUCTS_TBL;

MIN(PRODUCT_DESC)
-------------------
ASSORTED COSTUMES
```

The final example combines aggregate functions with the use of arithmetic operators:

```
SELECT COUNT(ORD_NUM), SUM(QTY),
       SUM(QTY) / COUNT(ORD_NUM) AVG_QTY
FROM ORDERS_TBL;

COUNT(ORD_NUM)    SUM(QTY)     AVG_QTY
--------------    --------     ---------
     7              160        22.857143
```

You have performed a count on all order numbers, figured the sum of all quantities ordered, and, by dividing the two figures, derived the average quantity of an item per order. You also created a column alias for the computation—AVG_QTY.

Summary

Aggregate functions can be useful and are quite simple to use. You have learned how to count values in columns, count rows of data in a table, get the maximum and minimum values for a column, figure the sum of the values in a column, and figure the average value for values in a column. Remember that NULL values are not considered when using aggregate functions, except when using the COUNT function in the format COUNT(*).

Aggregate functions are the first functions in SQL that you have learned, but more follow. You can also use aggregate functions for group values, which are discussed during the next hour. As you learn about other functions, you see that the syntaxes of most functions are similar to one another and that their concepts of use are relatively easy to understand.

Q&A

Q. *Why are NULL values ignored when using the MAX or MIN function?*

A. A NULL value means that nothing is there.

Q. *Why don't data types matter when using the COUNT function?*

A. The COUNT function only counts rows.

Workshop

The following workshop is composed of a series of quiz questions and practical exercises. The quiz questions are designed to test your overall understanding of the current material. The practical exercises are intended to afford you the opportunity to apply the concepts discussed during the current hour, as well as build upon the knowledge acquired in previous hours of study. Please take time to complete the quiz questions and exercises before continuing. Refer to Appendix C, "Answers to Quizzes and Exercises," for answers.

Quiz

1. True or false: The AVG function returns an average of all rows from a SELECT column, including any NULL values.

2. True or false: The SUM function adds column totals.

3. True or false: The COUNT(*) function counts all rows in a table.

4. Will the following SELECT statements work? If not, what fixes the statements?

   a.
   ```
   SELECT COUNT *
   FROM EMPLOYEE_PAY_TBL;
   ```

   b.
   ```
   SELECT COUNT(EMPLOYEE_ID), SALARY
   FROM EMPLOYEE_PAY_TBL;
   ```

   c.
   ```
   SELECT MIN(BONUS), MAX(SALARY)
   FROM EMPLOYEE_PAY_TBL
   WHERE SALARY > 20000;
   ```

   d.
   ```
   SELECT COUNT(DISTINCT PROD_ID) FROM PRODUCTS_TBL;
   ```

   e.
   ```
   SELECT AVG(LAST_NAME) FROM EMPLOYEE_TBL;
   ```

   f.
   ```
   SELECT AVG(PAGER) FROM EMPLOYEE_TBL;
   ```

Exercises

1. Use EMPLOYEE_PAY_TBL to construct SQL statements to solve the following exercises:

   A. What is the average salary?

   B. What is the maximum bonus?

   C. What are the total salaries?

   D. What is the minimum pay rate?

   E. How many rows are in the table?

2. Write a query to determine how many employees are in the company whose last names begin with a G.

3. Write a query to determine the total dollar amount for all the orders in the system. Rewrite the query to determine the total dollar amount if we set the price of each item as $10.00.

4. Write two sets of queries to find the first employee name and last employee name when they are listed in alphabetical order.

5. Write a query to perform an AVG function on the employee names. Does the statement work? Determine why it is that you got that result.

HOUR 10

Sorting and Grouping Data

What You'll Learn in This Hour:

▶ Why you would want to group data

▶ The GROUP BY clause

▶ Group value functions

▶ The how and why of group functions

▶ Grouping by columns

▶ GROUP BY versus ORDER BY

▶ The HAVING clause

You have learned how to query the database and return data in an organized fashion. You have also learned how to sort data from a query. During this hour, you learn how to break returned data from a query into groups for improved readability.

Why Group Data?

Grouping data is the process of combining columns with duplicate values in a logical order. For example, a database might contain information about employees; many employees live in different cities, but some employees live in the same city. You might want to execute a query that shows employee information for each particular city. You are grouping employee information by city and creating a summarized report.

Or perhaps you want to figure the average salary paid to employees according to each city. You can do this by using the aggregate function AVG on the SALARY column, as you learned in the previous hour, and by using the GROUP BY clause to group the output by city.

Grouping data is accomplished through the use of the GROUP BY clause of a SELECT statement (query). In Hour 9, "Summarizing Data Results from a Query," you learned how to use aggregate functions. In this lesson, you see how to use aggregate functions in conjunction with the GROUP BY clause to display results more effectively.

The GROUP BY Clause

The GROUP BY clause is used in collaboration with the SELECT statement to arrange identical data into groups. This clause follows the WHERE clause in a SELECT statement and precedes the ORDER BY clause.

The position of the GROUP BY clause in a query is as follows:

```
SELECT
FROM
WHERE
GROUP BY
ORDER BY
```

The following is the SELECT statement's syntax, including the GROUP BY clause:

```
SELECT COLUMN1, COLUMN2
FROM TABLE1, TABLE2
WHERE CONDITIONS
GROUP BY COLUMN1, COLUMN2
ORDER BY COLUMN1, COLUMN2
```

This ordering normally takes a little getting used to when writing your first queries with the GROUP BY clause; however, it is logical. The GROUP BY clause is normally a much more CPU-intensive operation, and if we do not constrain the rows provided to it we are grouping unnecessary data that would later be discarded. So we intentionally reduce the data set with the WHERE clause so that we perform our grouping only on the rows we need.

You can use the ORDER BY statement, but normally the *relational database management system (RDBMS)* also orders the results by the column ordering in the GROUP BY clause, which is discussed more in depth later in this hour. So unless you need to order the values in a different pattern than the GROUP BY clause, the ORDER BY clause is redundant. However, sometimes it is provided because you are using aggregate functions in the SELECT statement that are not in the GROUP BY clause or because your particular RDBMS functions slightly differently from the standard.

The following sections give examples and explanations of the GROUP BY clause's use in a variety of situations.

Group Functions

Typical group functions—those that the GROUP BY clause uses to arrange data in groups—include AVG, MAX, MIN, SUM, and COUNT. These are the aggregate functions that you learned about in Hour 9. Remember that the aggregate functions were used for single values in Hour 9; now you use the aggregate functions for group values.

Grouping Selected Data

Grouping data is simple. The selected columns (the column list following the SELECT keyword in a query) are the columns you can reference in the GROUP BY clause. If a column is not in the SELECT statement, you cannot use it in the GROUP BY clause. How can you group data on a report if the data is not displayed?

If the column name has been qualified, the qualified name must go into the GROUP BY clause. The column name can also be represented by a number, which is discussed later in the "Representing Column Names with Numbers" section. When grouping the data, the order of columns grouped does not have to match the column order in the SELECT clause.

Creating Groups and Using Aggregate Functions

The SELECT clause has conditions that must be met when using GROUP BY. Specifically, whatever columns are selected must appear in the GROUP BY clause, except for any aggregate values. The columns in the GROUP BY clause do not necessarily have to be in the same order as they appear in the SELECT clause. Should the columns in the SELECT clause be qualified, the qualified names of the columns must be used in the GROUP BY clause. Some examples of syntax for the GROUP BY clause are shown next.

The following SQL statement selects the EMP_ID and the CITY from the EMPLOYEE_TBL and groups the data returned by CITY and then EMP_ID:

```
SELECT EMP_ID, CITY
```

```
FROM EMPLOYEE_TBL
GROUP BY CITY, EMP_ID;
```

This SQL statement returns the EMP_ID and the total of the SALARY column. Then it groups the results by both the salaries and employee IDs:

```
SELECT EMP_ID, SUM(SALARY)
FROM EMPLOYEE_PAY_TBL
GROUP BY SALARY, EMP_ID;
```

This SQL statement returns the total of all the salaries from EMPLOYEE_PAY_TBL:

```
SELECT SUM(SALARY) AS TOTAL_SALARY
FROM EMPLOYEE_PAY_TBL;

TOTAL_SALARY
90000.00

1 row selected
```

This SQL statement returns the totals for the different groups of salaries:

```
SELECT SUM(SALARY)
FROM EMPLOYEE_PAY_TBL
GROUP BY SALARY;

SUM(SALARY)
(null)
20000.00
30000.00
40000.00

4 rows selected
```

Practical examples using real data follow. In this first example, you can see three distinct cities in the EMPLOYEE_TBL table:

```
SELECT CITY
FROM EMPLOYEE_TBL;
```

> **Column Ordering in the Group By Statement Matters**
> Note the order of the columns selected, versus the order of the columns in the GROUP BY clause.

```
CITY
- - - - - - - - - - -
GREENWOOD
INDIANAPOLIS
WHITELAND
```

```
INDIANAPOLIS
INDIANAPOLIS
INDIANAPOLIS

6 rows selected.
```

In the following example, you select the city and a count of all records for each city. You see a count on each of the three distinct cities because you are using a GROUP BY clause:

```
SELECT CITY, COUNT(*)
FROM EMPLOYEE_TBL
GROUP BY CITY;

CITY                 COUNT(*)
-------------        --------
GREENWOOD            1
INDIANAPOLIS         4
WHITELAND            1

3 rows selected.
```

The following is a query from a temporary table created based on EMPLOYEE_TBL and EMPLOYEE_PAY_TBL. You soon learn how to join two tables for a query:

```
SELECT *
FROM EMP_PAY_TMP;

CITY           LAST_NAM      FIRST_NA      PAY_RATE      SALARY
------------   --------      ---------     --------      ------
GREENWOOD      STEPHENS      TINA                        30000
INDIANAPOLIS   PLEW          LINDA         14.75
WHITELAND      GLASS         BRANDON                     40000
INDIANAPOLIS   GLASS         JACOB                       20000
INDIANAPOLIS   WALLACE       MARIAH        11
INDIANAPOLIS   SPURGEON      TIFFANY       15

6 rows selected.
```

In the following example, you retrieve the average pay rate and salary on each distinct city using the aggregate function AVG. There is no average pay rate for GREENWOOD or WHITELAND because no employees living in those cities are paid hourly:

```
SELECT CITY, AVG(PAY_RATE), AVG(SALARY)
FROM EMP_PAY_TMP
GROUP BY CITY;

CITY           AVG(PAY_RATE)     AVG(SALARY)
------------   -------------     -----------
GREENWOOD                        30000
INDIANAPOLIS   13.5833333        20000
```

```
WHITELAND                                      40000
```

3 rows selected.

In the next example, you combine the use of multiple components in a query to return grouped data. You still want to see the average pay rate and salary, but only for INDIANAPOLIS and WHITELAND. You group the data by CITY—you have no choice because you are using aggregate functions on the other columns. Lastly, you want to order the report by 2 and then 3, which are the average pay rate and then average salary, respectively. Study the following details and output:

```
SELECT CITY, AVG(PAY_RATE), AVG(SALARY)
FROM EMP_PAY_TMP
WHERE CITY IN ('INDIANAPOLIS','WHITELAND')
GROUP BY CITY
ORDER BY 2,3;
```

```
CITY                AVG(PAY_RATE)        AVG(SALARY)
------------        -------------        -----------
INDIANAPOLIS        13.5833333           20000
WHITELAND                                40000
```

Values are sorted before NULL values; therefore, the record for INDIANAPOLIS is displayed first. GREENWOOD is not selected, but if it was, its record would have been displayed before the WHITELAND record because the average salary for GREENWOOD is $30,000. (The second sort in the ORDER BY clause was on average salary.)

The last example in this section shows the use of the MAX and MIN aggregate functions with the GROUP BY clause:

```
SELECT CITY, MAX(PAY_RATE), MIN(SALARY)
FROM EMP_PAY_TMP
GROUP BY CITY;
```

```
CITY                MAX(PAY_RATE)       MIN(SALARY)
------------        -------------       -----------
GREENWOOD                               30000
INDIANAPOLIS        15                  20000
WHITELAND                               40000
```

3 rows selected.

Representing Column Names with Numbers

Like the ORDER BY clause, you can order the GROUP BY clause by using an integer to represent the column name. The following is an example of representing column names with numbers:

```
SELECT YEAR(DATE_HIRE) as YEAR_HIRED, SUM(SALARY)
FROM EMPLOYEE_PAY_TBL
GROUP BY 1;

YEAR_HIRED      SUM(SALARY)
- - - - - - - - - - -      - - - - - - - - - - - - -
1999            40000.00
2000
2001
2004            30000.00
2006
2007            20000.00

6 rows selected.
```

This SQL statement returns the SUM of the employee salaries grouped by the year in which the employees were hired. The GROUP BY clause is performed on the entire result set. The order for the groupings is 1, representing EMP_ID.

GROUP BY Versus ORDER BY

You should understand that the GROUP BY clause works the same as the ORDER BY clause in that both sort data. Specifically, you use the ORDER BY clause to sort data from a query. The GROUP BY clause also sorts data from a query to properly group the data.

However, there are some differences and disadvantages of using GROUP BY instead of ORDER BY for sorting operations:

▶ All nonaggregate columns selected must be listed in the GROUP BY clause.

▶ The GROUP BY clause is generally not necessary unless you're using aggregate functions.

An example of performing sort operations utilizing the GROUP BY clause in place of the ORDER BY clause is shown next:

```
SELECT LAST_NAME, FIRST_NAME, CITY
FROM EMPLOYEE_TBL
GROUP BY LAST_NAME;

SELECT LAST_NAME, CITY
                *
ERROR at line 1:
ORA-00979: not a GROUP BY expression
```

By the
Way

> **Error Messages Differ**
> Different SQL implementations return errors in different formats.

In this example, an Oracle database server received an error stating that FIRST_NAME is not a GROUP BY expression. Remember that all columns and expressions in the SELECT statement must be listed in the GROUP BY clause, with the exception of aggregate columns (those columns targeted by an aggregate function).

In the next example, the previous problem is solved by adding all the expressions in the SELECT statement to the GROUP BY clause:

```
SELECT LAST_NAME, FIRST_NAME, CITY
FROM EMPLOYEE_TBL
GROUP BY LAST_NAME, FIRST_NAME, CITY;
```

```
LAST_NAME           FIRST_NAME          CITY
----------          -----------         ------------
GLASS               BRANDON             WHITELAND
GLASS               JACOB               INDIANAPOLIS
PLEW                LINDA               INDIANAPOLIS
SPURGEON            TIFFANY             INDIANAPOLIS
STEPHENS            TINA                GREENWOOD
WALLACE             MARIAH              INDIANAPOLIS

6 rows selected.
```

In this example, the same columns were selected from the same table, but all columns in the GROUP BY clause are listed as they appeared after the SELECT keyword. The results are ordered by LAST_NAME first, FIRST_NAME second, and CITY third. These results could have been accomplished easier with the ORDER BY clause; however, it might help you better understand how the GROUP BY clause works if you can visualize how it must first sort data to group data results.

The following example shows a SELECT statement from EMPLOYEE_TBL and uses the GROUP BY clause to order by CITY:

```
SELECT CITY, LAST_NAME
FROM EMPLOYEE_TBL
GROUP BY CITY, LAST_NAME;
```

```
CITY                LAST_NAME
------------        ----------
GREENWOOD           STEPHENS
INDIANAPOLIS        GLASS
INDIANAPOLIS        PLEW
INDIANAPOLIS        SPURGEON
```

```
INDIANAPOLIS          WALLACE
WHITELAND             GLASS

6 rows selected.
```

Notice the order of data in the previous results, as well as the LAST_NAME of the individual for each CITY. In the following example, all employee records in the EMPLOYEE_TBL table are now counted, and the results are grouped by CITY but ordered by the count on each city first:

```
SELECT CITY, COUNT(*)
FROM EMPLOYEE_TBL
GROUP BY CITY
ORDER BY 2,1;
```

```
CITY                  COUNT(*)
-------------         --------
GREENWOOD             1
WHITELAND             1
INDIANAPOLIS          4

3 rows selected.
```

Check out the order of the results. The results were first sorted by the count on each city (1–4) and then sorted by city. The count for the first two cities in the output is 1. Because the count is the same, which is the first expression in the ORDER BY clause, the city is then sorted; GREENWOOD is placed before WHITELAND.

Although GROUP BY and ORDER BY perform a similar function, there is one major difference. The GROUP BY clause is designed to group identical data, whereas the ORDER BY clause is designed merely to put data into a specific order. You can use GROUP BY and ORDER BY in the same SELECT statement, but you must follow a specific order.

You Can't Use the ORDER BY Clause in a View

You can use the GROUP BY clause in the CREATE VIEW statement to sort data, but the ORDER BY clause is not allowed in the CREATE VIEW statement. The CREATE VIEW statement is discussed in depth in Hour 20, "Creating and Using Views and Synonyms."

CUBE and ROLLUP Expressions

Sometimes it is advantageous to get summary totals within a certain group. For instance, you might want to have a breakdown of the SUM of sales per year, country, and product type but also want to see the totals in each year and country. Luckily, the ANSI SQL standard provides for such functionality using the CUBE and ROLLUP expressions.

The ROLLUP expression is used to get subtotals, or what is commonly referred to as *super-aggregate* rows, along with a grand total row. The ANSI syntax is as follows:

```
GROUP BY ROLLUP(ordered column list of grouping sets)
```

The way the ROLLUP expression works is that, for every change in the LAST column provided for the grouping set, an additional row is inserted into the result set with a NULL value for that column and the subtotal of the values in the set. Additionally, a row is inserted at the end of the result set with NULL values for each of the group columns and a grand total for the aggregate information. Both Microsoft SQL Server and Oracle follow the ANSI-compliant format, but MySQL follows the following slightly different format:

```
GROUP BY order column list of grouping sets WITH ROLLUP
```

Let's first examine a result set of a simple GROUP BY statement in which we examine average employee pay by CITY and ZIP:

```
SELECT CITY,ZIP, AVG(PAY_RATE), AVG(SALARY)
FROM EMPLOYEE_TBL E
INNER JOIN EMPLOYEE_PAY_TBL P
ON E.EMP_ID=P.EMP_ID
GROUP BY CITY,ZIP
ORDER BY CITY,ZIP;
```

CITY	ZIP	AVG(PAY_RATE)	AVG(SALARY)
GREENWOOD	47890	NULL	40000
INDIANAPOLIS	45734	NULL	20000
INDIANAPOLIS	46224	14.75	NULL
INDIANAPOLIS	46234	15.00	NULL
INDIANAPOLIS	46741	11.00	NULL
WHITELAND	47885	NULL	30000

6 rows selected.

The following is an example of using the ROLLUP expression to get subtotals of sales:

```
SELECT CITY,ZIP, AVG(PAY_RATE), AVG(SALARY)
FROM EMPLOYEE_TBL E
INNER JOIN EMPLOYEE_PAY_TBL P
ON E.EMP_ID=P.EMP_ID
GROUP BY ROLLUP(CITY,ZIP);
```

CITY	ZIP	AVG(PAY_RATE)	AVG(SALARY)
GREENWOOD	47890	NULL	40000
GREENWOOD	NULL	NULL	40000
INDIANAPOLIS	45734	NULL	20000
INDIANAPOLIS	46224	14.75	NULL
INDIANAPOLIS	46234	15.00	NULL
INDIANAPOLIS	46741	11.00	NULL
INDIANAPOLIS	NULL	13.58	20000
WHITELAND	47885	NULL	30000
WHITELAND	NULL	NULL	30000
NULL	NULL	13.58	30000

10 rows selected.

Notice how we now get an average super-aggregate row for each one of the cities and an overall average for the entire set as the last row.

The CUBE expression is different. It returns a single row of data with every combination of the columns in the column list along with a row for the grand total of the whole set. The syntax for the CUBE expression is as follows:

```
GROUP BY CUBE(column list of grouping sets)
```

CUBE is often used to create crosstab reports due to its unique nature. For instance, if we want to have sales use the following columns in the GROUP BY CUBE expression list, CITY, STATE, REGION, we receive rows for each of the following:

```
CITY
CITY, STATE
CITY, REGION
CITY, STATE, REGION
REGION
STATE,REGION
STATE
<grand total row>
```

This expression is supported in both Microsoft SQL Server and Oracle, but as of the time of this writing it is not available in MySQL. The following statement shows an example of using the CUBE expression:

```
SELECT CITY,ZIP, AVG(PAY_RATE), AVG(SALARY)
FROM EMPLOYEE_TBL E
INNER JOIN EMPLOYEE_PAY_TBL P
ON E.EMP_ID=P.EMP_ID
GROUP BY CUBE(CITY,ZIP);
```

CITY	ZIP	AVG(PAY_RATE)	AVG(SALARY)
INDIANAPOLIS	45734	NULL	20000
NULL	45734	NULL	20000
INDIANAPOLIS	46224	14.75	NULL
NULL	46224	14.75	NULL
INDIANAPOLIS	46234	15.00	NULL
NULL	46234	15.00	NULL
INDIANAPOLIS	46741	11.00	NULL
NULL	46741	11.00	NULL
WHITELAND	47885	NULL	30000
NULL	47885	NULL	30000
GREENWOOD	47890	NULL	40000
NULL	47890	NULL	40000
GREENWOOD	NULL	NULL	40000
INDIANAPOLIS	NULL	13.58	20000
WHITELAND	NULL	NULL	30000
NULL	NULL	13.58	30000

16 rows selected.

Now you can see that with the CUBE expression, there are even more rows because the statement needs to return each combination of columns within the column set that we provided.

The HAVING Clause

The HAVING clause, when used in conjunction with the GROUP BY clause in a SELECT statement, tells GROUP BY which groups to include in the output. HAVING is to GROUP BY as WHERE is to SELECT. In other words, the WHERE clause places conditions on the selected columns, and the HAVING clause places conditions on groups created by the GROUP BY clause. Therefore, when you use the HAVING clause, you are effectively including or excluding, as the case might be, whole groups of data from the query results.

The following is the position of the HAVING clause in a query:

```
SELECT
FROM
WHERE
GROUP BY
HAVING
ORDER BY
```

The following is the syntax of the SELECT statement, including the HAVING clause:

```
SELECT COLUMN1, COLUMN2
FROM TABLE1, TABLE2
```

```
WHERE CONDITIONS
GROUP BY COLUMN1, COLUMN2
HAVING CONDITIONS
ORDER BY COLUMN1, COLUMN2
```

In the following example, you select the average pay rate and salary for all cities except GREENWOOD. You group the output by CITY, but you only want to display those groups (cities) that have an average salary greater than $20,000. You sort the results by average salary for each city:

```
SELECT CITY, AVG(PAY_RATE), AVG(SALARY)
FROM EMP_PAY_TMP
WHERE CITY <> 'GREENWOOD'
GROUP BY CITY
HAVING AVG(SALARY) > 20000
ORDER BY 3;
```

CITY	AVG(PAY_RATE)	AVG(SALARY)
WHITELAND		40000

1 row selected.

Why was only one row returned by this query?

▶ The city GREENWOOD was eliminated from the WHERE clause.

▶ INDIANAPOLIS was deducted from the output because the average salary was 20000, which is not greater than 20000.

Summary

You have learned how to group the results of a query using the GROUP BY clause. The GROUP BY clause is primarily used with aggregate SQL functions, such as SUM, AVG, MAX, MIN, and COUNT. The nature of GROUP BY is like that of ORDER BY in that both sort query results. The GROUP BY clause must sort data to group results logically, but you can also use it exclusively to sort data. However, an ORDER BY clause is much simpler for this purpose.

The HAVING clause, an extension to the GROUP BY clause, places conditions on the established groups of a query. The WHERE clause places conditions on a query's SELECT clause. During the next hour, you learn a new arsenal of functions that enable you to further manipulate query results.

Q&A

Q. *Is using the GROUP BY clause mandatory when using the ORDER BY clause in a SELECT statement?*

A. No. Using the GROUP BY clause is strictly optional, but it can be helpful when used with ORDER BY.

Q. *What is a group value?*

A. Take the CITY column from the EMPLOYEE_TBL. If you select the employee's name and city and then group the output by city, all the cities that are identical are arranged together.

Q. *Must a column appear in the SELECT statement to use a GROUP BY clause on it?*

A. Yes, a column must be in the SELECT statement to use a GROUP BY clause on it.

Workshop

The following workshop is composed of a series of quiz questions and practical exercises. The quiz questions are designed to test your overall understanding of the current material. The practical exercises are intended to afford you the opportunity to apply the concepts discussed during the current hour, as well as build upon the knowledge acquired in previous hours of study. Please take time to complete the quiz questions and exercises before continuing. Refer to Appendix C, "Answers to Quizzes and Exercises," for answers.

Quiz

1. Will the following SQL statements work?

   a.
   ```
   SELECT SUM(SALARY), EMP_ID
   FROM EMPLOYEE_PAY_TBL
   GROUP BY 1 and 2;
   ```

   b.
   ```
   SELECT EMP_ID, MAX(SALARY)
   FROM EMPLOYEE_PAY_TBL
   GROUP BY SALARY, EMP_ID;
   ```

c.
```
SELECT EMP_ID, COUNT(SALARY)
FROM EMPLOYEE_PAY_TBL
ORDER BY EMP_ID
GROUP BY SALARY;
```

d.
```
SELECT YEAR(DATE_HIRE) AS YEAR_HIRED,SUM(SALARY)
FROM EMPLOYEE_PAY_TBL
GROUP BY 1
HAVING SUM(SALARY)>20000;
```

2. True or false: You must also use the GROUP BY clause when using the HAVING clause.

3. True or false: The following SQL statement returns a total of the salaries by groups:

```
SELECT SUM(SALARY)
FROM EMPLOYEE_PAY_TBL;
```

4. True or false: The columns selected must appear in the GROUP BY clause in the same order.

5. True or false: The HAVING clause tells the GROUP BY which groups to include.

Exercises

1. Invoke the database and enter the following query to show all cities in EMPLOYEE_TBL:

```
SELECT CITY
FROM EMPLOYEE_TBL;
```

2. Enter the following query and compare the results to the query in Exercise 2:

```
SELECT CITY, COUNT(*)
FROM EMPLOYEE_TBL
GROUP BY CITY;
```

3. The HAVING clause works like the WHERE clause in that it enables the user to specify conditions on data returned. The WHERE clause is the main filter on the query, and the HAVING clause is the filter used after groups of data have been established using the GROUP BY clause. Enter the following query to see how the HAVING clause works:

```
SELECT CITY, COUNT(*)
FROM EMPLOYEE_TBL
GROUP BY CITY
HAVING COUNT(*) > 1;
```

4. Modify the query in Exercise 3 to order the results in descending order, from highest count to lowest.

5. Write a query to list the average pay rate and salary by position from the EMPLOYEE_PAY_TBL table.

6. Write a query to list the average salary by position from the EMPLOYEE_PAY_TBL table where the average salary is greater than 20000.

HOUR 11

Restructuring the Appearance of Data

What You'll Learn in This Hour:

▶ Introduction to character functions

▶ How and when to use character functions

▶ Examples of ANSI SQL functions

▶ Examples of common implementation-specific functions

▶ Overview of conversion functions

▶ How and when to use conversion functions

In this hour, you learn how to restructure the appearance of output results using some *American National Standards Institute (ANSI)* standard functions, other functions based on the standard, and several variations used by some major SQL implementations.

The ANSI Standard Is Not Rigid

The ANSI concepts discussed in this book are just that—concepts. Standards provided by ANSI are simply guidelines for how the use of SQL in a relational database should be implemented. With that thought, keep in mind that the specific functions discussed in this hour are not necessarily the exact functions that you might use in your particular implementation. Yes, the concepts are the same, and the way the functions work are generally the same, but function names and actual syntax might differ.

By the Way

ANSI Character Functions

Character functions are functions that represent strings in SQL in formats different from the way they are stored in the table. The first part of this hour discusses the concepts for character functions as covered by ANSI.

The second part of this hour shows real-world examples using functions that are specific to various SQL implementations. The most common forms of ANSI character functions deal with operations for concatenation, substrings, and TRANSLATE.

Concatenation is the process of combining two strings into one. For example, you might want to concatenate an individual's first and last names into a single string for the complete name.

JOHN concatenated with SMITH produces JOHN SMITH.

The concept of *substring* is the capability to extract part of a string, or a "sub" of the string. For example, the following values are substrings of JOHNSON:

- J
- JOHN
- JO
- ON
- SON

The TRANSLATE function translates a string, character by character, into another string. There are normally three arguments with the TRANSLATE function: the string to be converted, a list of the characters to convert, and a list of the substitution characters. Implementation examples are shown in the next part of this hour.

Common Character Functions

You use character functions mainly to compare, join, search, and extract a segment of a string or a value in a column. Several character functions are available to the SQL programmer.

The following sections illustrate the application of ANSI concepts in some of the leading implementations of SQL, such as Microsoft SQL Server, MySQL, and Oracle.

The CONCAT Function

The CONCAT function, along with most other functions, is represented slightly differently among various implementations. The following examples show the use of concatenation in Oracle and SQL Server.

Let's say you want to concatenate JOHN and SON to produce JOHNSON. In Oracle, your code looks like this:

```
SELECT 'JOHN' || 'SON'
```

In SQL Server, your code appears as follows:

```
SELECT 'JOHN' + 'SON'
```

In MySQL, your code looks like this:

```
SELECT CONCAT('JOHN' , 'SON')
```

Now for an overview of the syntaxes. The syntax for Oracle is

```
COLUMN_NAME || [ '' || ] COLUMN_NAME [ COLUMN_NAME ]
```

The syntax for SQL Server is

```
COLUMN_NAME + [ '' + ] COLUMN_NAME [ COLUMN_NAME ]
```

The syntax for MySQL is

```
CONCAT(COLUMN_NAME , [ '' , ] COLUMN_NAME [ COLUMN_NAME ])
```

Both MySQL as well as Oracle employ the CONCAT function. You can use it to get the concatenation of pairs of strings just like the shortened syntax of + for SQL Server and the double pipe (||) for Oracle. The main difference between the two versions is that the Oracle version is limited to two values to be concatenated, whereas you can use the MySQL version for large numbers of values. In addition, remember that, because this operation is for string values, any numeric values must be converted to strings before concatenation. Unfortunately, Microsoft SQL Server does not support the CONCAT function. Some examples of utilizing concatenation in its various formats are shown next.

This SQL Server statement concatenates the values for city and state into one value:

```
SELECT CITY + STATE FROM EMPLOYEE_TBL;
```

This Oracle statement concatenates the values for city and state into one value, placing a comma between the values for city and state:

```
SELECT CITY ||', '|| STATE FROM EMPLOYEE_TBL;
```

Alternatively for Oracle, if you wanted to use the CONCAT statement to achieve the preceding result, you would be unable to do so because you are concatenating more than two values.

> **Use of Quotation Marks for Special Characters**
>
> Notice the use of single quotation marks and a comma in the preceding SQL statement. Most characters and symbols are allowed if they're enclosed by single quotations marks. Some implementations might use double quotation marks for literal string values.

This SQL Server statement concatenates the values for city and state into one value, placing a space between the two original values:

```
SELECT CITY + '' + STATE FROM EMPLOYEE_TBL;
```

This SQL Server statement concatenates the last name with the first name and inserts a comma between the two original values:

```
SELECT LAST_NAME + ', ' + FIRST_NAME NAME
FROM EMPLOYEE_TBL;

NAME
----------------
STEPHENS, TINA
PLEW, LINDA
GLASS, BRANDON
GLASS, JACOB
WALLACE, MARIAH
SPURGEON, TIFFANY

6 rows selected.
```

The TRANSLATE Function

The TRANSLATE function searches a string of characters and checks for a specific character, makes note of the position found, searches the replacement string at the same position, and then replaces that character with the new value. The syntax is

```
TRANSLATE(CHARACTER SET, VALUE1, VALUE2)
```

The next SQL statement substitutes every occurrence of I in the string with A, every occurrence of N with B, and all occurrences of D with C:

```
SELECT TRANSLATE (CITY,'IND','ABC' FROM EMPLOYEE_TBL) CITY_TRANSLATION
```

The following example illustrates the use of TRANSLATE with real data:

```
SELECT CITY, TRANSLATE(CITY,'IND','ABC')
FROM EMPLOYEE_TBL;

CITY          CITY_TRANSLATION
----------    -----------------
```

```
GREENWOOD     GREEBWOOC
INDIANAPOLIS  ABCAABAPOLAS
WHITELAND     WHATELABC
INDIANAPOLIS  ABCAABAPOLAS
INDIANAPOLIS  ABCAABAPOLAS
INDIANAPOLIS  ABCAABAPOLAS

6 rows selected.
```

Notice in this example that all occurrences of I were replaced with A, N with B, and D with C. In the city INDIANAPOLIS, IND was replaced with ABC, but in GREENWOOD, D was replaced with C. Also notice how the value WHITELAND was translated.

Both MySQL and Oracle support the use of the TRANSLATE function. Microsoft SQL Server does not currently support the use of TRANSLATE.

The REPLACE Function

The REPLACE function replaces every occurrence of a character or string with another specified character or string. The use of this function is similar to the TRANSLATE function except only one specific character or string is replaced within another string. The syntax is

```
REPLACE('VALUE', 'VALUE', [ NULL ] 'VALUE')
```

This statement returns all the first names and changes any occurrence of T to B:

```
SELECT REPLACE(FIRST_NAME,'T', 'B') FROM EMPLOYEE_TBL
```

This statement returns all the cities in EMPLOYEE_TBL and returns the same cities with each I replaced with a Z:

```
SELECT CITY, REPLACE(CITY,'I','Z')
FROM EMPLOYEE_TBL;
```

```
CITY          REPLACE(CITY)
------------  -------------
GREENWOOD     GREENWOOD
INDIANAPOLIS  ZNDZANAPOLZS
WHITELAND     WHZTELAND
INDIANAPOLIS  ZNDZANAPOLZS
INDIANAPOLIS  ZNDZANAPOLZS
INDIANAPOLIS  ZNDZANAPOLZS

6 rows selected.
```

Microsoft SQL Server, MySQL, and Oracle all support the ANSI version of the syntax.

The UPPER Function

Most implementations have a way to control the case of data by using functions. The UPPER function converts lowercase letters to uppercase letters for a specific string.

The syntax is as follows:

```
UPPER(character string)
```

This SQL statement converts all characters in the column to uppercase:

```
SELECT UPPER(CITY)
FROM EMPLOYEE_TBL;

UPPER(CITY)
- - - - - - - - - - - - -
GREENWOOD
INDIANAPOLIS
WHITELAND
INDIANAPOLIS
INDIANAPOLIS
INDIANAPOLIS

6 rows selected.
```

Microsoft SQL Server, MySQL, and Oracle all support this syntax. Additionally, MySQL supports a synonym for the UPPER function by using UCASE. Because both functions accomplish the same task, you are better served to follow the ANSI syntax.

The LOWER Function

The converse of the UPPER function, the LOWER function, converts uppercase letters to lowercase letters for a specific string.

The syntax is as follows:

```
LOWER(character string)
```

This SQL statement converts all characters in the column to lowercase:

```
SELECT LOWER(CITY)
FROM EMPLOYEE_TBL;

LOWER(CITY)
- - - - - - - - - - - - -
greenwood
indianapolis
whiteland
indianapolis
indianapolis
indianapolis

6 rows selected.
```

The LOWER function is supported in Microsoft SQL Server, Oracle, and MySQL. Like the UPPER function, MySQL supports a synonym LCASE, but as discussed with the UPPER function, it is often better to follow the ANSI standard.

The SUBSTR Function

Taking an expression's substring is common in most implementations of SQL, but the function name might differ, as shown in the following Oracle and SQL Server examples.

The syntax for Oracle is

```
SUBSTR(COLUMN NAME, STARTING POSITION, LENGTH)
```

The syntax for SQL Server is

```
SUBSTRING(COLUMN NAME, STARTING POSITION, LENGTH)
```

The only difference between the two implementations is the spelling of the function name.

This SQL statement returns the first three characters of EMP_ID:

```
SELECT SUBSTRING(EMP_ID,1,3) FROM EMPLOYEE_TBL
```

This SQL statement returns the fourth and fifth characters of EMP_ID:

```
SELECT SUBSTRING(EMP_ID,4,2) FROM EMPLOYEE_TBL
```

This SQL statement returns the sixth through the ninth characters of EMP_ID:

```
SELECT SUBSTRING(EMP_ID,6,4) FROM EMPLOYEE_TBL
```

The following is an example that is compatible with Microsoft SQL Server and MySQL:

```
SELECT EMP_ID, SUBSTRING(EMP_ID,1,3)
FROM EMPLOYEE_TBL;

EMP_ID
------------
311549902 311
442346889 442
213764555 213
313782439 313
220984332 220
443679012 443

6 rows affected.
```

The following SQL statement is what you use for Oracle:

```
SELECT EMP_ID, SUBSTR(EMP_ID,1,3)
FROM EMPLOYEE_TBL;
```

```
EMP_ID
- - - - - - - - - - - - -
311549902 311
442346889 442
213764555 213
313782439 313
220984332 220
443679012 443

6 rows selected.
```

> **Output Statements Differ Between Implementations**
>
> Notice the difference in the feedback of the two queries. The first example
> returns the feedback 6 rows affected, and the second returns 6 rows
> selected. You will see differences such as this between the various implementa-
> tions.

The INSTR Function

The INSTR function searches a string of characters for a specific set of characters and reports the position of those characters. The syntax is as follows:

```
INSTR(COLUMN NAME, 'SET',
[ START POSITION [ , OCCURRENCE ] ]);
```

This SQL statement returns the position of the first occurrence of the letter I
for each state in EMPLOYEE_TBL:

```
SELECT INSTR(STATE,'I',1,1) FROM EMPLOYEE_TBL;
```

This SQL statement looks for the first occurrence of the letter A in the
PROD_DESC column:

```
SELECT PROD_DESC,
       INSTR(PROD_DESC,'A',1,1)
FROM PRODUCTS_TBL;
```

```
PROD_DESC                      INSTR(PROD_DESC,'A',1,1)
- - - - - - - - - - - - - - - - - - - - - -    - - - - - - - - - - - - - - - - - - - - - - - -
WITCH COSTUME                                         0
PLASTIC PUMPKIN 18 INCH                               3
FALSE PARAFFIN TEETH                                  2
LIGHTED LANTERNS                                     10
ASSORTED COSTUMES                                     1
CANDY CORN                                            2
```

```
PUMPKIN CANDY                        10
PLASTIC SPIDERS                       3
ASSORTED MASKS                        1
KEY CHAIN                             7
OAK BOOKSHELF                         2
```

```
11 rows selected.
```

Notice that if the searched character A is not found in a string, the value 0 is returned for the position.

The INSTR function is specific to the MySQL and Oracle implementations, although you can use a similar function, CHARINDEX, for Microsoft SQL Server implementations.

The LTRIM Function

The LTRIM function is another way of clipping part of a string. This function and SUBSTRING are in the same family. LTRIM trims characters from the left of a string. The syntax is

```
LTRIM(CHARACTER STRING [ ,'set' ])
```

This SQL statement trims the characters LES from the left of all names that are LESLIE:

```
SELECT LTRIM(FIRST_NAME,'LES') FROM CUSTOMER_TBL WHERE FIRST_NAME
='LESLIE';
```

This SQL statement returns the position of the employee with the word SALES trimmed from the left side of the character string:

```
SELECT POSITION, LTRIM(POSITION,'SALES')
FROM EMPLOYEE_PAY_TBL;
```

```
POSITION           LTRIM(POSITION,
- - - - - - - - - - - - -    - - - - - - - - - - - - - - -
MARKETING          MARKETING
TEAM LEADER        TEAM LEADER
SALES MANAGER      MANAGER
SALESMAN           MAN
SHIPPER            HIPPER
SHIPPER            HIPPER
```

```
6 rows selected.
```

The S in SHIPPER was trimmed off, even though SHIPPER does not contain the string SALES. The first four characters of SALES were ignored. The searched characters must appear in the same order of the search string and must be on the far left of the string. In other words, LTRIM trims off all characters to the left of the last occurrence in the search string.

The LTRIM function is supported in Microsoft SQL Server, MySQL, and Oracle.

The RTRIM Function

Like LTRIM, the RTRIM function trims characters, but this time from the right of a string. The syntax is

```
RTRIM(CHARACTER STRING [ ,'set' ])
```

This SQL statement returns the first name BRANDON and trims the ON, leaving BRAND as a result:

```
SELECT RTRIM(FIRST_NAME, 'ON') FROM EMPLOYEE_TBL WHERE FIRST_NAME =
'BRANDON';
```

This SQL statement returns a list of the positions in PAY_TBL as well as the positions with the letters ER trimmed from the right of the character string:

```
SELECT POSITION, RTRIM(POSITION,'ER')
FROM EMPLOYEE_PAY_TBL;
```

```
POSITION            RTRIM(POSITION,
- - - - - - - - - - - -     - - - - - - - - - - - - - -
MARKETING           MARKETING
TEAM LEADER         TEAM LEAD
SALES MANAGER       SALES MANAG
SALESMAN            SALESMAN
SHIPPER             SHIPP
SHIPPER             SHIPP

6 rows selected.
```

The string ER was trimmed from the right of all applicable strings.

The RTRIM function is supported in Microsoft SQL Server, MySQL, and Oracle.

The DECODE Function

The DECODE function is not ANSI—at least not at the time of this writing—but its use is shown here because of its great power. This function is used mainly in Oracle and PostgreSQL implementations. DECODE searches a string for a value or string; if the string is found, an alternative string is displayed as part of the query results.

The syntax is

```
DECODE(COLUMN NAME, 'SEARCH1', 'RETURN1',[ 'SEARCH2', 'RETURN2', 'DEFAULT
VALUE'])
```

This query searches the value of all last names in EMPLOYEE_TBL; if the value SMITH is found, JONES is displayed in its place. Any other names are displayed as OTHER, which is called the *default value*:

```
SELECT DECODE(LAST_NAME,'SMITH','JONES','OTHER') FROM EMPLOYEE_TBL;
```

In the following example, DECODE is used on the values for CITY in EMPLOYEE_TBL:

```
SELECT CITY,
       DECODE(CITY,'INDIANAPOLIS','INDY',
                   'GREENWOOD','GREEN','OTHER')
FROM EMPLOYEE_TBL;
```

```
CITY          DECOD
------------  ------
GREENWOOD     GREEN
INDIANAPOLIS  INDY
WHITELAND     OTHER
INDIANAPOLIS  INDY
INDIANAPOLIS  INDY
INDIANAPOLIS  INDY

6 rows selected.
```

The output shows the value INDIANAPOLIS displayed as INDY, GREENWOOD displayed as GREEN, and all other cities displayed as OTHER.

Miscellaneous Character Functions

The following sections show a few other character functions worth mentioning. Once again, these are functions that are fairly common among major implementations.

The LENGTH Function

The LENGTH function is a common one that finds the length of a string, number, date, or expression in bytes. The syntax is

```
LENGTH(CHARACTER STRING)
```

This SQL statement returns the product description and its corresponding length:

```
SELECT PROD_DESC, LENGTH(PROD_DESC)
FROM PRODUCTS_TBL;
```

```
PROD_DESC                              LENGTH(PROD_DESC)
------------------------               -----------------
WITCH COSTUME                          15
PLASTIC PUMPKIN 18 INCH                23
FALSE PARAFFIN TEETH                   19
LIGHTED LANTERNS                       16
ASSORTED COSTUMES                      17
CANDY CORN                             10
PUMPKIN CANDY                          13
PLASTIC SPIDERS                        15
ASSORTED MASKS                         14
KEY CHAIN                               9
OAK BOOKSHELF                          13

11 rows selected.
```

The LENGTH function is supported in both MySQL and Oracle. Microsoft SQL Server uses a shortened version LEN instead, but the functionality is the same.

The IFNULL Function (NULL Value Checker)

The IFNULL function returns data from one expression if another expression is NULL. You can use IFNULL with most data types; however, the value and the substitute must be the same data type. The syntax is

```
IFNULL('VALUE', 'SUBSTITUTION')
```

This SQL statement finds NULL values and substitutes 9999999999 for them:

```
SELECT PAGER, IFNULL(PAGER,9999999999)
FROM EMPLOYEE_TBL;
```

```
PAGER          IFNULL(PAGER,
----------     -------------
               9999999999
               9999999999
3175709980     3175709980
8887345678     8887345678
               9999999999
               9999999999

6 rows selected.
```

Only NULL values were represented as 9999999999.

IFNULL is supported only in the MySQL implementation. However, Microsoft SQL Server uses a similar function, ISNULL, that achieves the same result. Oracle utilizes the COALESCE function.

The COALESCE Function

The COALESCE function is similar to the IFNULL function in that it specifically replaces NULL values within the result set. The COALESCE function, however, can accept a whole set of values and checks each one in order until it finds a non-NULL result. If a non-NULL result is not present, COALESCE returns a NULL value.

The following example demonstrates the COALESCE function by giving us the first non-NULL value of BONUS, SALARY, and PAY_RATE:

```
SELECT EMP_ID, COALESCE(BONUS,SALARY,PAY_RATE)
FROM EMPLOYEE_PAY_TBL;


EMP_ID            COALESCE(BONUS,SALARY,PAY_RATE)
----------        -----------------------------------------------------
213764555         2000.00
220984332         11.00
311549902         40000.00
313782439         1000.00
442346889         14.75
443679012         15.00

6 rows selected.
```

The COALESCE function is supported in Microsoft SQL Server, MySQL, and Oracle.

The LPAD Function

LPAD (left pad) is used to add characters or spaces to the left of a string. The syntax is

```
LPAD(CHARACTER SET)
```

The following example pads periods to the left of each product description, totaling 30 characters between the actual value and padded periods:

```
SELECT LPAD(PROD_DESC,30,'.') PRODUCT
FROM PRODUCTS_TBL;

PRODUCT
------------------------------
.................WITCH COSTUME
.......PLASTIC PUMPKIN 18 INCH
..........FALSE PARAFFIN TEETH
..............LIGHTED LANTERNS
.............ASSORTED COSTUMES
...................CANDY CORN
................PUMPKIN CANDY
...............PLASTIC SPIDERS
...............ASSORTED MASKS
```

```
....................KEY CHAIN
.................OAK BOOKSHELF
```

11 rows selected.

The LPAD function is supported in both MySQL and Oracle. Unfortunately, no alternative is available for Microsoft SQL Server.

The RPAD Function

The RPAD (right pad) function adds characters or spaces to the right of a string. The syntax is

RPAD(*CHARACTER SET*)

The following example pads periods to the right of each product description, totaling 30 characters between the actual value and padded periods:

```
SELECT RPAD(PROD_DESC,30,'.') PRODUCT
FROM PRODUCTS_TBL;

PRODUCT
-------------------------------
WITCH COSTUME.................
PLASTIC PUMPKIN 18 INCH.......
FALSE PARAFFIN TEETH..........
LIGHTED LANTERNS..............
ASSORTED COSTUMES.............
CANDY CORN....................
PUMPKIN CANDY.................
PLASTIC SPIDERS...............
ASSORTED MASKS................
KEY CHAIN.....................
OAK BOOKSHELF.................

11 rows selected.
```

The RPAD function is available in both MySQL and Oracle. Unfortunately, no substitute is available for Microsoft SQL Server.

The ASCII Function

The ASCII function returns the *ASCII* representation of the leftmost character of a string. The syntax is

ASCII(*CHARACTER SET*)

The following are some examples:

▶ ASCII('A') returns 65

- ASCII('B') returns 66

- ASCII('C') returns 67

- ASCII('a') returns 97

For more information, you may refer to the ASCII chart located at www. asciitable.com.

The ASCII function is supported in Microsoft SQL Server, MySQL, and Oracle.

Mathematical Functions

Mathematical functions are standard across implementations. Mathematical functions enable you to manipulate numeric values in a database according to mathematical rules.

The most common functions include the following:

- Absolute value (ABS)

- Rounding (ROUND)

- Square root (SQRT)

- Sign values (SIGN)

- Power (POWER)

- Ceiling and floor values (CEIL(ING), FLOOR)

- Exponential values (EXP)

- SIN, COS, TAN

The general syntax of most mathematical functions is

FUNCTION(*EXPRESSION*)

All the mathematical functions are supported in Microsoft SQL Server, MySQL, and Oracle.

Conversion Functions

Conversion functions convert a data type into another data type. For example, perhaps you have data that is normally stored in character format, but occasionally you want to convert the character format to numeric to make calculations. Mathematical functions and computations are not allowed on data that is represented in character format.

The following are general types of data conversions:

▶ Character to numeric

▶ Numeric to character

▶ Character to date

▶ Date to character

The first two types of conversions are discussed in this hour. The remaining conversion types are discussed in Hour 12, "Understanding Dates and Times."

Converting Character Strings to Numbers

You should notice two things regarding the differences between numeric data types and character string data types:

> **Converting to Numeric Values**
>
> For a character string to be converted to a number, the characters must typically be 0 through 9. The addition symbol (+), minus symbol (−), and period (.) can also be used to represent positive numbers, negative numbers, and decimals. For example, the string STEVE cannot be converted to a number, whereas an individual's Social Security number can be stored as a character string but can easily be converted to a numeric value via use of a conversion function.

▶ You can use arithmetic expressions and functions on numeric values.

▶ Numeric values are right-justified in the output results, whereas character string data types are left-justified.

When a character string is converted to a numeric value, the value takes on the two attributes just mentioned.

Some implementations might not have functions to convert character strings to numbers, whereas others have such conversion functions. In either case, consult your implementation documentation for specific syntax and rules for conversions.

> **Some Systems Do the Conversions for You**
>
> Some implementations might implicitly convert data types when necessary. This means that the system makes the conversion for you when changing between data types. In these cases, the use of conversion functions is unnecessary. Check your implementation's documentation to see which types of implicit conversions are supported.

The following is an example of a numeric conversion using an Oracle conversion function:

```
SELECT EMP_ID, TO_NUMBER(EMP_ID)
FROM EMPLOYEE_TBL;
```

```
EMP_ID                TO_NUMBER(EMP_ID)
. . . . . . . . .     . . . . . . . . . . . . . . . .
311549902             311549902
442346889             442346889
213764555             213764555
313782439             313782439
220984332             220984332
443679012             443679012

6 rows selected.
```

The employee identification is right-justified following the conversion.

Converting Numbers to Character Strings

Converting numeric values to character strings is precisely the opposite of converting characters to numbers.

The following is an example of converting a numeric value to a character string using a Transact-SQL conversion function for Microsoft SQL Server:

```
SELECT PAY = PAY_RATE, NEW_PAY = STR(PAY_RATE)
FROM EMPLOYEE_PAY_TBL
WHERE PAY_RATE IS NOT NULL;
```

```
PAY           NEW_PAY
. . . . . . . . . .   . . . . . . .
17.5          17.5
14.75         14.75
18.25         18.25
12.8          12.8
11            11
15            15
6 rows affected.
```

The following is the same example using an Oracle conversion function:

```
SELECT PAY_RATE, TO_CHAR(PAY_RATE)
FROM EMPLOYEE_PAY_TBL
WHERE PAY_RATE IS NOT NULL;
```

```
    PAY_RATE            TO_CHAR(PAY_RATE)
    ----------          -----------------
    17.5                17.5
    14.75               14.75
    18.25               18.25
    12.8                12.8
    11                  11
    15                  15

6 rows selected.
```

Combining Character Functions

You can combine most functions in an SQL statement. SQL would be far too
limited if function combinations were not allowed. The following example
combines two functions in the query (concatenation with substring). By
pulling the EMP_ID column apart into three pieces, you can concatenate those
pieces with dashes to render a readable Social Security number. This example
uses the CONCAT function to combine the strings for output:

```
SELECT CONCAT(LAST_NAME,', ',FIRST_NAME) NAME,
       CONCAT(SUBSTR(EMP_ID,1,3),'-',
       SUBSTR(EMP_ID,4,2),'-',
       SUBSTR(EMP_ID,6,4)) AS ID
FROM EMPLOYEE_TBL;
```

```
NAME                    ID
------------------      ----------
STEPHENS, TINA          311-54-9902
PLEW, LINDA             442-34-6889
GLASS, BRANDON          213-76-4555
GLASS, JACOB            313-78-2439
WALLACE, MARIAH         220-98-4332
SPURGEON, TIFFANY       443-67-9012

6 rows selected.
```

This example uses the LENGTH function and the addition arithmetic operator (+) to add the length of the first name to the length of the last name for each column; the SUM function then finds the total length of all first and last names:

```
SELECT SUM(LENGTH(LAST_NAME) + LENGTH(FIRST_NAME)) TOTAL
FROM EMPLOYEE_TBL;

     TOTAL
- - - - - - - - - - -
71

1 row selected.
```

How Embedded Functions Are Resolved

When embedding functions within functions in an SQL statement, remember that the innermost function is resolved first, and then each function is subsequently resolved from the inside out.

By the Way

Summary

You have been introduced to various functions used in an SQL statement—usually a query—to modify or enhance the way output is represented. Those functions include character, mathematical, and conversion functions. It is important to realize that the ANSI standard is a guideline for how SQL should be implemented by vendors, but it does not dictate the exact syntax or necessarily place limits on vendors' innovations. Most vendors have standard functions and conform to the ANSI concepts, but each vendor has its own specific list of available functions. The function name might differ and the syntax might differ, but the concepts with all functions are the same.

Q&A

Q. *Are all functions in the ANSI standard?*

A. No, not all functions are exactly ANSI SQL. Functions, like data types, are often implementation dependent. Most implementations contain supersets of the ANSI functions; many have a wide range of functions with extended capability, whereas other implementations seem to be somewhat limited. Several examples of functions from selected implementations are included in this hour. However, because so many implementations use similar functions (although they might slightly differ), check your particular implementation for available functions and their usage.

Q. *Is the data actually changed in the database when using functions?*

A. No. Data is not changed in the database when using functions. Functions are typically used in queries to manipulate the output's appearance.

Workshop

The following workshop is composed of a series of quiz questions and practical exercises. The quiz questions are designed to test your overall understanding of the current material. The practical exercises are intended to afford you the opportunity to apply the concepts discussed during the current hour, as well as build upon the knowledge acquired in previous hours of study. Please take time to complete the quiz questions and exercises before continuing. Refer to Appendix C, "Answers to Quizzes and Exercises," for answers.

Quiz

1. Match the descriptions with the possible functions.

Description		Function
a.	Used to select a portion of a character string	||
b.	Used to trim characters from either the right or left of a string	RPAD
c.	Used to change all letters to lowercase	LPAD
d.	Used to find the length of a string	RTRIM

Description	Function
e. Used to combine strings	UPPER
	LTRIM
	LENGTH
	LOWER
	SUBSTR

2. True or false: Using functions in a SELECT statement to restructure the appearance of data in output also affects the way the data is stored in the database.

3. True or false: The outermost function is always resolved first when functions are embedded within other functions in a query.

Exercises

1. Type the following code at the mysql> prompt to concatenate each employee's last name and first name:

```
SELECT CONCAT(LAST_NAME, ', ', FIRST_NAME)
FROM EMPLOYEE_TBL;
```

How would the same statement be applied in Oracle and SQL Server?

2. Type the following MySQL code to print each employee's concatenated name and his or her area code:

```
SELECT CONCAT(LAST_NAME, ', ', FIRST_NAME), SUBSTRING(PHONE, 1, 3)
FROM EMPLOYEE_TBL;
```

Try writing the same code in SQL Server and Oracle.

3. Write an SQL statement that lists employee email addresses. Email is not a stored column. The email address for each employee should be as follows:

```
FIRST.LAST@PERPTECH.COM
```

For example, John Smith's email address is JOHN.SMITH@PERPTECH.COM.

4. Write an SQL statement that lists each employee's name, employee ID, and phone number in the following formats:

a. The name should be displayed as SMITH, JOHN.

b. The employee ID should be displayed as 999-99-9999.

c. The phone number should be displayed as (999)999-9999.

HOUR 12

Understanding Dates and Times

What You'll Learn in This Hour:

- ▶ Understanding dates and time
- ▶ How date and time are stored
- ▶ Typical date and time formats
- ▶ How to use date functions
- ▶ How to use date conversions

In this hour, you learn about the nature of dates and time in SQL. Not only does this hour discuss the DATETIME data type in more detail, but you also see how some implementations use dates, how to extract the date and time in a desired format, and some of the common rules.

By the Way

> **Variations in the SQL Syntax**
>
> As you know by now, there are many different SQL implementations. This book shows the *American National Standards Institute (ANSI)* standard and the most common nonstandard functions, commands, and operators. MySQL is used for the examples. Even in MySQL, the date can be stored in different formats. You must check your particular implementation for the date storage. No matter how it is stored, your implementation should have functions that convert date formats.

How Is a Date Stored?

Each implementation has a default storage format for the date and time. This default storage often varies among different implementations, as do other data types for each implementation. The following sections begin by reviewing the standard format of the DATETIME data type and its elements. Then you see the data types for date and time in some popular implementations of SQL, including Oracle, MySQL, and Microsoft SQL Server.

Standard Data Types for Date and Time

There are three standard SQL data types for date and time (DATETIME) storage:

▶ **DATE**—Stores date literals. DATE is formatted as YYYY-MM-DD and ranges from 0001-01-01 to 9999-12-31.

▶ **TIME**—Stores time literals. TIME is formatted as HH:MI:SS.nn... and ranges from 00:00:00... to 23:59:61.999....

▶ **TIMESTAMP**—Stores date and time literals. TIMESTAMP is formatted as YYYY-MM-DD HH:MI:SS.nn... and ranges from 0001-01-01 00:00:00... to 9999-12-31 23:59:61.999....

DATETIME Elements

DATETIME elements are those elements pertaining to date and time that are included as part of a DATETIME definition. The following is a list of the constrained DATETIME elements and a valid range of values for each element:

DATETIME Element	Valid Ranges
YEAR	0001 to 9999
MONTH	01 to 12
DAY	01 to 31
HOUR	00 to 23
MINUTE	00 to 59
SECOND	00.000... to 61.999...

Each of these elements is an element of time that we deal with on a daily basis. Seconds can be represented as a decimal, allowing the expression of tenths of a second, hundredths of a second, milliseconds, and so on. You might question the fact that a minute can contain more than 60 seconds. According to the ANSI standard, this 61.999 seconds is due to the possible insertion or omission of a leap second in a minute, which in itself is a rare occurrence. Refer to your implementation on the allowed values because date and time storage might vary widely.

Did You Know?

Databases Handle Leap Years

Date variances such as leap seconds and leap years are handled internally by the database if the data is stored in a DATETIME data type.

Implementation-Specific Data Types

As with other data types, each implementation provides its own representation and syntax. Table 12.1 shows how three products (Microsoft SQL Server, MySQL, and Oracle) have been implemented with date and time.

TABLE 12.1 DATETIME Types Across Platforms

Product	Data Type	Use
Oracle	DATE	Stores both date and time information
SQL Server	DATETIME	Stores both date and time information
	SMALLDATETIME	Same as DATETIME except it has a small range
	DATE	Stores a date value
	TIME	Stores a time value
MySQL	DATETIME	Stores both date and time information
	TIMESTAMP	Stores both date and time information
	DATE	Stores a date value
	TIME	Stores a time value
	YEAR	One byte type that represents the year

Date Functions

Even Date and Time Types Can Differ

Each implementation has its own specific data type(s) for date and time information. However, most implementations comply with the ANSI standard in the fact that all elements of the date and time are included in their associated data types. The way the date is internally stored is implementation dependent.

Did You Know?

Date functions are available in SQL depending on the options with each specific implementation. *Date functions*, similar to character string functions, are used to manipulate the representation of date and time data. Available date functions are often used to format the output of dates and time in an appealing format, compare date values with one another, compute intervals between dates, and so on.

The Current Date

You might have already raised the question, "How do I get the current date from the database?" The need to retrieve the current date from the database might originate from several situations, but the current date is normally returned either to compare it to a stored date or to return the value of the current date as some sort of timestamp.

The current date is ultimately stored on the host computer for the database and is called the *system date*. The database, which interfaces with the appropriate operating system, has the capability to retrieve the system date for its own purpose or to resolve database requests, such as queries.

Take a look at a couple of methods of attaining the system date based on commands from two different implementations.

Microsoft SQL Server uses a function called GETDATE() to return the system date. This function is used in a query as follows. The output is what would return if today's current date were New Year's Eve for 2010.

```
SELECT GETDATE()
```

```
Dec 31, 2010
```

MySQL uses the NOW function to retrieve the current date and time. NOW is called a *pseudocolumn* because it acts as any other column in a table and can be selected from any table in the database although it is not actually part of the table's definition.

The following MySQL statement returns the output if today were New Year's Eve before 2011:

```
SELECT NOW ();
```

```
31-DEC-11 13:41:45
```

Oracle uses a function known as SYSDATE and looks like this if using the DUAL table, which is a dummy table in Oracle:

```
SELECT SYSDATE FROM DUAL;
```

```
31-DEC-11 13:41:45
```

Time Zones

The use of time zones might be a factor when dealing with date and time information. For instance, a time of 6:00 p.m. in the central United States does not equate to the same time in Australia, although the actual point in time is the same. Some of us who live within the daylight saving time zone are used to adjusting our clocks twice a year. If time zones are considerations when maintaining data in your case, you might find it necessary to consider time zones and perform time conversions, if available with your SQL implementation.

The following are some common time zones and their abbreviations.

Abbreviation	Time Zone
AST, ADT	Atlantic standard time, Atlantic daylight time
BST, BDT	Bering standard time, Bering daylight time
CST, CDT	Central standard time, Central daylight time
EST, EDT	Eastern standard time, Eastern daylight time
GMT	Greenwich mean time
HST, HDT	Alaska/Hawaii standard time, Alaska/Hawaii daylight time
MST, MDT	Mountain standard time, Mountain daylight time
NST	Newfoundland standard time, Newfoundland daylight time
PST, PDT	Pacific standard time, Pacific daylight time
YST, YDT	Yukon standard time, Yukon daylight time

The following table shows examples of time zone differences based on a given time.

Time Zone	Time
AST	June 12, 2010 at 1:15 p.m.
BST	June 12, 2010 at 6:15 a.m.
CST	June 12, 2010 at 11:15 a.m.
EST	June 12, 2010 at 12:15 p.m.
GMT	June 12, 2010 at 5:15 p.m.
HST	June 12, 2010 at 7:15 a.m.
MST	June 12, 2010 at 10:15 a.m.
NST	June 12, 2010 at 1:45 p.m.
PST	June 12, 2010 at 9:15 a.m.
YST	June 12, 2010 at 8:15 a.m.

Handling Time Zones

Some implementations have functions that enable you to deal with different time zones. However, not all implementations support the use of time zones. Be sure to verify the use of time zones in your particular implementation, as well as the need to deal with them in the case of your database.

Adding Time to Dates

Days, months, and other parts of time can be added to dates for the purpose of comparing dates to one another or to provide more specific conditions in the WHERE clause of a query.

Intervals can be used to add periods of time to a DATETIME value. As defined by the standard, intervals can manipulate the value of a DATETIME value, as in the following examples:

```
DATE '2010-12-31' + INTERVAL '1' DAY
```

```
'2011-01-01'
```

```
DATE '2010-12-31' + INTERVAL '1' MONTH
```

```
'2011-01-31'
```

The following is an example using the SQL Server function DATEADD:

```
SELECT DATE_HIRE, DATEADD(MONTH, 1, DATE_HIRE)
FROM EMPLOYEE_PAY_TBL;
```

```
DATE_HIRE ADD_MONTH
--------- ---------
23-MAY-99 23-JUN-99
17-JUN-00 17-JUL-00
14-AUG-04 14-SEP-04
28-JUN-07 28-JUL-07
22-JUL-06 22-AUG-06
14-JAN-01 14-FEB-01

6 rows affected.
```

The following example uses the Oracle function ADD_MONTHS:

```
SELECT DATE_HIRE, ADD_MONTHS(DATE_HIRE,1)
FROM EMPLOYEE_PAY_TBL;
```

```
DATE_HIRE          ADD_MONTH
---------          ---------
23-MAY-99          23-JUN-99
```

```
17-JUN-00              17-JUL-00
14-AUG-04              14-SEP-04
28-JUN-07              28-JUL-07
22-JUL-06              22-AUG-06
14-JAN-01              14-FEB-01

6 rows selected.
```

To add one day to a date in Oracle, use the following:

```
SELECT DATE_HIRE, DATE_HIRE + 1
FROM EMPLOYEE_PAY_TBL
WHERE EMP_ID = '311549902';

DATE_HIRE      DATE_HIRE
---------      ---------
23-MAY-99      24-MAY-99

1 row selected.
```

If you wanted to do the same query in MySQL, you would use the ANSI standard INTERVAL command, as follows. Otherwise, MySQL would convert the date to an integer and try to perform the operation.

```
SELECT DATE_HIRE, DATE_ADD(DATE_HIRE, INTERVAL 1 DAY), DATE_HIRE + 1
FROM EMPLOYEE_PAY_TBL
WHERE EMP_ID = '311549902';

DATE_HIRE      DATE_ADD            DATE_HIRE+1
---------      ---------------     ---------------
23-MAY-99      24-MAY-99           1990524

1 row selected.
```

Notice that these examples in MySQL, SQL Server, and Oracle, although they differ syntactically from the ANSI examples, derive their results based on the same concept as described by the SQL standard.

Miscellaneous Date Functions

Table 12.2 shows some powerful date functions that exist in the implementations for SQL Server, Oracle, and MySQL.

TABLE 12.2   Date Functions by Platform

Product	Date Function	Use
SQL Server	DATEPART	Returns the integer value of a DATEPART for a date
	DATENAME	Returns the text value of a DATEPART for a date
	GETDATE()	Returns the system date
	DATEDIFF	Returns the difference between two dates for specified date parts, such as days, minutes, and seconds
Oracle	NEXT_DAY	Returns the next day of the week as specified (for example, FRIDAY) since a given date
	MONTHS_BETWEEN	Returns the number of months between two given dates
MySQL	DAYNAME(date)	Displays day of week
	DAYOFMONTH(date)	Displays day of month
	DAYOFWEEK(date)	Displays day of week
	DAYOFYEAR(date)	Displays day of year

Date Conversions

The conversion of dates can take place for any number of reasons. Conversions are mainly used to alter the data type of values defined as a DATETIME value or any other valid data type of a particular implementation.

Typical reasons for date conversions are as follows:

▶ To compare date values of different data types

▶ To format a date value as a character string

▶ To convert a character string into a date format

The ANSI CAST operator converts data types into other data types. The basic syntax is as follows:

```
CAST ( EXPRESSION AS NEW_DATA_TYPE )
```

Specific syntax examples of some implementations are illustrated in the following subsections, covering

- ▶ The representation of parts of a DATETIME value
- ▶ Conversions of dates to character strings
- ▶ Conversions of character strings to dates

Date Pictures

A *date picture* is composed of formatting elements used to extract date and time information from the database in a desired format. Date pictures might not be available in all SQL implementations.

Without the use of a date picture and some type of conversion function, the date and time information is retrieved from the database in a default format, such as

```
2010-12-31
31-DEC-10
2010-12-31 23:59:01.11
...
```

What if you want the date to be displayed as the following?

```
December 31, 2010
```

You would have to convert the date from a DATETIME format into a character string format. This is accomplished by implementation-specific functions for this very purpose, further illustrated in the following sections.

Table 12.3 displays some of the common date parts used in various implementations. This aids you in using the date picture in the following sections to extract the proper DATETIME information from the database.

TABLE 12.3 Continued

Product	Syntax	Date Part
SQL Server	yy	Year
	qq	Quarter
	mm	Month
	dy	Day of year
	wk	Week
	dw	Weekday
	hh	Hour
	mi	Minute
	ss	Second
	ms	Millisecond
Oracle	AD	Anno Domini
	AM	Ante meridian
	BC	Before Christ
	CC	Century
	D	Number of the day in the week
	DD	Number of the day in the month
	DDD	Number of the day in the year
	DAY	The day spelled out (MONDAY)
	Day	The day spelled out (Monday)
	day	The day spelled out (monday)
	DY	The three-letter abbreviation of the day (MON)
	Dy	The three-letter abbreviation of the day (Mon)
	dy	The three-letter abbreviation of the day (mon)
	HH	Hour of the day
	HH12	Hour of the day
	HH24	Hour of the day for a 24-hour clock
	J	Julian days since 12-31-4713 B.C.
	MI	Minute of the hour

TABLE 12.3 Continued

Product	Syntax	Date Part
	MM	The number of the month
	MON	The three-letter abbreviation of the month (JAN)
	Mon	The three-letter abbreviation of the month (Jan)
	mon	The three-letter abbreviation of the month (jan)
	MONTH	The month spelled out (JANUARY)
	Month	The month spelled out (January)
	month	The month spelled out (january)
	PM	Post meridian
	Q	The number of the quarter
	RM	The Roman numeral for the month
	RR	The two digits of the year
	SS	The second of a minute
	SSSSS	The seconds since midnight
	SYYYY	The signed year; if B.C. 500, B.C. = −500
	W	The number of the week in a month
	WW	The number of the week in a year
	Y	The last digit of the year
	YY	The last two digits of the year
	YYY	The last three digits of the year
	YYYY	The year
	YEAR	The year spelled out (TWO-THOUSAND-TEN)
	Year	The year spelled out (Two-Thousand-Ten)
	year	The year spelled out (two-thousand-ten)
MySQL	SECOND	Seconds
	MINUTE	Minutes
	HOUR	Hours

TABLE 12.3   Continued

Product	Syntax	Date Part
	DAY	Days
	MONTH	Months
	YEAR	Years
	MINUTE_SECOND	Minutes and seconds
	HOUR_MINUTE	Hours and minutes
	DAY_HOUR	Days and hours
	YEAR_MONTH	Years and months
	HOUR_SECOND	Hours, minutes, and seconds
	DAY_MINUTE	Days and minutes
	DAY_SECOND	Days and seconds

Converting Dates to Character Strings

DATETIME values are converted to character strings to alter the appearance of output from a query. A conversion function achieves this. Two examples of converting date and time data into a character string as designated by a query follow. The first uses SQL Server:

```
SELECT DATE_HIRE = DATENAME(MONTH, DATE_HIRE)
FROM EMPLOYEE_PAY_TBL;

DATE_HIRE
---------
May
June
August
June
July
January

6 rows affected.
```

The second example is an Oracle date conversion using the TO_CHAR function:

```
SELECT DATE_HIRE, TO_CHAR(DATE_HIRE,'Month dd, yyyy') HIRE
FROM EMPLOYEE_PAY_TBL;

DATE_HIRE           HIRE
---------           ---------------
```

```
23-MAY-99        May       23, 1999
17-JUN-00        June      17, 2000
14-AUG-04        August    14, 2004
28-JUN-07        June      28, 2007
22-JUL-06        July      22, 2006
14-JAN-01        January   14, 2001
```

6 rows selected.

By the
Way

Date Parts in MySQL

These are some of the most common date parts for MySQL. Other date parts might be available depending on the version of MySQL.

Converting Character Strings to Dates

The following example illustrates a method from a MySQL or Oracle implementation of converting a character string into a date format. When the conversion is complete, the data can be stored in a column defined as having some form of a DATETIME data type.

```
SELECT STR_TO_DATE('01/01/2010 12:00:00 AM', '%m/%d/%Y %h:%i:%s %p') AS
FORMAT_DATE
FROM EMPLOYEE_PAY_TBL;
```

```
FORMAT_DATE
-----------
01-JAN-10
01-JAN-10
01-JAN-10
01-JAN-10
01-JAN-10
01-JAN-10
```

6 rows selected.

You might be wondering why six rows were selected from this query when only one date value was provided. It's because the conversion of the literal string was selected from the EMPLOYEE_PAY_TBL, which has six rows of data. Hence, the conversion of the literal string was selected against each record in the table.

In Microsoft SQL Server we instead use the CONVERT function:

```
SELECT CONVERT(DATETIME,'02/25/2010 12:00:00 AM') AS FORMAT_DATE
FROM EMPLOYEE_PAY_TBL;
FORMAT_DATE
--------------------
2010-02-25 00:00:00.000
2010-02-25 00:00:00.000
```

```
2010-02-25 00:00:00.000
2010-02-25 00:00:00.000
2010-02-25 00:00:00.000
2010-02-25 00:00:00.000

6 rows selected.
```

Summary

You have an understanding of DATETIME values based on the fact that ANSI has provided a standard. However, as with many SQL elements, most implementations have deviated from the exact functions and syntax of standard SQL commands, although the concepts remain the same as far as the basic representation and manipulation of date and time information. In Hour 11, "Restructuring the Appearance of Data," you saw how functions varied depending on each implementation. This hour, you have seen some of the differences between date and time data types, functions, and operators. Keep in mind that not all examples discussed in this hour work with your particular implementation, but the concepts of dates and times are the same and should be applicable to any implementation.

Q&A

Q. *Why do implementations choose to deviate from a single standard set of data types and functions?*

A. Implementations differ as far as the representation of data types and functions mainly because of the way each vendor has chosen to internally store data and provide the most efficient means of data retrieval. However, all implementations should provide the same means for the storage of date and time values based on the required elements prescribed by ANSI, such as the year, month, day, hour, minute, second, and so on.

Q. *What if I want to store date and time information differently than what is available in my implementation?*

A. Dates can be stored in nearly any type of format if you choose to define the column for a date as a variable length character. The main thing to remember is that when comparing date values to one another, you are usually required to first convert the character string representation of the date to a valid DATETIME format for your implementation—that is, if appropriate conversion functions are available.

Workshop

The following workshop is composed of a series of quiz questions and practical exercises. The quiz questions are designed to test your overall understanding of the current material. The practical exercises are intended to afford you the opportunity to apply the concepts discussed during the current hour, as well as build upon the knowledge acquired in previous hours of study. Please take time to complete the quiz questions and exercises before continuing. Refer to Appendix C, "Answers to Quizzes and Exercises," for answers.

Quiz

1. From where is the system date and time normally derived?

2. What are the standard internal elements of a DATETIME value?

3. What could be a major factor concerning the representation and comparison of date and time values if your company is an international organization?

4. Can a character string date value be compared to a date value defined as a valid DATETIME data type?

5. What would you use in SQL Server, MySQL, and Oracle to get the current date and time?

Exercises

1. Type the following SQL code into the sql prompt in each of the implementations to display the current date from the database:

   a. MySQL : SELECT CURRENT_DATE;
   b. SQL Server : SELECT GETDATE();
   c. Oracle : SELECT SYSDATE FROM DUAL;

2. Type the following SQL code to display each employee's hire date:

   ```
   SELECT EMP_ID, DATE_HIRE
   FROM EMPLOYEE_PAY_TBL;
   ```

3. In MySQL, dates can be displayed in various formats using the EXTRACT function in conjunction with the MySQL date pictures. Type the following code to display the year that each employee was hired:

   ```
   SELECT EMP_ID, EXTRACT(YEAR FROM DATE_HIRE)
   FROM EMPLOYEE_PAY_TBL;
   ```

4. Try the following similar syntax in Microsoft SQL Server:

```
SELECT EMP_ID, YEAR( DATE_HIRE)
FROM EMPLOYEE_PAY_TBL;
```

5. Type in a statement similar to this MySQL implementation to display each of the employees' hire dates along with today's date:

```
SELECT EMP_ID, DATE_HIRE, CURRENT_DATE
FROM EMPLOYEE_PAY_TBL;
```

6. On what day of the week was each employee hired?

7. What is today's Julian date (day of year)?

8. Type in three SQL statements. The first to get the current system DATETIME as you did in Exercise 1, the second to convert the system DATETIME to a date value, and the third to convert the system DATETIME to a pure time value.

HOUR 13

Joining Tables in Queries

What You'll Learn in This Hour:

▶ An introduction to the table joins
▶ The different types of joins
▶ How and when joins are used
▶ Numerous practical examples of table joins
▶ The effects of improperly joined tables
▶ Renaming tables in a query using an alias

To this point, all database queries you have executed have extracted data from a single table. During this hour, you learn how to join tables in a query so you can retrieve data from multiple tables.

Selecting Data from Multiple Tables

Having the capability to select data from multiple tables is one of SQL's most powerful features. Without this capability, the entire relational database concept would not be feasible. Single-table queries are sometimes quite informative, but in the real world, the most practical queries are those whose data is acquired from multiple tables within the database.

As you witnessed in Hour 4, "The Normalization Process," a relational database is broken into smaller, more manageable tables for simplicity and the sake of overall management ease. As tables are divided into smaller tables, the related tables are created with common columns—*primary keys* and *foreign keys*. These keys are used to join related tables to one another.

You might ask why you should normalize tables if, in the end, you are only going to rejoin the tables to retrieve the data you want. You rarely select all data from all tables, so it is better to pick and choose according to the needs of each query. Although performance might suffer slightly due to a normalized database, overall coding and maintenance are much simpler. Remember that you generally normalize the database to reduce redundancy and increase data integrity. Your overreaching task as a database administrator is to ensure the safeguarding of data.

Understanding Joins

A *join* combines two or more tables to retrieve data from multiple tables. Although different implementations have many ways of joining tables, you concentrate on the most common joins in this lesson. The types of joins that you learn are

- ▶ Equijoins or inner joins
- ▶ Non-equijoins
- ▶ Outer joins
- ▶ Self joins

Component of a Join Condition

As you have learned from previous hours, both the SELECT and FROM clauses are required SQL statement elements; the WHERE clause is a required element of an SQL statement when joining tables. The tables being joined are listed in the FROM clause. The join is performed in the WHERE clause. Several operators can be used to join tables, such as =, <, >, <>, <=, >=, !=, BETWEEN, LIKE, and NOT. However, the most common operator is the equal symbol.

Joins of Equality

Perhaps the most used and important of the joins is the *equijoin*, also referred to as an *inner join*. The equijoin joins two tables with a common column in which each is usually the primary key.

The syntax for an equijoin is

```
SELECT TABLE1.COLUMN1, TABLE2.COLUMN2...
FROM TABLE1, TABLE2 [ , TABLE3 ]
WHERE TABLE1.COLUMN_NAME = TABLE2.COLUMN_NAME
[ AND TABLE1.COLUMN_NAME = TABLE3.COLUMN_NAME ]
```

Look at the following example:

```
SELECT EMPLOYEE_TBL.EMP_ID,
       EMPLOYEE_PAY_TBL.DATE_HIRE
FROM EMPLOYEE_TBL,
```

```
       EMPLOYEE_PAY_TBL
WHERE EMPLOYEE_TBL.EMP_ID = EMPLOYEE_PAY_TBL.EMP_ID;
```

This SQL statement returns the employee identification and the employee's date of hire. The employee identification is selected from EMPLOYEE_TBL (although it exists in both tables, you must specify one table), and the hire date is selected from EMPLOYEE_PAY_TBL. Because the employee identification exists in both tables, you must justify both columns with the table name. By justifying the columns with the table names, you tell the database server where to get the data.

Using Indentation in SQL Statements

Take note of the sample SQL statements. Indentation is used in the SQL statements to improve overall readability. Indentation is not required; however, it is recommended.

By the Way

Data in the following example is selected from EMPLOYEE_TBL and EMPLOYEE_PAY_TBL because desired data resides in each of the two tables. An equijoin is used.

```
SELECT EMPLOYEE_TBL.EMP_ID, EMPLOYEE_TBL.LAST_NAME,
       EMPLOYEE_PAY_TBL.POSITION
FROM EMPLOYEE_TBL, EMPLOYEE_PAY_TBL
WHERE EMPLOYEE_TBL.EMP_ID = EMPLOYEE_PAY_TBL.EMP_ID;

EMP_ID     LAST_NAM POSITION
---------- -------- -------------
311549902 STEPHENS MARKETING
442346889 PLEW     TEAM LEADER
213764555 GLASS    SALES MANAGER
313782439 GLASS    SALESMAN
220984332 WALLACE  SHIPPER
443679012 SPURGEON SHIPPER

6 rows selected.
```

Notice that each column in the SELECT clause is preceded by the associated table name to identify each column. This is called *qualifying columns* in a query. Qualifying columns is only necessary for columns that exist in more than one table referenced by a query. You usually qualify all columns for consistency and to avoid questions when debugging or modifying SQL code.

Additionally, the SQL syntax provides for a more readable version of the previous syntax by introducing the JOIN syntax. The JOIN syntax is as follows:

```
SELECT TABLE1.COLUMN1, TABLE2.COLUMN2...
FROM TABLE1
INNER JOIN TABLE2 ON TABLE1.COLUMN_NAME = TABLE2.COLUMN_NAME
```

As you can see, the join operator is removed from the WHERE clause and instead replaced with the JOIN syntax. The table being joined is added after the JOIN syntax, and then the JOIN operators are placed after the ON qualifier. In the following example, the previous query for employee identification and hire date is rewritten to use the JOIN syntax:

```
SELECT EMPLOYEE_TBL.EMP_ID,
       EMPLOYEE_PAY_TBL.DATE_HIRE
FROM EMPLOYEE_TBL
INNER JOIN EMPLOYEE_PAY_TBL
ON EMPLOYEE_TBL.EMP_ID = EMPLOYEE_PAY_TBL.EMP_ID;
```

Notice that this query returns the same set of data as the previous version, even though the syntax is different. So you may use either version of the syntax without fear of coming up with different results.

Using Table Aliases

You use table aliases to rename a table in a particular SQL statement. The renaming is a temporary; the actual table name does not change in the database. As you learn later in the "Self Joins" section, giving the tables aliases is a necessity for the self join. Giving tables aliases is most often for saving keystrokes, which results in a shorter and easier-to-read SQL statement. In addition, fewer keystrokes means fewer keystroke errors. Also, programming errors are typically less frequent if you can refer to an alias, which is often shorter in length and more descriptive of the data with which you are working. Giving tables aliases also means that the columns being selected must be qualified with the table alias. The following are some examples of table aliases and the corresponding columns:

```
SELECT E.EMP_ID, EP.SALARY, EP.DATE_HIRE, E.LAST_NAME
FROM EMPLOYEE_TBL E,
     EMPLOYEE_PAY_TBL EP
WHERE E.EMP_ID = EP.EMP_ID
AND EP.SALARY > 20000;
```

The tables have been given aliases in the preceding SQL statement. EMPLOYEE_TBL has been renamed E. EMPLOYEE_PAY_TBL has been renamed EP. The choice of what to rename the tables is arbitrary. The letter E is chosen because EMPLOYEE_TBL starts with E. Because EMPLOYEE_PAY_TBL also begins with the letter E, you cannot use E again. Instead, the first letter (E) and the first letter of the second word in the name (PAY) are used as the alias. The selected columns were justified with the corresponding table alias. Note that SALARY was used in the WHERE clause and must be justified with the table alias.

Joins of Non-Equality

A *non-equijoin* joins two or more tables based on a specified column value not equaling a specified column value in another table. The syntax for the non-equijoin is

```
FROM TABLE1, TABLE2 [, TABLE3 ]
WHERE TABLE1.COLUMN_NAME != TABLE2.COLUMN_NAME
[ AND TABLE1.COLUMN_NAME != TABLE2.COLUMN_NAME ]
```

An example is as follows:

```
SELECT EMPLOYEE_TBL.EMP_ID, EMPLOYEE_PAY_TBL.DATE_HIRE
FROM EMPLOYEE_TBL,
     EMPLOYEE_PAY_TBL
WHERE EMPLOYEE_TBL.EMP_ID != EMPLOYEE_PAY_TBL.EMP_ID;
```

The preceding SQL statement returns the employee identification and the date of hire for all employees who do not have a corresponding record in both tables. The following example is a join of non-equality:

```
SELECT E.EMP_ID, E.LAST_NAME, P.POSITION
FROM EMPLOYEE_TBL E,
     EMPLOYEE_PAY_TBL P
WHERE E.EMP_ID <> P.EMP_ID;
```

```
EMP_ID     LAST_NAM POSITION
---------  -------- ------------
442346889  PLEW     MARKETING
213764555  GLASS    MARKETING
313782439  GLASS    MARKETING
220984332  WALLACE  MARKETING
443679012  SPURGEON MARKETING
311549902  STEPHENS TEAM LEADER
213764555  GLASS    TEAM LEADER
313782439  GLASS    TEAM LEADER
220984332  WALLACE  TEAM LEADER
443679012  SPURGEON TEAM LEADER
311549902  STEPHENS SALES MANAGER
442346889  PLEW     SALES MANAGER
313782439  GLASS    SALES MANAGER
220984332  WALLACE  SALES MANAGER
443679012  SPURGEON SALES MANAGER
311549902  STEPHENS SALESMAN
442346889  PLEW     SALESMAN
213764555  GLASS    SALESMAN
220984332  WALLACE  SALESMAN
443679012  SPURGEON SALESMAN
311549902  STEPHENS SHIPPER
442346889  PLEW     SHIPPER
213764555  GLASS    SHIPPER
313782439  GLASS    SHIPPER
443679012  SPURGEON SHIPPER
```

> **Non-Equijoins Can Add Data**
>
> When using non-equijoins, you might receive several rows of data that are of no use to you. Check your results carefully.

You might be curious why 30 rows were retrieved when only 6 rows exist in each table. Every record in EMPLOYEE_TBL has a corresponding record in EMPLOYEE_PAY_TBL. Because non-equality was tested in the join of the two tables, each row in the first table is paired with all rows from the second table, except for its own corresponding row. This means that each of the 6 rows is paired with 5 unrelated rows in the second table; 6 rows multiplied by 5 rows equals 30 rows total.

In the earlier section's test for equality example, each of the six rows in the first table were paired with only one row in the second table (each row's corresponding row); six rows multiplied by one row yields a total of six rows.

Outer Joins

> **Join Syntax Varies Widely**
>
> You must check your particular implementation for exact usage and syntax of the outer join. The (+) symbol is used by some major implementations, but it is non-standard. In fact, this varies somewhat between versions of implementations. For example, Microsoft SQL Server 2000 supports this type of join syntax, but SQL Server 2005 and newer versions do not. Be sure to carefully consider using this syntax before implementing.

An *outer join* returns all rows that exist in one table, even though corresponding rows do not exist in the joined table. The (+) symbol denotes an outer join in a query. The (+) is placed at the end of the table name in the WHERE clause. The table with the (+) should be the table that does not have matching rows. In many implementations, the outer join is broken into joins called *left outer join*, *right outer join*, and *full outer join*. The outer join in these implementations is normally optional.

The general syntax for an outer join is

```
FROM TABLE1
{RIGHT | LEFT | FULL} [OUTER] JOIN
ON TABLE2
```

> **Use of Outer Joins**
>
> You can use the outer join on only one side of a JOIN condition; however, you can use an outer join on more than one column of the same table in the JOIN condition.

The Oracle syntax is

```
FROM TABLE1, TABLE2 [, TABLE3 ]
WHERE TABLE1.COLUMN_NAME[(+)] = TABLE2.COLUMN_NAME[(+)]
[ AND TABLE1.COLUMN_NAME[(+)] = TABLE3.COLUMN_NAME[(+)]]
```

The concept of the outer join is explained in the next two examples. In the first example, the product description and the quantity ordered are selected; both values are extracted from two separate tables. One important factor to keep in mind is that there might not be a corresponding record in ORDERS_TBL for every product. A regular join of equality is performed:

```
SELECT P.PROD_DESC, O.QTY
FROM PRODUCTS_TBL P,
     ORDERS_TBL O
WHERE P.PROD_ID = O.PROD_ID;
```

PROD_DESC	QTY
PLASTIC PUMPKIN 18 INCH	2
LIGHTED LANTERNS	10
PLASTIC SPIDERS	30
LIGHTED LANTERNS	20
FALSE PARAFFIN TEETH	20
PUMPKIN CANDY	10
FALSE PARAFFIN TEETH	10
WITCH COSTUME	5
CANDY CORN	45
LIGHTED LANTERNS	25
PLASTIC PUMPKIN 18 INCH	25
WITCH COSTUME	30
FALSE PARAFFIN TEETH	15
PLASTIC SPIDERS	50
PLASTIC PUMPKIN 18 INCH	25
PLASTIC PUMPKIN 18 INCH	25
WITCH COSTUME	1

```
17 rows selected.
```

Only 17 rows were selected with only 7 products listed, but there are 9 distinct products. You want to display all products, whether they have been placed on order or not.

The next example accomplishes the desired output through the use of an outer join. Oracle's syntax is used here:

```
SELECT P.PROD_DESC, O.QTY
FROM PRODUCTS_TBL P,
     ORDERS_TBL O
WHERE P.PROD_ID = O.PROD_ID(+);
```

```
PROD_DESC                               QTY
------------------------------------    ----------
WITCH COSTUME                              5
WITCH COSTUME                             30
WITCH COSTUME                              1
ASSORTED MASKS                          NULL
FALSE PARAFFIN TEETH                     20
FALSE PARAFFIN TEETH                     10
FALSE PARAFFIN TEETH                     15
ASSORTED COSTUMES                       NULL
PLASTIC PUMPKIN 18 INCH                   2
PLASTIC PUMPKIN 18 INCH                  25
PLASTIC PUMPKIN 18 INCH                  25
PLASTIC PUMPKIN 18 INCH                  25
PUMPKIN CANDY                            10
PLASTIC SPIDERS                          30
PLASTIC SPIDERS                          50
CANDY CORN                               45
LIGHTED LANTERNS                         10
LIGHTED LANTERNS                         20
LIGHTED LANTERNS                         25

19 rows selected.
```

You can also use the more verbose standard join syntax discussed earlier to achieve the same result. The following code achieves the same result but uses the more verbose version of the join syntax, which makes it easier to read.

```
SELECT P.PROD_DESC, O.QTY
FROM PRODUCTS_TBL P
LEFT OUTER JOIN  ORDERS_TBL O
ON P.PROD_ID = O.PROD_ID;
```

```
PROD_DESC                               QTY
------------------------------------    ----------
WITCH COSTUME                              5
WITCH COSTUME                             30
WITCH COSTUME                              1
ASSORTED MASKS                          NULL
FALSE PARAFFIN TEETH                     20
FALSE PARAFFIN TEETH                     10
FALSE PARAFFIN TEETH                     15
ASSORTED COSTUMES                       NULL
PLASTIC PUMPKIN 18 INCH                   2
PLASTIC PUMPKIN 18 INCH                  25
PLASTIC PUMPKIN 18 INCH                  25
PLASTIC PUMPKIN 18 INCH                  25
PUMPKIN CANDY                            10
PLASTIC SPIDERS                          30
PLASTIC SPIDERS                          50
CANDY CORN                               45
```

```
LIGHTED LANTERNS                        10
LIGHTED LANTERNS                        20
LIGHTED LANTERNS                        25

19 rows selected.
```

All products were returned by the query, even though they might not have had a quantity ordered. The outer join is inclusive of all rows of data in PRODUCTS_TBL, whether a corresponding row exists in ORDERS_TBL or not.

Self Joins

The *self join* joins a table to itself, as if the table were two tables, temporarily renaming at least one table in the SQL statement using a table alias. The syntax is as follows:

```
SELECT A.COLUMN_NAME, B.COLUMN_NAME, [ C.COLUMN_NAME ]
FROM TABLE1 A, TABLE2 B [, TABLE3 C ]
WHERE A.COLUMN_NAME = B.COLUMN_NAME
[ AND A.COLUMN_NAME = C.COLUMN_NAME ]
```

The following is an example:

```
SELECT A.LAST_NAME, B.LAST_NAME, A.FIRST_NAME
FROM EMPLOYEE_TBL A,
     EMPLOYEE_TBL B
WHERE A.LAST_NAME = B.LAST_NAME;
```

The preceding SQL statement returns the employees' first names for all the employees with the same last name from EMPLOYEE_TBL. Self joins are useful when all the data you want to retrieve resides in one table, but you must somehow compare records in the table to other records in the table.

You may also use the alternate INNER JOIN syntax as shown here to obtain the same result:

```
SELECT A.LAST_NAME, B.LAST_NAME, A.FIRST_NAME
FROM EMPLOYEE_TBL A
INNER JOIN EMPLOYEE_TBL B
ON A.LAST_NAME = B.LAST_NAME;
```

Another common example used to explain a self join follows: Suppose you have a table that stores an employee identification number, the employee's name, and the employee identification number of the employee's manager. You might want to produce a list of all employees and their managers' names. The problem is that the manager name does not exist as a category in the table:

```
SELECT * FROM EMP;

ID    NAME      MGR_ID
---   ------    --------
1     JOHN      0
2     MARY      1
3     STEVE     1
4     JACK      2
5     SUE       2
```

In the following example, we have included the table EMP twice in the FROM clause of the query, giving the table two aliases for the purpose of the query. By providing two aliases, it is as if you are selecting from two distinct tables. All managers are also employees, so the JOIN condition between the two tables compares the value of the employee identification number from the first table with the manager identification number in the second table. The first table acts as a table that stores employee information, whereas the second table acts as a table that stores manager information:

```
SELECT E1.NAME, E2.NAME
FROM EMP E1, EMP E2
WHERE E1.MGR_ID = E2.ID;

NAME      NAME
-------   -------
MARY      JOHN
STEVE     JOHN
JACK      MARY
SUE       MARY
```

Joining on Multiple Keys

Most join operations involve the merging of data based on a key in one table and a key in another table. Depending on how your database has been designed, you might have to join on more than one key field to accurately depict that data in your database. You might have a table that has a primary key that is composed of more than one column. You might also have a foreign key in a table that consists of more than one column, which references the multiple column primary key.

Consider the following Oracle tables that are used here for examples only:

```
SQL> desc prod
 Name                                      Null?    Type
 ----------------------------------------- -------- ----------------------
 ------
 SERIAL_NUMBER                             NOT NULL NUMBER(10)
 VENDOR_NUMBER                             NOT NULL NUMBER(10)
 PRODUCT_NAME                              NOT NULL VARCHAR2(30)
```

```
COST                                           NOT NULL NUMBER(8,2)

SQL> desc ord
 Name                                          Null?    Type
 -------------------------------------------   -------  ---------------------
 ------
 ORD_NO                                        NOT NULL NUMBER(10)
 PROD_NUMBER                                   NOT NULL NUMBER(10)
 VENDOR_NUMBER                                 NOT NULL NUMBER(10)
 QUANTITY                                      NOT NULL NUMBER(5)
 ORD_DATE                                      NOT NULL DATE
```

The primary key in PROD is the combination of the columns SERIAL_NUMBER and VENDOR_NUMBER. Perhaps two products can have the same serial number within the distribution company, but each serial number is unique per vendor.

The foreign key in ORD is also the combination of the columns SERIAL_NUMBER and VENDOR_NUMBER.

When selecting data from both tables (PROD and ORD), the join operation might appear as follows:

```
SELECT P.PRODUCT_NAME, O.ORD_DATE, O.QUANTITY
FROM PROD P, ORD O
WHERE P.SERIAL_NUMBER = O.SERIAL_NUMBER
  AND P.VENDOR_NUMBER = O.VENDOR_NUMBER;
```

Similarly, if you were using the INNER JOIN syntax, you would merely list the multiple join operations after the ON keyword, as shown here:

```
SELECT P.PRODUCT_NAME, O.ORD_DATE, O.QUANTITY
FROM PROD P,
INNER JOIN ORD O ON P.SERIAL_NUMBER = O.SERIAL_NUMBER
  AND P.VENDOR_NUMBER = O.VENDOR_NUMBER;
```

Join Considerations

You should consider several things before using joins: what columns(s) to join on, whether there is no common column to join on, and what the performance issues are. More joins in a query means the database server has to do more work, which means that more time is taken to retrieve data. You cannot avoid joins when retrieving data from a normalized database, but it is imperative to ensure that joins are performed correctly from a logical standpoint. Incorrect joins can result in serious performance degradation and inaccurate query results. Performance issues are discussed in more detail in Hour 18, "Managing Database Users."

Using a Base Table

What should you join on? Should you have the need to retrieve data from two tables that do not have a common column to join, you must join on another table that has a common column or columns to both tables. That table becomes the base table. A *base table* joins one or more tables that have common columns, or joins tables that do not have common columns. Use the following three tables for an example of a base table:

```
CUSTOMER_TBL
CUST_ID          VARCHAR(10)    NOT NULL      primary key
CUST_NAME        VARCHAR(30)    NOT NULL
CUST_ADDRESS     VARCHAR(20)    NOT NULL
CUST_CITY        VARCHAR(15)    NOT NULL
CUST_STATE       VARCHAR(2)     NOT NULL
CUST_ZIP         INTEGER(5)     NOT NULL
CUST_PHONE       INTEGER(10)
CUST_FAX         INTEGER(10)


ORDERS_TBL
ORD_NUM            VARCHAR(10)      NOT NULL    primary key
CUST_ID            VARCHAR(10)      NOT NULL
PROD_ID            VARCHAR(10)      NOT NULL
QTY                INTEGER(6)       NOT NULL
ORD_DATE           DATETIME


PRODUCTS_TBL
PROD_ID            VARCHAR(10)      NOT NULL    primary key
PROD_DESC          VARCHAR(40)      NOT NULL
COST               DECIMAL(6,2)     NOT NULL
```

Say you have a need to use CUSTOMERS_TBL and PRODUCTS_TBL. There is no common column in which to join the tables. Now look at ORDERS_TBL. ORDERS_TBL has a CUST_ID column to join with CUSTOMERS_TBL, which also has a CUST_ID column. PRODUCTS_TBL has a PROD_ID column, which is also in ORDERS_TBL. The JOIN conditions and results look like the following:

```
SELECT C.CUST_NAME, P.PROD_DESC
FROM CUSTOMER_TBL C,
     PRODUCTS_TBL P,
     ORDERS_TBL O
WHERE C.CUST_ID = O.CUST_ID
  AND P.PROD_ID = O.PROD_ID;
```

```
CUST_NAME                         PROD_DESC
--------------------------------  --------------------------
LESLIE GLEASON                    WITCH COSTUME
SCHYLERS NOVELTIES                PLASTIC PUMPKIN 18 INCH
WENDY WOLF                        PLASTIC PUMPKIN 18 INCH
GAVINS PLACE                      LIGHTED LANTERNS
```

SCOTTYS MARKET   FALSE PARAFFIN TEETH
ANDYS CANDIES   KEY CHAIN

6 rows selected.

Using Aliases on Tables and Columns

Note the use of table aliases and their use on the columns in the WHERE clause.

By the
Way

The Cartesian Product

The *Cartesian product* is a result of a Cartesian join or "no join." If you select from two or more tables and do not join the tables, your output is all possible rows from all the tables selected. If your tables were large, the result could be hundreds of thousands, or even millions, of rows of data. A WHERE clause is highly recommended for SQL statements retrieving data from two or more tables. The Cartesian product is also known as a *cross join*.

The syntax is

```
FROM TABLE1, TABLE2 [ , TABLE3 ]
WHERE TABLE1, TABLE2 [ , TABLE3 ]
```

The following is an example of a cross join, or the dreaded Cartesian product:

```
SELECT E.EMP_ID, E.LAST_NAME, P.POSITION
FROM EMPLOYEE_TBL E,
    EMPLOYEE_PAY_TBL P;
```

EMP_ID	LAST_NAM	POSITION
311549902	STEPHENS	MARKETING
442346889	PLEW	MARKETING
213764555	GLASS	MARKETING
313782439	GLASS	MARKETING
220984332	WALLACE	MARKETING
443679012	SPURGEON	MARKETING
311549902	STEPHENS	TEAM LEADER
442346889	PLEW	TEAM LEADER
213764555	GLASS	TEAM LEADER
313782439	GLASS	TEAM LEADER
220984332	WALLACE	TEAM LEADER
443679012	SPURGEON	TEAM LEADER
311549902	STEPHENS	SALES MANAGER
442346889	PLEW	SALES MANAGER
213764555	GLASS	SALES MANAGER
313782439	GLASS	SALES MANAGER
220984332	WALLACE	SALES MANAGER

```
443679012 SPURGEON SALES MANAGER
311549902 STEPHENS SALESMAN
442346889 PLEW     SALESMAN
213764555 GLASS    SALESMAN
313782439 GLASS    SALESMAN
220984332 WALLACE  SALESMAN
443679012 SPURGEON SALESMAN
311549902 STEPHENS SHIPPER
442346889 PLEW     SHIPPER
213764555 GLASS    SHIPPER
313782439 GLASS    SHIPPER
220984332 WALLACE  SHIPPER
443679012 SPURGEON SHIPPER
311549902 STEPHENS SHIPPER
442346889 PLEW     SHIPPER
213764555 GLASS    SHIPPER
313782439 GLASS    SHIPPER
220984332 WALLACE  SHIPPER
443679012 SPURGEON SHIPPER

36 rows selected.
```

Data is being selected from two separate tables, yet no JOIN operation is performed. Because you have not specified how to join rows in the first table with rows in the second table, the database server pairs every row in the first table with every row in the second table. Because each table has 6 rows of data each, the product of 36 rows selected is achieved from 6 rows multiplied by 6 rows.

To fully understand exactly how the Cartesian product is derived, study the following example:

```
SQL> SELECT X FROM TABLE1;

X
-
A
B
C
D

4 rows selected.

SQL> SELECT V FROM TABLE2;

X
-
A
B
C
D
```

```
4 rows selected.

SQL> SELECT TABLE1.X, TABLE2.X
  2* FROM TABLE1, TABLE2;

X X
- -
A A
B A
C A
D A
A B
B B
C B
D B
A C
B C
C C
D C
A D
B D
C D
D D

16 rows selected.
```

Ensure That All Tables Are Joined

Be careful to join all tables in a query. If two tables in a query have not been joined and each table contains 1,000 rows of data, the Cartesian product consists of 1,000 rows multiplied by 1,000 rows, which results in a total of 1,000,000 rows of data returned. Cartesian products, when dealing with large amounts of data, can cause the host computer to stall or crash in some cases, based on resource usage on the host computer. Therefore, it is important for the *database administrator (DBA)* and system administrator to closely monitor for long-running queries.

Watch
Out!

Summary

You have been introduced to one of the most robust features of SQL—the table join. Imagine the limits if you were not able to extract data from more than one table in a single query. You were shown several types of joins, each serving its own purpose depending on conditions placed on the query. Joins are used to link data from tables based on equality and non-equality. Outer joins are powerful, allowing data to be retrieved from one table, even though associated data is not found in a joined table. Self joins are used to join a table to itself. Beware of the cross join, more commonly known as the Cartesian product. The Cartesian product is the resultset of a multiple table query without a join, often yielding a large amount of unwanted output. When selecting data from more than one table, be sure to properly join the tables according to the related columns (normally primary keys). Failure to properly join tables could result in incomplete or inaccurate output.

Q&A

Q. *When joining tables, must they be joined in the same order that they appear in the FROM clause?*

A. No, they do not have to appear in the same order; however, performance might benefit depending on the order of tables in the FROM clause and the order in which tables are joined.

Q. *When using a base table to join unrelated tables, must I select any columns from the base table?*

A. No, the use of a base table to join unrelated tables does not mandate that columns from the base table be selected.

Q. *Can I join on more than one column between tables?*

A. Yes, some queries might require you to join on more than one column per table to provide a complete relationship between rows of data in the joined tables.

Workshop

The following workshop is composed of a series of quiz questions and practical exercises. The quiz questions are designed to test your overall understanding of the current material. The practical exercises are intended to afford you the opportunity to apply the concepts discussed during the current hour, as well as build upon the knowledge acquired in previous hours of study. Please take time to complete the quiz questions and exercises before continuing. Refer to Appendix C, "Answers to Quizzes and Exercises," for answers.

Quiz

1. What type of join would you use to return records from one table, regardless of the existence of associated records in the related table?

2. The `join` conditions are located in which parts of the SQL statement?

3. What type of `join` do you use to evaluate equality among rows of related tables?

4. What happens if you select from two different tables but fail to join the tables?

5. Use the following tables:

```
ORDERS_TBL
ORD_NUM      VARCHAR(10)    NOT NULL    primary key
CUST_ID      VARCHAR(10)    NOT NULL
PROD_ID      VARCHAR(10)    NOT NULL
QTY          Integer(6)     NOT NULL
ORD_DATE     DATETIME


PRODUCTS_TBL
PROD_ID      VARCHAR(10)    NOT NULL    primary key
PROD_DESC    VARCHAR(40)    NOT NULL
COST         DECIMAL(,2)    NOT NULL
```

Is the following syntax correct for using an outer join?

```
SELECT C.CUST_ID, C.CUST_NAME, O.ORD_NUM
FROM CUSTOMER_TBL C, ORDERS_TBL O
WHERE C.CUST_ID(+) = O.CUST_ID(+)
```

What would the query look like if you used the verbose JOIN syntax?

Exercises

1. Type the following code into the database and study the resultset (Cartesian product):

```
SELECT E.LAST_NAME, E.FIRST_NAME, EP.DATE_HIRE
FROM EMPLOYEE_TBL E,
     EMPLOYEE_PAY_TBL EP;
```

2. Type the following code to properly join EMPLOYEE_TBL and EMPLOYEE_PAY_TBL:

```
SELECT E.LAST_NAME, E.FIRST_NAME, EP.DATE_HIRE
FROM EMPLOYEE_TBL E,
     EMPLOYEE_PAY_TBL EP
WHERE E.EMP_ID = EP.EMP_ID;
```

3. Rewrite the SQL query from Exercise 2, using the INNER JOIN syntax.

4. Write an SQL statement to return the EMP_ID, LAST_NAME, and FIRST_NAME columns from EMPLOYEE_TBL and SALARY and BONUS columns from EMPLOYEE_PAY_TBL. Use both types of INNER JOIN techniques. Once that's completed, use the queries to determine what the average employee salary per city is.

5. Write a few queries with join operations on your own.

HOUR 14

Using Subqueries to Define Unknown Data

What You'll Learn in This Hour:

▶ What a subquery is

▶ The justifications of using subqueries

▶ Examples of subqueries in regular database queries

▶ Using subqueries with data manipulation commands

▶ Embedded subqueries

In this hour, you are introduced to the concept of subqueries. Using subqueries enables you to more easily preform complex queries.

What Is a Subquery?

A *subquery*, also known as a *nested query*, is a query embedded within the WHERE clause of another query to further restrict data returned by the query. A subquery returns data that is used in the main query as a condition to further restrict the data to be retrieved. Subqueries are employed with the SELECT, INSERT, UPDATE, and DELETE statements.

You can use a subquery in some cases in place of a join operation by indirectly linking data between the tables based on one or more conditions. When you have a subquery in a query, the subquery is resolved first, and then the main query is resolved according to the condition(s) resolved by the subquery. The results of the subquery process expressions in the WHERE clause of the main query. You can use the subquery either in the WHERE clause or the HAVING clause of the main query. You can use logical and relational operators, such as =, >, <, <>,!=, IN, NOT IN, AND, OR, and so on, within the subquery as well as to evaluate a subquery in the WHERE or HAVING clause.

The Rules of Using Subqueries

The same rules that apply to standard queries also apply to subqueries. You can use join operations, functions, conversions, and other options within a subquery.

Use Indentation for Neater Statement Syntax

Notice the use of indentation in our examples. The use of indentation is merely for readability. The neater your statements are, the easier it is to read and find syntax errors.

Subqueries must follow a few rules:

▶ Subqueries must be enclosed within parentheses.

▶ A subquery can have only one column in the SELECT clause, unless multiple columns are in the main query for the subquery to compare its selected columns.

▶ You cannot use an ORDER BY clause in a subquery, although the main query can use an ORDER BY clause. You can use the GROUP BY clause to perform the same function as the ORDER BY clause in a subquery.

▶ You can only use subqueries that return more than one row with multiple value operators, such as the IN operator.

▶ The SELECT list cannot include references to values that evaluate to a BLOB, ARRAY, CLOB, or NCLOB.

▶ You cannot immediately enclose a subquery in a SET function.

▶ You cannot use the BETWEEN operator with a subquery; however, you can use the BETWEEN operator within the subquery.

The basic syntax for a subquery is as follows:

```
SELECT COLUMN_NAME
FROM TABLE
WHERE COLUMN_NAME = (SELECT COLUMN_NAME
                     FROM TABLE
                     WHERE CONDITIONS);
```

The following examples show how you can and cannot use the BETWEEN operator with a subquery. Here is an example of a correct use of BETWEEN in the subquery:

```
SELECT COLUMN_NAME
FROM TABLE_A
```

```
WHERE COLUMN_NAME OPERATOR (SELECT COLUMN_NAME
                            FROM TABLE_B)
                            WHERE VALUE BETWEEN VALUE)
```

You cannot use BETWEEN as an operator outside the subquery. The following is an example of an illegal use of BETWEEN with a subquery:

```
SELECT COLUMN_NAME
FROM TABLE_A
WHERE COLUMN_NAME BETWEEN VALUE AND (SELECT COLUMN_NAME
                                     FROM TABLE_B)
```

Subqueries with the SELECT Statement

Subqueries are most frequently used with the SELECT statement, although you can use them within a data manipulation statement as well. The subquery, when employed with the SELECT statement, retrieves data for the main query to use.

The basic syntax is as follows:

```
SELECT COLUMN_NAME [, COLUMN_NAME ]
FROM TABLE1 [, TABLE2 ]
WHERE COLUMN_NAME OPERATOR
                  (SELECT COLUMN_NAME [, COLUMN_NAME ]
                   FROM TABLE1 [, TABLE2 ]
                   [ WHERE ])
```

The following is an example:

```
SELECT E.EMP_ID, E.LAST_NAME, E.FIRST_NAME, EP.PAY_RATE
FROM EMPLOYEE_TBL E, EMPLOYEE_PAY_TBL EP
WHERE E.EMP_ID = EP.EMP_ID
AND EP.PAY_RATE < (SELECT PAY_RATE
                   FROM EMPLOYEE_PAY_TBL
                   WHERE EMP_ID = '443679012');
```

The preceding SQL statement returns the employee identification, last name, first name, and pay rate for all employees who have a pay rate greater than that of the employee with the identification 443679012. In this case, you do not necessarily know (or care) what the exact pay rate is for this particular employee; you only care about the pay rate for the purpose of getting a list of employees who bring home more than the employee specified in the subquery.

Using Subqueries for Unknown Values

Subqueries are frequently used to place conditions on a query when the exact conditions are unknown. The pay rate for 220984332 was unknown, but the subquery was designed to do the footwork for you.

The next query selects the pay rate for a particular employee. This query is used as the subquery in the following example.

```
SELECT PAY_RATE
FROM EMPLOYEE_PAY_TBL
WHERE EMP_ID = '220984332';
```

```
  PAY_RATE
----------
11
```

```
1 row selected.
```

The previous query is used as a subquery in the WHERE clause of the following query:

```
SELECT E.EMP_ID, E.LAST_NAME, E.FIRST_NAME, EP.PAY_RATE
FROM EMPLOYEE_TBL E, EMPLOYEE_PAY_TBL EP
WHERE E.EMP_ID = EP.EMP_ID
  AND EP.PAY_RATE > (SELECT PAY_RATE
                     FROM EMPLOYEE_PAY_TBL
                     WHERE EMP_ID = '220984332');
```

EMP_ID	LAST_NAME	FIRST_NAME	PAY_RATE
442346889	PLEW	LINDA	14.75
443679012	SPURGEON	TIFFANY	15

```
2 rows selected.
```

The result of the subquery is 11 (shown in the last example), so the last condition of the WHERE clause is evaluated as

```
AND EP.PAY_RATE > 11
```

You did not know the value of the pay rate for the given individual when you executed the query. However, the main query was able to compare each individual's pay rate to the subquery results.

Subqueries with the INSERT Statement

By the Way

Always Remember to COMMIT Your DML

Remember to use the COMMIT and ROLLBACK commands when using DML commands such as the INSERT statement.

You can also use subqueries in conjunction with *Data Manipulation Language (DML)* statements. The INSERT statement is the first instance you examine. It uses the data returned from the subquery to insert into another table. You can modify the selected data in the subquery with any of the character, date, or number functions.

The basic syntax is as follows:

```
INSERT INTO TABLE_NAME [ (COLUMN1 [, COLUMN2 ]) ]
SELECT [ *|COLUMN1 [, COLUMN2 ]
FROM TABLE1 [, TABLE2 ]
[ WHERE VALUE OPERATOR ]
```

The following is an example of the INSERT statement with a subquery:

```
INSERT INTO RICH_EMPLOYEES
SELECT E.EMP_ID, E.LAST_NAME, E.FIRST_NAME, EP.PAY_RATE
FROM EMPLOYEE_TBL E, EMPLOYEE_PAY_TBL EP
WHERE E.EMP_ID = EP.EMP_ID
  AND EP.PAY_RATE > (SELECT PAY_RATE
                     FROM EMPLOYEE_PAY_TBL
                     WHERE EMP_ID = '220984332');

2 rows created.
```

This INSERT statement inserts the EMP_ID, LAST_NAME, FIRST_NAME, and PAY_RATE into a table called RICH_EMPLOYEES for all records of employees who have a pay rate greater than the pay rate of the employee with identification 220984332.

Subqueries with the UPDATE Statement

You can use subqueries in conjunction with the UPDATE statement to update single or multiple columns in a table. The basic syntax is as follows:

```
UPDATE TABLE
SET COLUMN_NAME [, COLUMN_NAME) ] =
    (SELECT ]COLUMN_NAME [, COLUMN_NAME) ]
    FROM TABLE
    [ WHERE ]
```

Examples showing the use of the UPDATE statement with a subquery follow. The first query returns the employee identification of all employees who reside in Indianapolis. You can see that four individuals meet this criterion.

```
SELECT EMP_ID
FROM EMPLOYEE_TBL
WHERE CITY = 'INDIANAPOLIS';

EMP_ID
---------
442346889
313782439
220984332
```

```
443679012
```

```
4 rows selected.
```

The first query is used as the subquery in the following statement; it proves how many employee identifications are returned by the subquery. The following is the UPDATE with the subquery:

```
UPDATE EMPLOYEE_PAY_TBL
SET PAY_RATE = PAY_RATE * 1.1
WHERE EMP_ID IN (SELECT EMP_ID
                 FROM EMPLOYEE_TBL
                 WHERE CITY = 'INDIANAPOLIS');
```

```
4 rows updated.
```

As expected, four rows are updated. One important thing to notice is that, unlike the example in the first section, this subquery returns multiple rows of data. Because you expect multiple rows to be returned, you use the IN operator instead of the equal sign. Remember that IN compares an expression to values in a list. If you had used the equal sign, an error would have been returned.

Subqueries with the DELETE Statement

You can also use subqueries in conjunction with the DELETE statement. The basic syntax is as follows:

```
DELETE FROM TABLE_NAME
[ WHERE OPERATOR [ VALUE ]
                 (SELECT COLUMN_NAME
                 FROM TABLE_NAME)
                 [ WHERE) ]
```

In the following example, you delete the BRANDON GLASS record from EMPLOYEE_PAY_TBL. You do not know Brandon's employee identification number, but you can use a subquery to get his identification number from EMPLOYEE_TBL, which contains the FIRST_NAME and LAST_NAME columns.

```
DELETE FROM EMPLOYEE_PAY_TBL
WHERE EMP_ID = (SELECT EMP_ID
                FROM EMPLOYEE_TBL
                WHERE LAST_NAME = 'GLASS'
                  AND FIRST_NAME = 'BRANDON');
```

```
1 row deleted.
```

Embedded Subqueries

By the Way

You can embed a subquery within another subquery, just as you can embed the subquery within a regular query. When a subquery is used, that subquery is resolved before the main query. Likewise, the lowest level subquery is resolved first in embedded or nested subqueries, working out to the main query.

The basic syntax for embedded subqueries is as follows:

```
SELECT COLUMN_NAME [, COLUMN_NAME ]
FROM TABLE1 [, TABLE2 ]
WHERE COLUMN_NAME OPERATOR (SELECT COLUMN_NAME
                           FROM TABLE
                           WHERE COLUMN_NAME OPERATOR
                                  (SELECT COLUMN_NAME
                                  FROM TABLE
                                  [ WHERE COLUMN_NAME OPERATOR VALUE ]))
```

The following example uses two subqueries, one embedded within the other. You want to find out what customers have placed orders in which the quantity multiplied by the cost of a single order is greater than the sum of the cost of all products.

```
SELECT CUST_ID, CUST_NAME
FROM CUSTOMER_TBL
WHERE CUST_ID IN (SELECT O.CUST_ID
                  FROM ORDERS_TBL O, PRODUCTS_TBL P
                  WHERE O.PROD_ID = P.PROD_ID
                  AND O.QTY + P.COST < (SELECT SUM(COST)
                                        FROM
                                             PRODUCTS_TBL));
```

CUST_ID	CUST_NAME
090	WENDY WOLF
232	LESLIE GLEASON
287	GAVINS PLACE
43	SCHYLERS NOVELTIES
432	SCOTTYS MARKET
560	ANDYS CANDIES

6 rows selected.

Always Use a WHERE Clause

Do not forget the use of the WHERE clause with the UPDATE and DELETE statements. All rows are updated or deleted from the target table if the WHERE clause is not used. You can utilize a SELECT statement with the WHERE clause first to ensure that you are modifying the correct rows. See Hour 5, "Manipulating Data."

Six rows that meet the criteria of both subqueries were selected.

The following two examples show the results of each of the subqueries to aid your understanding of how the main query was resolved:

```
SELECT SUM(COST) FROM PRODUCTS_TBL;

 SUM(COST)
----------
 138.08

1 row selected.

SELECT O.CUST_ID
FROM ORDERS_TBL O, PRODUCTS_TBL P
WHERE O.PROD_ID = P.PROD_ID
  AND O.QTY + P.COST > 138.08;

CUST_ID
-------
43
287

2 rows selected.
```

In essence, the main query, after the substitution of the second subquery, is evaluated as shown in the following example:

```
SELECT CUST_ID, CUST_NAME
FROM CUSTOMER_TBL
WHERE CUST_ID IN (SELECT O.CUST_ID
                  FROM ORDERS_TBL O, PRODUCTS_TBL P
                  WHERE O.PROD_ID = P.PROD_ID
                    AND O.QTY + P.COST > 138.08);
```

The following shows how the main query is evaluated after the substitution of the first subquery:

```
SELECT CUST_ID, CUST_NAME
FROM CUSTOMER_TBL
WHERE CUST_ID IN (287,43);
```

The following is the final result:

```
CUST_ID        CUST_NAME
...........    ..................


43             SCHYLERS NOVELTIES
287            GAVINS PLACE

2 rows selected.
```

Multiple Subqueries Can Cause Problems

The use of multiple subqueries results in slower response time and might result in reduced accuracy of the results due to possible mistakes in the statement coding.

Correlated Subqueries

Correlated subqueries are common in many SQL implementations. The concept of correlated subqueries is discussed as an ANSI-standard SQL topic and is covered briefly in this hour. A correlated subquery is a subquery that is dependent upon information in the main query. This means that tables in a subquery can be related to tables in the main query.

In the following example, the table join between CUSTOMER_TBL and ORDERS_TBL in the subquery is dependent on the alias for CUSTOMER_TBL (C) in the main query. This query returns the name of all customers who have ordered more than 10 units of one or more items.

```
SELECT C.CUST_NAME
FROM CUSTOMER_TBL C
WHERE 10 < (SELECT SUM(O.QTY)
            FROM ORDERS_TBL O
            WHERE O.CUST_ID = C.CUST_ID);

CUST_NAME
.................


SCOTTYS MARKET
SCHYLERS NOVELTIES
MARYS GIFT SHOP

3 rows selected.
```

You can extract and slightly modify the subquery from the previous statement in the next statement to show you the total quantity of units ordered for each customer, allowing the previous results to be verified:

```
SELECT C.CUST_NAME, SUM(O.QTY)
FROM CUSTOMER_TBL C,
     ORDERS_TBL O
WHERE C.CUST_ID = O.CUST_ID
GROUP BY C.CUST_NAME;
```

```
CUST_NAME                        SUM(O.QTY)
-----------------------          ----------
ANDYS CANDIES                    1
GAVINS PLACE                     10
LESLIE GLEASON                   1
MARYS GIFT SHOP                  100
SCHYLERS NOVELTIES               25
SCOTTYS MARKET                   20
WENDY WOLF                       2

7 rows selected.
```

The GROUP BY clause in this example is required because another column is being selected with the aggregate function SUM. This gives you a sum for each customer. In the original subquery, a GROUP BY clause is not required because SUM achieves a total for the entire query, which is run against the record for each customer.

Subquery Performance

Subqueries do have performance implications when used within a query. You must consider those implications prior to implementing them in a production environment. Consider that a subquery must be evaluated prior to the main part of the query, so the time that it takes to execute the subquery has a direct effect on the time it takes for the main query to execute. Let's look at our previous example:

Proper Use of Correlated Subqueries
In the case of a correlated subquery, you must reference the table in the main query before you can resolve the subquery.

```
SELECT CUST_ID, CUST_NAME
FROM CUSTOMER_TBL
WHERE CUST_ID IN (SELECT O.CUST_ID
                  FROM ORDERS_TBL O, PRODUCTS_TBL P
                  WHERE O.PROD_ID = P.PROD_ID
                  AND O.QTY + P.COST < (SELECT SUM(COST)
                                        FROM
                                             PRODUCTS_TBL));
```

Imagine what would happen if PRODUCTS_TBL contained a couple thousand product lines and ORDERS_TBL contained a few million lines of customer orders. The resulting effect of having to do a SUM across PRODUCTS_TBL and then join it with ORDERS_TBL could slow the query down quite considerably. So always remember to evaluate the effect that using a subquery has on performance when deciding on a course of action to take for getting information out of the database.

Summary

By simple definition and general concept, a subquery is a query that is performed within another query to place further conditions on a query. You can use a subquery in an SQL statement's WHERE clause or HAVING clause. Queries are typically used within other queries (Data Query Language), but you can also use them in the resolution of DML statements such as INSERT, UPDATE, and DELETE. All basic rules for DML apply when using subqueries with DML commands.

The subquery's syntax is virtually the same as that of a standalone query, with a few minor restrictions. One of these restrictions is that you cannot use the ORDER BY clause within a subquery; you can use a GROUP BY clause, however, which renders virtually the same effect. Subqueries are used to place conditions that are not necessarily known for a query, providing more power and flexibility with SQL.

Q&A

Q. *In the examples of subqueries, I noticed quite a bit of indentation. Is this necessary in the syntax of a subquery?*

A. Absolutely not. The indentation is used merely to break the statement into separate parts, making the statement more readable and easier to follow.

Q. *Is there a limit on the number of embedded subqueries that can be used in a single query?*

A. Limitations such as the number of embedded subqueries allowed and the number of tables joined in a query are specific to each implementation. Some implementations might not have limits, although the use of too many embedded subqueries could drastically hinder SQL statement performance. Most limitations are affected by the actual hardware, CPU speed, and system memory available, although there are many other considerations.

Q. *It seems that debugging a query with subqueries can prove to be confusing, especially with embedded subqueries. What is the best way to debug a query with subqueries?*

A. The best way to debug a query with subqueries is to evaluate the query in sections. First evaluate the lowest-level subquery, and then work your way to the main query (the same way the database evaluates the query). When you evaluate each subquery individually, you can substitute the returned values for each subquery to check your main query's logic. An error with a subquery often results from the use of the operator that evaluates the subquery, such as (=), IN, >, <, and so on.

Workshop

The following workshop is composed of a series of quiz questions and practical exercises. The quiz questions are designed to test your overall understanding of the current material. The practical exercises are intended to afford you the opportunity to apply the concepts discussed during the current hour, as well as build upon the knowledge acquired in previous hours of study. Please take time to complete the quiz questions and exercises before continuing. Refer to Appendix C, "Answers to Quizzes and Exercises," for answers.

Quiz

1. What is the function of a subquery when used with a SELECT statement?

2. Can you update more than one column when using the UPDATE statement in conjunction with a subquery?

3. Do the following have the correct syntax? If not, what is the correct syntax?

   a.
   ```
   SELECT CUST_ID, CUST_NAME
          FROM CUSTOMER_TBL
          WHERE CUST_ID =
                      (SELECT CUST_ID
                          FROM ORDERS_TBL
                          WHERE ORD_NUM = '16C17');
   ```

   b.
   ```
   SELECT EMP_ID, SALARY
          FROM EMPLOYEE_PAY_TBL
          WHERE SALARY BETWEEN '20000'
                      AND (SELECT SALARY
                              FROM EMPLOYEE_ID
                              WHERE SALARY = '40000');
   ```

c.
```
UPDATE PRODUCTS_TBL
   SET COST = 1.15
   WHERE CUST_ID =
                    (SELECT CUST_ID
                     FROM ORDERS_TBL
                     WHERE ORD_NUM = '32A132');
```

4. What would happen if you ran the following statement?

```
DELETE FROM EMPLOYEE_TBL
WHERE EMP_ID IN
              (SELECT EMP_ID
               FROM EMPLOYEE_PAY_TBL);
```

Exercises

1. Write the SQL code for the requested subqueries, and compare your results to ours. Use the following tables to complete the exercises:

```
EMPLOYEE_TBL
EMP_ID          VARCHAR(9)      NOT NULL     primary key
LAST_NAME       VARCHAR(15)     NOT NULL
FIRST_NAME      VARCHAR(15)     NOT NULL
MIDDLE_NAME     VARCHAR(15)
ADDRESS         VARCHAR(30)     NOT NULL
CITY            VARCHAR(15)     NOT NULL
STATE           VARCHAR(2)      NOT NULL
ZIP             INTEGER(5)      NOT NULL
PHONE           VARCHAR(10)
PAGER           VARCHAR(10)


EMPLOYEE_PAY_TBL
EMP_ID            VARCHAR(9)      NOT NULL     primary key
POSITION          VARCHAR(15)     NOT NULL
DATE_HIRE         DATETIME
PAY_RATE          DECIMAL(4,2)    NOT NULL
DATE_LAST_RAISE   DATETIME
CONSTRAINT EMP_FK   FOREIGN KEY (EMP_ID_ REFERENCES
EMPLOYEE_TBL (EMP_ID)


CUSTOMER_TBL
CUST_ID         VARCHAR(10)     NOT NULL     primary key
CUST_NAME       VARCHAR(30)     NOT NULL
CUST_ADDRESS    VARCHAR(20)     NOT NULL
CUST_CITY       VARCHAR(15)     NOT NULL
CUST_STATE      VARCHAR(2)      NOT NULL
CUST_ZIP        INTEGER(5)      NOT NULL
CUST_PHONE      INTEGER(10)
CUST_FAX        INTEGER(10)
```

```
ORDERS_TBL
ORD_NUM        VARCHAR(10)     NOT NULL        primary key
CUST_ID        VARCHAR(10)     NOT NULL
PROD_ID        VARCHAR(10)     NOT NULL
QTY            INTEGER(6)      NOT NULL
ORD_DATE       DATETIME


PRODUCTS_TBL
PROD_ID        VARCHAR(10)     NOT NULL        primary key
PROD_DESC      VARCHAR(40)     NOT NULL
COST           DECIMAL(6,2)    NOT NULL
```

2. Using a subquery, write an SQL statement to update CUSTOMER_TBL. Find the customer with the order number 23E934, contained in the field ORD_NUM, and change the customer name to DAVIDS MARKET.

3. Using a subquery, write a query that returns the names of all employees who have a pay rate greater than JOHN DOE, whose employee identification number is 343559876.

4. Using a subquery, write a query that lists all products that cost more than the average cost of all products.

HOUR 15

Combining Multiple Queries into One

In this hour, you learn how to combine SQL queries by using the UNION, UNION ALL, INTERSECT, and EXCEPT operators. Once again, you must check your particular implementation for any variations in the use of these operators.

Single Queries Versus Compound Queries

The single query is one SELECT statement, whereas the *compound query* includes two or more SELECT statements.

You form compound queries by using some type of operator to join the two queries. The UNION operator in the following examples joins two queries.

A single SQL statement could be written as follows:

```
SELECT EMP_ID, SALARY, PAY_RATE
FROM EMPLOYEE_PAY_TBL
WHERE SALARY IS NOT NULL OR
PAY_RATE IS NOT NULL;
```

This is the same statement using the UNION operator:

```
SELECT EMP_ID, SALARY
FROM EMPLOYEE_PAY_TBL
WHERE SALARY IS NOT NULL
UNION
SELECT EMP_ID, PAY_RATE
FROM EMPLOYEE_PAY_TBL
WHERE PAY_RATE IS NOT NULL;
```

The previous statements return pay information for all employees who are paid either hourly or on a salary.

Compound operators are used to combine and restrict the results of two SELECT statements. You can use these operators to return or suppress the output of duplicate records. Compound operators can bring together similar data that is stored in different fields.

> **How UNION Works**
>
> If you executed the second query, the output has two column headings: EMP_ID and SALARY. Each individual's pay rate is listed under the SALARY column. When using the UNION operator, column headings are determined by column names or column aliases used in the first SELECT statement.

Compound queries enable you to combine the results of more than one query to return a single set of data. Compound queries are often simpler to write than a single query with complex conditions. Compound queries also allow for more flexibility regarding the never-ending task of data retrieval.

Compound Query Operators

The compound query operators vary among database vendors. The *American National Standards Institute (ANSI)* standard includes the UNION, UNION ALL, EXCEPT, and INTERSECT operators, all of which are discussed in the following sections.

The UNION Operator

The UNION operator combines the results of two or more SELECT statements without returning duplicate rows. In other words, if a row of output exists in the results of one query, the same row is not returned, even though it exists in the second query. To use the UNION operator, each SELECT statement must have the same number of columns selected, the same number of column expressions, the same data type, and the same order—but they do not have to be the same length.

The syntax is as follows:

```
SELECT COLUMN1 [, COLUMN2 ]
FROM TABLE1 [, TABLE2 ]
[ WHERE ]
UNION
SELECT COLUMN1 [, COLUMN2 ]
FROM TABLE1 [, TABLE2 ]
[ WHERE ]
```

Look at the following example:

```
SELECT EMP_ID FROM EMPLOYEE_TBL
UNION
SELECT EMP_ID FROM EMPLOYEE_PAY_TBL;
```

Those employee IDs that are in both tables appear only once in the results.

This hour's examples begin with a simple SELECT statement from two tables:

```
SELECT PROD_DESC FROM PRODUCTS_TBL;
```

```
PROD_DESC
----------------------
WITCH COSTUME
PLASTIC PUMPKIN 18 INCH
FALSE PARAFFIN TEETH
LIGHTED LANTERNS
ASSORTED COSTUMES
CANDY CORN
PUMPKIN CANDY
PLASTIC SPIDERS
ASSORTED MASKS
KEY CHAIN
OAK BOOKSHELF

11 rows selected.
```

```
SELECT PROD_DESC FROM PRODUCTS_TMP;
```

```
PROD_DESC
--------------------
WITCH COSTUME
PLASTIC PUMPKIN 18 INCH
FALSE PARAFFIN TEETH
LIGHTED LANTERNS
ASSORTED COSTUMES
CANDY CORN
PUMPKIN CANDY
PLASTIC SPIDERS
```

```
ASSORTED MASKS
KEY CHAIN
OAK BOOKSHELF
```

```
11 rows selected.
```

Now, combine the same two queries with the UNION operator, making a compound query:

```
SELECT PROD_DESC FROM PRODUCTS_TBL
UNION
SELECT PROD_DESC FROM PRODUCTS_TMP;
```

```
PROD_DESC
-----------------------
ASSORTED COSTUMES
ASSORTED MASKS
CANDY CORN
FALSE PARAFFIN TEETH
LIGHTED LANTERNS
PLASTIC PUMPKIN 18 INCH
PLASTIC SPIDERS
PUMPKIN CANDY
WITCH COSTUME
KEY CHAIN
OAK BOOKSHELF
```

```
11 rows selected.
```

Where the PRODUCTS_TMP Table Came From

The PRODUCTS_TMP table was created in Hour 3, "Managing Database Objects." Refer to Hour 3 if you need to re-create this table.

In the first query, eleven rows of data were returned, and eleven rows of data were returned from the second query. Eleven rows of data are returned when the UNION operator combines the two queries. Only eleven rows are returned because duplicate rows of data are not returned when using the UNION operator.

The following code shows an example of combining two unrelated queries with the UNION operator:

```
SELECT PROD_DESC FROM PRODUCTS_TBL
UNION
SELECT LAST_NAME FROM EMPLOYEE_TBL;
```

```
PROD_DESC
----------------------
ASSORTED COSTUMES
ASSORTED MASKS
CANDY CORN
FALSE PARAFFIN TEETH
GLASS
KEY CHAIN
LIGHTED LANTERNS
OAK BOOKSHELF
PLASTIC PUMPKIN 18 INCH
PLASTIC SPIDERS
PLEW
PUMPKIN CANDY
SPURGEON
STEPHENS
WALLACE
WITCH COSTUME

16 rows selected.
```

The PROD_DESC and LAST_NAME values are listed together, and the column heading is taken from the column name in the first query.

The UNION ALL Operator

You use the UNION ALL operator to combine the results of two SELECT statements, including duplicate rows. The same rules that apply to UNION apply to the UNION ALL operator. The UNION and UNION ALL operators are the same, although one returns duplicate rows of data where the other does not.

The syntax is as follows:

```
SELECT COLUMN1 [, COLUMN2 ]
FROM TABLE1 [, TABLE2 ]
[ WHERE ]
UNION ALL
SELECT COLUMN1 [, COLUMN2 ]
FROM TABLE1 [, TABLE2 ]
[ WHERE ]
```

The following SQL statement returns all employee IDs from both tables and shows duplicates:

```
SELECT EMP_ID FROM EMPLOYEE_TBL
UNION ALL
SELECT EMP_ID FROM EMPLOYEE_PAY_TBL
```

The following is the same compound query in the previous section with the
UNION ALL operator:

```
SELECT PROD_DESC FROM PRODUCTS_TBL
UNION ALL
SELECT PROD_DESC FROM PRODUCTS_TMP;


PROD_DESC
----------------------
WITCH COSTUME
PLASTIC PUMPKIN 18 INCH
FALSE PARAFFIN TEETH
LIGHTED LANTERNS
ASSORTED COSTUMES
CANDY CORN
PUMPKIN CANDY
PLASTIC SPIDERS
ASSORTED MASKS
KEY CHAIN
OAK BOOKSHELF
WITCH COSTUME
PLASTIC PUMPKIN 18 INCH
FALSE PARAFFIN TEETH
LIGHTED LANTERNS
ASSORTED COSTUMES
CANDY CORN
PUMPKIN CANDY
PLASTIC SPIDERS
ASSORTED MASKS
KEY CHAIN
OAK BOOKSHELF

22 rows selected.
```

Notice that there were 22 rows returned in this query (11+11) because duplicate records are retrieved with the UNION ALL operator.

The INTERSECT Operator

You use the INTERSECT operator to combine two SELECT statements, but it
returns only rows from the first SELECT statement that are identical to a row
in the second SELECT statement. The same rules apply when using the
INTERSECT operator as when you used the UNION operator. Currently, the
INTERSECT operator is not supported by MySQL 5.0 but is supported by both
SQL Server and Oracle.

The syntax is as follows:

```
SELECT COLUMN1 [, COLUMN2 ]
FROM TABLE1 [, TABLE2 ]
[ WHERE ]
```

```
INTERSECT
SELECT COLUMN1 [ , COLUMN2 ]
FROM TABLE1 [ , TABLE2 ]
[ WHERE ]
```

The following SQL statement returns the customer identification for those customers who have placed an order:

```
SELECT CUST_ID FROM CUSTOMER_TBL
INTERSECT
SELECT CUST_ID FROM ORDERS_TBL;
```

The following example illustrates the INTERSECT operator using the two original queries in this hour:

```
SELECT PROD_DESC FROM PRODUCTS_TBL
INTERSECT
SELECT PROD_DESC FROM PRODUCTS_TMP;
```

```
PROD_DESC
--------------------
ASSORTED COSTUMES
ASSORTED MASKS
CANDY CORN
FALSE PARAFFIN TEETH
KEY CHAIN
LIGHTED LANTERNS
OAK BOOKSHELF
PLASTIC PUMPKIN 18 INCH
PLASTIC SPIDERS
PUMPKIN CANDY
WITCH COSTUME

11 rows selected.
```

Only 11 rows are returned because only 11 rows were identical between the output of the two single queries.

The EXCEPT Operator

The EXCEPT operator combines two SELECT statements and returns rows from the first SELECT statement that are not returned by the second SELECT statement. Once again, the same rules that apply to the UNION operator also apply to the EXCEPT operator. The EXCEPT operator is not currently supported in MySQL. In Oracle the EXCEPT operator is referenced by using the term MINUS but performs the same functionality.

The syntax is as follows:

```
SELECT COLUMN1 [, COLUMN2 ]
FROM TABLE1 [, TABLE2 ]
[ WHERE ]
EXCEPT
SELECT COLUMN1 [, COLUMN2 ]
FROM TABLE1 [, TABLE2 ]
[ WHERE ]
```

Study the following example, which would work in an SQL Server implementation:

```
SELECT PROD_DESC FROM PRODUCTS_TBL
EXCEPT
SELECT PROD_DESC FROM PRODUCTS_TMP;


PROD_DESC
---------------------
PLASTIC PUMPKIN 18 INCH
PLASTIC SPIDERS
PUMPKIN CANDY

3 rows selected.
```

According to the results, three rows of data were returned by the first query that were not returned by the second query.

The following example demonstrates the use of the MINUS operator as a replacement for the EXCEPT operator:

```
SELECT PROD_DESC FROM PRODUCTS_TBL
MINUS
SELECT PROD_DESC FROM PRODUCTS_TMP;


PROD_DESC
---------------------
PLASTIC PUMPKIN 18 INCH
PLASTIC SPIDERS
PUMPKIN CANDY

3 rows selected.
```

Using ORDER BY with a Compound Query

You can use the ORDER BY clause with a compound query. However, you can only use the ORDER BY clause to order the results of both queries. Therefore, there can be only one ORDER BY clause in a compound query, even though the compound query might consist of multiple individual queries or SELECT statements. The ORDER BY clause must reference the columns being ordered by an alias or by the column number.

The syntax is as follows:

```
SELECT COLUMN1 [, COLUMN2 ]
FROM TABLE1 [, TABLE2 ]
[ WHERE ]
OPERATOR{UNION | EXCEPT | INTERSECT | UNION ALL}
SELECT COLUMN1 [, COLUMN2 ]
FROM TABLE1 [, TABLE2 ]
[ WHERE ]
[ ORDER BY ]
```

The following SQL statement returns the employee ID from EMPLOYEE_TBL and EMPLOYEE_PAY_TBL, but it does not show duplicates and it orders by EMP_ID:

```
SELECT EMP_ID FROM EMPLOYEE_TBL
UNION
SELECT EMP_ID FROM EMPLOYEE_PAY_TBL
ORDER BY 1;
```

> **Using Numbers in the ORDER BY Clause**
>
> The column in the ORDER BY clause is referenced by the number 1 instead of the actual column name.

By the Way

The results of the compound query are sorted by the first column of each query. Sorting compound queries lets you easily recognize duplicate records.

The following example shows the use of the ORDER BY clause with a compound query. You can use the column name in the ORDER BY clause if the column sorted by has the same name in all individual queries of the statement.

```
SELECT PROD_DESC FROM PRODUCTS_TBL
UNION
SELECT PROD_DESC FROM PRODUCTS_TBL
ORDER BY PROD_DESC;

PROD_DESC
----------------------
ASSORTED COSTUMES
ASSORTED MASKS
CANDY CORN
FALSE PARAFFIN TEETH
KEY CHAIN
LIGHTED LANTERNS
OAK BOOKSHELF
PLASTIC PUMPKIN 18 INCH
PLASTIC SPIDERS
```

PUMPKIN CANDY
WITCH COSTUME

11 rows selected.

The following query uses a numeric value in place of the actual column name in the ORDER BY clause:

```
SELECT PROD_DESC FROM PRODUCTS_TBL
UNION
SELECT PROD_DESC FROM PRODUCTS_TBL;
```

```
PROD_DESC
----------------------
ASSORTED COSTUMES
ASSORTED MASKS
CANDY CORN
FALSE PARAFFIN TEETH
KEY CHAIN
LIGHTED LANTERNS
OAK BOOKSHELF
PLASTIC PUMPKIN 18 INCH
PLASTIC SPIDERS
PUMPKIN CANDY
WITCH COSTUME

11 rows selected.
```

Using GROUP BY with a Compound Query

Unlike ORDER BY, you can use GROUP BY in each SELECT statement of a compound query, but you also can use it following all individual queries. In addition, you can use the HAVING clause (sometimes used with the GROUP BY clause) in each SELECT statement of a compound statement.

The syntax is as follows:

```
SELECT COLUMN1 [, COLUMN2 ]
FROM TABLE1 [, TABLE2 ]
[ WHERE ]
[ GROUP BY ]
[ HAVING ]
OPERATOR {UNION | EXCEPT | INTERSECT | UNION ALL}
SELECT COLUMN1 [, COLUMN2 ]
FROM TABLE1 [, TABLE2 ]
[ WHERE ]
[ GROUP BY ]
[ HAVING ]
[ ORDER BY ]
```

In the following example, you select a literal string to represent customer records, employee records, and product records. Each query is simply a count of all records in each appropriate table. The GROUP BY clause groups the results of the entire report by the numeric value 1, which represents the first column in each query.

```
SELECT 'CUSTOMERS' TYPE, COUNT(*)
FROM CUSTOMER_TBL
UNION
SELECT 'EMPLOYEES' TYPE, COUNT(*)
FROM EMPLOYEE_TBL
UNION
SELECT 'PRODUCTS' TYPE, COUNT(*)
FROM PRODUCTS_TBL
GROUP BY 1;


TYPE          COUNT(*)
----------- --------
CUSTOMERS         15
EMPLOYEES          6
PRODUCTS           9

3 rows selected.
```

The following query is identical to the previous query, except that the ORDER BY clause is used as well:

```
SELECT 'CUSTOMERS' TYPE, COUNT(*)
FROM CUSTOMER_TBL
UNION
SELECT 'EMPLOYEES' TYPE, COUNT(*)
FROM EMPLOYEE_TBL
UNION
SELECT 'PRODUCTS' TYPE, COUNT(*)
FROM PRODUCTS_TBL
GROUP BY 1
ORDER BY 2;


TYPE          COUNT(*)
----------- --------
EMPLOYEES          6
PRODUCTS           9
CUSTOMERS         15

3 rows selected.
```

This is sorted by column 2, which was the count on each table. Hence, the final output is sorted by the count from least to greatest.

> **Bad Data Results**
>
> Incomplete data returned by a query qualifies as incorrect data.

Retrieving Accurate Data

Be cautious when using the compound operators. Incorrect or incomplete data might be returned if you use the INTERSECT operator and you use the wrong SELECT statement as the first individual query. In addition, consider whether you want duplicate records when using the UNION and UNION ALL operators. What about EXCEPT? Do you need any of the rows that the second query did not return? As you can see, the wrong compound query operator or the wrong order of individual queries in a compound query can easily cause misleading data to be returned.

Summary

This hour introduced you to compound queries. All SQL statements previous to this hour have consisted of a single query. Compound queries allow multiple individual queries to be used together as a single query to achieve the data resultset desired as output. The compound query operators discussed included UNION, UNION ALL, INTERSECT, and EXCEPT (MINUS). UNION returns the output of two single queries without displaying duplicate rows of data. UNION ALL simply displays all output of single queries, regardless of existing duplicate rows. INTERSECT returns identical rows between two queries. EXCEPT (the same as MINUS) returns the results of one query that do not exist in another query. Compound queries provide greater flexibility when trying to satisfy the requirements of various queries, which, without the use of compound operators, could result in complex queries.

Q&A

Q. *How are the columns referenced in the GROUP BY clause in a compound query?*

A. The columns can be referenced by the actual column name or by the number of the column placement in the query if the column names are not identical in the two queries.

Q. *I understand what the EXCEPT operator does, but would the outcome change if I were to reverse the SELECT statements?*

A. Yes. The order of the individual queries is important when using the EXCEPT or MINUS operator. Remember that all rows are returned from the first query that are not returned by the second query. Changing the order of the two individual queries in the compound query could definitely affect the results.

Q. *Must the data type and the length of columns in a compound query be the same in both queries?*

A. No. Only the data type must be the same. The length can differ.

Q. *What determines the column names when using the UNION operator?*

A. The first query set determines the column names for the data returned when using a UNION operator.

Workshop

The following workshop is composed of a series of quiz questions and practical exercises. The quiz questions are designed to test your overall understanding of the current material. The practical exercises are intended to afford you the opportunity to apply the concepts discussed during the current hour, as well as build upon the knowledge acquired in previous hours of study. Please take time to complete the quiz questions and exercises before continuing. Refer to Appendix C, "Answers to Quizzes and Exercises," for answers.

Quiz

Refer to the syntax covered in this hour for the following quiz questions when referring to the INTERSECT and EXCEPT operators. Remember that MySQL does not currently support these two operators.

1. Is the syntax correct for the following compound queries? If not, what would correct the syntax? Use EMPLOYEE_TBL and EMPLOYEE_PAY_TBL as follows:

```
EMPLOYEE_TBL
EMP_ID        VARCHAR(9)    NOT NULL,
LAST_NAME     VARCHAR(15)   NOT NULL,
FIRST_NAME    VARCHAR(15)   NOT NULL,
MIDDLE_NAME   VARCHAR(15),
```

```
ADDRESS       VARCHAR(30)    NOT NULL,
CITY          VARCHAR(15)    NOT NULL,
STATE         VARCHAR(2)     NOT NULL,
ZIP           INTEGER(5)     NOT NULL,
PHONE         VARCHAR(10),
PAGER         VARCHAR(10),
CONSTRAINT EMP_PK PRIMARY KEY (EMP_ID)

EMPLOYEE_PAY_TBL
EMP_ID            VARCHAR(9)    NOT NULL    primary key,
POSITION          VARCHAR(15)   NOT NULL,
DATE_HIRE         DATETIME,
PAY_RATE          DECIMAL(4,2)  NOT NULL,
DATE_LAST_RAISE   DATE,
SALARY            DECIMAL(8,2),
BONUS             DECIMAL(6,2),
CONSTRAINT EMP_FK FOREIGN KEY (EMP_ID)
REFERENCES EMPLOYEE_TBL (EMP_ID)
```

a. SELECT EMP_ID, LAST_NAME, FIRST_NAME
   FROM EMPLOYEE_TBL
   UNION
   SELECT EMP_ID, POSITION, DATE_HIRE
   FROM EMPLOYEE_PAY_TBL;

b. SELECT EMP_ID FROM EMPLOYEE_TBL
   UNION ALL
   SELECT EMP_ID FROM EMPLOYEE_PAY_TBL
   ORDER BY EMP_ID;

c. SELECT EMP_ID FROM EMPLOYEE_PAY_TBL
   INTERSECT
   SELECT EMP_ID FROM EMPLOYEE_TBL
   ORDER BY 1;

2. Match the correct operator to the following statements.

Statement	Operator
a. Show duplicates	UNION
b. Return only rows from the first query that match those in the second query	INTERSECT
c. Return no duplicates	UNION ALL
d. Return only rows from the first query not returned by the second	EXCEPT

Exercises

Refer to the syntax covered in this hour for the following exercises. You might have to write your queries by hand because MySQL does not support some of the operators covered in this hour. When you are finished, compare your results to ours.

Use CUSTOMER_TBL and ORDERS_TBL as listed:

```
CUSTOMER_TBL
CUST_IN        VARCHAR(10)    NOT NULL    primary key,
CUST_NAME      VARCHAR(30)    NOT NULL,
CUST_ADDRESS   VARCHAR(20)    NOT NULL,
CUST_CITY      VARCHAR(15)    NOT NULL,
CUST_STATE     VARCHAR(2)     NOT NULL,
CUST_ZIP       INTEGER(5)     NOT NULL,
CUST_PHONE     INTEGER(10),
CUST_FAX       INTEGER(10)


ORDERS_TBL
ORD_NUM        VARCHAR(10)    NOT NULL    primary key,
CUST_ID        VARCHAR(10)    NOT NULL,
PROD_ID        VARCHAR(10)    NOT NULL,
QTY            INTEGER(6)     NOT NULL,
ORD_DATE       DATETIME
```

1. Write a compound query to find the customers who have placed an order.

2. Write a compound query to find the customers who have not placed an order.

Using Indexes to Improve Performance

What You'll Learn in This Hour:

▶ How indexes work

▶ How to create an index

▶ The different types of indexes

▶ When to use indexes

▶ When not to use indexes

In this hour, you learn how to improve SQL statement performance by creating and using indexes. You begin with the CREATE INDEX command and learn how to use indexes that have been created on tables.

What Is an Index?

Simply put, an *index* is a pointer to data in a table. An index in a database is similar to an index in the back of a book. For example, if you want to reference all pages in a book that discuss a certain topic, you first refer to the index, which lists all topics alphabetically, and it refers you to one or more specific page numbers. An index in a database works the same way in that a query is pointed to the exact physical location of data in a table. You are actually being directed to the data's location in an underlying file of the database, but as far as you are concerned, you are referring to a table.

Which would be faster, looking through a book page by page for some information or searching the book's index and getting a page number? Of course, using the book's index is the most efficient method. It can save a lot of time, especially if the book is large. If you have a book of just a few pages, however, it might be faster to check the pages for the information than to flip back and forth between the index and pages of the book. When a database does not use an index, it is performing what is typically called a *full table scan*, the same as flipping through a book page by page. Full table scans are discussed in Hour 17, "Improving Database Performance."

An index is typically stored separately from the table for which the index was created. An index's main purpose is to improve the performance of data retrieval. Indexes can be created or dropped with no effect on the data. However, after an index is dropped, performance of data retrieval might be slowed. Indexes do take up physical space and can often grow larger than the table. Therefore, you should consider them when estimating your database storage needs.

How Do Indexes Work?

When an index is created, it records the location of values in a table that are associated with the column that is indexed. Entries are added to the index when new data is added to the table. When a query is executed against the database and a condition is specified on a column in the WHERE clause that is indexed, the index is first searched for the values specified in the WHERE clause. If the value is found in the index, the index returns the exact location of the searched data in the table. Figure 16.1 illustrates the functioning of an index.

Suppose the following query was issued:

```
SELECT *
FROM TABLE_NAME
WHERE NAME = 'SMITH';
```

FIGURE 16.1
Table access using an index.

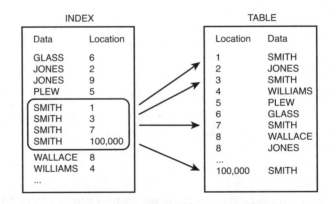

As shown in Figure 16.1, the NAME index is referenced to resolve the location of all names equal to SMITH. After the location is determined, the data can quickly be retrieved from the table. The data, in this case, names is alphabetized in the index.

Variations of Index Creation

Indexes can be created during table creation in certain implementations. Most implementations accommodate a command, aside from the CREATE TABLE command, used to create indexes. Check your particular implementation for the exact syntax for the command, if any, that is available to create an index.

By the Way

A full table scan occurs if there is no index on the table and the same query is executed, which means that every row of data in the table is read to retrieve information pertaining to all individuals with the name SMITH.

An index is faster because it typically stores information in an orderly tree-like format. Consider if we have a list of books upon which we place an index. The index has a root node, which is the beginning point of each query. Then it is split into branches. Maybe in our case there are two branches, one for letters A-L and the other for letters M-Z. Now if you ask for a book with a name that starts with the letter M, you enter the index at the root node and immediately travel to the branch containing letters M-Z. This effectively cuts your time to find the book by eliminating close to half the possibilities.

The CREATE INDEX Command

The CREATE INDEX statement, as with many other statements in SQL, varies greatly among different relational database vendors. Most relational database implementations use the CREATE INDEX statement:

```
CREATE INDEX INDEX_NAME ON TABLE_NAME
```

The syntax is where the vendors start varying greatly on the CREATE INDEX statement options. Some implementations allow the specification of a storage clause (as with the CREATE TABLE statement), ordering (DESC||ASC), and the use of clusters. You must check your particular implementation for its correct syntax.

Types of Indexes

You can create different types of indexes on tables in a database, all of which serve the same goal: to improve database performance by expediting data retrieval. This hour discusses single-column indexes, composite indexes, and unique indexes.

Single-Column Indexes

Best Places for Single-Column Indexes

Single-column indexes are most effective when used on columns that are frequently used alone in the WHERE clause as query conditions. Good candidates for a single-column index are an individual identification number, a serial number, or a system-assigned key.

Indexing on a single column of a table is the simplest and most common manifestation of an index. Obviously, a *single-column index* is one that is created based on only one table column. The basic syntax is as follows:

```
CREATE INDEX INDEX_NAME
ON TABLE_NAME (COLUMN_NAME)
```

For example, if you want to create an index on EMPLOYEE_TBL for employees' last names, the command used to create the index looks like the following:

```
CREATE INDEX NAME_IDX
ON EMPLOYEE_TBL (LAST_NAME);
```

Unique Indexes

You use *unique indexes* for performance and data integrity. A unique index does not allow duplicate values to be inserted into the table. Otherwise, the unique index performs the same way a regular index performs. The syntax is as follows:

```
CREATE UNIQUE INDEX INDEX_NAME
ON TABLE_NAME (COLUMN_NAME)
```

If you want to create a unique index on EMPLOYEE_TBL for an employee's last name, the command used to create the unique index looks like the following:

```
CREATE UNIQUE INDEX NAME_IDX
ON EMPLOYEE_TBL (LAST_NAME);
```

The only problem with this index is that every individual's last name in EMPLOYEE_TBL must be unique, which is impractical. However, a unique index should be created for a column, such as an individual's Social Security number, because that number would be unique for each individual.

You might be wondering, "What if an employee's Social Security number is the primary key for a table?" An index is usually implicitly created when you define a primary key for a table. However, a company can use a fictitious number for an employee ID but maintain each employee's Social Security number for tax purposes. You probably want to index this column and ensure that all entries into this column are unique values.

When working with objects such as unique indexes, it is often beneficial to create the indexes on empty tables during the creation of the database structure. This ensures that the data going into the structure already meets the demand of the constraints you want to place on it. If you are working with existing data, you will want to analyze the impact of whether the data needs to be adjusted to be able to properly apply the index.

Composite Indexes

A *composite index* is an index on two or more columns of a table. You should consider performance when creating a composite index, because the order of columns in the index has a measurable effect on the data retrieval speed. Generally, the most restrictive value should be placed first for optimum performance. However, the columns that are always specified in your queries should be placed first. The syntax is as follows:

```
CREATE INDEX INDEX_NAME
ON TABLE_NAME (COLUMN1, COLUMN2)
```

An example of a composite index follows:

```
CREATE INDEX ORD_IDX
ON ORDERS_TBL (CUST_ID, PROD_ID);
```

In this example, you create a composite index based on two columns in the ORDERS_TBL: CUST_ID and PROD_ID. You assume that these two columns are frequently used together as conditions in the WHERE clause of a query.

Unique Index Constraints

You can only create a unique index on a column in a table whose values are unique. In other words, you cannot create a unique index on an existing table with data that already contains records on the indexed key that are nonunique. Similarly, you cannot create a unique index on a column that allows for NULL values. If you attempt to create a unique index on a column that violates one of these principles, the statement fails.

Did You Know?

In deciding whether to create a single-column index or a composite index, consider the column(s) that you might use frequently in a query's WHERE clause as filter conditions. If only one column is used, choose a single-column index. If two or more columns are frequently used in the WHERE clause as filters, a composite index would be the best choice.

Implicit Indexes

Implicit indexes are indexes that are automatically created by the database server when an object is created. Indexes are automatically created for primary key constraints and unique constraints.

Why are indexes automatically created for these constraints? Imagine that you are the database server. A user adds a new product to the database. The product identification is the primary key on the table, which means that it must be a unique value. To efficiently make sure the new value is unique among hundreds or thousands of records, the product identifications in the table must be indexed. Therefore, when you create a primary key or unique constraint, an index is automatically created for you.

Did You Know?

> **Best Places for Composite Indexes**
>
> Composite indexes are most effective on table columns that are used together frequently as conditions in a query's WHERE clause.

When Should Indexes Be Considered?

Unique indexes are implicitly used in conjunction with a primary key for the primary key to work. Foreign keys are also excellent candidates for an index because you often use them to join the parent table. Most, if not all, columns used for table joins should be indexed.

Columns that you frequently reference in the ORDER BY and GROUP BY clauses should be considered for indexes. For example, if you are sorting on an individual's name, it is quite beneficial to have an index on the name column. It renders an automatic alphabetical order on every name, thus simplifying the actual sort operation and expediting the output results.

Furthermore, you should create indexes on columns with a high number of unique values, or columns that, when used as filter conditions in the WHERE clause, return a low percentage of rows of data from a table. This is where trial and error might come into play. Just as you should always test production code and database structures before implementing them into production, so should you test indexes. Your testing should center on trying different combinations of indexes, no indexes, single-column indexes, and composite indexes. There is no cut-and-dried rule for using indexes. The effective use of indexes requires a thorough knowledge of table relationships, query and transaction requirements, and the data itself.

When Should Indexes Be Avoided?

Plan for Indexing Accordingly

You should plan your tables and indexes. Don't assume that because an index has been created, all performance issues are resolved. The index might not help at all (it might actually hinder performance) and might just take up disk space.

By the Way

Although indexes are intended to enhance a database's performance, sometimes you should avoid them. The following guidelines indicate when you should reconsider using an index:

▶ You should not use indexes on small tables. This is because indexes have an overhead associated with them in terms of query time to access them. In the case of small tables, it is usually faster for the query engine to do a quick scan over the table rather than look at an index first.

▶ You should not use indexes on columns that return a high percentage of data rows when used as a filter condition in a query's WHERE clause. For instance, you would not have an entry for the words the or and in the index of a book.

▶ You can index tables that have frequent, large batch update jobs run. However, the batch job's performance is slowed considerably by the index. You can correct the conflict of having an index on a table that is frequently loaded or manipulated by a large batch process by dropping the index before the batch job and then re-creating the index after the job has completed. This is because the indexes are also updated as the data is inserted, causing additional overhead.

▶ You should not use indexes on columns that contain a high number of NULL values. This is because indexes operate best on columns that have a higher uniqueness of the data between rows. If there are a lot of NULL values, the index will be skewed toward the NULL values and might affect performance.

▶ You should not index columns that are frequently manipulated.
Maintenance on the index can become excessive.

You can see in Figure 16.2 that an index on a column, such as gender,
might not prove beneficial. For example, suppose the following query was
submitted to the database:

```
SELECT *
FROM TABLE_NAME
WHERE GENDER = 'FEMALE';
```

FIGURE 16.2
An example of
an ineffective
index.

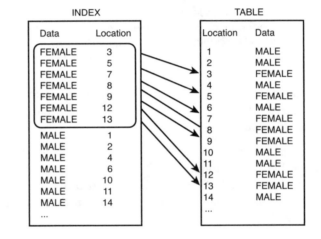

By referring to Figure 16.2, which is based on the previous query, you can
see that there is constant activity between the table and its index. Because a
high number of data rows is returned for WHERE GENDER = 'FEMALE' (or
'MALE'), the database server constantly has to read the index, and then the
table, and then the index, and then the table, and so on. In this case, it
might be more efficient for a full table scan to occur because a high percentage of the table must be read anyway.

Indexes Can Sometimes Lead to Performance Problems
Caution should be taken when creating indexes on a table's extremely long keys because performance is inevitably slowed by high I/O costs.

As a general rule, do not use an index on a column used in a query's condition that returns a high percentage of data rows from the table. In other
words, do not create an index on a column such as gender, or any column

that contains few distinct values. This is often referred to as a column's *cardinality,* or the uniqueness of the data. High cardinality means very unique and therefore describes things such as identification numbers. Low-cardinality values are not very unique and refer to columns such as the gender example.

Altering an Index

You can alter an index after it has been created using syntax that is similar to the CREATE INDEX syntax. The types of alterations that you can manage with the statement differ between implementations but handle all the basic variations of an index in terms of columns, ordering, and such. The syntax is as follows:

```
ALTER INDEX INDEX_NAME
```

You should take care when altering an existing index on production systems. This is because in most cases the index is immediately rebuilt, which obviously creates an overhead in terms of resources. Additionally, on most basic implementations, while the index is being rebuilt it cannot be utilized for queries that might put an additional hindrance upon the performance of your system.

Dropping an Index

An index can be dropped rather simply. Check your particular implementation for the exact syntax, but most major implementations use the DROP command. You should take care when dropping an index because performance might be slowed drastically (or improved!). The syntax is as follows:

```
DROP INDEX INDEX_NAME
```

MySQL uses a slightly different syntax; you also specify the table name of the table that you are dropping the index from:

```
DROP INDEX INDEX_NAME ON TABLE_NAME
```

The most common reason for dropping an index is an attempt to improve performance. Remember that if you drop an index, you can re-create it later. You might need to rebuild an indexes to reduce fragmentation. It is often necessary to experiment with the use of indexes in a database to determine the route to best performance, which might involve creating an index, dropping it, and eventually re-creating it, with or without modifications.

Be Careful with Your Indexes

Indexes are often good for performance, but that's not always true. Refrain from creating indexes on columns that contain few unique values, such as gender and state of residence.

Differences in How to Drop Indexes

MySQL uses the ALTER TABLE command to drop indexes. However, you can still use the DROP INDEX syntax and MySQL maps it to an appropriate ALTER TABLE statement. Again, different SQL implementations might vary widely in syntax, especially when dealing with indexes and data storage.

Summary

You have learned that you can use indexes to improve the overall perform-ance of queries and transactions performed within the database. Database indexes, like an index of a book, enable specific data to be quickly refer-enced from a table. The most common method for creating indexes is through use of the CREATE INDEX command. Different types of indexes are available among SQL implementations. Unique indexes, single-column indexes, and composite indexes are among those types of indexes. You need to consider many factors when deciding on the index type that best meets the needs of your database. The effective use of indexes often requires some experimentation, a thorough knowledge of table relation-ships and data, and a little patience—but patience when you create an index can save minutes, hours, or even days of work later.

Q&A

Q. *Does an index actually take up space the way a table does?*

A. Yes. An index takes up physical space in a database. In fact, an index can become much larger than the table for which the index was created.

Q. *If you drop an index so a batch job can complete faster, how long does it take to re-create the index?*

A. Many factors are involved, such as the size of the index being dropped, the CPU usage, and the machine's power.

Q. *Should all indexes be unique?*

A. No. Unique indexes allow no duplicate values. There might be a need for the allowance of duplicate values in a table.

Workshop

The following workshop is composed of a series of quiz questions and practical exercises. The quiz questions are designed to test your overall understanding of the current material. The practical exercises are intended to afford you the opportunity to apply the concepts discussed during the current hour, as well as build upon the knowledge acquired in previous hours of study. Please take time to complete the quiz questions and exercises before continuing. Refer to Appendix C, "Answers to Quizzes and Exercises," for answers.

Quiz

1. What are some major disadvantages of using indexes?

2. Why is the order of columns in a composite important?

3. Should a column with a large percentage of NULL values be indexed?

4. Is the main purpose of an index to stop duplicate values in a table?

5. True or false: The main reason for a composite index is for aggregate function usage in an index.

6. What does cardinality refer to? What is considered a column of high-cardinality?

Exercises

1. For the following situations, decide whether an index should be used and, if so, what type of index should be used.

   a. Several columns, but a rather small table

   b. Medium-sized table; no duplicates should be allowed

   c. Several columns, very large table, several columns used as filters in the WHERE clause

   d. Large table, many columns, a lot of data manipulation

2. Write the SQL statement to create an index called EP_POSITION in EMPLOYEE_PAY_TBL on the POSITION column.

3. Create a statement to alter the index you just created to make it unique. What do you need to do to create a unique index on the SALARY column? Write the SQL statements that you need to run them in the sequence.

4. Study the tables used in this book. What are some good candidates for indexed columns based on how a user might search for data?

5. Create a multicolumn index on ORDERS_TBL. Include the following columns: CUST_ID, PROD_ID, and ORD_DATE.

6. Create some additional indexes on your tables as desired.

HOUR 17

Improving Database Performance

What You'll Learn in This Hour:

▶ What SQL statement tuning is

▶ Database tuning versus SQL statement tuning

▶ Formatting your SQL statement

▶ Properly joining tables

▶ The most restrictive condition

▶ Full table scans

▶ Invoking the use of indexes

▶ Avoiding the use of OR and HAVING

▶ Avoiding large sort operations

In this hour, you learn how to tune your SQL statement for maximum performance using some simple methods.

What Is SQL Statement Tuning?

SQL statement tuning is the process of optimally building SQL statements to achieve results in the most effective and efficient manner. SQL tuning begins with the basic arrangement of the elements in a query. Simple formatting can play a rather large role in the optimization of a statement.

SQL statement tuning mainly involves tweaking a statement's FROM and WHERE clauses. It is mostly from these two clauses that the database server decides how to evaluate a query. To this point, you have learned the FROM and WHERE clauses' basics. Now it is time to learn how to fine-tune them for better results and happier users.

Database Tuning Versus SQL Statement Tuning

Before this hour continues with your SQL statement tuning lesson, you need to understand the difference between tuning a database and tuning the SQL statements that access the database.

Database tuning is the process of tuning the actual database, which encompasses the allocated memory, disk usage, CPU, I/O, and underlying database processes. Tuning a database also involves the management and manipulation of the database structure, such as the design and layout of tables and indexes. In addition, database tuning often involves the modification of the database architecture to optimize the use of the hardware resources available. You need to consider many other things when tuning a database, but the *database administrator (DBA)* in conjunction with a system administrator normally accomplishes these tasks. The objective of database tuning is to ensure that the database has been designed in a way that best accommodates expected activity within the database.

SQL tuning is the process of tuning the SQL statements that access the database. These SQL statements include database queries and transactional operations, such as inserts, updates, and deletes. The objective of SQL statement tuning is to formulate statements that most effectively access the database in its current state, taking advantage of database and system resources and indexes. The objective is to reduce the operational overhead of executing the query on the database.

By the Way

> **Tuning Is Not One Dimensional**
>
> You must perform both database tuning and SQL statement tuning to achieve optimal results when accessing the database. A poorly tuned database might render your efforts in SQL tuning as wasted, and vice versa. Ideally, it is best to first tune the database, ensure that indexes exist where needed, and then tune the SQL code.

Formatting Your SQL Statement

Formatting your SQL statement sounds like an obvious task, but it is worth mentioning. A newcomer to SQL will probably neglect to consider several things when building an SQL statement. The upcoming sections discuss the following considerations; some are common sense, others are not so obvious:

▶ The format of SQL statements for readability

▶ The order of tables in the FROM clause

▶ The placement of the most restrictive conditions in the WHERE clause

▶ The placement of join conditions in the WHERE clause

Formatting a Statement for Readability

It's All About the Optimizer

Most relational database implementations have what is called an *SQL optimizer*, which evaluates an SQL statement and determines the best method for executing the statement based on the way an SQL statement is written and the availability of indexes in the database. Not all optimizers are the same. Check your implementation or consult the database administrator to learn how the optimizer reads SQL code. You should understand how the optimizer works to effectively tune an SQL statement.

Did You Know?

Formatting an SQL statement for readability is fairly obvious, but many SQL statements have not been written neatly. Although the neatness of a statement does not affect the actual performance (the database does not care how neat the statement appears), careful formatting is the first step in tuning a statement. When you look at an SQL statement with tuning intentions, making the statement readable is always the first priority. How can you determine whether the statement is written well if it is difficult to read?

Some basic rules for making a statement readable include

▶ Always begin a new line with each clause in the statement. For example, place the FROM clause on a separate line from the SELECT clause. Then place the WHERE clause on a separate line from the FROM clause, and so on.

▶ Use tabs or spaces for indentation when arguments of a clause in the statement exceed one line.

▶ Use tabs and spaces consistently.

▶ Use table aliases when multiple tables are used in the statement. The use of the full table name to qualify each column in the statement quickly clutters the statement and makes reading it difficult.

▶ Use remarks sparingly in SQL statements if they are available within your specific implementation. Remarks are great for documentation, but too many of them clutter a statement.

▶ Begin a new line with each column name in the SELECT clause if many columns are being selected.

▶ Begin a new line with each table name in the FROM clause if many tables are being used.

▶ Begin a new line with each condition of the WHERE clause. You can easily see all conditions of the statement and the order in which they are used.

The following is an example of a statement that would be hard for you to decipher:

```
SELECT CUSTOMER_TBL.CUST_ID, CUSTOMER_TBL.CUST_NAME,
CUSTOMER_TBL.CUST_PHONE, ORDERS_TBL.ORD_NUM, ORDERS_TBL.QTY
FROM CUSTOMER_TBL, ORDERS_TBL
WHERE CUSTOMER_TBL.CUST_ID = ORDERS_TBL.CUST_ID
AND ORDERS_TBL.QTY > 1 AND CUSTOMER_TBL.CUST_NAME LIKE 'G%'
ORDER BY CUSTOMER_TBL.CUST_NAME;
```

CUST_ID	CUST_NAME	CUST_PHONE	ORD_NUM	QTY
287	GAVINS PLACE	3172719991	18D778	10

1 row selected.

Here the statement has been reformatted for improved readability:

```
SELECT C.CUST_ID,
       C.CUST_NAME,
       C.CUST_PHONE,
       O.ORD_NUM,
       O.QTY
FROM ORDERS_TBL O,
     CUSTOMER_TBL C
WHERE O.CUST_ID = C.CUST_ID
  AND O.QTY > 1
  AND C.CUST_NAME LIKE 'G%'
ORDER BY 2;
```

CUST_ID	CUST_NAME	CUST_PHONE	ORD_NUM	QTY
287	GAVINS PLACE	3172719991	18D778	10

1 row selected.

Both statements have the same content, but the second statement is much more readable. It has been greatly simplified through the use of table aliases, which have been defined in the query's FROM clause. In addition, the second statement aligns the elements of each clause with spacing, making each clause stand out.

Again, making a statement more readable does not directly improve its performance, but it assists you in making modifications and debugging a lengthy and otherwise complex statement. Now you can easily identify the columns being selected, the tables being used, the table joins being performed, and the conditions being placed on the query.

> **Check for Performance When Using Multiple Tables**
>
> Check your particular implementation for performance tips, if any, when listing multiple tables in the FROM clause.

Arranging Tables in the FROM Clause

The arrangement or order of tables in the FROM clause might make a difference, depending on how the optimizer reads the SQL statement. For example, it might be more beneficial to list the smaller tables first and the larger tables last. Some users with lots of experience have found that listing the larger tables last in the FROM clause is more efficient.

The following is an example of the FROM clause:

```
FROM SMALLEST TABLE,
     LARGEST TABLE
```

> **Always Establish Standards**
>
> It is especially important to establish coding standards in a multiuser programming environment. If all code is consistently formatted, shared code and modifications to code are much easier to manage.

Ordering Join Conditions

As you learned in Hour 13, "Joining Tables in Queries," most joins use a base table to link tables that have one or more common columns on which to join. The base table is the main table that most or all tables are joined to in a query. The column from the base table is normally placed on the right side of a join operation in the WHERE clause. The tables being joined to the base table are normally in order from smallest to largest, similar to the tables listed in the FROM clause.

If a base table doesn't exist, the tables should be listed from smallest to largest, with the largest tables on the right side of the join operation in the WHERE clause. The join conditions should be in the first position(s) of the WHERE clause followed by the filter clause(s), as shown in the following:

```
FROM TABLE1,            Smallest table
     TABLE2,            to
     TABLE3             Largest table, also base table
```

```
WHERE TABLE1.COLUMN = TABLE3.COLUMN        Join condition
  AND TABLE2.COLUMN = TABLE3.COLUMN        Join condition
[ AND CONDITION1 ]                         Filter condition
[ AND CONDITION2 ]                         Filter condition
```

Watch
~~Out!~~

> **Be Restrictive with Your Joins**
>
> Because joins typically return a high percentage of rows of data from the table(s),
> you should evaluate join conditions after more restrictive conditions.

In this example, TABLE3 is used as the base table. TABLE1 and TABLE2 are
joined to TABLE3 for both simplicity and proven efficiency.

The Most Restrictive Condition

The most restrictive condition is typically the driving factor in achieving
optimal performance for an SQL query. What is the most restrictive condition? The condition in the WHERE clause of a statement that returns the
fewest rows of data. Conversely, the least restrictive condition is the condition in a statement that returns the most rows of data. This hour is concerned with the most restrictive condition simply because it filters the data
that is to be returned by the query the most.

It should be your goal for the SQL optimizer to evaluate the most restrictive
condition first, because a smaller subset of data is returned by the condition, thus reducing the query's overhead. The effective placement of the
most restrictive condition in the query requires knowledge of how the optimizer operates. The optimizers, in some cases, seem to read from the bottom of the WHERE clause up. Therefore, you want to place the most restrictive
condition last in the WHERE clause, which is the condition that the optimizer
reads first. The following example shows how to structure the WHERE clause
based on the restrictiveness of the conditions and the FROM clause on the size
of the tables:

```
FROM TABLE1,                               Smallest table
     TABLE2,                               to
     TABLE3                                Largest table, also base table
WHERE TABLE1.COLUMN = TABLE3.COLUMN        Join condition
  AND TABLE2.COLUMN = TABLE3.COLUMN        Join condition
[ AND CONDITION1 ]                         Least restrictive
[ AND CONDITION2 ]                         Most restrictive
```

The following is an example using a phony table:

Watch
Out!

Always Test Your WHERE Clauses

If you do not know how your particular implementation's SQL optimizer works, the DBA does not know, or you do not have sufficient documentation, you can execute a large query that takes a while to run and then rearrange conditions in the WHERE clause. Be sure to record the time it takes the query to complete each time you make changes. You should only have to run a couple of tests to figure out whether the optimizer reads the WHERE clause from the top to bottom or bottom to top. Turn off database caching during the testing for more accurate results.

Table:	TEST
Row count:	95,867
Conditions:	WHERE LAST_NAME = 'SMITH'
	returns 2,000 rows
	WHERE CITY = 'INDIANAPOLIS'
	returns 30,000 rows
Most restrictive condition:	WHERE LAST_NAME = 'SMITH'

The following is the first query:

```
SELECT COUNT(*)
FROM TEST
WHERE LAST_NAME = 'SMITH'
  AND CITY = 'INDIANAPOLIS';

  COUNT(*)
----------
     1,024
```

The following is the second query:

```
SELECT COUNT(*)
FROM TEST
WHERE CITY = 'INDIANAPOLIS'
  AND LAST_NAME = 'SMITH';

  COUNT(*)
----------
     1,024
```

Suppose that the first query completed in 20 seconds, whereas the second query completed in 10 seconds. Because the second query returned faster results and the most restrictive condition was listed last in the WHERE clause, it is safe to assume that the optimizer reads the WHERE clause from the bottom up.

> **Try to Use Indexed Columns**
>
> It is a good practice to use an indexed column as the most restrictive condition in a query. Indexes generally improve a query's performance.

Full Table Scans

A full table scan occurs when an index is not used by the query engine or there is no index on the table(s) being used. Full table scans usually return data much slower than when an index is used. The larger the table, the slower that data is returned when a full table scan is performed. The query optimizer decides whether to use an index when executing the SQL statement. The index is used—if it exists—in most cases.

Some implementations have sophisticated query optimizers that can decide whether to use an index. Decisions such as this are based on statistics that are gathered on database objects, such as the size of an object and the estimated number of rows that are returned by a condition with an indexed column. Refer to your implementation documentation for specifics on the decision-making capabilities of your relational database's optimizer.

You should avoid full table scans when reading large tables. For example, a full table scan is performed when a table that does not have an index is read, which usually takes a considerably longer time to return the data. An index should be considered for the majority of larger tables. On small tables, as previously mentioned, the optimizer might choose the full table scan over using the index, if the table is indexed. In the case of a small table with an index, you should consider dropping the index and reserving the space that was used for the index for other needy objects in the database.

Did You
Know?

> **There Are Simple Ways to Avoid Table Scans**
>
> The easiest and most obvious way to avoid a full table scan—outside of ensuring that indexes exist on the table—is to use conditions in a query's WHERE clause to filter data to be returned.

The following is a reminder of data that should be indexed:

- ▶ Columns used as primary keys
- ▶ Columns used as foreign keys
- ▶ Columns frequently used to join tables

- ▶ Columns frequently used as conditions in a query
- ▶ Columns that have a high percentage of unique values

Table Scans Are Not Always Bad

Sometimes full table scans are good. You should perform them on queries against small tables or queries whose conditions return a high percentage of rows. The easiest way to force a full table scan is to avoid creating an index on the table.

Did You Know?

Other Performance Considerations

There are other performance considerations that you should note when tuning SQL statements. The following concepts are discussed in the next sections:

- ▶ Using the LIKE operator and wildcards
- ▶ Avoiding the OR operator
- ▶ Avoiding the HAVING clause
- ▶ Avoiding large sort operations
- ▶ Using stored procedures
- ▶ Disabling indexes during batch loads

Using the LIKE Operator and Wildcards

The LIKE operator is a useful tool that places conditions on a query in a flexible manner. Using wildcards in a query can eliminate many possibilities of data that should be retrieved. Wildcards are flexible for queries that search for similar data (data that is not equivalent to an exact value specified).

Suppose you want to write a query using EMPLOYEE_TBL selecting the EMP_ID, LAST_NAME, FIRST_NAME, and STATE columns. You need to know the employee identification, name, and state for all the employees with the last name Stevens. Three SQL statement examples with different wildcard placements serve as examples.

The following is Query 1:

```
SELECT EMP_ID, LAST_NAME, FIRST_NAME, STATE
FROM EMPLOYEE_TBL
WHERE LAST_NAME LIKE 'STEVENS';
```

Next is Query 2:

```
SELECT EMP_ID, LAST_NAME, FIRST_NAME, STATE
FROM EMPLOYEE_TBL
WHERE LAST_NAME LIKE '%EVENS%';
```

Here is the last query, Query 3:

```
SELECT EMP_ID, LAST_NAME, FIRST_NAME, STATE
FROM EMPLOYEE_TBL
WHERE LAST_NAME LIKE 'ST%';
```

The SQL statements do not necessarily return the same results. More than likely, Query 1 will return fewer rows than the other two queries and will take advantage of indexing. Query 2 and Query 3 are less specific as to the desired returned data, thus making them slower than Query 1. Additionally, Query 3 is probably faster than Query 2 because the first letters of the string for which you are searching are specified (and the column LAST_NAME is likely to be indexed). So Query 3 could potentially take advantage of an index.

> **Try to Account for Differences in the Data**
>
> With Query 1, you might retrieve all individuals with the last name Stevens; but can't Stevens be spelled different ways? Query 2 picks up all individuals with the last name Stevens and its various spellings. Query 3 also picks up any last name starting with ST; this is the only way to ensure that you receive all the Stevens (or Stephens).

Avoiding the OR Operator

Rewriting the SQL statement using the IN predicate instead of the OR operator consistently and substantially improves data retrieval speed. Your implementation tells you about tools you can use to time or check the performance between the OR operator and the IN predicate. An example of how to rewrite an SQL statement by taking the OR operator out and replacing the OR operator with the IN predicate follows.

> **How to Use OR and IN**
>
> Refer to Hour 8, "Using Operators to Categorize Data," for the use of the OR operator and the IN predicate.

The following is a query using the OR operator:

```
SELECT EMP_ID, LAST_NAME, FIRST_NAME
FROM EMPLOYEE_TBL
WHERE CITY = 'INDIANAPOLIS'
```

```
OR CITY = 'BROWNSBURG'
OR CITY = 'GREENFIELD';
```

The following is the same query using the IN operator:

```
SELECT EMP_ID, LAST_NAME, FIRST_NAME
FROM EMPLOYEE_TBL
WHERE CITY IN ('INDIANAPOLIS', 'BROWNSBURG',
               'GREENFIELD');
```

The SQL statements retrieve the same data; however, through testing and experience, you find that the data retrieval is measurably faster by replacing OR conditions with the IN predicate, as in the second query.

Avoiding the HAVING Clause

The HAVING clause is a useful clause for paring down the result of a GROUP BY clause; however, you can't use it without cost. Using the HAVING clause gives the SQL optimizer extra work, which results in extra time. Not only will the query be concerned with grouping result sets, it also will be concerned with parsing those result sets down via the restrictions of the HAVING clause. For example, observe the following statement:

```
SELECT C.CUST_ID, C.CUST_NAME, P.PROD_DESC,
       SUM(O.QTY) AS QTY, SUM(P.COST) AS COST,
       SUM(O.QTY * P.COST) AS TOTAL
FROM CUSTOMER_TBL AS C
    INNER JOIN ORDERS_TBL AS O ON C.CUST_ID = O.CUST_ID
    INNER JOIN PRODUCTS_TBL AS P ON O.PROD_ID = P.PROD_ID
WHERE PROD_DESC LIKE ('P%')
GROUP BY C.CUST_ID, C.CUST_NAME, P.PROD_DESC
HAVING SUM(O.QTY * P.COST)>25.00
```

Here we are trying to determine which customers have sales of specific products over the total of $25.00. Although this query is fairly simple and our sample database is small, the addition of the HAVING clause introduces some overhead, especially when the HAVING clause has more complex logic and a higher number of groupings to be applied. If possible, you should write SQL statements without using the HAVING clause or design the HAVING clause restrictions so they are as simple as possible.

Avoiding Large Sort Operations

Large sort operations mean using the ORDER BY, GROUP BY, and HAVING clauses. Subsets of data must be stored in memory or to disk (if there is not enough space in allotted memory) whenever sort operations are performed. You must sort data often. The main point is that these sort operations affect an SQL statement's response time. Because you cannot always avoid large sort operations, it is best to schedule queries with large sorts as periodic batch processes during off-peak database usage so that the performance of most user processes is not affected.

Using Stored Procedures

You should create stored procedures for SQL statements executed on a regular basis—particularly large transactions or queries. Stored procedures are simply SQL statements that are compiled and permanently stored in the database in an executable format.

Normally, when an SQL statement is issued in the database, the database must check the syntax and convert the statement into an executable format within the database (called *parsing*). The statement, after it is parsed, is stored in memory; however, it is not permanent. This means that when other operations need memory, the statement might be ejected from memory. In the case of stored procedures, the SQL statement is always available in an executable format and remains in the database until it is dropped like any other database object. Stored procedures are discussed in more detail in Hour 22, "Advanced SQL Topics."

Disabling Indexes During Batch Loads

When a user submits a transaction to the database (INSERT, UPDATE, or DELETE), an entry is made to both the database table and any indexes associated with the table being modified. This means that if there is an index on the EMPLOYEE table, and a user updates the EMPLOYEE table, an update also occurs to the index associated with the EMPLOYEE table. In a transactional environment, having a write to an index occur every time a write to the table occurs is usually not an issue.

During batch loads, however, an index can actually cause serious performance degradation. A batch load might consist of hundreds, thousands, or millions of manipulation statements or transactions. Because of their volume, batch loads take a long time to complete and are normally scheduled during off-peak hours—usually during weekends or evenings. To optimize performance during a batch load—which might equate to decreasing the time it takes the batch load to complete from 12 hours to 6 hours—it is recommended that the indexes associated with the table affected during the load are dropped. When you drop the indexes, changes are written to the tables much faster, so the job completes faster. When the batch load is complete, you should rebuild the indexes. During the rebuild, the indexes are populated with all the appropriate data from the tables. Although it might take a while for an index to be created on a large table, the overall time expended if you drop the index and rebuild it is less.

Another advantage to rebuilding an index after a batch load completes is the reduction of fragmentation that is found in the index. When a database grows, records are added, removed, and updated, and fragmentation can occur. For any database that experiences a lot of growth, it is a good idea to periodically drop and rebuild large indexes. When you rebuild an index, the number of physical extents that comprise the index is decreased, there is less disk I/O involved to read the index, the user gets results more quickly, and everyone is happy.

Cost-Based Optimization

Often you inherit a database that is in need of SQL statement tuning attention. These existing systems might have thousands of SQL statements executing at any given time. To optimize the amount of time spent on performance tuning, you need a way to determine what queries are most beneficial to concentrate on. This is where cost-based optimization comes into play. Cost-based optimization attempts to determine which queries are most costly in relation to the overall system resources spent. For instance, say we measure cost by execution duration and we have the following two queries with their corresponding run times:

```
SELECT * FROM CUSTOMER_TBL
WHERE CUST_NAME LIKE '%LE%'          2 sec

SELECT * FROM EMPLOYEE_TBL
WHERE LAST_NAME LIKE 'G%';           1 sec
```

At first, it might appear that the first statement is the one you need to concentrate your efforts on. However, what if the second statement is executed 1,000 times an hour but the first is performed only 10 times in the same hour? Doesn't this make a huge difference in how you allocate your time?

Cost-based optimization ranks SQL statements in order of total computational cost. Computational cost is easily determined based on some measure of query execution (duration, number of reads, and so on) multiplied by the number of executions over a given period:

Total Computational Cost = Execution Measure * (number of executions)

This is important because you get the most overall benefit from tuning the queries with the most total computational cost first. Looking at the previous example, if we are able to cut each statement execution time in half, you can easily figure out the total computational savings:

Statement #1: 1 sec * 10 executions = 10 sec of computational savings

Statement #2: .5 sec * 1000 executions = 500 sec of computational savings

Now it is much easier to understand why your valuable time should be spent on the second statement instead of the first. Not only have you worked to optimize your database, but you've optimized your time as well.

Performance Tools

Many relational databases have built-in tools that assist in SQL statement database performance tuning. For example, Oracle has a tool called EXPLAIN PLAN that shows the user the execution plan of an SQL statement. Another tool in Oracle that measures the actual elapsed time of an SQL statement is TKPROF. In SQL Server, the Query Analyzer has several options to provide you with an estimated execution plan or statistics from the executed query. Check with your DBA and implementation documentation for more information on tools that might be available to you.

Summary

You have learned the meaning of tuning SQL statements in a relational database. You have learned that there are two basic types of tuning: database tuning and SQL statement tuning—both of which are vital to the efficient operation of the database and SQL statements within it. Each is equally important and cannot be optimally tuned without the other.

You have read about methods for tuning an SQL statement, starting with a statement's actual readability, which does not directly improve performance but aids the programmer in the development and management of statements. One of the main issues in SQL statement performance is the use of indexes. There are times to use indexes and times to avoid using them. For all measures taken to improve SQL statement performance, you need to understand the data itself, the database design and relationships, and the users' needs as far as accessing the database.

Q&A

Q. *By following what I have learned about performance, what realistic perform-ance gains, as far as data retrieval time, can I really expect to see?*

A. Realistically, you could see performance gains from fractions of a sec-ond to minutes, hours, or even days.

Q. *How can I test my SQL statements for performance?*

A. Each implementation should have a tool or system to check perform-ance. Oracle7 was used to test the SQL statements in this book. Oracle has several tools for checking performance. Some of these tools include the EXPLAIN PLAN, TKPROF, and SET commands. Check your particular implementation for tools that are similar to Oracle's.

Workshop

The following workshop is composed of a series of quiz questions and practi-cal exercises. The quiz questions are designed to test your overall under-standing of the current material. The practical exercises are intended to afford you the opportunity to apply the concepts discussed during the cur-rent hour, as well as build upon the knowledge acquired in previous hours of study. Please take time to complete the quiz questions and exercises before continuing. Refer to Appendix C, "Answers to Quizzes and Exercises," for answers.

Quiz

1. Would the use of a unique index on a small table be of any benefit?

2. What happens when the optimizer chooses not to use an index on a table when a query has been executed?

3. Should the most restrictive clause(s) be placed before the join condi-tion(s) or after the join conditions in the WHERE clause?

Exercises

1. Rewrite the following SQL statements to improve their performance.
Use EMPLOYEE_TBL and EMPLOYEE_PAY_TBL as described here:

```
EMPLOYEE_TBL
EMP_ID          VARCHAR(9)      NOT NULL      Primary key,
LAST_NAME       VARCHAR(15)     NOT NULL,
FIRST_NAME      VARCHAR(15)     NOT NULL,
MIDDLE_NAME     VARCHAR(15),
ADDRESS         VARCHAR(30)     NOT NULL,
CITY            VARCHAR(15)     NOT NULL,
STATE           VARCHAR(2)      NOT NULL,
ZIP             INTEGER(5)      NOT NULL,
PHONE           VARCHAR(10),
PAGER           VARCHAR(10),
CONSTRAINT EMP_PK PRIMARY KEY (EMP_ID)


EMPLOYEE_PAY_TBL
EMP_ID              VARCHAR(9)      NOT NULL      primary key,
POSITION            VARCHAR(15)     NOT NULL,
DATE_HIRE           DATETIME,
PAY_RATE            DECIMAL(4,2)    NOT NULL,
DATE_LAST_RAISE     DATETIME,
SALARY              DECIMAL(8,2),
BONUS               DECIMAL(8,2),
CONSTRAINT EMP_FK FOREIGN KEY (EMP_ID)
REFERENCES EMPLOYEE_TBL (EMP_ID)
```

a. SELECT EMP_ID, LAST_NAME, FIRST_NAME,
            PHONE
    FROM EMPLOYEE_TBL
    WHERE SUBSTRING(PHONE, 1, 3) = '317' OR
          SUBSTRING(PHONE, 1, 3) = '812' OR
          SUBSTRING(PHONE, 1, 3) = '765';

b. SELECT LAST_NAME, FIRST_NAME
    FROM EMPLOYEE_TBL
    WHERE LAST_NAME LIKE '%ALL%;

c. SELECT E.EMP_ID, E.LAST_NAME, E.FIRST_NAME,
            EP.SALARY
    FROM EMPLOYEE_TBL E,
    EMPLOYEE_PAY_TBL EP
    WHERE LAST_NAME LIKE 'S%'
          AND E.EMP_ID = EP.EMP_ID;

2. Add another table called EMPLOYEE_PAYHIST_TBL that contains a large amount of pay history data. Use the table that follows to write the series of SQL statements to address the following problems:

```
EMPLOYEE_PAYHIST_TBL
PAYHIST_ID          VARCHAR(9)     NOT NULL      primary key,
EMP_ID              VARCHAR(9)     NOT NULL,
START_DATE          DATETIME       NOT NULL,
     END_DATE           DATETIME,
PAY_RATE            DECIMAL(4,2)   NOT NULL,
SALARY              DECIMAL(8,2)   NOT NULL,
BONUS               DECIMAL(8,2)   NOT NULL,
CONSTRAINT EMP_FK FOREIGN KEY (EMP_ID)
REFERENCES EMPLOYEE_TBL (EMP_ID)
```

What steps did you take to ensure that the queries you wrote perform well?

a. Find the SUM of the salaried versus nonsalaried employees by the year in which their pay started.

b. Find the difference in the yearly pay of salaried employees versus nonsalaried employees by the year in which their pay started. Consider the nonsalaried employees to be working full time during the year (PAY_RATE * 52 * 40).

c. Find the difference in what employees make now versus what they made when they started with the company. Again, consider the nonsalaried employees to be full-time. Also consider that the employees' current pay is reflected in the EMPLOYEE_PAY_TBL as well as the EMPLOYEE_PAYHIST_TBL. In the pay history table, the current pay is reflected as a row with the END_DATE for pay equal to NULL.

HOUR 18

Managing Database Users

What You'll Learn in This Hour:

▶ Types of users

▶ User management

▶ The user's place in the database

▶ The user versus the schema

▶ User sessions

▶ Altering a user's attributes

▶ User profiles

▶ Dropping users from the database

▶ Tools utilized by users

In this hour, you learn about one of the most critical administration functions for any relational database: managing database users. Managing users ensures that your database is available to the required people and application while keeping external entities out. Considering the amount of sensitive commercial and personal data that is stored in databases, this hour is definitely one that you should pay careful attention to.

User Management in the Database

Users are the reason for the season—the season of designing, creating, implementing, and maintaining any database. Their needs are considered when the database is designed, and the final goal in implementing a database is making the database available to users, who in turn utilize the database that you, and possibly many others, have had a hand in developing.

Some believe that if there were no users, nothing bad would ever happen to the database. Although this statement reeks with truth, the database was actually created to hold data so users could function in their day-to-day jobs.

Although user management is often the database administrator's implicit task, other individuals sometimes take a part in the user management process. User management is vital in the life of a relational database and is ultimately managed through the use of SQL concepts and commands, although they vary from vendor to vendor. The ultimate goal of the database administrator in terms of user management is to strike the proper balance between giving users access to the data they need and maintaining the integrity of the data within the system.

Roles Vary Widely

Titles, roles, and duties of users vary widely (and wildly) from workplace to workplace, depending on the size of each organization and each organization's specific data processing needs. One organization's database administrator might be another organization's "computer guy."

Types of Users

There are several types of database users:

- Data entry clerks
- Programmers
- System engineers
- Database administrators
- System analysts
- Developers
- Testers
- Managers
- End users

Each type of user has a unique set of job functions (and problems), all of which are critical to the user's daily survival and job security. Furthermore, each type of user has different levels of authority and a special place in the database.

Who Manages Users?

A company's management staff is responsible for the day-to-day management of users; however, the *database administrator (DBA)* or other assigned individuals are ultimately responsible for the management of users within the database.

The DBA usually handles creating the database user accounts, roles, privileges, and profiles, as well as dropping those user accounts from the database. Because it can become an overwhelming task in a large and active environment, some companies have a security officer who assists the DBA with the user management process.

The *security officer*, if one is assigned, is usually responsible for the paperwork, relaying to the DBA a user's job requirements and letting the DBA know when a user no longer requires access to the database.

The *system analyst*, or system administrator, is usually responsible for the operating system security, which entails creating users and assigning appropriate privileges. The security officer also might assist the system analyst in the same way he does the database administrator.

Maintaining an orderly way in which to assign and remove permissions as well as to document the changes makes the process much easier to maintain. Documentation also enables you to have a paper trail to point to when the security of your system needs to be audited either internally or externally. We expand on the user management system throughout this hour.

The User's Place in the Database

Make Sure You Follow a Systematic Approach to User Management

User account management is vital to the protection and success of any database; when not managed systematically, it often fails. User account management is one of the simplest database management tasks, theoretically, but it is often complicated by politics and communication problems.

By the Way

A user should be given the roles and privileges necessary to accomplish her job. No user should have database access that extends beyond the scope of her job duties. Protecting the data is the entire reason for setting up user accounts and security. Data can be damaged or lost, even if unintentionally, if the wrong user has access to the wrong data. When the user no longer requires database access, that user's account should be either removed from the database or disabled as quickly as possible.

All users have their place in the database, yet some have more responsibilities and duties than others. Database users are like parts of a human body—all work together in unison to accomplish some goal.

How Does a User Differ from a Schema?

A database's objects are associated with database user accounts, called schemas. A *schema* is a collection of database objects that a database user owns. This database user is called the *schema owner*. Often schemas logically group like objects in a database and then assign them to a particular schema owner to manage. You could think of it in terms of possibly grouping all the personnel tables under a schema called HR for human resources. The difference between a regular database user and a schema owner is that a schema owner owns objects within the database, whereas most users do not own objects. Most users are given database accounts to access data that is contained in other schemas. Because the schema owner actually owns these objects, he has complete control over them.

Microsoft SQL Server actually goes one step further by having a database owner. The database owner basically owns all objects within the database and has complete control over everything stored within. Within the database are one or more schemas. The default schema is always dbo and is normally the default for the database owner. There may be as many schemas as necessary to logically group the database objects and assign schema owners.

By the Way

> **User Creation and Management Varies Between Systems**
>
> You must check your particular implementation for the creation of users. Also refer to company policies and procedures when creating and managing users. The following section compares the user creation processes in Oracle, MySQL, and Microsoft SQL Server.

The Management Process

A stable user management system is mandatory for data security in any database system. The user management system starts with the new user's immediate supervisor, who should initiate the access request and then go through the company's approval authorities. If management accepts the request, it is routed to the security officer or database administrator, who takes action. A good notification process is necessary; the supervisor and the user must be notified that the user account has been created and that access to the database has been granted. The user account password should only be given to the user, who should immediately change the password upon initial login to the database.

Creating Users

The creation of database users involves the use of SQL commands within the database. There is no one standard command for creating database users in SQL; each implementation has a method for doing so. The basic concept is the same, regardless of the implementation. There are several *graphical user interface (GUI)* tools on the market that can be used for user management.

When the DBA or assigned security officer receives a user account request, the request should be analyzed for the necessary information. The information should include your particular company's requirements for establishing a user account.

Some items that should be included are Social Security number, full name, address, phone number, office or department name, assigned database, and, sometimes, a suggested user account name.

Syntactical examples of creating users compared among the different implementations are shown in the following sections.

Creating Users in Oracle

Following are the steps for creating a user account in an Oracle database:

1. Create the database user account with default settings.

2. Grant appropriate privileges to the user account.

The following is the syntax for creating a user:

```
CREATE USER USER_ID
IDENTIFIED BY [PASSWORD | EXTERNALLY ]
[ DEFAULT TABLESPACE TABLESPACE_NAME ]
[ TEMPORARY TABLESPACE TABLESPACE_NAME ]
[ QUOTA (INTEGER (K | M) | UNLIMITED) ON TABLESPACE_NAME ]
[ PROFILE PROFILE_TYPE ]
[PASSWORD EXPIRE |ACCOUNT [LOCK | UNLOCK]
```

If you are not using Oracle, do not overly concern yourself with some of the options in this syntax. A *tablespace* is a logical area managed by the DBA that houses database objects, such as tables and indexes. The DEFAULT TABLE-SPACE is the tablespace in which objects created by the particular user reside. The TEMPORARY TABLESPACE is the tablespace used for sort operations (table joins, ORDER BY, GROUP BY) from queries the user executes. The QUOTA is the space limit placed on a particular tablespace to which the user has access. PROFILE is a particular database profile that has been assigned to the user.

The following is the syntax for granting privileges to the user account:

```
GRANT PRIV1 [ , PRIV2, ... ] TO USERNAME | ROLE [ , USERNAME ]
```

> **Even the CREATE USER Command Has Differences**
>
> You can use the preceding syntax for creating users to add a user to an Oracle database, as well as a few other major relational database implementations.
>
> MySQL does not support the CREATE USER command. Users can be managed using the mysqladmin tool. After a local user account is set up on a Windows computer, a login is not required. However, you should set up a user for each user requiring access to the database in a multiuser environment using mysqladmin.

The GRANT statement can grant one or more privileges to one or more users in the same statement. The privilege(s) can also be granted to a role, which in turn can be granted to a user(s).

In MySQL, the GRANT command can grant users access on the local computer to the current database. For example:

```
GRANT USAGE ON *.* TO USER@LOCALHOST IDENTIFIED BY 'PASSWORD';
```

Additional privileges can be granted to a user as follows:

```
GRANT SELECT ON TABLENAME TO USER@LOCALHOST;
```

For the most part, multiuser setup and access for MySQL is required only in multiuser environments.

Creating Users in Microsoft SQL Server

The steps for creating a user account in a Microsoft SQL Server database follow:

1. Create the login user account for SQL Server, and assign a password and a default database for the user.

2. Add the user to the appropriate database(s) so that a database user account is created.

3. Grant appropriate privileges to the database user account.

The following is the syntax for creating the user account:

```
SP_ADDLOGIN USER_ID ,PASSWORD [ , DEFAULT_DATABASE ]
```

There's a Lot More to Assigning Privileges

The discussion of privileges within a relational database is further elaborated on in Hour 19, "Managing Database Security."

By the Way

The following is the syntax for adding the user to a database:

```
SP_ADDUSER USER_ID [ , NAME_IN_DB [ , GRPNAME ] ]
```

As you can see, SQL Server distinguishes between a login account that is granted access to log into the SQL Server instance and a database user account that grants access to database objects. You can view this for yourself by looking at the security folders in SQL Server Management Studio after you have created the login account and then at the database level when you issue the SP_ADDUSER command. This is an important distinction with SQL Server because you can create a login account that does not have access to any of the databases on the instance.

A common error when creating accounts on SQL Server is forgetting to assign them access to their default database. So when you set up accounts, ensure that they have access to at least their default database or you might be setting up the users to receive an error when logging into your system.

The following is the syntax for granting privileges to the user account:

```
GRANT PRIV1 [ , PRIV2, ... ] TO USER_ID
```

Creating Users in MySQL

The steps for creating a user account in MySQL follow:

1. Create the user account within the database.

2. Grant the appropriate privileges to the user account.

The syntax for creating the user account is similar to the syntax used in Oracle:

```
SELECT USER user [IDENTIFIED BY [PASSWORD] 'password']
```

The syntax for granting the user's privileges is also similar to the Oracle version:

```
GRANT priv_type [(column_list)] [, priv_type [(column_list)]] ...
    ON [object_type]
        {tbl_name | * | *.* | db_name.* | db_name.routine_name}
        TO user
```

Creating Schemas

Schemas are created via the CREATE SCHEMA statement.

The syntax is as follows:

```
CREATE SCHEMA [ SCHEMA_NAME ] [ USER_ID ]
              [ DEFAULT CHARACTER SET CHARACTER_SET ]
              [PATH SCHEMA NAME [ ,SCHEMA NAME] ]
              [ SCHEMA_ELEMENT_LIST ]
```

The following is an example:

```
CREATE SCHEMA USER1
CREATE TABLE TBL1
   (COLUMN1    DATATYPE    [NOT NULL],
    COLUMN2    DATATYPE    [NOT NULL]...)
CREATE TABLE TBL2
   (COLUMN1    DATATYPE    [NOT NULL],
    COLUMN2    DATATYPE    [NOT NULL]...)
GRANT SELECT ON TBL1 TO USER2
GRANT SELECT ON TBL2 TO USER2
[ OTHER DDL COMMANDS ... ]
```

The following is the application of the CREATE SCHEMA command in one implementation:

```
CREATE SCHEMA AUTHORIZATION USER1
CREATE TABLE EMP
   (ID       NUMBER         NOT NULL,
    NAME     VARCHAR2(10)   NOT NULL)
CREATE TABLE CUST
   (ID       NUMBER         NOT NULL,
    NAME     VARCHAR2(10)   NOT NULL)
GRANT SELECT ON TBL1 TO USER2
GRANT SELECT ON TBL2 TO USER2;
Schema created.
```

The AUTHORIZATION keyword is added to the CREATE SCHEMA command. This example was performed in an Oracle database. This goes to show you, as you have also seen in this book's previous examples, that vendors' syntax for commands often varies in their implementations.

Implementations that do support the creation of schemas often assign a default schema to a user. Most often this is aligned with the user's account. So a user with the account BethA2 normally has a default schema of BethA2. This is important to remember because objects are created in the user's default schema unless otherwise directed by providing a schema name at the time of creation. If we issue the following CREATE TABLE statement using BethA2's account, it is created in the BethA2 schema:

```
CREATE TABLE MYTABLE(
  NAME VARCHAR(50)  NOT NULL );
```

This might not be the desired location. If this is SQL Server, we might have permissions to the dbo schema and want to create it there. In that case, we need to qualify our object with the schema as shown here:

```
CREATE TABLE DBO.MYTABLE(
  NAME VARCHAR(50) NOT NULL):
```

It is important to remember these caveats when creating users and assigning them permissions so that you can maintain proper order within your database systems without having unintended consequences.

Dropping a Schema

> **CREATE SCHEMA Is Not Always Supported**
>
> Some implementations might not support the CREATE SCHEMA command. However, schemas can be implicitly created when a user creates objects. The CREATE SCHEMA command is simply a single-step method of accomplishing this task. After a user creates objects, the user can grant privileges that allow access to the user's objects to other users.
>
> MySQL does not support the CREATE SCHEMA command. A schema in MySQL is considered to be a database. So you use the CREATE DATABASE command to essentially create a schema to populate with objects.

You can remove a schema from the database using the DROP SCHEMA statement. You must consider two things when dropping a schema: the RESTRICT option and the CASCADE option. If RESTRICT is specified, an error occurs if objects currently exist in the schema. You must use the CASCADE option if any objects currently exist in the schema. Remember that when you drop a schema, you also drop all database objects associated with that schema.

The syntax is as follows:

```
DROP SCHEMA SCHEMA_NAME { RESTRICT | CASCADE }
```

> **There Are Different Ways to Remove a Schema**
>
> The absence of objects in a schema is possible because objects, such as tables, can be dropped using the DROP TABLE command. Some implementations have a

procedure or command that drops a user and can also drop a schema. If the
DROP SCHEMA command is not available in your implementation, you can remove a
schema by removing the user who owns the schema objects.

Altering Users

An important part of managing users is the ability to alter a user's attributes
after user creation. Life for the DBA would be a lot simpler if personnel with
user accounts were never promoted, never left the company, or if the addition of new employees was minimized. In the real world, high personnel
turnover and changes in users' responsibilities are a reality and a significant
factor in user management. Nearly everyone changes jobs or job duties.
Therefore, user privileges in a database must be adjusted to fit a user's needs.

The following is Oracle's example of altering the current state of a user:

```
ALTER USER USER_ID [ IDENTIFIED BY PASSWORD | EXTERNALLY |GLOBALLY AS
'CN=USER']
[ DEFAULT TABLESPACE TABLESPACE_NAME ]
[ TEMPORARY TABLESPACE TABLESPACE_NAME ]
[ QUOTA  INTEGER K|M |UNLIMITED ON TABLESPACE_NAME ]
[ PROFILE PROFILE_NAME ]
[ PASSWORD EXPIRE]
[ ACCOUNT [LOCK |UNLOCK]]
[ DEFAULT ROLE ROLE1 [, ROLE2 ] | ALL
[ EXCEPT ROLE1 [, ROLE2 | NONE ] ]
```

You can alter many of the user's attributes in this syntax. Unfortunately,
not all implementations provide a simple command that allows the manipulation of database users.

MySQL, for instance, uses several means to modify the user account. For
example, you use the following syntax to reset the user's password in MySQL:

```
UPDATE mysql.user SET Password=PASSWORD('new password')
WHERE user='username';
```

Additionally, you might want to change the username for the user. You
could accomplish this with the following syntax:

```
RENAME USER old_username TO new_username;
```

Some implementations also provide GUI tools that enable you to create,
modify, and remove users.

Some Databases and Tools Obscure the Underlying Commands

Remember that the syntax varies between implementations. In addition, most database users do not manually issue the commands to connect or disconnect from the database. Most users access the database through a vendor-provided or third-party tool that prompts the user for a username and password, which in turn connects to the database and initiates a database user session.

By the Way

User Sessions

A user database *session* is the time that begins at database login and ends when a user logs out. During the user session, the user can perform various actions that have been granted, such as queries and transactions.

Upon the establishment of the connection and the initiation of the session, the user can start and perform any number of transactions until the connection is disconnected; at that time, the database user session terminates.

Users can explicitly connect and disconnect from the database, starting and terminating SQL sessions, using commands such as the following:

```
CONNECT TO DEFAULT | STRING1 [ AS STRING2 ] [ USER STRING3 ]
DISCONNECT DEFAULT | CURRENT | ALL | STRING
SET CONNECTION DEFAULT | STRING
```

User sessions can be—and often are—monitored by the DBA or other personnel having interest in user activities. A user session is associated with a particular user account when a user is monitored. A database user session is ultimately represented as a process on the host operating system.

Removing User Access

You can remove a user from the database or disallow a user's access through a couple of simple commands. Once again, however, variations among implementations are numerous, so you must check your particular implementation for the syntax or tools to accomplish user removal or access revocation.

Following are methods for removing user database access:

▶ Change the user's password

▶ Drop the user account from the database

▶ Revoke appropriate previously granted privileges from the user

You can use the DROP command in some implementations to drop a user from the database:

```
DROP USER USER_ID [ CASCADE ]
```

The REVOKE command is the counterpart of the GRANT command in many implementations, allowing privileges that have been granted to a user to be revoked. An example syntax for this command for SQL Server, Oracle, and MySQL is as follows:

```
REVOKE PRIV1 [ ,PRIV2, ... ] FROM USERNAME
```

Tools Utilized by Database Users

Some people say that you do not need to know SQL to perform database queries. In a sense, they are correct; however, knowing SQL definitely helps when querying a database, even when using GUI tools. Even though GUI tools are good and should be used when available, it is most beneficial to understand what is happening behind the scenes so you can maximize the efficiency of utilizing these user-friendly tools.

Many GUI tools that aid the database user automatically generate SQL code by navigating through windows, responding to prompts, and selecting options. There are reporting tools that generate reports. Forms can be created for users to query, update, insert, or delete data from a database. There are tools that convert data into graphs and charts. Certain database administration tools monitor database performance, and others allow remote connectivity to a database. Database vendors provide some of these tools, whereas others are provided as third-party tools from other vendors.

Summary

All databases have users, whether one or thousands. The user is the reason for the database.

There are three necessities for managing users in the database. First, you must be able to create database user accounts for the proper individuals and services. Second, you must be able to grant privileges to the accounts to accommodate the tasks that must be performed within the database. Finally, you must be able to either remove a user account from the database or revoke certain privileges within the database from an account.

Some of the most common tasks of managing users have been touched on; much detail is avoided here, because most databases differ in how users are managed. However, it is important to discuss user management due to its relationship with SQL. The American National Standards Institute (ANSI) has not defined or discussed in detail many of the commands to manage users, but the concept remains the same.

Q&A

Q. *Is there an SQL standard for adding users to a database?*

A. ANSI provides some commands and concepts, although each implementation and each company has its own commands, tools, and rules for creating or adding users to a database.

Q. *Can user access be temporarily suspended without removing the user ID completely from the database?*

A. Yes. You can temporarily suspend user access by simply changing the user's password or revoking privileges that allow the user to connect to the database. You can reinstate the functionality of the user account by changing and issuing the password to the user or granting privileges to the user that might have been revoked.

Q. *Can a user change his own password?*

A. Yes, in most major implementations. Upon user creation or addition to the database, a generic password is given to the user, who must change it as quickly as possible to a password of his choice. After the user changes his password, even the DBA does not know the new password.

Workshop

The following workshop is composed of a series of quiz questions and practical exercises. The quiz questions are designed to test your overall understanding of the current material. The practical exercises are intended to afford you the opportunity to apply the concepts discussed during the current hour, as well as build upon the knowledge acquired in previous hours of study. Please take time to complete the quiz questions and exercises before continuing. Refer to Appendix C, "Answers to Quizzes and Exercises," for answers.

Quiz

1. Which command establishes a session?

2. Which option drops a schema that still contains database objects?

3. Which command in MySQL creates a schema?

4. Which statement removes a database privilege?

5. Which command creates a grouping or collection of tables, views, and privileges?

6. What is the difference in SQL Server between a login account and a database user account?

Exercises

1. Describe how you would create a new user 'John' in your learnsql database.

2. How would you grant access to the Employee_tbl to your new user 'John'?

3. Describe how you would assign permissions to all objects within the learnsql database to 'John'.

4. Describe how you would revoke the previous privileges from 'John' and then remove his account.

Managing Database Security

What You'll Learn in This Hour:

▶ Database security

▶ Security versus user management

▶ Database system privileges

▶ Database object privileges

▶ Granting privileges to users

▶ Revoking privileges from users

▶ Security features in the database

In this hour, you learn the basics of implementing and managing security within a relational database using SQL and SQL-related commands. Each major implementation differs on syntax with its security commands, but the overall security for the relational database follows the same basic guidelines discussed in the ANSI standard. You must check your particular implementation for syntax and any special guidelines for security.

What Is Database Security?

Database security is simply the process of protecting the data from unauthorized usage. Unauthorized usage includes data access by database users who should have access to part of the database, but not all parts. This protection also includes the act of policing against unauthorized connectivity and distribution of privileges. Many user levels exist in a database, from the database creator to individuals responsible for maintaining the database (such as the *database administrator [DBA]*) to database programmers to end users. Although end users have the most limited access, they are the users for which the database exists. A user should be granted the fewest number of privileges needed to perform his particular job.

You might be wondering what the difference between user management and database security is. After all, the previous hour discussed user management, which seems to cover security. Although user management and database security are definitely related, each has its own purpose, and the two work together to achieve a secure database.

A well-planned and maintained user management program goes hand in hand with the overall security of a database. Users are assigned user accounts and passwords that give them general access to the database. The user accounts within the database should be stored with information, such as the user's actual name, the office and department in which the user works, a telephone number or extension, and the database name to which the user has access. Personal user information should only be accessible to the DBA. A DBA or security officer assigns an initial password for the database user; the user should change this password immediately. Remember that the DBA does not need, and should not want to know, the individual's password. This ensures a separation of duties and protects the DBA's integrity should problems with a user's account arise.

If a user no longer requires certain privileges granted to her, those privileges should be revoked. If a user no longer requires access to the database, the user account should be dropped from the database.

Generally, *user management* is the process of creating user accounts, removing user accounts, and keeping track of users' actions within the database. *Database security* is going a step further by granting privileges for specific database access, revoking certain privileges from users, and taking measures to protect other parts of the database, such as the underlying database files.

By the Way

There Are More Aspects to Database Security Than Privileges

Because this is an SQL book, not a database book, it focuses on database privileges. However, you should keep in mind other aspects to database security, such as the protection of underlying database files, which holds equal importance with the distribution of database privileges. High-level database security can become complex and differs immensely among relational database implementations. If you would like to learn more about database security, you can find information on The Center for Internet Security's web page: www.cisecurity.org/.

What Are Privileges?

Privileges are authority levels used to access the database, access objects within the database, manipulate data in the database, and perform various administrative functions within the database. Privileges are issued via the GRANT command and are taken away via the REVOKE command.

Just because a user can connect to a database does not mean that the user can access data within a database. Access to data within the database is handled through these privileges. The two types of privileges are system privileges and object privileges.

System Privileges

System privileges are those that allow database users to perform administrative actions within the database, such as creating a database, dropping a database, creating user accounts, dropping users, dropping and altering database objects, altering the state of objects, altering the state of the database, and other actions that could result in serious repercussions if not carefully used.

System privileges vary greatly among the different relational database vendors, so you must check your particular implementation for all the available system privileges and their correct usage.

The following are some common system privileges in SQL Server:

- ▶ CREATE DATABASE—Allows for the creation of a new database
- ▶ CREATE PROCEDURE—Allows for the creation of stored procedures
- ▶ CREATE VIEW—Allows for the creation of views
- ▶ BACKUP DATABASE—Allows the user to control backup of the database system
- ▶ CREATE TABLE—Allows the user to create new tables
- ▶ CREATE TRIGGER—Allows the user to create triggers on tables
- ▶ EXECUTE—Allows the user to execute given stored procedures within the specific database

The following are some common system privileges in Oracle:

- ▶ CREATE TABLE—Allows the user to create new tables in the specified schema

- ▶ CREATE ANY TABLE—Allows the user to create tables in any schema

- ▶ ALTER ANY TABLE—Allows the user to alter table structure in any schema

- ▶ DROP TABLE—Allows the user to drop table objects in the specified schema

- ▶ CREATE USER—Allows the user to create other user accounts

- ▶ DROP USER—Allows the user to drop existing user accounts

- ▶ ALTER USER—Allows the user to make alterations to existing user accounts

- ▶ ALTER DATABASE—Allows the user to alter database properties

- ▶ BACKUP ANY TABLE—Allows the user to backup data from any table in any schema

- ▶ SELECT ANY TABLE—Allows the user to perform a select on any table from any schema

The following are some common global (system) privileges in MySQL:

- ▶ CREATE—Allows the user to create a specific object type such as a database, table, or index

- ▶ DROP—Allows the user to delete a specific object type

- ▶ GRANT—Allows the user to grant permissions on specific object types

- ▶ RELOAD—Allows the user to perform a FLUSH operation to purge items such as log files

- ▶ SHUTDOWN—Allows the user to shut down the MySQL instance

By the Way

> **There Can Be Many Layers of Privileges**
>
> MySQL has global privileges and object privileges. Global privileges, similar to system privileges, deal with user access to all database objects.

Object Privileges

Object privileges are authority levels on objects, meaning you must have been granted the appropriate privileges to perform certain operations on database objects. For example, to select data from another user's table, the user must first grant you access to do so. Object privileges are granted to users in the database by the object's owner. Remember that this owner is also called the *schema owner*.

The ANSI standard for privileges includes the following object privileges:

▶ USAGE—Authorizes usage of a specific domain.

▶ SELECT—Allows access to a specific table.

▶ INSERT(*column_name*)—Allows data insertion to a specific column of a specified table.

▶ INSERT—Allows insertion of data into all columns of a specific table.

▶ UPDATE(*column_name*)—Allows a specific column of a specified table to be updated.

▶ UPDATE—Allows all columns of a specified table to be updated.

▶ REFERENCES(*column_name*)—Allows a reference to a specified column of a specified table in integrity constraints; this privilege is required for all integrity constraints.

▶ REFERENCES—Allows references to all columns of a specified table.

Some Privileges Are Granted Automatically

The owner of an object has been automatically granted all privileges that relate to the objects owned. These privileges have also been granted with the GRANT OPTION, which is a nice feature available in some SQL implementations. This feature is discussed in the "GRANT OPTION" section later this hour.

Did You Know?

Most implementations of SQL adhere to the standard list of object privileges for controlling access to database objects.

You should use these object-level privileges to grant and restrict access to objects in a schema. These privileges can protect objects in one schema from database users who have access to another schema in the same database.

A variety of object privileges are available among different implementations not listed in this section. The capability to delete data from another user's object is another common object privilege available in many implementations. Be sure to check your implementation documentation for all the available object-level privileges.

Who Grants and Revokes Privileges?

The DBA is usually the one who issues the GRANT and REVOKE commands, although a security administrator, if one exists, might have the authority to do so. The authority on what to grant or revoke would come from management and normally should be carefully tracked to ensure that only authorized individuals are allowed access to these types of permissions.

The owner of an object must grant privileges to other users in the database on the object. Even the DBA cannot grant database users privileges on objects that do not belong to the DBA, although there are ways to work around that.

Controlling User Access

User access is primarily controlled by a user account and password, but that is not enough to access the database in most major implementations. The creation of a user account is only the first step in allowing and controlling access to the database.

After the user account has been created, the database administrator, security officer, or designated individual must be able to assign appropriate system-level privileges to a user for that user to be allowed to perform actual functions within the database, such as creating tables or selecting from tables. Furthermore, the schema owner usually needs to grant database users access to objects in the schema so that the user can do his job.

Two commands in SQL allow database access control involving the assignment of privileges and the revocation of privileges. The GRANT and REVOKE commands distribute both system and object privileges in a relational database.

The GRANT Command

The GRANT command grants both system-level and object-level privileges to an existing database user account.

The syntax is as follows:

```
GRANT PRIVILEGE1 [, PRIVILEGE2 ][ ON OBJECT ]
TO USERNAME [ WITH GRANT OPTION | ADMIN OPTION]
```

Granting one privilege to a user is as follows:

```
GRANT SELECT ON EMPLOYEE_TBL TO USER1;
Grant succeeded.
```

Granting multiple privileges to a user is as follows:

```
GRANT SELECT, INSERT ON EMPLOYEE_TBL TO USER1;
Grant succeeded.
```

Notice that when granting multiple privileges to a user in a single statement, each privilege is separated by a comma.

Be Sure to Understand the Feedback the System Is Giving You

Notice the phrase Grant succeeded, denoting the successful completion of each grant statement. This is the feedback that you receive when you issue these statements in the implementation used for the book examples (Oracle). Most implementations have some sort of feedback, although the phrase used might vary.

Granting privileges to multiple users is as follows:

```
GRANT SELECT, INSERT ON EMPLOYEE_TBL TO USER1, USER2;
Grant succeeded.
```

GRANT OPTION

GRANT OPTION is a powerful GRANT command option. When an object's owner grants privileges on an object to another user with GRANT OPTION, the new user can also grant privileges on that object to other users, even though the user does not actually own the object. An example follows:

```
GRANT SELECT ON EMPLOYEE_TBL TO USER1 WITH GRANT OPTION;
Grant succeeded.
```

ADMIN OPTION

ADMIN OPTION is similar to GRANT OPTION in that the user who has been granted the privileges also inherits the ability to grant those privileges to another user. GRANT OPTION is used for object-level privileges, whereas ADMIN OPTION is used for system-level privileges. When a user grants system privileges to another user with ADMIN OPTION, the new user can also grant the system-level privileges to any other user. An example follows:

```
GRANT CREATE TABLE TO USER1 WITH ADMIN OPTION;
Grant succeeded.
```

The REVOKE Command

Dropping a User Can Drop Granted Privileges

When a user who has granted privileges using either GRANT OPTION or ADMIN OPTION has been dropped from the database, the privileges that the user granted are disassociated with the users to whom the privileges were granted.

The REVOKE command removes privileges that have been granted to database users. The REVOKE command has two options: RESTRICT and CASCADE. When the RESTRICT option is used, REVOKE succeeds only if the privileges specified explicitly in the REVOKE statement leave no other users with abandoned privileges. The CASCADE option revokes any privileges that would otherwise be left with other users. In other words, if the owner of an object granted USER1 privileges with GRANT OPTION, USER1 granted USER2 privileges with GRANT OPTION, and then the owner revokes USER1's privileges, CASCADE also removes the privileges from USER2.

Abandoned privileges are privileges that are left with a user who was granted privileges with the GRANT OPTION from a user who has been dropped from the database or had her privileges revoked.

The syntax for REVOKE is as follows:

```
REVOKE PRIVILEGE1 [, PRIVILEGE2 ] [ GRANT OPTION FOR ] ON OBJECT
FROM USER { RESTRICT | CASCADE }
```

The following is an example:

```
REVOKE INSERT ON EMPLOYEE_TBL FROM USER1;
Revoke succeeded.
```

Controlling Access on Individual Columns

Instead of granting object privileges (INSERT, UPDATE, or DELETE) on a table as a whole, you can grant privileges on specific columns in the table to restrict user access, as shown in the following example:

```
GRANT UPDATE (NAME) ON EMPLOYEES TO PUBLIC;
Grant succeeded.
```

The PUBLIC Database Account

The PUBLIC database user account is a database account that represents all users in the database. All users are part of the PUBLIC account. If a privilege is granted to the PUBLIC account, all database users have the privilege. Likewise, if a privilege is revoked from the PUBLIC account, the privilege is revoked from all database users, unless that privilege was explicitly granted to a specific user. The following is an example:

```
GRANT SELECT ON EMPLOYEE_TBL TO PUBLIC;
Grant succeeded.
```

Groups of Privileges

Some implementations have groups of privileges in the database. These groups of permissions are referred to with different names. Having a group of privileges allows simplicity for granting and revoking common privileges to and from users. For example, if a group consists of ten privileges, the group can be granted to a user instead of individually granting all ten privileges.

Oracle has groups of privileges that are called *roles*. Oracle includes the following groups of privileges with their implementations:

▶ CONNECT—Allows a user to connect to the database and perform operations on any database objects to which the user has access.

Database Privilege Groups Vary Between Systems

Each implementation differs on the use of groups of database privileges. If available, this feature should be used for ease of database security administration.

▶ RESOURCE—Allows a user to create objects, drop objects he owns, grant privileges to objects he owns, and so on.

▶ DBA—Allows a user to perform any function within the database. The user can access any database object and perform any operation with this group.

PUBLIC Privileges Can Grant Unintended Access

Use extreme caution when granting privileges to PUBLIC; all database users acquire the privileges granted. Therefore, by granting permissions to PUBLIC, you might unintentionally give access to data to users who have no business accessing it. For example, giving PUBLIC access to SELECT from the employee salary table would give everyone who has access to the database the rights to see what everyone in the company is being paid!

An example for granting a group of privileges to a user follows:

```
GRANT DBA TO USER1;
Grant succeeded.
```

SQL Server has several groups of permissions at the server level and the database level. Some of the database level permission groups are

▶ DB_DDLADMIN

▶ DB_DATAREADER

▶ DB_DATAWRITER

The DB_DDLADMIN role allows the user to manipulate any of the objects within the database through any legal data definition language command. The DB_DATAREADER role allows the user to select from any of the tables within the database from which it is assigned.

The DB_DATAWRITER role allows the user to perform any data manipulation syntax—INSERT, UPDATE, or DELETE—on any of the tables within the database.

Controlling Privileges Through Roles

A *role* is an object created in the database that contains group-like privileges. Roles can reduce security maintenance by not having to grant explicit privileges directly to a user. Group privilege management is much easier to handle with roles. A role's privileges can be changed, and such a change is transparent to the user.

If a user needs SELECT and UPDATE table privileges on a table at a specified time within an application, a role with those privileges can temporarily be assigned until the transaction is complete.

When a role is created, it has no real value other than being a role within a database. It can be granted to users or other roles. Let's say that a schema named APP01 grants the SELECT table privilege to the RECORDS_CLERK role on the EMPLOYEE_PAY table. Any user or role granted the RECORDS_CLERK role now would have SELECT privileges on the EMPLOYEE_PAY table.

Likewise, if APP01 revoked the SELECT table privilege from the RECORDS_CLERK role on the EMPLOYEE_PAY table, any user or role granted the RECORDS_CLERK role would no longer have SELECT privileges on that table.

When assigning permissions in a database, ensure that you think through what permissions a user needs and if other users need the same sets of permissions. For example, a set of accounting tables might need to be accessed by several members of an accounting team. In this case, unless they each need drastically different permissions to these tables, it is far easier to set up a role, assign the role the appropriate conditions, and then assign the users to the role.

If a new object is created and needs to have permissions granted now to the accounting group, you can do it in one location instead of having to update each account. Likewise, if the accounting team brings on a new member or decides someone else needs the same access to its tables, you only have to assign the role to the new user and you are good to go. Roles are an excellent tool to enable the DBA to work smarter and not harder when dealing with complex database security protocols.

The CREATE ROLE Statement

A role is created with the CREATE ROLE statement.

```
CREATE ROLE role_name;
```

Granting privileges to roles is the same as granting privileges to a user. Study the following example:

```
CREATE ROLE RECORDS_CLERK;
Role created.
GRANT SELECT, INSERT, UPDATE, DELETE ON EMPLOYEE_PAY TO RECORDS_CLERK;
Grant succeeded.
GRANT RECORDS_CLERK TO USER1;
Grant succeeded.
```

The DROP ROLE Statement

A role is dropped using the DROP_ROLE statement:

```
DROP ROLE role_name;
```

The following is an example:

```
DROP ROLE RECORDS_CLERK;
Role dropped.
```

Roles Are Not Supported in MySQL

MySQL does not support roles. The lack of role usage is a weakness in some implementations of SQL.

By the Way

The SET ROLE Statement

A role can be set for a user SQL session using the SET_ROLE statement:

```
SET ROLE role_name;
```

The following is an example:

```
SET ROLE RECORDS_CLERK;
Role set.
```

You can set more than one role at once:

```
SET ROLE RECORDS_CLERK, ROLE2, ROLE3;
Role set.
```

SET ROLE Is Not Always Used

In some implementations, such as Microsoft SQL Server and Oracle, all roles granted to a user are automatically default roles, which means they are set and available to the user as soon as the user logs in to the database. The SET ROLE syntax here is shown so that you can understand what the ANSI standard for setting a role is.

By the Way

Summary

You were shown the basics on implementing security in an SQL database or a relational database. You learned the basics of managing database users. The first step in implementing security at the database level for users is to create the user. Then the user must be assigned certain privileges that allow her access to specific parts of the database. ANSI allows the use of roles as discussed during this hour. Privileges can be granted to users or roles.

The two types of privileges are system and object. System privileges are those that allow the user to perform various tasks within the database, such as actually connecting to the database, creating tables, creating users, and altering the state of the database. Object privileges are those that allow a user access to specific objects within the database, such as the ability to select data or manipulate data in a specific table.

Two commands in SQL allow a user to grant and revoke privileges to and from other users or roles in the database: GRANT and REVOKE. These two commands control the overall administration of privileges in the database. Although there are many other considerations for implementing security in a relational database, this hour discussed the basics that relate to the language of SQL.

Q&A

Q. *If a user forgets her password, what should she do to gain access to the database again?*

A. The user should go to her immediate management or an available help desk. A help desk should be able to reset a user's password. If not, the DBA or security officer can reset the password. The user should change the password to a password of her choosing as soon as the password is reset and the user is notified. Sometimes the DBA can affect this by setting a specific property that forces the user to change her password on the next login. Check your particular implementation's documentation for specifics.

Q. *What can I do if I want to grant* CONNECT *to a user, but the user does not need all the privileges that are assigned to the* CONNECT *role?*

A. You would simply not grant CONNECT, but only the privileges required. Should you ever grant CONNECT and the user no longer needs all the privileges that go with it, simply revoke CONNECT from the user and grant the specific privileges required.

Q. *Why is it so important for the new user to change the password when received from whoever created the new user?*

A. An initial password is assigned upon creation of the user ID. No one, not even the DBA or management, should know a user's password. The password should be kept a secret at all times to prevent another user from logging on to the database under another user's account.

Workshop

The following workshop is composed of a series of quiz questions and practical exercises. The quiz questions are designed to test your overall understanding of the current material. The practical exercises are intended to afford you the opportunity to apply the concepts discussed during the current hour, as well as build upon the knowledge acquired in previous hours of study. Please take time to complete the quiz questions and exercises before continuing. Refer to Appendix C, "Answers to Quizzes and Exercises," for answers.

Quiz

1. What option must a user have to grant another user privileges on an object not owned by the user?

2. When privileges are granted to PUBLIC, do all database users acquire the privileges, or only specified users?

3. What privilege is required to look at data in a specific table?

4. What type of privilege is SELECT?

5. What option revokes a user's privilege to an object as well as the other users that they might have granted privileges to by use of the GRANT option?

Exercises

1. Log in to your database instance and switch the database instance to use the learnsql database if it is not set as your default.

2. Type the following at the database prompt to get a list of the default tables depending on your implementation:

```
MySQL:           SHOW TABLES;
   SQL Server:       SELECT NAME FROM SYS.TABLES;
       Oracle:                SELECT * FROM USER_TABLES;
```

3. Create a new database user as follows:

```
Username: Steve
Password: Steve123
Access: learnsql database, SELECT on all tables
```

4. Get a list of all database users by typing the following depending on your implementation:

```
MySQL:        SELECT * FROM USER;
SQL Server:   SELECT * FROM SYS.DATABSE_PRINCIPALS WHERE TYPE='S';
Oracle:       SELECT * FROM DBA_USERS;
```

Creating and Using Views and Synonyms

What You'll Learn in This Hour:

▶ What views are

▶ How views are used

▶ Views and security

▶ Storing views

▶ Creating views

▶ Joining views

▶ Data manipulation in a view

▶ Performance of nested views

▶ What synonyms are

▶ Managing synonyms

▶ Creating synonyms

▶ Dropping synonyms

In this hour, you learn about performance, as well as how to create and drop views, how to use views for security, and how to provide simplicity in data retrieval for end users and reports. This hour also includes a discussion on synonyms.

What Is a View?

A *view* is a virtual table. That is, a view looks like a table and acts like a table as far as a user is concerned, but it doesn't require physical storage. A view is actually a composition of a table in the form of a predefined query, which is stored in the database. For example, you can create a view from EMPLOYEE_TBL that contains only the employee's name and address, instead of all columns in EMPLOYEE_TBL. A view can contain all rows of a table or select rows from a table. You can create a view from one or many tables.

When you create a view, a SELECT statement is actually run against the database, which defines the view. The SELECT statement that defines the view might simply contain column names from the table, or it can be more explicitly written using various functions and calculations to manipulate or summarize the data that the user sees. Study the illustration of a view in Figure 20.1.

FIGURE 20.1
The view.

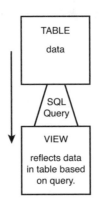

A view is considered a database object, although the view takes up no storage space on its own. The main difference between a view and a table is that data in a table consumes physical storage, whereas a view does not require physical storage because it is actually referring to data from a table.

A view is used in the same manner that a table is used in the database, meaning that data can be selected from a view as it is from a table. Data can also be manipulated in a view, although there are some restrictions. The following sections discuss some common uses for views and how they are stored in the database.

Watch Out!

Dropping Tables Used by Views

If a table that created a view is dropped, the view becomes inaccessible. You receive an error when trying to query against the view.

Utilizing Views to Simplify Data Access

Sometimes, through the process of normalizing your database or just as a process of database design, the data might be contained in a table format that does not easily lend itself to querying by end users. In this instance, you could create a series of views to make the data simpler for your end users to query. Your users might need to query the employee salary information from the `learnsql` database. However, they might not totally understand how to create joins between `EMPLOYEE_TBL` and `EMPLOYEE_PAY_TBL`. To bridge this gap, you create a view that contains the join and gives the end users the right to select from the view.

Utilizing Views as a Form of Security

> **Views Can Be Used as a Form of Security**
>
> Views can restrict user access to particular columns in a table or to rows in a table that meet specific conditions as defined in the WHERE clause of the view definition.

Views can be utilized as a form of security in the database. Let's say you have a table called `EMPLOYEE_TBL`. `EMPLOYEE_TBL` includes employee names, addresses, phone numbers, emergency contacts, department, position, and salary or hourly pay. You have some temporary help come in to write a report of employees' names, addresses, and phone numbers. If you give access to `EMPLOYEE_TBL` to the temporary help, they can see how much each of your employees receives in compensation—you do not want this to happen. To prevent that, you have created a view containing only the required information: employee name, address, and phone numbers. You can then give the temporary help access to the view to write the report without giving them access to the compensation columns in the table.

Utilizing Views to Maintain Summarized Data

If you have a summarized data report in which the data in the table or tables is updated often and the report is created often, a view with summarized data might be an excellent choice.

For example, suppose that you have a table containing information about individuals, such as city of residence, gender, salary, and age. You could create a view based on the table that shows summarized figures for individuals for each city, such as the average age, average salary, total number of males, and total number of females. To retrieve this information from the base table(s) after the view is created, you can simply query the view instead of composing a SELECT statement that might, in some cases, turn out to be very complex.

The only difference between the syntax for creating a view with summarized data and creating a view from a single or multiple tables is the use of aggregate functions. Review Hour 9, "Summarizing Data Results from a Query," for the use of aggregate functions.

A view is stored in memory only. It takes up no storage space—as do other database objects—other than the space required to store the view definition. The view's creator or the schema owner owns the view. The view owner automatically has all applicable privileges on that view and can grant privileges on the view to other users, as with tables. The GRANT command's GRANT OPTION privilege works the same as on a table. See Hour 19, "Managing Database Security," for more information.

Creating Views

Views are created using the CREATE VIEW statement. You can create views from a single table, multiple tables, or another view. To create a view, a user must have the appropriate system privilege according to the specific implementation.

The basic CREATE VIEW syntax is as follows:

```
CREATE [RECURSIVE]VIEW VIEW_NAME
[COLUMN NAME [,COLUMN NAME]]
[OF UDT NAME [UNDER TABLE NAME]
[REF IS COLUMN NAME SYSTEM GENERATED |USER GENERATED | DERIVED]
[COLUMN NAME WITH OPTIONS SCOPE TABLE NAME]]
 AS
{SELECT STATEMENT}
[WITH [CASCADED | LOCAL] CHECK OPTION]
```

The following subsections explore different methods for creating views using the CREATE VIEW statement.

ANSI SQL Has No ALTER VIEW Statement

There is no provision for an ALTER VIEW statement in ANSI SQL, although most database implementations do provide for that capability. For example, in older versions of MySQL, you use REPLACE VIEW to alter a current view. However, the newest versions of MySQL, SQL Server, and Oracle support the ALTER VIEW statement. Check with your specific database implementation's documentation to see what is supported.

Creating a View from a Single Table

You can create a view from a single table.

The syntax is as follows:

```
CREATE VIEW VIEW_NAME AS
SELECT * | COLUMN1 [, COLUMN2 ]
FROM TABLE_NAME
[ WHERE EXPRESSION1 [, EXPRESSION2 ]]
[ WITH CHECK OPTION ]
[ GROUP BY ]
```

The simplest form for creating a view is one based on the entire contents of a single table, as in the following example:

```
CREATE VIEW CUSTOMERS_VIEW AS
SELECT *
FROM CUSTOMER_TBL;
View created.
```

The next example narrows the contents for a view by selecting only specified columns from the base table:

```
CREATE VIEW EMP_VIEW AS
SELECT LAST_NAME, FIRST_NAME, MIDDLE_NAME
FROM EMPLOYEE_TBL;
View created.
```

The following is an example of how columns from the base table can be combined or manipulated to form a column in a view. The view column is titled NAMES by using an alias in the SELECT clause.

```
CREATE VIEW NAMES AS
SELECT LAST_NAME || ', ' ||FIRST_NAME || ' ' || MIDDLE_NAME NAME
FROM EMPLOYEE_TBL;
View created.
```

Now you select all data from the NAMES view that you created:

```
SELECT *
FROM NAMES;
NAME
----------------
STEPHENS, TINA D
PLEW, LINDA C
GLASS, BRANDON S
GLASS, JACOB
WALLACE, MARIAH
SPURGEON, TIFFANY
6 rows selected.
```

The following example shows how to create a view with summarized data from one or more underlying tables:

```
CREATE VIEW CITY_PAY AS
SELECT E.CITY, AVG(P PAY_RATE) AVG_PAY
FROM EMPLOYEE_TBL E,
     EMPLOYEE_PAY_TBL P
WHERE E.EMP_ID = P.EMP_ID
GROUP BY E.CITY;
View created.
```

Now you can select from your summarized view:

```
SELECT *
FROM CITY_PAY;
CITY            AVG_PAY
--------------- -------
GREENWOOD
INDIANAPOLIS    13.33333
WHITELAND
3 rows selected.
```

By summarizing a view, SELECT statements that might occur in the future are simplified against the underlying table of the view.

Creating a View from Multiple Tables

You can create a view from multiple tables by using a JOIN in the SELECT statement. The syntax is as follows:

```
CREATE VIEW VIEW_NAME AS
SELECT * | COLUMN1 [, COLUMN2 ]
FROM TABLE_NAME1, TABLE_NAME2 [, TABLE_NAME3 ]
WHERE TABLE_NAME1 = TABLE_NAME2
[ AND TABLE_NAME1 = TABLE_NAME3 ]
[ EXPRESSION1 ][, EXPRESSION2 ]
[ WITH CHECK OPTION ]
[ GROUP BY ]
```

The following is an example of creating a view from multiple tables:

```
CREATE VIEW EMPLOYEE_SUMMARY AS
SELECT E.EMP_ID, E.LAST_NAME, P.POSITION, P.DATE_HIRE, P.PAY_RATE
FROM EMPLOYEE_TBL E,
     EMPLOYEE PAY_TBL P
WHERE E.EMP_ID = P.EMP_ID;
View created.
```

Remember that when selecting data from multiple tables, the tables must be joined by common columns in the WHERE clause. A view is nothing more than a SELECT statement; therefore, tables are joined in a view definition the same as they are in a regular SELECT statement. Recall the use of table aliases to simplify the readability of a multiple-table query.

A view can also be joined with tables and with other views. The same principles apply to joining views with tables and other views that apply to joining tables to other tables. Review Hour 13, "Joining Tables in Queries," for more information.

Creating a View from a View

You can create a view from another view using the following format:

```
CREATE VIEW2 AS
SELECT * FROM VIEW1
```

You can create a view from a view many layers deep (a view of a view of a view, and so on). How deep you can go is implementation specific. The only problem with creating views based on other views is their manageability. For example, suppose that you create VIEW2 based on VIEW1 and then create VIEW3 based on VIEW2. If VIEW1 is dropped, VIEW2 and VIEW3 are no good. The underlying information that supports these views no longer exists. Therefore, always maintain a good understanding of the views in the database and on which other objects those views rely (see Figure 20.2).

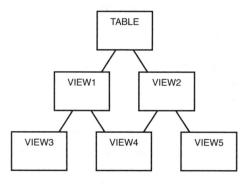

VIEW DEPENDENCIES

FIGURE 20.2
View dependencies.

Figure 20.2 shows the relationship of views that are dependent not only on tables, but on other views. VIEW1 and VIEW2 are dependent on the TABLE. VIEW3 is dependent on VIEW1. VIEW4 is dependent on both VIEW1 and VIEW2. VIEW5 is dependent on VIEW2. Based on these relationships, the following can be concluded:

▶ If VIEW1 is dropped, VIEW3 and VIEW4 are invalid.

▶ If VIEW2 is dropped, VIEW4 and VIEW5 are invalid.

▶ If the TABLE is dropped, none of the views is valid.

> **Choose Carefully How You Implement Your Views**
>
> If a view is as easy and efficient to create from the base table as from another view, preference should go to the view being created from the base table.

WITH CHECK OPTION

WITH CHECK OPTION is a CREATE VIEW statement option. The purpose of WITH CHECK OPTION is to ensure that all UPDATE and INSERT commands satisfy the condition(s) in the view definition. If they do not satisfy the condition(s), the UPDATE or INSERT returns an error. WITH CHECK OPTION actually enforces referential integrity by checking the view's definition to see that it is not violated.

The following is an example of creating a view with WITH CHECK OPTION:

```
CREATE VIEW EMPLOYEE_PAGERS AS
SELECT LAST_NAME, FIRST_NAME, PAGER
FROM EMPLOYEE_TBL
WHERE PAGER IS NOT NULL
WITH CHECK OPTION;
View created.
```

WITH CHECK OPTION in this case should deny the entry of any NULL values in the view's PAGER column because the view is defined by data that does not have a NULL value in the PAGER column.

Try to insert a NULL value into the PAGER column:

```
INSERT INTO EMPLOYEE PAGERS
VALUES ('SMITH','JOHN',NULL);
insert into employee_pagers
            *
ERROR at line 1:
ORA-01400: mandatory (NOT NULL) column is missing or NULL during insert
```

When you choose to use WITH CHECK OPTION during creation of a view from a view, you have two options: CASCADED and LOCAL. CASCADED is the default and is assumed if neither is specified. CASCADED is the ANSI standard for the syntax, however, Microsoft SQL Server and Oracle use the slightly different keyword CASCADE. The CASCADED option checks all underlying views, all integrity constraints during an update for the base table, and against defining conditions in the second view. The LOCAL option checks only integrity constraints against both views and the defining conditions in the second view, not the underlying base table. Therefore, it is safer to create views with the CASCADED option because the base table's referential integrity is preserved.

Creating a Table from a View

You can create a table from a view, just as you can create a table from another table (or a view from another view).

The syntax is as follows:

```
CREATE TABLE TABLE_NAME AS
SELECT {* | COLUMN1 [, COLUMN2 ]
FROM VIEW_NAME
[ WHERE CONDITION1 [, CONDITION2 ]
[ ORDER BY ]
```

Subtle Differences Between Tables and Views

Remember that the main difference between a table and a view is that a table contains actual data and consumes physical storage, whereas a view contains no data and requires no storage other than to store the view definition (the query).

First, create a view based on two tables:

```
CREATE VIEW ACTIVE_CUSTOMERS AS
SELECT C.*
FROM CUSTOMER_TBL C,
     ORDERS_TBL O
WHERE C.CUST_ID = O.CUST_ID;
View created.
```

Next, create a table based on the previously created view:

```
CREATE TABLE CUSTOMER_ROSTER_TBL AS
SELECT CUST_ID, CUST_NAME
FROM ACTIVE_CUSTOMERS;
Table created.
```

Defer the Use of the GROUP BY Clause in Your Views

Using the ORDER BY clause in the SELECT statement that is querying the view is better and simpler than using the GROUP BY clause in the CREATE VIEW statement.

Finally, select data from the table, the same as any other table:

```
SELECT *
FROM CUSTOMER_ROSTER_TBL;
CUST_ID    CUST_NAME
---------- ------------------
232        LESLIE GLEASON
12         MARYS GIFT SHOP
43         SCHYLERS NOVELTIES
```

```
090        WENDY WOLF
287        GAVINS PLACE
432        SCOTTYS MARKET

6 rows selected.
```

Views and the ORDER BY Clause

You cannot use the ORDER BY clause in the CREATE VIEW statement; however, the GROUP BY clause has the same effect as an ORDER BY clause when it's used in the CREATE VIEW statement.

The following is an example of a GROUP BY clause in a CREATE VIEW statement:

```
CREATE VIEW NAMES2 AS
SELECT LAST_NAME || ', ' || FIRST_NAME || ' ' ||MIDDLE_NAME NAME
FROM EMPLOYEE_TBL
GROUP BY LAST_NAME || ', ' || FIRST_NAME || ' ' || MIDDLE_NAME;
View created.
```

If you select all data from the view, the data is in alphabetical order (because you grouped by NAME):

```
SELECT *
FROM NAMES2;
NAME
-----------------
GLASS, BRANDON S
GLASS, JACOB
PLEW, LINDA C
SPURGEON, TIFFANY
STEPHENS, TINA D
WALLACE, MARIAH

6 rows selected.
```

Updating Data Through a View

You can update the underlying data of a view under certain conditions:

▶ The view must not involve joins.

▶ The view must not contain a GROUP BY clause.

▶ The view must not contain a UNION statement.

▶ The view cannot contain a reference to the pseudocolumn ROWNUM.

▶ The view cannot contain group functions.

▶ The DISTINCT clause cannot be used.

▶ The WHERE clause cannot include a nested table expression that includes a reference to the same table as referenced in the FROM clause.

▶ This means that the view can perform INSERTS, UPDATES, and DELETES as long as they honor these caveats.

Review Hour 14, "Using Subqueries to Define Unknown Data," for the UPDATE command's syntax.

Dropping a View

You use the DROP VIEW command to drop a view from the database. The two options for the DROP VIEW command are RESTRICT and CASCADE. If a view is dropped with the RESTRICT option and other views are referenced in a constraint, the DROP VIEW errs. If the CASCADE option is used and another view or constraint is referenced, the DROP VIEW succeeds and the underlying view or constraint is dropped. An example follows:

```
DROP VIEW NAMES2;
View dropped.
```

Performance Impact of Using Nested Views

Views adhere to the same performance characteristics as tables when they are used in queries. As such, you need to be cognizant of the fact that hiding complex logic behind a view does not negate the fact that the data must be parsed and assembled by the system querying the underlying tables. Views must be treated as any other SQL statement in terms of performance tuning. If the query that makes up your view is not preformant, the view itself experiences performance issues.

Additionally, some users employ views to break down complex queries into multiple units of views and views that are created on top of other views. Although this might seem to be an excellent idea to break down the logic into simpler steps, it can present some performance degradation. This is because the query engine must break down and translate each sublayer of view to determine what exactly it needs to do for the query request.

The more layers you have, the more the query engine has to work to come up with an execution plan. In fact, most query engines do not guarantee that you get the best overall plan but merely that you get a decent plan in the shortest amount of time. So it is always best practice to keep the levels of code in your query as flat as possible and to test and tune the statements that make up your views.

> **Synonyms Are Not ANSI SQL Standard**
>
> Synonyms are not American National Standards Institute (ANSI) SQL standard; however, because several major implementations use synonyms, it is best we discuss them briefly here. You must check your particular implementation for the exact use of synonyms, if available. Note, however, that MySQL does not support synonyms. However, you might be able to implement the same type of functionality using a view instead.

What Is a Synonym?

A *synonym* is merely another name for a table or a view. Synonyms are usually created so a user can avoid having to qualify another user's table or view to access the table or view. Synonyms can be created as PUBLIC or PRIVATE. Any user of the database can use a PUBLIC synonym; only the owner of a database and any users that have been granted privileges can use a PRIVATE synonym.

Either a database administrator (or another designated individual) or individual users manage synonyms. Because there are two types of synonyms, PUBLIC and PRIVATE, different system-level privileges might be required to create one or the other. All users can generally create a PRIVATE synonym. Typically, only a DBA or privileged database user can create a PUBLIC synonym. Refer to your specific implementation for required privileges when creating synonyms.

Creating Synonyms

The general syntax to create a synonym is as follows:

```
CREATE [PUBLIC|PRIVATE] SYNONYM SYNONYM_NAME FOR TABLE|VIEW
```

You create a synonym called CUST, short for CUSTOMER_TBL, in the following example. This frees you from having to spell out the full table name.

```
CREATE SYNONYM CUST FOR CUSTOMER_TBL;
Synonym created.
SELECT CUST_NAME
```

```
FROM CUST;
CUST_NAME
--------------------------
LESLIE GLEASON
NANCY BUNKER
ANGELA DOBKO
WENDY WOLF
MARYS GIFT SHOP
SCOTTYS MARKET
JASONS AND DALLAS GOODIES
MORGANS CANDIES AND TREATS
SCHYLERS NOVELTIES
GAVINS PLACE
HOLLYS GAMEARAMA
HEATHERS FEATHERS AND THINGS
RAGANS HOBBIES INC
ANDYS CANDIES
RYANS STUFF
15 rows selected.
```

It is also common for a table owner to create a synonym for the table to which you have been granted access so you do not have to qualify the table name by the name of the owner:

```
CREATE SYNONYM PRODUCTS_TBL FOR USER1.PRODUCTS_TBL;
Synonym created.
```

Dropping Synonyms

Dropping synonyms is like dropping almost any other database object. The general syntax to drop a synonym is as follows:

```
DROP [PUBLIC|PRIVATE] SYNONYM SYNONYM_NAME
```

The following is an example:

```
DROP SYNONYM CUST;
Synonym dropped.
```

Summary

This hour discusses two important features in SQL: views and synonyms. In many cases, these features are not used when they could aid in the overall functionality of relational database users. Views were defined as virtual tables—objects that look and act like tables but do not take physical space like tables. Views are actually defined by queries against tables and possible other views in the database. Administrators typically use views to restrict data that a user sees and to simplify and summarize data. You can create views from views, but take care not to embed views too deeply to avoid losing control over their management. There are various options when creating views; some are implementation specific.

Synonyms are objects in the database that represent other objects. They simplify the name of another object in the database, either by creating a synonym with a short name for an object with a long name or by creating a synonym on an object owned by another user to which you have access. There are two types of synonyms: PUBLIC and PRIVATE. A PUBLIC synonym is one that is accessible to all database users, whereas a PRIVATE synonym is accessible to a single user. A DBA typically creates a PUBLIC synonym, whereas each user normally creates her own PRIVATE synonyms.

Q&A

Q. *How can a view contain data but take no storage space?*

A. A view does not contain data. A view is a virtual table or a stored query. The only space required for a view is for the actual view creation statement, called the view definition.

Q. *What happens to the view if a table from which a view was created is dropped?*

A. The view is invalid because the underlying data for the view no longer exists.

Q. *What are the limits on naming the synonym when creating synonyms?*

A. This is implementation specific. However, the naming convention for synonyms in most major implementations follows the same rules that apply to the tables and other objects in the database.

Workshop

The following workshop is composed of a series of quiz questions and practical exercises. The quiz questions are designed to test your overall understanding of the current material. The practical exercises are intended to afford you the opportunity to apply the concepts discussed during the current hour, as well as build upon the knowledge acquired in previous hours of study. Please take time to complete the quiz questions and exercises before continuing. Refer to Appendix C, "Answers to Quizzes and Exercises," for answers.

Quiz

1. Can you delete a row of data from a view that you created from multiple tables?

2. When creating a table, the owner is automatically granted the appropriate privileges on that table. Is this true when creating a view?

3. Which clause orders data when creating a view?

4. Which option can you use when creating a view from a view to check integrity constraints?

5. You try to drop a view and receive an error because of one or more underlying views. What must you do to drop the view?

Exercises

1. Write a statement to create a view based on the total contents of EMPLOYEE_TBL.

2. Write a statement that creates a summarized view containing the average pay rate and average salary for each city in EMPLOYEE_TBL.

3. Create another view for the same summarized data, except use the view you created in Exercise 1 instead of the base EMPLOYEE_TBL. Compare the two results.

4. Use the view in Exercise 2 to create a table called EMPLOYEE_PAY_SUMMARIZED. Verify that the view and the table contain the same data.

5. Write a statement that drops the table and the three views that you created.

Working with the System Catalog

What You'll Learn in This Hour:

▶ What the system catalog is

▶ How the system catalog is created

▶ What data is contained in the system catalog

▶ Examples of system catalog tables

▶ Querying the system catalog

▶ Updating the system catalog

In this hour, you learn about the system catalog, commonly referred to as the *data dictionary* in some relational database implementations. By the end of this hour, you will understand the purpose and contents of the system catalog and will be able to query it to find information about the database based on commands that you have learned in previous hours. Each major implementation has some form of a system catalog that stores information about the database. This hour shows examples of the elements contained in a few of the different system catalogs for the implementations discussed in this book.

What Is the System Catalog?

The *system catalog* is a collection of tables and views that contain important information about a database. A system catalog is available for each database. Information in the system catalog defines the structure of the database and information on the data contained therein. For example, the *Data Definition Language (DDL)* for all tables in the database is stored in the system catalog. See Figure 21.1 for an example of the system catalog within the database.

FIGURE 21.1
The system catalog.

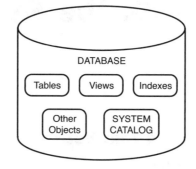

As you can see in Figure 21.1, the system catalog for a database is actually part of the database. Within the database are objects, such as tables, indexes, and views. The system catalog is basically a group of objects that contain information that defines other objects in the database, the structure of the database, and various other significant information.

The system catalog for your implementation might be divided into logical groups of objects to provide tables that are accessible by the *Database Administrator (DBA)* and any other database user. For example, a user might need to view the particular database privileges that she has been granted but doesn't care how this is internally structured in the database. A user typically queries the system catalog to acquire information on the user's own objects and privileges, whereas the DBA needs to be able to inquire about any structure or event within the database. In some implementations, system catalog objects are accessible only to the DBA.

The system catalog is crucial to the DBA or any other database user who needs to know about the database's structure and nature. It is especially important in those instances in which the database user is not presented with a *Graphical User Interface (GUI)*. The system catalog allows orders to be kept, not only by the DBA and users, but by the database server.

Did You Know?

Database System Catalogs Vary

Each implementation has its own naming conventions for the system catalog's tables and views. The naming is *not* important; however, learning what the system catalog does *is* important, as is what it contains and how and where to retrieve the information.

How Is the System Catalog Created?

The system catalog is created either automatically with the creation of the database, or by the DBA immediately following the creation of the database. For example, a set of predefined, vendor-provided SQL scripts in Oracle is executed, which builds all the database tables and views in the system catalog that are accessible to a database user.

The system catalog tables and views are system-owned and not specific to any one schema. In Oracle, for example, the system catalog owner is a user account called SYS, which has full authority in the database. In Microsoft SQL Server, the system catalog for the SQL server is located in the master database. In MySQL the database is contained in the mysql system database. Check with your specific vendor documentation to find where the system catalogs are stored.

What Is Contained in the System Catalog?

The system catalog contains a variety of information accessible to many users and is sometimes used for different specific purposes by each of those users.

The system catalog contains information such as the following:

- User accounts and default settings
- Privileges and other security information
- Performance statistics
- Object sizing
- Object growth
- Table structure and storage
- Index structure and storage
- Information on other database objects, such as views, synonyms, triggers, and stored procedures
- Table constraints and referential integrity information
- User sessions
- Auditing information

- ▸ Internal database settings
- ▸ Locations of database files

The database server maintains the system catalog. For example, when a table is created, the database server inserts the data into the appropriate system catalog table or view. When a table's structure is modified, appropriate objects in the data dictionary are updated. The following sections describe, by category, the types of data that are contained in the system catalog.

User Data

All information about individual users is stored in the system catalog: the system and object privileges a user has been granted, the objects a user owns, and the objects not owned by the user to which the user has access. The user tables or views are accessible to the individual to query for information. See your implementation documentation on the system catalog objects.

Security Information

The system catalog also stores security information, such as user identifications, encrypted passwords, and various privileges and groups of privileges that database users utilize to access the data. Audit tables exist in some implementations for tracking actions that occur within the database, as well as by whom, when, and so on. Database user sessions can be closely monitored through the use of the system catalog in many implementations.

Database Design Information

The system catalog contains information regarding the actual database. That information includes the database's creation date, name, object sizing, size and location of data files, referential integrity information, indexes that exist in the database, and specific column information and column attributes for each table in the database.

Performance Statistics

Performance statistics are typically maintained in the system catalog as well. Performance statistics include information concerning the performance of SQL statements, both elapsed time and the execution method of an SQL statement taken by the optimizer. Other information for performance concerns memory allocation and usage, free space in the database, and information that allows table and index fragmentation to be controlled within the database. You can use this performance information to properly tune the database, rearrange SQL queries, and redesign methods of access to data to achieve better overall performance and SQL query response time.

System Catalog Tables by Implementation

Each implementation has several tables and views that compose the system catalog, some of which are categorized by user level, system level, and DBA level. For your particular implementation, you should query these tables and read your implementation's documentation for more information on system catalog tables. Table 21.1 has examples of six major implementations.

TABLE 21.1 Major Implementation System Catalog Objects

Microsoft SQL Server

Table Name	Information On...
SYSUSERS	Database users
SYS.DATABASES	All database segments
SYS.DATABASE_PERMISSIONS	All database permissions
SYS.DATABASE_FILES	All database files
SYSINDEXES	All indexes
SYSCONSTRAINTS	All constraints
SYS.TABLES	All database tables
SYS.VIEWS	All database views
Oracle	
ALL_TABLES	Tables accessible by a user
USER_TABLES	Tables owned by a user
DBA_TABLES	All tables in the database
DBA_SEGMENTS	Segment storage
DBA_INDEXES	All indexes
DBA_USERS	All users of the database
DBA_ROLE_PRIVS	Roles granted
DBA_ROLES	Roles in the database
DBA_SYS_PRIVS	System privileges granted
DBA_FREE_SPACE	Database free space

TABLE 21.1   Continued

Microsoft SQL Server

Table Name	Information On...
V$DATABASE	The creation of the database
V$SESSION	Current sessions
MySQL	
COLUMNS_PRIV	Column privileges
DB	Database privileges
FUNC	The management of user-defined functions
HOST	Hostnames related to MySQL
TABLES_PRIV	Table privileges
USER	User information

These are just a few of the system catalog objects from the main relational database implementations that we cover in the book. Many of the system catalog objects that are similar between implementations are shown here, but this hour strives to provide some variety. Overall, each implementation is specific to the organization of the system catalog's contents.

Querying the System Catalog

The system catalog tables or views are queried as any other table or view in the database using SQL. A user can usually query the user-related tables but might be denied access to various system tables accessible only by privileged database user accounts, such as the DBA.

You create an SQL query to retrieve data from the system catalog just as you create a query to access any other table in the database. For example, the following query returns all rows of data from the Microsoft SQL Server table SYS.TABLES:

```
SELECT * FROM SYS.TABLES;
GO
```

The following query lists all user accounts in the database and is run from the MySQL system database:

```
SELECT USER
FROM ALL_USER;
USER
----------------
ROOT
SYSTEM
RYAN
SCOTT
DEMO
RON
USER1
USER2
8 rows selected.
```

A Word About the Following Examples

The following examples use MySQL's system catalog. MySQL is chosen for no particular reason other than to give you some examples from one of the database implementations talked about in the book.

The following query lists all tables within our learnsql schema and is run from the Information_schema:

```
SELECT TABLE_NAME
FROM TABLES WHERE   TABLE_SCHEMA='learnsql';
TABLE_NAME
----------------
CUSTOMER_TBL
EMPLOYEE_PAY_TBL
EMPLOYEE_TBL
PRODUCTS_TBL
ORDERS_TBL
5 rows selected.
```

Manipulating System Catalog Tables Can Be Dangerous

Never directly manipulate tables in the system catalog in any way (only the DBA has access to manipulate system catalog tables). Doing so might compromise the database's integrity. Remember that information concerning the structure of the database, as well as all objects in the database, is maintained in the system catalog. The system catalog is typically isolated from all other data in the database. Some implementations, such as Microsoft SQL Server, do not allow the user to manipulate the system catalog directly in order to maintain the integrity of the system.

The next query returns all the system privileges that have been granted to the database user BRANDON:

```
SELECT GRANTEE, PRIVILEGE_TYPE
FROM USER_PRIVILEGES
WHERE GRANTEE = 'BRANDON';
```

```
GRANTEE                 PRIVILEGE
--------------------    --------------------
BRANDON                 SELECT
BRANDON                 INSERT
BRANDON                 UPDATE
BRANDON                 CREATE
4 rows selected.
```

By the
Way

These Are Just a Few of the System Catalog Tables Available

The examples shown in this section are a drop in the bucket compared to the information that you can retrieve from any system catalog. You might find it extremely helpful to dump data dictionary information using queries to a file that can be printed and used as a reference. Refer to your implementation documentation for specific system catalog tables and columns within those available tables.

Updating System Catalog Objects

The system catalog is used only for query operations—even when the DBA is using it. The database server makes updates to the system catalog automatically. For example, a table is created in the database when a database user issues a CREATE TABLE statement. The database server then places the DDL that created the table in the system catalog under the appropriate system catalog table.

There is never a need to manually update a table in the system catalog even though you might have the power to do so. The database server for each implementation performs these updates according to actions that occur within the database, as shown in Figure 21.2.

FIGURE 21.2
Updates to the system catalog.

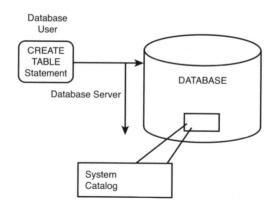

Summary

You have learned about the system catalog for a relational database. The system catalog is, in a sense, a database within a database. The system catalog is essentially a database that contains all information about the database in which it resides. It is a way of maintaining the database's overall structure, tracking events and changes that occur within the database, and providing the vast pool of information necessary for overall database management. The system catalog is only used for query operations. Database users should *not* make changes directly to system tables. However, changes are implicitly made each time a change is made to the database structure itself, such as the creation of a table. The database server makes these entries in the system catalog automatically.

Q&A

Q. *As a database user, I realize I can find information about my objects. How can I find information about other users' objects?*

A. Users can employ sets of tables and views to query in most system catalogs. One set of these tables and views includes information on what objects you have access to. To find out about other users' access, you need to check the system catalogs containing that information. For example, in Oracle you could check the DBA_TABLES and DBA_USERS system catalogs.

Q. *If a user forgets his password, is there a table that the DBA can query to get the password?*

A. Yes and no. The password is maintained in a system table, but it is typically encrypted so that even the DBA cannot read the password. The password has to be reset if the user forgets it, which the DBA can easily accomplish.

Q. *How can I tell which columns are in a system catalog table?*

A. You can query the system catalog tables as you query any other table. Simply query the table holding that particular information.

Workshop

The following workshop is composed of a series of quiz questions and practical exercises. The quiz questions are designed to test your overall understanding of the current material. The practical exercises are intended to afford you the opportunity to apply the concepts discussed during the current hour, as well as build upon the knowledge acquired in previous hours of study. Please take time to complete the quiz questions and exercises before continuing. Refer to Appendix C, "Answers to Quizzes and Exercises," for answers.

Quiz

1. In some implementations, the system catalog is also known as what?

2. Can a regular user update the system catalog?

3. Which Microsoft SQL Server system table retrieves information about views that exist in the database?

4. Who owns the system catalog?

5. What is the difference between the Oracle system objects ALL_TABLES and DBA_TABLES?

6. Who makes modifications to the system tables?

Exercises

1. In Hour 19, "Managing Database Security," you looked at the tables in your learnsql database. Now find some of the system tables that we discussed earlier in this chapter. Review them.

2. At the prompt, type in queries to bring up each of the following:

   ▸ Information on all the tables

   ▸ Information on all the views

   ▸ All the usernames in the database

3. Write a query using multiple system tables to retrieve all the users and their associated privileges in your learnsql database.

HOUR 22

Advanced SQL Topics

What You'll Learn in This Hour:

- ▶ What cursors are
- ▶ Using stored procedures
- ▶ What triggers are
- ▶ Basics of dynamic SQL
- ▶ Using SQL to generate SQL
- ▶ Direct SQL versus embedded SQL
- ▶ Call-level interface

In this hour, you are introduced to some advanced SQL topics that extend beyond the basic operations that you have learned so far, such as querying data from the database, building database structures, and manipulating data within the database. By the end of the hour, you should understand the concepts behind cursors, stored procedures, triggers, dynamic SQL, direct versus embedded SQL, and SQL generated from SQL. These advanced topics are features available in many implementations, all of which provide enhancements to the parts of SQL discussed so far.

Some Topics Are Not ANSI SQL Related

Not all topics are ANSI SQL, so you must check your particular implementation for variations in syntax and rules. A few major vendors' syntax is shown in this hour for comparison.

By the Way

Cursors

Normally, database operations are commonly referred to as set-based operations. This means that the majority of ANSI SQL commands are geared toward working on a block of data. A cursor, on the other hand, is typically used to retrieve a subset of data from the database in a row-based operation. Thereby, each row in the cursor can be evaluated by a program, one row at a time. Cursors are normally used in SQL that is embedded in procedural-type programs. Some cursors are created implicitly by the database server, whereas others are defined by the SQL programmer. Each SQL implementation might define the use of cursors differently.

This section shows syntax examples from three popular implementations that we have tracked throughout the book: MySQL, Microsoft SQL Server, and Oracle.

The syntax to declare a cursor in MySQL is as follows:

```
DECLARE CURSOR_NAME CURSOR
FOR SELECT_STATEMENT
```

The syntax to declare a cursor for Microsoft SQL Server is as follows:

```
DECLARE CURSOR_NAME CURSOR
FOR SELECT_STATEMENT
[ FOR [READ ONLY | UPDATE {[ COLUMN_LIST ]}]
```

The syntax for Oracle is as follows:

```
DECLARE CURSOR CURSOR_NAME
IS {SELECT_STATEMENT}
```

The following cursor contains the result subset of all records from
`EMPLOYEE_TBL`:

```
DECLARE CURSOR EMP_CURSOR IS
SELECT * FROM EMPLOYEE_TBL
{ OTHER PROGRAM STATEMENTS }
```

According to the ANSI standard, you use the following operations to access a cursor after it has been defined:

- OPEN: Opens a defined cursor
- FETCH: Fetches rows from a cursor into a program variable
- CLOSE: Closes the cursor when operations against the cursor are complete

Opening a Cursor

You cannot access a cursor until you have opened it. When a cursor is opened, the specified cursor's SELECT statement is executed, and the results of the query are stored in a staging area in memory.

The syntax to open a cursor in MySQL and Microsoft SQL Server is as follows:

```
OPEN CURSOR_NAME
```

The syntax in Oracle is as follows:

```
OPEN CURSOR_NAME [ PARAMETER1 [, PARAMETER2 ]]
```

To open the EMP_CURSOR, use the following statement:

```
OPEN EMP_CURSOR
```

Fetching Data from a Cursor

You can retrieve the contents of the cursor (results from the query) through the FETCH statement after you have opened the cursor.

The syntax for the FETCH statement in Microsoft SQL Server is as follows:

```
FETCH NEXT FROM CURSOR_NAME [ INTO FETCH_LIST ]
```

The syntax for Oracle is as follows:

```
FETCH CURSOR_NAME {INTO : HOST_VARIABLE
[[ INDICATOR ] : INDICATOR_VARIABLE ]
[, : HOST_VARIABLE
[[ INDICATOR ] : INDICATOR_VARIABLE ]]
| USING DESCRIPTOR DESCRIPTOR ] }
```

The syntax for MySQL is as follows:

```
FETCH CURSOR_NAME into VARIABLE_NAME,[VARIABLE_NAME] ...
```

To fetch the contents of EMP_CURSOR into a variable called EMP_RECORD, your FETCH statement might appear as follows:

```
FETCH EMP_CURSOR INTO EMP_RECORD
```

When fetching data from a cursor, note that at some time you will come to the end of the cursor. Each implementation has a different way to set up handling of this so that you can gracefully close the cursor without receiving an error. Following are pseudocode examples from MySQL, Microsoft SQL Server, and Oracle on how to handle these situations. The syntax is meant to give you a feel for the process of handling cursors.

The syntax for MySQL is as follows:

```
BEGIN
    DECLARE done INT DEFAULT 0;
    DECLARE custname VARCHAR(30);
    DECLARE namecursor CURSOR FOR SELECT CUST_NAME FROM TBL_CUSTOMER;
```

```
        OPEN namecursor;
        read_loop: LOOP
                FETCH namecursor INTO custname;
                IF done THEN
                        LEAVE read_loop;
                END IF;
                -- Do something with the variable
        END LOOP;
        CLOSE namecursor;
END;
```

The syntax for Microsoft SQL Server is as follows:

```
BEGIN
        DECLARE @custname VARCHAR(30);
        DECLARE namecursor CURSOR FOR SELECT CUST_NAME FROM TBL_CUSTOMER;
        OPEN namecursor;
        FETCH NEXT FROM namecursor INTO @custname
        WHILE (@@FETCH_STATUS<>-1)
                BEGIN
                        IF (@@FETCH_STATUS<>-2)
                        BEGIN
                                -- Do something with the variable
                        END
        FETCH NEXT FROM namecursor INTO @custname
        END
        CLOSE namecursor
        DEALLOCATE namecursor
END;
```

The syntax for Oracle is as follows:

```
custname  varchar(30);
CURSOR namecursor
IS
SELECT CUST_NAME FROM TBL_CUSTOMER;
BEGIN
        OPEN namecursor;
        FETCH namecursor INTO custname;
        IF namecursor%notfound THEN
                -- Do some handling as you are at the end of the cursor
        END IF;
        -- Do something with the variable
        CLOSE namecursor;
END;
```

Closing a Cursor

You can obviously close a cursor if you can open one. After it's closed, it is no longer available to user programs. Closing a cursor is quite simple.

The Microsoft SQL Server syntax for the closing of a cursor and the deallocation of a cursor is as follows:

```
CLOSE CURSOR_NAME
DEALLOCATE CURSOR CURSOR_NAME
```

When a cursor is closed in Oracle, the resources and name are released without the DEALLOCATE statement. The syntax for Oracle is as follows:

```
CLOSE CURSOR_NAME
```

The same is true for the MySQL cursor. There is no DEALLOCATE statement available because the resources are released when the cursor is closed. The syntax for MySQL is as follows:

```
CLOSE CURSOR_NAME
```

By the Way

More Variations Exist in Advanced Features

As you can see from the previous examples, variations among the implementations are extensive, especially with advanced features of and extensions to SQL, which are covered in Hour 24, "Extensions to Standard SQL." You must check your particular implementation for the exact usage of a cursor.

Stored Procedures and Functions

By the Way

You Need to Deallocate a Cursor to Free Its Resources

Closing a cursor does not necessarily free the memory associated with the cursor. In some implementations, the memory used by a cursor must be deallocated by using the DEALLOCATE statement. When the cursor is deallocated, the associated memory is freed, and the name of the cursor can then be reused. In other implementations, memory is implicitly deallocated when the cursor is closed. Memory is available for other operations, such as opening another cursor, when space used by a cursor is reclaimed. If you do not deallocate the memory a cursor uses, the database could hold onto that memory even if other processes need it. This normally leads to poor performance as the system fights over limited computing resources.

Stored procedures are groupings of related SQL statements—commonly referred to as *functions* and *subprograms*—that allow ease and flexibility for a programmer. This ease and flexibility are derived from the fact that a stored procedure is often easier to execute than a number of individual SQL statements. Stored procedures can be nested within other stored procedures.

That is, a stored procedure can call another stored procedure, which can call another stored procedure, and so on.

Stored procedures allow for procedural programming. The basic *SQL DDL (Data Definition Language)*, *DML (Data Manipulation Language)*, and *DQL (Data Query Language)* statements (CREATE TABLE, INSERT, UPDATE, SELECT, and so on) allow you the opportunity to tell the database what needs to be done, but not how to do it. By coding stored procedures, you tell the database engine how to go about processing the data.

A *stored procedure* is a group of one or more SQL statements or functions that are stored in the database, compiled, and ready to be executed by a database user. A *stored function* is the same as a stored procedure, but a function returns a value.

Functions are called by procedures. When a function is called by a procedure, parameters can be passed into a function like a procedure, a value is computed, and then the value is passed back to the calling procedure for further processing.

When a stored procedure is created, the various subprograms and functions that compose the stored procedure are actually stored in the database. These stored procedures are preparsed and are immediately ready to execute when the user invokes them.

The MySQL syntax for creating a stored procedure is as follows:

```
CREATE [ OR REPLACE ] PROCEDURE PROCEDURE_NAME
[ (ARGUMENT [{IN | OUT | IN OUT} ] TYPE,
ARGUMENT [{IN | OUT | IN OUT} ] TYPE) ] { AS}
PROCEDURE_BODY
```

The Microsoft SQL Server syntax for creating a stored procedure is as follows:

```
CREATE PROCEDURE PROCEDURE_NAME
[ [(] @PARAMETER_NAME
DATATYPE [(LENGTH) | (PRECISION] [, SCALE ])
[ = DEFAULT ][ OUTPUT ]]
[, @PARAMETER_NAME
DATATYPE [(LENGTH) | (PRECISION [, SCALE ])
[ = DEFAULT ][ OUTPUT ]] [)]]
[ WITH RECOMPILE ]
AS SQL_STATEMENTS
```

The syntax for Oracle is as follows:

```
CREATE [ OR REPLACE ] PROCEDURE PROCEDURE_NAME
[ (ARGUMENT [{IN | OUT | IN OUT} ] TYPE,
ARGUMENT [{IN | OUT | IN OUT} ] TYPE) ] {IS | AS}
PROCEDURE_BODY
```

An example of a simple stored procedure to insert new rows into the
PRODUCTS_TBL table is as follows:

```
CREATE PROCEDURE NEW_PRODUCT
(PROD_ID IN VARCHAR2, PROD_DESC IN VARCHAR2, COST IN NUMBER)
AS
BEGIN
  INSERT INTO PRODUCTS_TBL
  VALUES (PROD_ID, PROD_DESC, COST);
  COMMIT;
END;
Procedure created.
```

The syntax for executing a stored procedure in Microsoft SQL Server is as
follows:

```
EXECUTE [ @RETURN_STATUS = ]
PROCEDURE_NAME
[[@PARAMETER_NAME = ] VALUE |
[@PARAMETER_NAME = ] @VARIABLE [ OUTPUT ]]
[WITH RECOMPILE]
```

The syntax for Oracle is as follows:

```
EXECUTE [ @RETURN STATUS =] PROCEDURE NAME
[[ @PARAMETER NAME = ] VALUE | [ @PARAMETER NAME = ] @VARIABLE [ OUTPUT ]]]
[ WITH RECOMPILE ]
```

The syntax for MySQL is as follows:

```
CALL PROCEDURE_NAME([PARAMETER[,.......]])
```

> **Basic SQL Commands Are Often the Same**
>
> You might find distinct differences between the allowed syntax used to code
> proce-dures in different implementations of SQL. The basic SQL commands
> should be the same, but the programming constructs (variables, conditional
> statements, cursors, loops) might vary drastically among implementations.

Now execute the procedure you have created:

```
CALL NEW_PRODUCT ('9999','INDIAN CORN',1.99);
PL/SQL procedure successfully completed.
```

Stored procedures provide several distinct advantages over individual SQL
statements exe-cuted in the database. Some of these advantages include
the following:

▶ The statements are already stored in the database.

▶ The statements are already parsed and in an executable format.

▶ Stored procedures support modular programming.

▶ Stored procedures can call other procedures and functions.

▶ Stored procedures can be called by other types of programs.

▶ Overall response time is typically better with stored procedures.

▶ Stored procedures increase the overall ease of use.

Triggers

A *trigger* is a compiled SQL procedure in the database that performs actions based on other actions occurring within the database. A trigger is a form of a stored procedure that is executed when a specified DML action is performed on a table. The trigger can be executed before or after an INSERT, DELETE, or UPDATE statement. Triggers can also check data integrity before an INSERT, DELETE, or UPDATE statement. Triggers can roll back transactions, and they can modify data in one table and read from another table in another database.

Triggers, for the most part, are very good functions to use; they can, however, cause more I/O overhead. Triggers should not be used when a stored procedure or a program can accomplish the same results with less overhead.

The CREATE TRIGGER Statement

You can create a trigger using the CREATE TRIGGER statement.

The ANSI standard syntax is

```
CREATE TRIGGER TRIGGER NAME
[[BEFORE | AFTER] TRIGGER EVENT ON TABLE NAME]
[REFERENCING VALUES ALIAS LIST]
[TRIGGERED ACTION
TRIGGER EVENT::=
INSERT | UPDATE | DELETE [OF TRIGGER COLUMN LIST]
TRIGGER COLUMN LIST ::= COLUMN NAME [,COLUMN NAME]
VALUES ALIAS LIST ::=
VALUES ALIAS LIST ::=
OLD [ROW] ´ OLD VALUES CORRELATION NAME |
NEW [ROW] ´ NEW VALUES CORRELATION NAME |
OLD TABLE ´ OLD VALUES TABLE ALIAS |
NEW TABLE ´ NEW VALUES TABLE ALIAS
OLD VALUES TABLE ALIAS ::= IDENTIFIER
NEW VALUES TABLE ALIAS ::= IDENTIFIER
TRIGGERED ACTION ::=
```

```
[FOR EACH [ROW | STATEMENT] [WHEN SEARCH CONDITION]]
TRIGGERED SQL STATEMENT
TRIGGERED SQL STATEMENT ::=
SQL STATEMENT | BEGIN ATOMIC [SQL STATEMENT;]
END
```

The MySQL syntax to create a trigger is as follows:

```
CREATE [DEFINER={user | CURRENT_USER }]
TRIGGER TRIGGER_NAME
{BEFORE | AFTER }
{ INSERT | UPDATE | DELETE [, ..]}
ON TABLE_NAME
AS
SQL_STATEMENTS
```

The Microsoft SQL Server syntax to create a trigger is as follows:

```
CREATE TRIGGER TRIGGER_NAME
ON TABLE_NAME
FOR { INSERT | UPDATE | DELETE [, ..]}
AS
SQL_STATEMENTS
[ RETURN ]
```

The basic syntax for Oracle is as follows:

```
CREATE [ OR REPLACE ] TRIGGER TRIGGER_NAME
[ BEFORE | AFTER]
[ DELETE | INSERT | UPDATE]
ON [ USER.TABLE_NAME ]
[ FOR EACH ROW ]
[ WHEN CONDITION ]
[ PL/SQL BLOCK ]
```

The following is an example trigger written in the Oracle syntax:

```
CREATE TRIGGER EMP_PAY_TRIG
AFTER UPDATE ON EMPLOYEE_PAY_TBL
FOR EACH ROW
BEGIN
  INSERT INTO EMPLOYEE_PAY_HISTORY
  (EMP_ID, PREV_PAY_RATE, PAY_RATE, DATE_LAST_RAISE,
   TRANSACTION_TYPE)
  VALUES
  (:NEW.EMP_ID, :OLD.PAY_RATE, :NEW.PAY_RATE,
   :NEW.DATE_LAST_RAISE, 'PAY CHANGE');
END;
/
Trigger created.
```

The preceding example shows the creation of a trigger called EMP_PAY_TRIG. This trigger inserts a row into the EMPLOYEE_PAY_HISTORY table, reflecting the changes made every time a row of data is updated in EMPLOYEE_PAY_TBL.

Did You Know?

> **Triggers Cannot Be Altered**
>
> You cannot alter the body of a trigger. You must either replace or re-create the trigger. Some implementations allow a trigger to be replaced (if the trigger with the same name already exists) as part of the CREATE TRIGGER statement.

The DROP TRIGGER Statement

You can drop a trigger using the DROP TRIGGER statement. The syntax for dropping a trigger is as follows:

```
DROP TRIGGER TRIGGER_NAME
```

The FOR EACH ROW Statement

Triggers in MySQL also have another piece of syntax that allows them to be scoped. The FOR EACH ROW syntax allows the developer to have the procedure fire for each row that is affected by the SQL statement or once for the statement as a whole. The syntax is as follows:

```
CREATE TRIGGER TRIGGER_NAME
ON TABLE_NAME FOR EACH ROW SQL_STATEMENT
```

The difference is how many times the trigger is executed. If you create a regular trigger and execute a statement against the table that affects 100 rows, the trigger is executed once. If instead you create the trigger with the FOR EACH ROW syntax and execute the statement again, the trigger is executed 100 times—once for each row that the statement affects.

Dynamic SQL

Dynamic SQL allows a programmer or end user to create an SQL statement's specifics at runtime and pass the statement to the database. The database then returns data into the program variables, which are bound at SQL runtime.

To comprehend dynamic SQL, review static SQL. Static SQL is what this book has discussed thus far. A *static SQL statement* is written and not meant to be changed. Although static SQL statements can be stored as files ready to be executed later or as stored procedures in the database, static SQL does not quite offer the flexibility that is allowed with dynamic SQL.

The problem with static SQL is that even though numerous queries might be available to the end user, there is a good chance that none of these "canned" queries will satisfy the users' needs on every occasion. Dynamic SQL is often used by ad hoc query tools, which allow an SQL statement to be created on-the-fly by a user to satisfy the particular query requirements for that particular situation. After the statement is customized according to the user's needs, the statement is sent to the database, checked for syntax errors and privileges required to execute the statement, and compiled in the database where the database server carries out the statement. Dynamic SQL can be created by using a call-level interface, which is explained in the next section.

Dynamic SQL Is Not Always the Most Performant

Although dynamic SQL provides more flexibility for the end user's query needs, the performance might not compare to that of a stored procedure whose code has already been analyzed by the SQL optimizer.

Call-Level Interface

A *call-level interface (CLI)* embeds SQL code in a host program, such as ANSI C. Application programmers should be familiar with the concept of a CLI. It is one of the methods that allows a programmer to embed SQL in different procedural programming languages. When using a CLI, you simply pass the text of an SQL statement into a variable using the rules of the host programming language. You can execute the SQL statement in the host program through the use of the variable into which you passed the SQL text.

EXEC SQL is a common host programming language command that enables you to call an SQL statement (CLI) from within the program.

The following are examples of programming languages that support CLI:

- ANSI C
- C#
- VB.NET
- Java

▶ Pascal

▶ Fortran

By the Way

> **CLIs Are Platform Specific**
>
> Refer to the syntax of the host programming language with which you are using CLI options. The CLI programming language is always platform specific. So an Oracle CLI will not work with an SQL Server CLI.

Using SQL to Generate SQL

Using SQL to generate SQL is a valuable time-budgeting method of writing SQL statements. Assume you have 100 users in the database already. A new role, ENABLE (a user-defined object that is granted privileges), has been created and must be granted to those 100 users. Instead of manually creating 100 GRANT statements, the following SQL statement generates each of those statements for you:

```
SELECT 'GRANT ENABLE TO '|| USERNAME||';'
FROM SYS.DBA_USERS;
```

This example uses Oracle's system catalog view (which contains information for users).

Notice the use of single quotation marks around GRANT ENABLE TO. The use of single quotation marks allows whatever is between the marks (including spaces) to be literal. Remember that literal values can be selected from tables, the same as columns from a table. USERNAME is the column in the system catalog table SYS.DBA_USERS. The double pipe signs (||) concatenate the columns. The use of double pipes followed by ; concatenates the semicolon to the end of the username, thus completing the statement.

The results of the SQL statement look like the following:

```
GRANT ENABLE TO RRPLEW;
GRANT ENABLE TO RKSTEP;
```

You should spool these results to a file, which can be sent to the database. The database, in turn, executes each SQL statement in the file, saving you many keystrokes and much time. The GRANT ENABLE TO USERNAME statement is repeated once for every user in the database.

The next time you are writing SQL statements and have repeated the same statement several times, allow your imagination to take hold, and let SQL do the work for you.

Direct Versus Embedded SQL

Direct SQL is where an SQL statement is executed from some form of an interactive terminal. The SQL results are returned directly to the terminal that issued the statement. Most of this book has focused on direct SQL. Direct SQL is also referred to as *interactive invocation* or *direct invocation*.

Embedded SQL is SQL code used within other programs, such as Pascal, Fortran, COBOL, and C. SQL code is actually embedded in a host programming language, as discussed previously, with a call-level interface. Embedded SQL statements in host programming language codes are commonly preceded by EXEC SQL and terminated by a semicolon. Other termination characters include END-EXEC and the right parenthesis.

The following is an example of embedded SQL in a host program, such as the ANSI C language:

```
{HOST PROGRAMMING COMMANDS}
EXEC SQL {SQL STATEMENT};
{MORE HOST PROGRAMMING COMMANDS}
```

Windowed Table Functions

Windowed table functions allow calculations to operate over a window of the table and return a value based upon that window. This allows for the calculation of values such as a running sum, ranks, and moving averages. The syntax for the table valued function follows:

```
ARGUMENT OVER ([PARTITION CLAUSE] [ORDER CLAUSE] [FRAME CLAUSE])
```

Almost all aggregate functions can act as windowed table functions. They provide five new windowed table functions:

- ▶ RANK() OVER

- ▶ DENSE_RANK() OVER

- ▶ PERCENT_RANK() OVER

- ▶ CUME_DIST() OVER

- ▶ ROW_NUMBER() OVER

Normally, it would be difficult to calculate something such as an individual's ranking within his pay year. Windowed table function would make this calculation a little easier, as seen in the following example for Microsoft SQL Server:

```
SELECT EMP_ID, SALARY, RANK() OVER (PARTITION BY YEAR(DATE_HIRE)
ORDER BY SALARY DESC) AS RANK_IN_DEPT
FROM EMPLOYEE_PAY_TBL;
```

Not all RDBM implementations currently support windowed table functions, so it is best to check the documentation of your specific implementation.

Working with XML

The ANSI standard presented an XML-related features section in its 2003 version. Since then, most database implementations have tried to support at least part of the released feature set. For example, one part of the ANSI standard is to provide for the output of XML-formatted output from a query. SQL Server provides such a method by using the FOR XML statement, as shown in the following example:

```
SELECT EMP_ID, HIRE_DATE, SALARY FROM
EMPLOYEE_TBL FOR XML AUTO
```

Another important feature of the XML feature set is being able to retrieve information from an XML document or fragment. MySQL provides this functionality through the EXTRACTVALUE function. This function takes two arguments. The first is an XML fragment, and the second is the locator, which returns the first value of the tags matched by the string. The syntax is shown here:

```
ExtractValue([XML Fragment],[locator string])
```

The following is an example of using the function to extract the value in the node a:

```
SELECT EXTRACTVALUE('<a>Red</a><b>Blue</b>','/a') as ColorValue;
ColorValue
Red
```

It is important to check with your individual database's documentation to see exactly what XML support is provided. Some implementations, such as SQL Server and Oracle, have advanced functionality such as specific XML data types. For example, Oracle's XMLTYPE provides a specific API to handle the most used functions with XML data, such as finding and extracting values. Microsoft SQL Server's XML data type allows for the application of templates to ensure that the XML data input into the column is complete.

Summary

Some advanced SQL concepts were discussed in this hour. Although this hour did not go into a lot of detail, it did provide you with a basic understanding of how you can apply the fundamental concepts that you have learned up to this point. You start with cursors, which pass a data set selected by a query into a location in memory. After a cursor is declared in a program, you must open it for accessibility. Then the contents of the cursor are fetched into a variable, at which time the data can be used for program processing. The resultset for the cursor is contained in memory until the cursor is closed and the memory is deallocated.

Stored procedures and triggers were covered next. Stored procedures are basically SQL statements that are stored together in the database. These statements, along with other implementation-specific commands, are compiled in the database and are ready for a database user to execute at any given time. Stored procedures typically provide better performance benefits than individual SQL statements.

This chapter also discussed dynamic SQL, using SQL to generate other SQL statements, and the differences between direct SQL and embedded SQL. Dynamic SQL is SQL code that a user dynamically creates during runtime, unlike static SQL.

Lastly, we discussed Windowed Table Functions and XML. These features may not yet be supported in your database version because they are relatively new but are good to know for future reference. The concepts of some of the advanced topics discussed during this hour illustrate the application of SQL in an enterprise, covered in Hour 23, "Extending SQL to the Enterprise, the Internet, and the Intranet."

Q&A

Q. *Can a stored procedure call another stored procedure?*

A. Yes. The stored procedure being called is referred to as being nested.

Q. *How do I execute a cursor?*

A. Simply use the OPEN CURSOR statement. This sends the results of the cursor to a staging area.

Workshop

The following workshop is composed of a series of quiz questions and practical exercises. The quiz questions are designed to test your overall understanding of the current material. The practical exercises are intended to afford you the opportunity to apply the concepts discussed during the current hour, as well as build upon the knowledge acquired in previous hours of study. Please take time to complete the quiz questions and exercises before continuing. Refer to Appendix C, "Answers to Quizzes and Exercises," for answers.

Quiz

1. Can a trigger be altered?

2. When a cursor is closed, can you reuse the name?

3. Which command retrieves the results after a cursor has been opened?

4. Are triggers executed before or after an INSERT, DELETE, or UPDATE statement?

5. Which MySQL function retrieves information from an XML fragment?

6. Why do Oracle and MySQL not support the DEALLOCATE syntax for cursors?

7. Why is a cursor not considered a set-based operation?

Exercises

1. Enter a command similar to the one that follows for MySQL to write out SQL statements to DESCRIBE each table in the database:

   ```
   SELECT CONCAT('DESCRIBE ',TABLE_NAME,';') FROM TABLES_PRIV;
   ```

2. Write a SELECT statement that generates the SQL code to count all rows in each of your tables. (Hint: It is similar to Exercise 1.)

3. Write a series of SQL commands to create a cursor that prints each customer name and the customer's total sales. Ensure that the cursor is properly closed and deallocated based on which implementation you are using.

Extending SQL to the Enterprise, the Internet, and the Intranet

---

What You'll Learn in This Hour:

▶ SQL and the enterprise
▶ Front-end and back-end applications
▶ Accessing a remote database
▶ SQL and the Internet
▶ SQL and the intranet

The previous hour covered some advanced SQL topics. These topics build on earlier hours in the book and show you practical applications for the SQL you have learned. In this hour, you focus on the concepts behind extending SQL to the enterprise, which involve SQL applications and making data available to all appropriate members of a company for daily use.

SQL and the Enterprise

Many commercial enterprises have specific data available to other enterprises, customers, and vendors. For example, the enterprise might have detailed information on its products available for customers to access in hopes of acquiring more purchases. Enterprise employee needs are included as well. For example, employee-specific data can be made available, such as for timesheet logs, vacation schedules, training schedules, company policies, and so on. A database can be created, and customers and employees can be allowed easy access to an enterprise's important data via SQL and an Internet language.

The Back-End Application

The heart of any application is the back-end application. This is where things happen behind the scenes, transparent to the database end user. The *back-end application* includes the actual database server, the data sources, and the appropriate middleware that connects an application to the Web or a remote database on the local network.

Determining your database implementation is typically the first step in deploying any application, either to the enterprise through a *local area network (LAN)*, to the enterprise's own intranet, or to the Internet. *Deploying* describes the process of implementing an application in an environment that is available for use. The database server should be established by an onsite *database administrator (DBA)* who understands the company's needs and the application's requirements.

The middleware for the application includes a web server and a tool capable of connecting the web server to the database server. The main objective is to have an application that can communicate with a corporate database.

The Front-End Application

The *front-end application* is the part of an application with which an end user interacts. The front-end application is either a commercial, off-the-shelf software product that a company purchases or an application that is developed in-house using other third-party tools. Commercial software can include applications that utilize a web browser to display content. In the Web environment, web browsers such as Firefox and Internet Explorer are often used to access database applications. This allows users to have access to the database without having to install special software.

Did You Know?

> **There Are Many Different Layers to an Application**
>
> The front-end application promotes simplicity for the database end user. The underlying database, code, and events that occur within the database are transparent to the user. The front-end application is developed to relieve the end user from guesswork and confusion, which might otherwise be caused by having to be too intuitive to the system. The new technologies allow the applications to be more intuitive, enabling the end users to focus on the true aspects of their particular jobs, thereby increasing overall productivity.

The tools available for developers today are user friendly and object oriented, by way of icons, wizards, and dragging and dropping with the mouse. Some of the popular tools to port applications to the Web include Borland's

C++Builder and IntraBuilder and Microsoft's Visual Studio. Other popular applications used to develop corporate-based applications on a LAN include PowerBuilder by Powersoft, Oracle Forms by Oracle Corporation, Visual Studio by Microsoft, and Delphi by Borland.

Figure 23.1 illustrates the back-end and front-end components of a database application. The back end resides on the host server, where the database resides. Back-end users include developers, programmers, DBAs, system administrators, and system analysts. The front-end application resides on the client machine, which is typically each end user's PC. End users are the vast audience for the front-end component of an application, which can include users such as data entry clerks and accountants. The end user is able to access the back-end database through a network connection—either a LAN or a *wide area network (WAN)*. Some type of middleware (such as an ODBC driver) provides a connection between the front and back ends through the network.

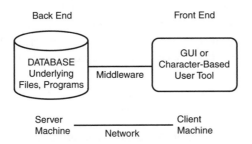

FIGURE 23.1
A database application.

Accessing a Remote Database

Sometimes the database you are accessing is a local one to which you are directly connected. For the most part, you will probably access some form of a remote database. A *remote database* is one that is nonlocal, or located on a server other than the server to which you are currently connected, meaning that you must utilize the network and some network protocol to interface with the database.

You can access a remote database in several ways. From a broad perspective, a remote database is accessed via the network or Internet connection using a middleware product. (Both ODBC and JDBC, standard middleware, are discussed in the next section.) Figure 23.2 shows three scenarios for accessing a remote database.

FIGURE 23.2
Scenarios for
accessing a
remote data-
base.

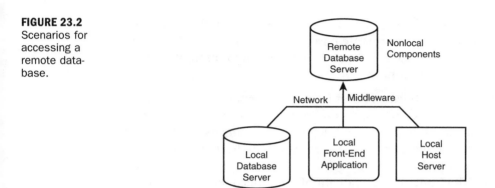

Local Components

Figure 23.2 shows access to a remote server from another local database server, a local front-end application, and a local host server. The local database server and local host server are often the same because the database normally resides on a local host server. However, you can usually connect to a remote database from a local server without a current local database connection. For the end user, the front-end application is the most typical method of remote database access. All methods must route their database requests through the network.

ODBC

Open Database Connectivity (ODBC) allows connections to remote databases through a library driver. A front-end application uses an *ODBC driver* to interface with a back-end database. A network driver might also be required for a connection to a remote database. An application calls the ODBC functions, and a driver manager loads the ODBC driver. The ODBC driver processes the call, submits the SQL request, and returns the results from the database.

As a part of ODBC, all the *relational database management system (RDBMS)* vendors have an *application programming interface (API)* with their database.

JDBC

JDBC is Java Database Connectivity. Like ODBC, JDBC allows connections to remote databases through a Java library driver. A front-end Java application uses the JDBC driver to interface with a back-end database.

OLE DB

OLE DB is a set of interfaces written using the *Component Object Model (COM)* by Microsoft as a replacement for ODBC. The implementation of OLE DB attempts to extend the feature set of ODBC and address connectivity not only to various database implementations but to nondatabase data stored such as spreadsheets.

Vendor Connectivity Products

In addition to drivers or an API, many vendors have their own products that allow a user to connect to a remote database. Each of these vendor products is specific to the particular vendor implementation and might not be portable to other types of database servers.

Oracle Corporation has a product called Oracle Fusion Middleware that allows connectivity to the Oracle database as well as other applications.

Microsoft produces several products for interacting with its database, such as Microsoft SharePoint Server and SQL Server Reporting Services.

Accessing a Remote Database Through a Web Interface

Accessing a remote database through a web interface is similar to accessing one through a local network. The main difference is that all requests to the database from the user are routed through the web server (see Figure 23.3).

You can see in Figure 23.3 that an end user accesses a database through a web interface by first invoking a web browser. The web browser connects to a particular URL, determined by the location of the web server. The web server authenticates user access and sends the user request, perhaps a query, to the remote database, which might also verify user authenticity. The database server then returns the results to the web server, which displays the results on the user's web browser. Using a firewall can control unauthorized access to a particular server.

Be Mindful of Security Concerns with the Internet

Be careful what information you make available on the Web. Always take precautions to properly implement security at all appropriate levels; that might include the web server, the host server, and the remote database. Be especially careful with Privacy Act data, such as individuals' Social Security numbers; protect that data, and don't broadcast it over the Web.

Watch
Out!

FIGURE 23.3
A web interface
to a remote
database.

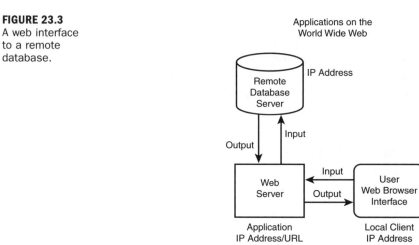

A *firewall* is a security mechanism that ensures against unauthorized connections to and from a server. One or multiple firewalls can be enabled to patrol access to a database or server.

Additionally, certain database implementations allow you to restrict access to them via IP address. This provides another layer of protection, because you can limit your traffic that has access to the database to the actual set of web servers that are acting as the application layer.

SQL and the Internet

You can embed SQL or use it in conjunction with programming languages such as C# and Java. You can also embed SQL in Internet programming languages, such as Java and ASP.NET. Text from *Hypertext Markup Language (HTML)*, another Internet language, can be translated into SQL to send a query to a remote database from a Web front end. After the database resolves the query, the output is translated back into HTML and displayed on the web browser of the individual executing the query. The following sections discuss the use of SQL on the Internet.

Making Data Available to Customers Worldwide

With the advent of the Internet, data became available to customers and vendors worldwide. The data is normally available for read-only access through a front-end tool.

The data that is available to customers can contain general customer information, product information, invoice information, current orders, back orders, and other pertinent information. Private information, such as corporate strategies and employee information, should not be available.

Home web pages on the Internet have become nearly a necessity for companies that want to keep pace with their competition. A web page is a powerful tool that can tell surfers all about a company—its services, products, and other information—with little overhead.

Making Data Available to Employees and Privileged Customers

A database can be made accessible, through the Internet or a company's intranet, to employees or its customers. Using Internet technologies is a valuable communication asset for keeping employees informed about company policies, benefits, training, and so on. However, you must be careful when making information available to web users. Confidential corporate or individual information should not be accessible on the Web if possible. Additionally, only a subset, or copy of a subset of a database, should be accessible online. The main production database(s) should be protected at all costs.

Internet Security Is a Far Less Stable Platform

Database security is much more stable than security on the Internet because database security can be fine-tuned down to the specific levels of the data contained in the system. Although you can implement some security features for data access through the Internet, these are generally limited and not as easily changed as those on the database. Always be sure to use the security features available to you through your database server.

Did You Know?

SQL and the Intranet

IBM originally created SQL for use between databases located on mainframe computers and the users on client machines. The users were connected to the mainframes via a LAN. SQL was adopted as the standard language of communication between databases and users. An *intranet* is basically a small Internet. The main difference is that an *intranet* is for a single organization's use, whereas the Internet is accessible to the general public. The user (client) interface in an intranet remains the same as that in a client/server environment. SQL requests are routed through the web server and languages (such as HTML) before being directed to the database for evaluation. An intranet is primarily used for inner-corporate applications, documents, forms, web pages, and email.

SQL requests made through the Internet must be extremely cognizant of performance. In these scenarios, not only must the data be retrieved from the database, but it must be presented to the user through her browser. This normally involves transforming the data into some kind of HTML-compliant code to be displayed on the user's browser. The web connection might be slower than a normal intranet connection; therefore, the sending of the data back and forth might be slower as well.

Security should play an important role in a database implementation that is exposed via the web. A couple of considerations must be taken into account to ensure that your data is protected. First, if the data is exposed over public networks, you must try to ensure that the data is protected from outside sources that may try to pick up that traffic. Normally, data is transferred in plain text format so that anyone can read it. You might consider as part of your security implementation use of *Secure Socket Layer (SSL)* to protect the communication. This method uses a certificate to encrypt the data between the client and the application and is typically identified by a website beginning with HTTPS, with the *S* on the end standing for secure.

Another typical consideration is protecting against unintended data entry through data validation. This can be simply from the user or application entering the wrong type of data into the wrong field or something more nefarious such as an SQL injection attack, where a hacker tries to inject his own SQL code onto the database to be run.

The best way to protect against these types of problems is to restrict access for the user accounts accessing the database from the application. A good way to accomplish this is trying to use stored procedures and functions whenever possibly for the calls against the database. This gives you more control over how the data gets out of the system and how the data gets in. Additionally, it allows you to perform whatever data validation steps may be necessary from the DBA's point of view to ensure that the data remains consistent.

Summary

Some concepts behind deploying SQL and database applications to the Internet were discussed in this hour. Companies need to remain competitive. To keep up with the rest of the world, it has proven beneficial—almost mandatory—to obtain a presence on the World Wide Web. In establishing this presence, applications must be developed and even migrated from client/server systems to the Internet on a web server. One of the greatest concerns when publishing any kind or any amount of corporate data on the Web is security. Security must be considered, adhered to, and strictly enforced.

This hour discussed accessing remote databases across local networks as well as over the Internet. Each major method for accessing any type of a remote database requires the use of the network and protocol adapters used to translate requests to the database. This has been a broad overview of the application of SQL over local networks, company intranets, and the Internet. After digesting a few quiz and exercise questions, you should be ready to venture into the last hour of your journey through SQL.

Q&A

Q. *Why is it important to know if your data is accessed over a public network via the Internet?*

A. The data that is sent between a client and a web application is often just plain text. That means that anyone could intercept the traffic and be able to see exactly what the individual saw, such as sensitive data like Social Security numbers or account numbers. You need to encrypt data whenever possible.

Q. *Is a back-end database for a web application any different from a back-end database for a client/server system?*

A. The back-end database itself for a web application is not necessarily different from that of a client/server system. However, other requirements must be met to implement a web-based application. For example, a web server is used to access the database with a web application. With a web application, end users do not typically connect directly to the database.

Workshop

The following workshop is composed of a series of quiz questions and practical exercises. The quiz questions are designed to test your overall understanding of the current material. The practical exercises are intended to afford you the opportunity to apply the concepts discussed during the current hour, as well as build upon the knowledge acquired in previous hours of study. Please take time to complete the quiz questions and exercises before continuing. Refer to Appendix C, "Answers to Quizzes and Exercises," for answers.

Quiz

1. Can a database on a server be accessed from another server?

2. What can a company use to disseminate information to its own employees?

3. Products that allow connections to databases are called what?

4. Can SQL be embedded into Internet programming languages?

5. How is a remote database accessed through a web application?

Exercises

1. Connect to the Internet and look at various companies' home pages. If your own company has a home page, compare it to the competition's home pages. Ask yourself these questions about the pages:

   ▶ Does any of the page content appear to be dynamic?

   ▶ What pages or areas on pages might be data from a back-end database?

   ▶ Do there appear to be security mechanisms on the web page? Can a login be entered to access data that might be stored in a database?

   ▶ Most modern browsers enable you to view the source code of the page returned. Use your web browser to view the source code. Is there any code that would give you a hint as to what the back-end database is?

   ▶ If you uncovered any information in the page's code, such as a server name or a database username, would you consider this a security flaw?

2. Visit the following websites and browse through the content, latest technologies, and companies' use of data on the Web (data that appears to be derived from a database):

- ▶ www.amazon.com
- ▶ www.informit.com
- ▶ www.mysql.com
- ▶ www.oracle.com
- ▶ www.ebay.com
- ▶ www.google.com

HOUR 24

Extensions to Standard SQL

What You'll Learn in This Hour:

▶ Various implementations
▶ Differences between implementations
▶ Compliance with ANSI SQL
▶ Interactive SQL statements
▶ Using variables
▶ Using parameters

This hour covers extensions to *American National Standards Institute (ANSI)*-standard SQL. Although most implementations conform to the standard, many vendors have provided extensions to standard SQL through various enhancements.

Various Implementations

Numerous SQL implementations are released by various vendors. All the relational database vendors could not possibly be mentioned; a few of the leading implementations, however, are discussed. The implementations discussed here are MySQL, Microsoft SQL Server, and Oracle. Other popular vendors providing database products include Sybase, IBM, Informix, Progress, PostgreSQL, and many more.

Differences Between Implementations

Although the implementations listed here are relational database products, there are specific differences between each. These differences stem from the design of the product and the way data is handled by the database engine; however, this book concentrates on the SQL aspect of the differences. All implementations use SQL as the language for communicating with the database, as directed by ANSI. Many have some sort of extension to SQL that is unique to that particular implementation.

> **Vendors Purposely Break with the ANSI Standard**
>
> Differences in SQL have been adopted by various vendors to enhance ANSI SQL for performance considerations and ease of use. Vendors also strive to make enhancements that provide them with advantages over other vendors, making their implementation more attractive to the customer.

Now that you know SQL, you should have little problem adjusting to the differences in SQL among the various vendors. In other words, if you can write SQL in a Sybase implementation, you should be able to write SQL in Oracle. Besides, knowing SQL for various vendors improves your résumé.

The following sections compare the SELECT statement's syntax from a few major vendors to the ANSI standard.

The following is the ANSI standard:

```
SELECT [DISTINCT ] [* | COLUMN1 [, COLUMN2 ]
FROM TABLE1 [, TABLE2 ]
[ WHERE SEARCH_ CONDITION ]
GROUP BY [ TABLE_ALIAS | COLUMN1 [, COLUMN2 ]
[ HAVING SEARCH_CONDITION ]]
[ ALL ]
[ CORRESPONDING [ BY (COLUMN1 [, COLUMN2 ]) ]
QUERY_SPEC | SELECT * FROM TABLE | TABLE_CONSTRUCTOR ]
[ORDER BY SORT_LIST ]
```

The following is the syntax for Microsoft SQL Server:

```
[WITH <COMMON_TABLE_EXPRESSION>]
SELECT [DISTINCT][*| COLUMN1 [, COLUMN2, .. ]
[INTO NEW_TABLE]
FROM TABLE1 [, TABLE2 ]
[WHERE SEARCH_CONDITION]
GROUP BY [COLUMN1, COLUMN2,... ]
[HAVING SEARCH_CONDITION]
[ {UNION | INTERSECT | EXCEPT} ][ ALL ]
[ ORDER BY SORT_LIST ]
[ OPTION QUERY_HINT ]
```

The following is the syntax for Oracle:

```
SELECT [ ALL | DISTINCT ] COLUMN1 [, COLUMN2 ]
FROM TABLE1 [, TABLE2 ]
[ WHERE SEARCH_CONDITION ]
[[ START WITH SEARCH_CONDITION ]
```

```
CONNECT BY SEARCH_CONDITION ]
[ GROUP BY COLUMN1 [, COLUMN2 ]
[ HAVING SEARCH_CONDITION ]]
[{UNION [ ALL ] | INTERSECT | MINUS} QUERY_SPEC ]
[ ORDER BY COLUMN1 [, COLUMN2 ]]
[ NOWAIT ]
```

As you can see by comparing the syntax examples, the basics are there. All have the SELECT, FROM, WHERE, GROUP BY, HAVING, UNION, and ORDER BY clauses. Each of these clauses works the same conceptually, but some have additional options that might not be found in other implementations. These options are called *enhancements*.

Compliance with ANSI SQL

Vendors do strive to comply with ANSI SQL; however, none is 100 percent ANSI SQL-standard. Some vendors have added commands or functions to ANSI SQL, and ANSI SQL has adopted many of these new commands or functions. It is beneficial for a vendor to comply with the standard for many reasons. One obvious benefit to standard compliance is that the vendor's implementation will be easy to learn, and the SQL code used is portable to other implementations. Portability is definitely a factor when a database is being migrated from one implementation to another.

For a database to be considered ANSI compliant, however, it only needs to correspond to a small subset of the functionality of the ANSI standard. The ANSI standard is written by a coalition of database companies. Therefore, most implementations are considered ANSI compliant even though their SQL implementations might vary widely between one another. Limiting your code to only strict ANSI-compliant statements would improve portability but would most likely severely limit database performance. So, in the end, you need to balance the demands of portability with the performance needs of your users. It is often best to forgo a lot of portability to ensure that your applications are taking advantage of the specific platform you are using to its full extent.

Extensions to SQL

Practically all the major vendors have an extension to SQL. An SQL extension is unique to a particular implementation and is generally not portable between implementations. However, popular standard extensions are reviewed by ANSI and are sometimes implemented as part of the new standard.

PL/SQL, which is a product of Oracle Corporation, and Transact-SQL, which is used by both Sybase and Microsoft SQL Server, are two examples of robust SQL extensions. Both extensions are discussed in relative detail for the examples during this hour.

Example Extensions

Both PL/SQL and Transact-SQL are considered fourth-generation programming languages. Both are procedural languages, whereas SQL is a nonprocedural language. We also briefly discuss MySQL.

The nonprocedural language SQL includes statements such as the following:

▶ INSERT

▶ UPDATE

▶ DELETE

▶ SELECT

▶ COMMIT

▶ ROLLBACK

An SQL extension considered a procedural language includes all the preceding statements, commands, and functions of standard SQL. In addition, extensions include statements such as

▶ Variable declarations

▶ Cursor declarations

▶ Conditional statements

▶ Loops

▶ Error handling

▶ Variable assignment

▶ Date conversions

▶ Wildcard operators

▶ Triggers

▶ Stored procedures

These statements allow the programmer to have more control over the way data is handled in a procedural language.

Transact-SQL

Transact-SQL is a procedural language used by Microsoft SQL Server, which means you tell the database how and where to find and manipulate data. SQL is nonprocedural, and the database decides how and where to select and manipulate data. Some highlights of Transact-SQL's capabilities include declaring local and global variables, cursors, error handling, triggers, stored procedures, loops, wildcard operators, date conversions, and summarized reports.

An example Transact-SQL statement follows:

```
IF (SELECT AVG(COST) FROM PRODUCTS_TBL) > 50
BEGIN
  PRINT 'LOWER ALL COSTS BY 10 PERCENT.'
END
ELSE
  PRINT 'COSTS ARE REASONABLE.'
```

This is a simple Transact-SQL statement. It states that if the average cost in PRODUCTS_TBL is greater than 50, the text LOWER ALL COSTS BY 10 PERCENT. will be printed. If the average cost is less than or equal to 50, the text COSTS ARE REASONABLE. will be printed.

Notice the use of the IF...ELSE statement to evaluate conditions of data values. The PRINT command is also a new command. These additional options are not even a drop in the bucket of Transact-SQL capabilities.

SQL Is Not Considered a Procedural Language

Standard SQL is primarily a *nonprocedural language*, which means that you issue statements to the database server. The database server decides how to optimally execute the statement. *Procedural languages* allow the programmer to request the data to be retrieved or manipulated and to tell the database server exactly how to carry out the request.

Did You Know?

PL/SQL

PL/SQL is Oracle's extension to SQL. Like Transact-SQL, PL/SQL is a procedural language. PL/SQL is structured in logical blocks of code. A PL/SQL block contains three sections, two of which are optional. The first section is the DECLARE section, which is optional. The DECLARE section contains variables, cursors, and constants. The second section is called the PROCEDURE section and is mandatory. The PROCEDURE section contains the conditional commands and SQL statements. This section is where the block is controlled. The third section is called the EXCEPTION section, and it is optional. The EXCEPTION section defines the way the program should handle errors and user-defined exceptions. Highlights of PL/SQL include the use of variables, constants, cursors, attributes, loops, handling exceptions, displaying output to the programmer, transactional control, stored procedures, triggers, and packages.

An example PL/SQL statement follows:

```
DECLARE
  CURSOR EMP_CURSOR IS SELECT EMP_ID, LAST_NAME, FIRST_NAME, MIDDLE_NAME
                       FROM EMPLOYEE_TBL;
  EMP_REC EMP_CURSOR%ROWTYPE;
BEGIN
  OPEN EMP_CURSOR;
  LOOP
    FETCH EMP_CURSOR INTO EMP_REC;
    EXIT WHEN EMP_CURSOR%NOTFOUND;
    IF (EMP_REC.MIDDLE_NAME IS NULL) THEN
      UPDATE EMPLOYEE_TBL
      SET MIDDLE_NAME = 'X'
      WHERE EMP_ID = EMP_REC.EMP_ID;
      COMMIT;
    END IF;
  END LOOP;
  CLOSE EMP_CURSOR;
END;
```

Two out of the three sections are being used in this example: the DECLARE section and the PROCEDURE section. First, a cursor called EMP_CURSOR is defined by a query. Second, a variable called EMP_REC is declared, whose values have the same data type (%ROWTYPE) as each column in the defined cursor. The first step in the PROCEDURE section (after BEGIN) is to open the cursor. After the cursor is opened, you use the LOOP command to scroll through each record of the cursor, which is eventually terminated by END LOOP. Update EMPLOYEE_TBL for all rows in the cursor. If the middle initial of an employee is NULL, the update sets the middle initial to 'X'. Changes are committed, and the cursor is eventually closed.

MySQL

MySQL is a multiuser, multithreaded SQL database client/server implementation. It consists of a server daemon, a terminal monitor client program, and several client programs and libraries. The main goals of MySQL are speed, robustness, and ease of use. MySQL was originally designed to provide faster access to large databases.

MySQL is often considered one of the more ANSI-compliant database implementations. From its beginnings, MySQL has been part of a semi-open-source development environment that has deliberately tried to maintain close adherence to the ANSI standards. Since version 5.0, MySQL has been available in both the open-source Community Edition as well as the closed-source Enterprise Edition. In 2009, MySQL was acquired as part of a deal in which Oracle bought Sun Microsystems, which was the original owner of the platform.

Currently, MySQL does not contain major extensions like Oracle or Microsoft SQL Server, but with its recent acquisition, this might change in the near future. To be certain, check your version's documentation for specific extensions that may become available.

Interactive SQL Statements

Interactive SQL statements ask you for a variable, parameter, or some form of data before fully executing. Say you have an SQL statement that is interactive. The statement is used to create users in a database. The SQL statement could prompt you for information such as user ID, name of user, and phone number. The statement could be for one or many users and is executed only once. Otherwise, each user has to be entered individually with the CREATE USER statement. The SQL statement could also prompt you for privileges. Not all vendors have interactive SQL statements; you must check your particular implementation.

Another interesting aspect of using interactive SQL statements is the ability to employ parameters. *Parameters* are variables that are written in SQL and reside within an application. Parameters can be passed into an SQL statement during runtime, allowing more flexibility for the user executing the statement. Many of the major implementations allow use of these parameters. The following sections show examples of passing parameters for Oracle and SQL Server.

Parameters in Oracle can be passed into an otherwise static SQL statement, as the following code shows:

```
SELECT EMP_ID, LAST_NAME, FIRST_NAME
FROM EMPLOYEE_TBL
WHERE EMP_ID = '&EMP_ID'
```

The preceding SQL statement returns the EMP_ID, LAST_NAME, and FIRST_NAME for whatever EMP_ID you enter at the prompt. The next statement prompts you for the city and the state. The query returns all data for those employees living in the city and state that you entered.

```
SELECT *
FROM EMPLOYEE_TBL
WHERE CITY = '&CITY'
AND STATE = '&STATE'
```

Parameters in Microsoft SQL Server can also be passed into a stored procedure:

```
CREATE PROC EMP_SEARCH
(@EMP_ID)
AS
SELECT LAST_NAME, FIRST_NAME
FROM EMPLOYEE_TBL
WHERE EMP_ID = @EMP_ID
```

Type the following to execute the stored procedure and pass a parameter:

```
SP_EMP_SEARCH "443679012"
```

Summary

This hour discussed extensions to standard SQL among vendors' implementations and their compliance with the ANSI standard. After you learn SQL, you can easily apply your knowledge—and your code—to other implementations of SQL. SQL is portable between vendors; implementations can use most SQL code with a few minor modifications.

The last part of this hour was spent showing two specific extensions used by three implementations. Microsoft SQL Server and Sybase use Transact-SQL, and Oracle uses PL/SQL. You should have seen some similarities between Transact-SQL and PL/SQL. One thing to note is that these two implementations have first sought their compliance with the standard, and then added enhancements to their implementations for better overall functionality and efficiency. Also discussed was MySQL, which was designed to increase performance for large database queries. This hour's intent was to make you aware that many SQL extensions do exist and to teach the importance of a vendor's compliance to the ANSI SQL standard.

If you take what you have learned in this book and apply it (build your code, test it, and build upon your knowledge), you are well on your way to mastering SQL. Companies have data and cannot function without databases. Relational databases are everywhere—and because SQL is the standard language with which to communicate and administer a relational database, you have made an excellent decision by learning SQL. Good luck!

Q&A

Q. Why do variations in SQL exist?

A. Variations in SQL exist among the various implementations because of the way data is stored, because of the various vendors' ambition for trying to get an advantage over competition, and because of new ideas that surface.

Q. After learning basic SQL, will I be able to use SQL in different implementations?

A. Yes. However, remember that there are differences and variations between the implementations. The basic framework for SQL is the same among most implementations.

Workshop

The following workshop is composed of a series of quiz questions and practical exercises. The quiz questions are designed to test your overall understanding of the current material. The practical exercises are intended to afford you the opportunity to apply the concepts discussed during the current hour, as well as build upon the knowledge acquired in previous hours of study. Please take time to complete the quiz questions and exercises before continuing. Refer to Appendix C, "Answers to Quizzes and Exercises," for answers.

Quiz

1. Is SQL a procedural or nonprocedural language?

2. What are the three basic operations of a cursor, outside of declaring the cursor?

3. Procedural or nonprocedural: With which does the database engine decide how to evaluate and execute SQL statements?

Exercises

1. Research the SQL variations among the various vendors. Go to the following websites and review the implementations of SQL that are available:

www.oracle.com

www.sybase.com

www.microsoft.com

www.mysql.com

www.informix.com

www.pgsql.com

www.ibm.com

APPENDIX A

Common SQL Commands

This appendix details some of the most common SQL commands that you will use. As we have stated throughout the book, check your database documentation, because some of the statements vary depending upon your implementation.

SQL Statements

ALTER TABLE

```
ALTER TABLE TABLE_NAME
[MODIFY | ADD | DROP]
   [COLUMN COLUMN_NAME][DATATYPE|NULL NOT NULL] [RESTRICT|CASCADE]
[ADD | DROP]   CONSTRAINT CONSTRAINT_NAME]
```

Description: Alters a table's columns.

COMMIT

```
COMMIT [ TRANSACTION ]
```

Description: Saves a transaction to the database.

CREATE INDEX

```
CREATE INDEX INDEX_NAME
ON TABLE_NAME (COLUMN_NAME)
```

Description: Creates an index on a table.

CREATE ROLE

```
CREATE ROLE ROLE NAME
[ WITH ADMIN [CURRENT_USER | CURRENT_ROLE]]
```

Description: Creates a database role to which system and object privileges can be granted.

CREATE TABLE

```
CREATE TABLE TABLE_NAME
( COLUMN1      DATA_TYPE      [NULL|NOT NULL],
  COLUMN2      DATA_TYPE      [NULL|NOT NULL])
```

Description: Creates a database table.

CREATE TABLE AS

```
CREATE TABLE TABLE_NAME AS
SELECT COLUMN1, COLUMN2,...
FROM TABLE_NAME
[ WHERE CONDITIONS ]
[ GROUP BY COLUMN1, COLUMN2,...]
[ HAVING CONDITIONS ]
```

Description: Creates a database table based on another table.

CREATE TYPE

```
CREATE TYPE typename AS OBJECT
( COLUMN1      DATA_TYPE      [NULL|NOT NULL],
  COLUMN2      DATA_TYPE      [NULL|NOT NULL])
```

Description: Creates a user-defined type that can define columns in a table.

CREATE USER

```
CREATE USER username IDENTIFIED BY password
```

Description: Creates a user account in the database.

CREATE VIEW

```
CREATE VIEW AS
SELECT COLUMN1, COLUMN2,...
FROM TABLE_NAME
[ WHERE CONDITIONS ]
[ GROUP BY COLUMN1, COLUMN2,... ]
[ HAVING CONDITIONS ]
```

Description: Creates a view of a table.

DELETE

```
DELETE
FROM TABLE_NAME
[ WHERE CONDITIONS ]
```

Description: Deletes rows of data from a table.

DROP INDEX

```
DROP INDEX INDEX_NAME
```

Description: Drops an index on a table.

DROP TABLE

```
DROP TABLE TABLE_NAME
```

Description: Drops a table from the database.

DROP USER

```
DROP USER user1 [, user2, ...]
```

Description: Drops a user account from the database.

DROP VIEW

```
DROP VIEW VIEW_NAME
```

Description: Drops a view of a table.

GRANT

```
GRANT PRIVILEGE1, PRIVILEGE2, ... TO USER_NAME
```

Description: Grants privileges to a user.

INSERT

```
INSERT INTO TABLE_NAME [ (COLUMN1, COLUMN2,...]
VALUES ('VALUE1','VALUE2',...)
```

Description: Inserts new rows of data into a table.

INSERT...SELECT

```
INSERT INTO TABLE_NAME
SELECT COLUMN1, COLUMN2
FROM TABLE_NAME
[ WHERE CONDITIONS ]
```

Description: Inserts new rows of data into a table based on data in another table.

REVOKE

```
REVOKE PRIVILEGE1, PRIVILEGE2, ... FROM USER_NAME
```

Description: Revokes privileges from a user.

ROLLBACK

```
ROLLBACK [ TO SAVEPOINT_NAME ]
```

Description: Undoes a database transaction.

SAVEPOINT

```
SAVEPOINT SAVEPOINT_NAME
```

Description: Creates transaction savepoints in which to roll back if necessary.

SELECT

```
SELECT [ DISTINCT ] COLUMN1, COLUMN2,...
FROM TABLE1, TABLE2,...
[ WHERE CONDITIONS ]
[ GROUP BY COLUMN1, COLUMN2,...]
[ HAVING CONDITIONS ]
[ ORDER BY COLUMN1, COLUMN2,...]
```

Description: Returns data from one or more database tables; used to create queries.

UPDATE

```
UPDATE TABLE_NAME
SET COLUMN1 = 'VALUE1',
    COLUMN2 = 'VALUE2',...
[ WHERE CONDITIONS ]
```

Description: Updates existing data in a table.

SQL Clauses

SELECT

```
SELECT *
SELECT COLUMN1, COLUMN2,...
SELECT DISTINCT (COLUMN1)
SELECT COUNT(*)
```

Description: Defines columns to display as part of query output.

FROM

```
FROM TABLE1, TABLE2, TABLE3,...
```

Description: Defines tables from which to retrieve data.

WHERE

```
WHERE COLUMN1 = 'VALUE1'
  AND COLUMN2 = 'VALUE2'
...
WHERE COLUMN1 = 'VALUE1'
   OR COLUMN2 = 'VALUE2'
...
WHERE COLUMN IN ('VALUE1' [, 'VALUE2'] )
```

Description: Defines conditions (criteria) placed on a query for data to be returned.

GROUP BY

```
GROUP BY GROUP_COLUMN1, GROUP_COLUMN2,...
```

Description: Divides output into logical groups; a form of sorting operation.

HAVING

```
HAVING GROUP_COLUMN1 = 'VALUE1'
   AND GROUP_COLUMN2 = 'VALUE2'
...
```

Description: Places conditions on the GROUP BY clause; similar to the WHERE clause.

ORDER BY

```
ORDER BY COLUMN1, COLUMN2,...
ORDER BY 1,2,...
```

Description: Sorts a query's results.

APPENDIX B

Using the Databases for Exercises

The instructions for installing MySQL, Microsoft SQL Server, and Oracle have been included in this appendix for your convenience for the Windows operating system. MySQL and Oracle are available on other operating systems as well, such as MacOS and Linux. These instructions are accurate as of the date this book was written. Neither the authors nor Sams Publishing place any warranties on the software or the software support. For any installation problems or to inquire about software support, refer to the particular implementation's documentation or contact customer support for the implementation.

By the Way

MySQL Install Instructions

You might want to review the current documentation for MySQL. To get to the online documentation, go to www.mysql.com and look under the Products category link on the MySQL.com tab for the link to the documentation.

Windows Installation Instructions for MySQL

Use the following instructions if you are installing MySQL on a computer with Microsoft Windows:

1. Go to www.mysql.com to download MySQL. WinZip, or an equivalent program, is required to unzip the download.

2. Select the Downloads (GA) tab on the website.

3. Select the latest stable version, currently MySQL Community Server 5.5.8. Find the appropriate msi download for your machine, and download it.

4. Double-click the msi to start the installation process. Click Next on the welcome screen shown in Figure B.1.

FIGURE B.1
MySQL
Installation wel-
come screen.

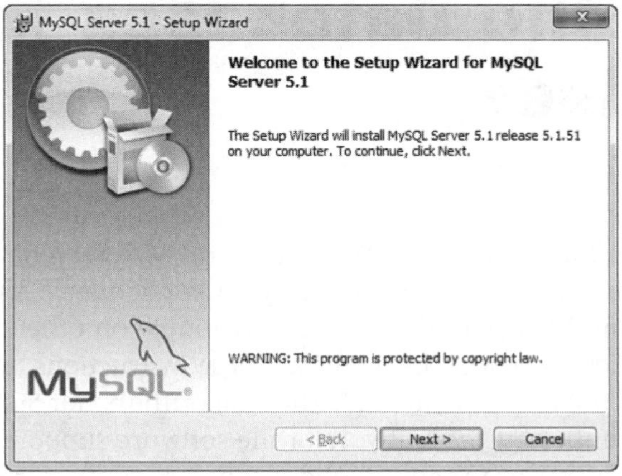

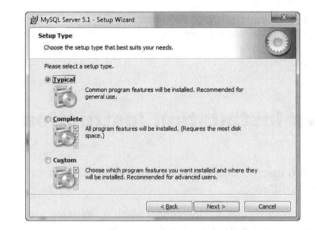

5. Select the Typical installation option shown in Figure B.2, and click Next.

FIGURE B.2
MySQL installa-
tion selection.

6. Select Install on the next screen to start the installation of the application.

7. After installation has completed successfully, click Next to complete the Setup Wizard.

8. On the Wizard Completed screen shown in Figure B.3, select the check box to configure your installed instance. Then click Finish. It

is much simpler to use the Configuration Wizard than try to manually configure yourself.

9. Select Next on the MySQL Server Instance Configuration Wizard screen.

10. Select the option to Reconfigure Instance, and click Next. The Reconfigure Instance option sets up a new instance.

11. Choose Standard Configuration, and click Next.

12. Check the box to include a path in your Windows installation to the MySQL application, and click Next. This enables you to run MySQL from the command line without having to know its exact installation path.

13. Check Modify Security Settings. Enter and confirm a root (administrator) password, and click Next as shown in Figure B.4.

14. Click Execute, and the configuration update begins.

If all the preceding steps were successful, you are ready to use MySQL for exercises in this book.

If you experience problems during the installation, uninstall MySQL and repeat steps 1–14. If you are still unable to obtain or install MySQL, contact MySQL for support and check the support forums at http://forums.mysql.com.

FIGURE B.4
MySQL security
configuration.

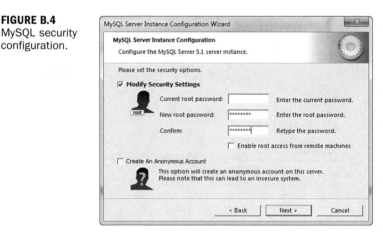

Windows Installation Instructions for Oracle

Use the following instructions if you are installing Oracle on a computer with Microsoft Windows:

By the
Way

Oracle Install Instructions

You might want to review the current documentation for Oracle. To access the online documentation, go to www.oracle.com and look under Products and Services for the link to the documentation.

---

1. Go to www.oracle.com and download the appropriate installation package for your machine from the Downloads tab. You will be using the Oracle 10g Express Edition for the examples in this book because this is the free version of the application.

2. Double-click the installation file to start the installation, and on the first screen click Next.

3. Click to agree to the license agreement, and click Next.

4. Select the default installation and install location on the screen shown in Figure B.5, and click Next.

5. Enter and confirm a password for the SYSTEM (administrator) account, as shown in Figure B.6, and select Next.

6. Click Install on the next screen. The installation process begins.

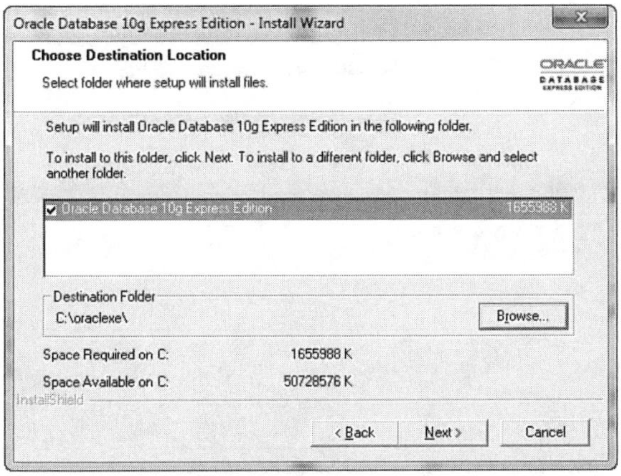

FIGURE B.5
Oracle installation location.

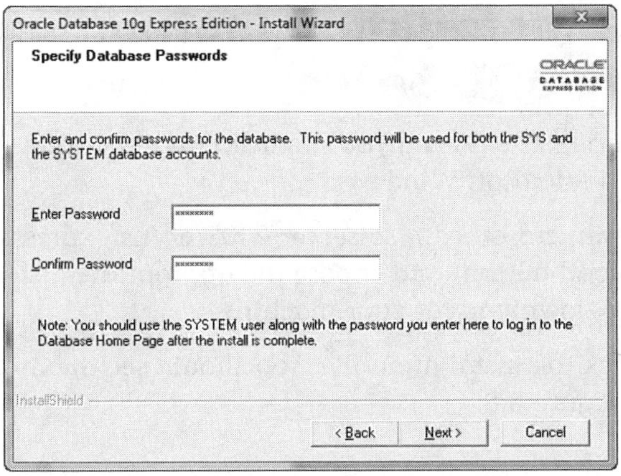

FIGURE B.6
Setting the system password.

If your installation is successful, you should see the completion screen shown in Figure B.7.

If all the preceding steps were successful, you are ready to use Oracle for exercises in this book.

If you experience problems during the installation, uninstall Oracle and repeat steps 1–6. If you are still unable to obtain or install Oracle, contact Oracle for support, and check the community support forums located on www.oracle.com.

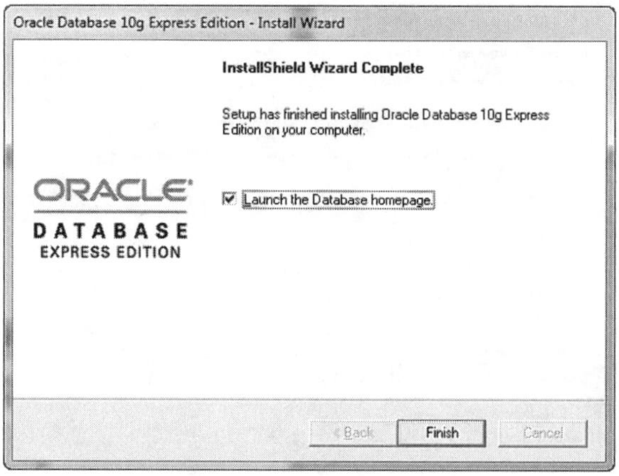

FIGURE B.7
Oracle installation completion screen.

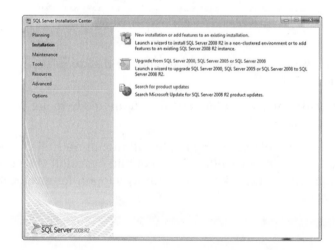

Windows Installation Instructions for Microsoft SQL Server

Use the following instructions if you are installing Microsoft SQL Server on a computer with Microsoft Windows:

1. Go to www.microsoft.com/sqlserver/2008/en/us/express.aspx, click the Download button, and choose the appropriate installation package to download for your machine.

2. Double-click the installation file. You should see the initial screen shown in Figure B.8.

FIGURE B.8
SQL Server initial installation screen.

3. Select the new installation option from the choices in the right pane, as shown in Figure B.9. This begins installing some setup and support files that are used during the main installation.

Microsoft SQL Server Install Instructions

You might want to review the current documentation for Microsoft SQL Server. To get to the online documentation, go to www.microsoft.com/sqlserver/2008/en/us/default.aspx and look under the Product Information tab for the link to the documentation.

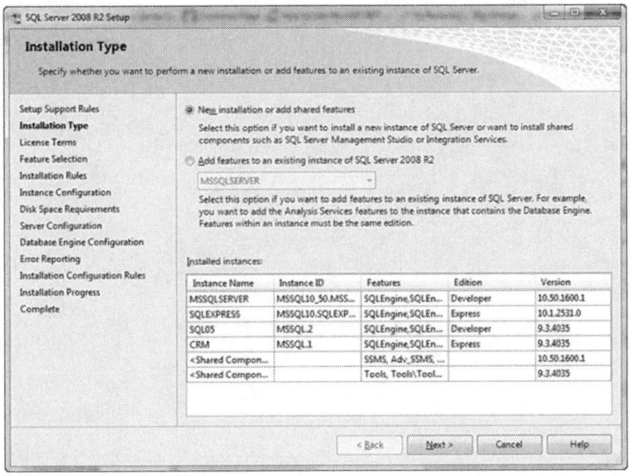

By the Way

FIGURE B.9
SQL Server installation selection screen.

4. Leave the radio button selected for a new installation, and click Next.

5. Accept the license terms, and click Next.

6. Select all of the features, and click Next.

7. Select Default instance, and click Next.

8. Click Next on the disk space requirements screen.

9. On the Database Engine Configuration screen, click the Add Current User button to add yourself as an administrator of the instance, and then click Next.

10. Click Next on the Error Reporting screen.

11. Click Next on the Installation Configuration Rules page to begin the installation.

If all the preceding steps were successful, you should see a completion screen. You will be ready to use Microsoft SQL Server for exercises in this book.

If you experience problems during the installation, uninstall SQL Server and repeat steps 1–11. If you are still unable to obtain or install Microsoft SQL Server, refer to the Microsoft website at www.microsoft.com.

APPENDIX C

Answers to Quizzes and Exercises

Hour 1, "Welcome to the World of SQL"

Quiz Answers

1. What does the acronym SQL stand for?

   A. SQL stands for Structured Query Language.

2. What are the six main categories of SQL commands?

   A. Data Definition Language (DDL)

   Data Manipulation Language (DML)

   Data Query Language (DQL)

   Data Control Language (DCL)

   Data administration commands (DAC)

   Transactional control commands (TCC)

3. What are the four transactional control commands?

   A. `COMMIT`
   `ROLLBACK`
   `SAVEPOINT`
   `SET TRANSACTIONS`

4. What is the main difference between client/server and web technologies as they relate to database access?

   A. The connection to the database is the main difference. Using the client to connect means you log on to the server directly to access the database. When using the Web, you log on to the Internet to reach the database.

5. If a field is defined as NULL, does something have to be entered into that field?

> **A.** No. If a column is defined as NULL, nothing has to be in the column. If a column is defined as NOT NULL, something *does* have to be entered.

Exercise Answers

1. Identify the categories in which the following SQL commands fall:

```
CREATE TABLE
DELETE
SELECT
INSERT
ALTER TABLE
UPDATE
```

> **A.** CREATE TABLE—DDL, Data Definition Language
>
> DELETE—DML, Data Manipulation Language
>
> SELECT—DQL, Data Query Language
>
> INSERT—DML, Data Manipulation Language
>
> ALTER TABLE—DDL, Data Definition Language
>
> UPDATE—DML, Data Manipulation Language

2. Study the following tables, and pick out the column that would be a good candidate for the primary key.

EMPLOYEE_TBL	INVENTORY_TBL	EQUIPMENT_TBL
name	item	model
phone	description	year
start date	quantity	serial number
address	item number	equipment number
employee number	location assigned to	

A. The primary key for EMPLOYEE_TBL is the employee number. Each employee is assigned a unique employee number. Employees could have the same name, phone, start date, and address.

The primary key for INVENTORY_TBL is the item number. The other columns could be duplicated.

The primary key for EQUIPMENT_TBL is the equipment number. Once again, the other columns could be duplicated.

3. No answer required.

Hour 2, "Defining Data Structures"

Quiz Answers

1. True or false: An individual's Social Security number, entered in the format '111111111', can be any of the following data types: constant length character, varying length character, or numeric.

   A. True, as long as the precision is the correct length.

2. True or false: The scale of a numeric value is the total length allowed for values.

   A. False. The precision is the total length, where the scale represents the number of places reserved to the right of a decimal point.

3. Do all implementations use the same data types?

   A. No. Most implementations differ in their use of data types. The data types prescribed by ANSI are adhered to but might differ among implementations according to storage precautions taken by each vendor.

4. What are the precision and scale of the following?

   ```
   DECIMAL(4,2)
   DECIMAL(10,2)
   DECIMAL(14,1)
   ```

   A. DECIMAL(4,2)—Precision = 4, scale = 2

   DECIMAL(10,2)—Precision = 10, scale = 2

   DECIMAL(14,1)—Precision = 14, scale = 1

5. Which numbers could be inserted into a column whose data type is DECIMAL(4,1)?

   a. 16.2

   b. 116.2

   c. 16.21

   d. 1116.2

   e. 1116.21

   A. The first three fit, although 16.21 is rounded off to 16.2. The numbers 1116.2 and 1116.21 exceed the maximum precision, which was set at 4.

6. What is data?

   A. Data is a collection of information stored in a database as one of several different data types.

Exercise Answers

1. Take the following column titles, assign them to a data type, decide on the proper length, and give an example of the data you would enter into that column.

   A. SSN—Constant-length character; '111111111'

   STATE—Varying-length character; 'INDIANA'

   CITY—Varying-length character; 'INDIANAPOLIS'

   PHONE_NUMBER—Constant-length character; '(555)555-5555'

   ZIP—Constant-length character; '46113'

   LAST_NAME—Varying-length character; 'JONES'

   FIRST_NAME—Varying-length character; 'JACQUELINE'

   MIDDLE_NAME—Varying-length character; 'OLIVIA'

   SALARY—Numeric data type; 30000

   HOURLY_PAY_RATE—Decimal; 35.00

   DATE_HIRED—Date; '01/01/2007'

2. Take the same column titles and decide if they should be NULL or NOT NULL, realizing that in some cases where a column would normally be NOT NULL, the column could be NULL or vice versa, depending on the application.

A. SSN—NOT NULL
STATE—NOT NULL
CITY—NOT NULL
PHONE_NUMBER—NULL
ZIP—NOT NULL
LAST_NAME—NOT NULL
FIRST_NAME—NOT NULL
MIDDLE_NAME—NULL
SALARY—NULL
HOURLY_PAY_RATE—NULL
DATE_HIRED—NOT NULL

2. Some individuals might not have a phone (however rare that might be), and not everyone has a middle name, so these columns should allow NULL values. In addition, not all employees are paid an hourly rate.

3. No answer required.

Hour 3, "Managing Database Objects"

Quiz Answers

1. Does the following CREATE TABLE statement work? If not, what needs to be done to correct the problem(s)? Are there limitations as to what database implementation it works in (MySQL, Oracle, SQL Server)?

```
CREATE TABLE EMPLOYEE_TABLE AS:
( SSN           NUMBER(9)     NOT NULL,
LAST_NAME     VARCHAR2(20)  NOT NULL,
FIRST_NAME    VARCHAR(20)   NOT NULL,
MIDDLE_NAME   VARCHAR2(20)  NOT NULL,
ST ADDRESS    VARCHAR2(20)  NOT NULL,
CITY          CHAR(20)      NOT NULL,
STATE         CHAR(2)       NOT NULL,
ZIP           NUMBER(4)     NOT NULL,
DATE HIRED    DATE);
```

A. The CREATE TABLE statement does not work because there are several errors in the syntax. The corrected statement follows and is given as an Oracle-specific version. A listing of what was incorrect follows a corrected statement.

```
CREATE TABLE EMPLOYEE_TABLE
  ( SSN           NUMBER()      NOT NULL,
  LAST_NAME       VARCHAR2(20)  NOT NULL,
  FIRST_NAME      VARCHAR2(20)  NOT NULL,
  MIDDLE_NAME     VARCHAR2(20),
  ST_ADDRESS      VARCHAR2(30)  NOT NULL,
  CITY            VARCHAR2(20)  NOT NULL,
  STATE           CHAR(2)       NOT NULL,
  ZIP             NUMBER(5)     NOT NULL,
  DATE_HIRED      DATE );
```

The following needs to be done:

1. The AS: should not be in this CREATE TABLE statement.

2. A comma is missing after the NOT NULL for the LAST_NAME column.

3. The MIDDLE_NAME column should be NULL because not everyone has a middle name.

4. The column ST ADDRESS should be ST_ADDRESS. With two words, the database looked at ST as being the column name, which would make the database look for a valid data type, where it would find the word ADDRESS.

5. The CITY column works, although it would be better to use the VARCHAR2 data type. If all city names were a constant length, CHAR would be okay.

6. The STATE column is missing a left parenthesis.

7. The ZIP column length should be (5), not (4).

8. The DATE HIRED column should be DATE_HIRED with an underscore to make the column name one continuous string.

2. Can you drop a column from a table?

A. Yes. However, even though it is an ANSI standard, you must check your particular implementation to see if it has been accepted.

3. What statement would you issue to create a primary key constraint on the preceding EMPLOYEE_TABLE?

> **A.** ALTER TABLE EMPLOYEE_TBL
> ADD CONSTRAINT EMPLOYEE_PK PRIMARY KEY(SSN);

4. What statement would you issue on the preceding EMPLOYEE_TABLE to allow the MIDDLE_NAME column to accept NULL values?

> **A.** ALTER TABLE EMPOYEE_TBL
> MODIFY MIDDLE_NAME VARCHAR(20), NOT NULL;

5. What statement would you use to restrict the people added into the preceding EMPLOYEE_TABLE to only reside in the state of New York ('NY')?

> **A.** ALTER TABLE EMPLOYEE_TBL
> ADD CONSTRAINT CHK_STATE CHECK(STATE='NY');

6. What statement would you use to add an auto-incrementing column called 'EMPID' to the preceding EMPLOYEE_TABLE using both the MySQL and SQL Server syntax?

> **A.** ALTER TABLE EMPLOYEE_TBL
> ADD COLUMN EMPID INT AUTO_INCREMENT;

Exercise Answers

No answer required.

Hour 4, "The Normalization Process"

Quiz Answers

1. True or false: Normalization is the process of grouping data into logical related groups.

> **A.** True.

2. True or false: Having no duplicate or redundant data in a database, and having everything in the database normalized, is always the best way to go.

> **A.** False. Not always; normalization can and does slow performance because more tables must be joined, which results in more I/O and CPU time.

3. True or false: If data is in the third normal form, it is automatically in the first and second normal forms.

   A. True.

4. What is a major advantage of a denormalized database versus a normalized database?

   A. The major advantage is improved performance.

5. What are some major disadvantages of denormalization?

   A. Having redundant and duplicate data takes up valuable space; it is harder to code, and much more data maintenance is required.

6. How do you determine if data needs to be moved to a separate table when normalizing your database?

   A. If the table has redundant groups of data, this data would be a candidate to remove into a separate table.

7. What are the disadvantages of overnormalizing your database design?

   A. Overnormalization can lead to excess CPU and memory utilization, which can put excess strain on the server.

Exercise Answers

1. You are developing a new database for a small company. Take the following data and normalize it. Keep in mind that there would be many more items for a small company than you are given here.

   Employees:

   Angela Smith, secretary, 317-545-6789, RR 1 Box 73, Greensburg, Indiana, 47890, $9.50 hour, date started January 22, 1996, SSN is 323149669.

   Jack Lee Nelson, salesman, 3334 N. Main St., Brownsburg, IN, 45687, 317-852-9901, salary of $35,000.00 year, SSN is 312567342, date started 10/28/95.

   Customers:

   Robert's Games and Things, 5612 Lafayette Rd., Indianapolis, IN, 46224, 317-291-7888, customer ID is 432A.

Reed's Dairy Bar, 4556 W 10th St., Indianapolis, IN, 46245, 317-271-9823, customer ID is 117A.

Customer Orders:

Customer ID is 117A, date of last order is February 20, 1999, the product ordered was napkins, and the product ID is 661.

A.

```
Employees         Customers        Orders
SSN               CUSTOMER ID      CUSTOMER ID
NAME              NAME             PRODUCT ID
STREET ADDRESS    STREET ADDRESS   PRODUCT
CITY              CITY             DATE ORDERED
STATE             STATE
ZIP  ZIP
PHONE NUMBER      PHONE NUMBER
SALARY
HOURLY PAY
START DATE
POSITION
```

2. No answer required.

Hour 5, "Manipulating Data"

Quiz Answers

1. Use the EMPLOYEE_TBL with the following structure:

```
           Column        data type      (not)null
last_name    varchar2(20)     not null
first_name   varchar2(20)     not null
ssn          char(9)          not null
phone        number(10)       null
LAST_NAME    FIRST_NAME     SSN            PHONE
SMITH        JOHN           312456788      3174549923
ROBERTS      LISA           232118857      3175452321
SMITH        SUE            443221989      3178398712
PIERCE       BILLY          310239856      3176763990
```

What would happen if the following statements were run?

a. INSERT INTO EMPLOYEE_TBL
    (''JACKSON', 'STEVE', '313546078', '3178523443');

A. The INSERT statement does not run because the keyword VALUES is missing in the syntax.

b. INSERT INTO EMPLOYEE_TBL VALUES
('JACKSON', 'STEVE', '313546078', '3178523443');

A. One row would be inserted into the EMPLOYEE_TBL.

c. INSERT INTO EMPLOYEE_TBL VALUES
('MILLER', 'DANIEL', '230980012', NULL);

A. One row would be inserted into the EMPLOYEE_TBL, with a NULL value in the PHONE column.

d. INSERT INTO EMPLOYEE_TBL VALUES
('TAYLOR', NULL, '445761212', '3179221331');

A. The INSERT statement would not process because the FIRST_NAME column is NOT NULL.

e. DELETE FROM RMPLOYEE_TBL;

A. All rows in EMPLOYEE_TBL would be deleted.

f. DELETE FROM EMPLOYEE_TBL
WHERE LAST_NAME = 'SMITH';

A. All employees with the last name of SMITH would be deleted from EMPLOYEE_TBL.

g. DELETE FROM EMPLOYEE_TBL
WHERE LAST_NAME = 'SMITH'
AND FIRST_NAME = 'JOHN';

A. Only JOHN SMITH would be deleted from the EMPLOYEE_TBL.

h. UPDATE EMPLOYEE_TBL
SET LAST_NAME - 'CONRAD';

A. All last names would be changed to CONRAD.

i. UPDATE EMPLOYEE_TBL
SET LAST_NAME = 'CONRAD'
WHERE LAST_NAME = 'SMITH';

A. Both JOHN and SUE SMITH would now be JOHN and SUE CONRAD.

j. UPDATE EMPLOYEE_TBL
SET LAST_NAME = 'CONRAD',
FIRST_NAME = 'LARRY';

A. All employees are now LARRY CONRAD.

> **k.** UPDATE EMPLOYEE_TBL
> SET LAST_NAME = 'CONRAD',
> FIRST_NAME = 'LARRY'
> WHERE SSN = '312456788';

A. JOHN SMITH is now LARRY CONRAD.

Exercise Answers

1. No answer required.

2. Use PRODUCTS_TBL for the next exercise.

> **a.** Add the following products to the product table:

PROD_ID	PROD_DESC	COST
301	FIREMAN COSTUME	24.99
302	POLICEMAN COSTUME	24.99
303	KIDDIE GRAB BAG	4.99

A. INSERT INTO PRODUCTS_TBL VALUES
('301','FIREMAN COSTUME',24.99);
INSERT INTO PRODUCTS_TBL VALUES
('302','POLICEMAN COSTUME',24.99);
INSERT INTO PRODUCTS_TBL VALUES
('303','KIDDIE GRAB BAG',4.99);

> **b.** Write DML to correct the cost of the two costumes added. The cost should be the same as the witch costume.'

A. UPDATE PRODUCTS_TBL
SET COST = 29.99
WHERE PROD_ID = '301';

UPDATE PRODUCTS_TBL
SET COST = 29.99
WHERE PROD_ID = '302';

> **c.** Now we have decided to cut our product line, starting with the new products. Remove the three products you just added.

A. DELETE FROM PRODUCTS_TBL WHERE PROD_ID = '301';
DELETE FROM PRODUCTS_TBL WHERE PROD_ID = '302';
DELETE FROM PRODUCTS_TBL WHERE PROD_ID = '303';

> **d.** Before you executed the statements to remove the products you added, what should you have done to ensure that you only delete the desired rows?

A. To ensure that you are deleting exactly what you want to delete, you need to perform a SELECT statement using the same FROM and WHERE clause.

Hour 6, "Managing Database Transactions"

Quiz Answers

1. True or false: If you have committed several transactions, have several more transactions that have not been committed, and issue a ROLLBACK command, all your transactions for the same session are undone.

   A. False. When a transaction is committed, the transaction cannot be rolled back.

2. True or false: A SAVEPOINT command actually saves transactions after a specified number of transactions have executed.

   A. False. A SAVEPOINT is used only as a point for a ROLLBACK to return to.

3. Briefly describe the purpose of each one of the following commands: COMMIT, ROLLBACK, and SAVEPOINT.

   A. COMMIT saves changes made by a transaction. ROLLBACK undoes changes made by a transaction. SAVEPOINT creates logical points in the transaction to which to roll back.

4. What are some differences in the implementation of transactions in Microsoft SQL Server?

   A. SQL Server auto-commits statements unless specifically placed in a transaction and has a different syntax for SAVEPOINT. Also, it does not support the RELEASE SAVEPOINT command.

5. What are some performance implications when using transactions?

   A. Transactions have implications on temporary storage space because the database server has to keep track of all the changes until they are committed in case of a ROLLBACK.

Exercise Answers

1. Take the following transactions and create a SAVEPOINT or a SAVE TRANSACTION command after the first three transactions. Then create a ROLLBACK statement for your SAVEPOINT at the end. Try to determine what CUSTOMER_TBL will look like after you are done.

   A. ```
INSERT INTO CUSTOMER_TBL VALUES(615,'FRED WOLF','109 MEMORY
LANE','PLAINFIELD','IN',46113,'3175555555',NULL);
INSERT INTO CUSTOMER_TBL VALUES(559,'RITA THOMPSON',
'125PEACHTREE','INDIANAPOLIS','IN',46248,'3171111111',NULL);
INSERT INTO CUSTOMER_TBL VALUES(715,'BOB DIGGLER',
'1102 HUNTINGTON ST','SHELBY','IN',41234,'3172222222',NULL);
SAVEPOINT SAVEPOINT1;
UPDATE CUSTOMER_TBL SET CUST_NAME='FRED WOLF' WHERE
CUST_ID='559';
UPDATE CUSTOMER_TBL SET CUST_ADDRESS='APT C 4556 WATERWAY'
WHERE CUST_ID='615';
UPDATE CUSTOMER_TBL SET CUST_CITY='CHICAGO' WHERE CUST_ID='715';
ROLLBACK;
```

2. Take the following group of transactions and create a SAVEPOINT after the first three transactions.

   Then place a COMMIT statement at the end followed by a ROLLBACK statement to your SAVEPOINT. What do you think should happen?

   A.  ```
UPDATE CUSTOMER_TBL SET CUST_NAME='FRED WOLF' WHERE
CUST_ID='559';
UPDATE CUSTOMER_TBL SET CUST_ADDRESS='APT C 4556 WATERWAY'
WHERE CUST_ID='615';
UPDATE CUSTOMER_TBL SET CUST_CITY='CHICAGO' WHERE CUST_ID='715';
SAVEPOINT SAVEPOINT1;
DELETE FROM CUSTOMER_TBL WHERE CUST_ID='615';
DELETE FROM CUSTOMER_TBL WHERE CUST_ID='559';
DELETE FROM CUSTOMER_TBL WHERE CUST_ID='615';
COMMIT;
ROLLBACK;
```

Because the statement is committed, the ROLLBACK statement doesn't have an effect.

Hour 7, "Introduction to the Database Query"

Quiz Answers

1. Name the required parts for any SELECT statement.

    A. The SELECT and FROM keywords, also called clauses, are required for all SELECT statements.

2. In the WHERE clause, are single quotation marks required for all the data?

    A. No. Single quotation marks are required when selecting alphanumeric data types. Number data types do not require single quotation marks.

3. Under what part of the SQL language does the SELECT statement (database query) fall?

    A. The SELECT statement is considered Data Query Language.

4. Can multiple conditions be used in the WHERE clause?

    A. Yes. Multiple conditions can be specified in the WHERE clause of SELECT, INSERT, UPDATE, and DELETE statements. Multiple conditions are used with the operators AND and OR, which are thoroughly discussed in Hour 8, "Using Operators to Categorize Data."

5. What is the purpose of the DISTINCT option?

    A. The DISTINCT option suppresses the display of duplicates.

6. Is the ALL option required?

    A. No. Even though the ALL option can be used, it is not really required.

7. How are numeric characters treated when ordering based upon a character field?

    A. They are sorted as ASCII characters. This means that numbers would be ordered like this: 1, 12, 2, 222, 22222, 3, 33.

8. How does Oracle handle its default case sensitivity differently from MySQL and Microsoft SQL Server?

    A. Oracle by default performs matches as case sensitive.

Exercise Answers

1. Invoke your RDBMS query editor on your computer. Using your
   learnsql database, enter the following SELECT statements.
   Determine whether the syntax is correct. If the syntax is incorrect,
   make corrections to the code as necessary. We are using the
   EMPLOYEE_TBL here.

   a. SELECT EMP_ID, LAST_NAME, FIRST_NAME,
   FROM EMPLOYEE_TBL;

A. This SELECT statement does not work because there is a comma
after the FIRST_NAME column that does not belong there. The correct
syntax follows:

   a. SELECT EMP_ID, LAST_NAME, FIRST_NAME
   FROM EMPLOYEE_TBL;

   b. SELECT EMP_ID, LAST_NAME
   ORDER BY EMP_ID
   FROM EMPLOYEE_TBL;

A. This SELECT statement does not work because the FROM and ORDER BY
clauses are in the incorrect order. The correct syntax follows:

```
SELECT EMP_ID, LAST_NAME
FROM EMPLOYEE_TBL
ORDER BY EMP_ID;
```

   c. SELECT EMP_ID, LAST_NAME, FIRST_NAME
   FROM EMPLOYEE_TBL
   WHERE EMP_ID = '213764555'
   ORDER BY EMP_ID;

A. The syntax for this SELECT statement is correct.

   d. SELECT EMP_ID SSN, LAST_NAME
   FROM EMPLOYEE_TBL
   WHERE EMP_ID = '213764555'
   ORDER BY 1;

A. The syntax for this SELECT statement is correct. Notice that the
EMP_ID column is renamed SSN.

   e. SELECT EMP_ID, LAST_NAME, FIRST_NAME
   FROM EMPLOYEE_TBL
   WHERE EMP_ID = '213764555'
   ORDER BY 3, 1, 2;

A. The syntax for this SELECT statement is correct. Notice the order of the columns in the ORDER BY. This SELECT statement returns records from the database that are sorted by FIRST_NAME, and then by EMP_ID, and finally by LAST_NAME.

2. Does the following SELECT statement work?

```
SELECT LAST_NAME, FIRST_NAME, PHONE
FROM EMPLOYEE_TBL
WHERE EMP_ID = '333333333';
```

A. The syntax is correct and the statement worked, even though no data was returned. No data was returned because there was no row with an EMP_ID of 333333333.

3. Write a SELECT statement that returns the name and cost of each product from the PRODUCTS_TBL. Which product is the most expensive?

A. SELECT PROD_DESC,COST FROM PRODUCTS_TBL;

The witch costume is the most expensive.

4. Write a query that generates a list of all customers and their telephone numbers.

A. SELECT CUST_NAME,CUST_PHONE FROM CUSTOMER_TBL;

5. Answers will vary.

Hour 8, "Using Operators to Categorize Data"

Quiz Answers

1. True or false: Both conditions when using the OR operator must be TRUE.

A. False. Only one of the conditions must be TRUE.

2. True or false: All specified values must match when using the IN operator.

A. False. Only one of the values must match.

3. True or false: The AND operator can be used in the SELECT and the WHERE clauses.

A. False. The AND operator can only be used in the WHERE clause.

4. True or false: The ANY operator can accept an expression list.

A. False. The ANY operator cannot take an expression list.

5. What is the logical negation of the IN operator?

A. NOT IN.

6. What is the logical negation of the ANY and ALL operators?

A. <>ANY and <>ALL.

7. What, if anything, is wrong with the following SELECT statements?

    a.
```
SELECT SALARY
FROM EMPLOYEE_PAY_TBL
WHERE SALARY BETWEEN 20000, 30000;
```

A. The AND is missing between 20000, 30000. The correct syntax is
```
SELECT SALARY
FROM EMPLOYEE_PAY_TBL
WHERE SALARY BETWEEN 20000 AND 30000;
```

    b.
```
SELECT SALARY + DATE_HIRE
FROM EMPLOYEE_PAY_TBL;
```

A. The DATE_HIRE column is a DATE data type and is in the incorrect format for arithmetic functions.

    c.
```
SELECT SALARY, BONUS
FROM EMPLOYEE_PAY_TBL
WHERE DATE_HIRE BETWEEN 1999-09-22
AND 1999-11-23
AND POSITION = 'SALES'
OR POSITION = 'MARKETING'
AND EMP_ID LIKE '%55%';
```

A. The syntax is correct.

Exercise Answers

1. Using the following CUSTOMER_TBL, write a SELECT statement that returns customer IDs and customer names (alpha order) for customers who live in Indiana, Ohio, Michigan, and Illinois, and whose names begin with the letters A or B:

```
DESCRIBE CUSTOMER_TBL
Name                                 Null?      Type
------------------------------------ ---------- ------------
CUST_ID                              NOT NULL   VARCHAR (10)
CUST_NAME                            NOT NULL   VARCHAR (30)
CUST_ADDRESS                         NOT NULL   VARCHAR (20)
CUST_CITY                            NOT NULL   VARCHAR (12)
CUST_STATE                           NOT NULL   VARCHAR (2)
CUST_ZIP                             NOT NULL   VARCHAR (5)
CUST_PHONE                                      VARCHAR (10)
CUST_FAX                                        VARCHAR (10)
```

A. SELECT CUST_ID, CUST_NAME, CUST_STATE
   FROM CUSTOMER_TBL
   WHERE CUST_STATE IN ('IN', 'OH', 'MI', 'IL')
   AND CUST_NAME LIKE 'A%'
   OR CUST_NAME LIKE 'B%'
   ORDER BY CUST_NAME;

2. Using the following PRODUCTS_TBL, write a SELECT statement that returns the product ID, product description, and product cost. Limit the product cost to between $1.00 and $12.50:

```
DESCRIBE PRODUCTS_TBL
Name                                 Null?      Type
------------------------------------ ---------- ------------
PROD_ID                              NOT NULL   VARCHAR (10)
PROD_DESC                            NOT NULL   VARCHAR (25)
COST                                 NOT NULL   DECIMAL(6,2)
```

A. SELECT *
   FROM PRODUCTS_TBL
   WHERE COST BETWEEN 1.00 AND 12.50;

3. Assuming that you used the BETWEEN operator in Exercise 2, rewrite your SQL statement to achieve the same results using different operators. If you did not use the BETWEEN operator, do so now.

A. SELECT *
   FROM PRODUCTS_TBL
   WHERE COST >= 1.00 AND COST <= 12.50;

   SELECT *
   FROM PRODUCTS_TBL
   WHERE COST BETWEEN 1.00 AND 12.50;

4. Write a SELECT statement that returns products that are either less than 1.00 or greater than 12.50. There are two ways to achieve the same results.

A.
```
SELECT *
FROM PRODUCTS_TBL
WHERE COST < 1.00 OR COST > 12.50;

SELECT *
FROM PRODUCTS_TBL
WHERE COST NOT BETWEEN 1.00 AND 12.50;
```

Also keep in mind that BETWEEN is inclusive of the upper and lower values, whereas NOT BETWEEN is not inclusive.

5. Write a SELECT statement that returns the following information from PRODUCTS_TBL: product description, product cost, and 5% sales tax for each product. List the products in order from most to least expensive.

A.
```
SELECT PROD_DESC, COST, COST * .05
FROM PRODUCTS_TBL
ORDER BY COST DESC;
```

6. Write a SELECT statement that returns the following information from PRODUCTS_TBL: product description, product cost, 5% sales tax for each product, and total cost with sales tax. List the products in order from most to least expensive. There are two ways to achieve the same results. Try both.

A.
```
SELECT PROD_DESC, COST, COST * .05, COST + (COST * .05)
FROM PRODUCTS_TBL
ORDER BY COST DESC;

SELECT PROD_DESC, COST, COST * .05, COST * 1.05
FROM PRODUCTS_TBL
ORDER BY COST DESC;
```

7. Pick three items from the PRODUCTS table. Now write a query to return the rows of data from the table associated with those three items. Now rewrite the query to return everything but those three items. For your query, use combinations of equality operators and conjunctive operators.

A.
```
SELECT   *
    FROM PRODUCTS_TBL
    WHERE PROD_ID=11235
    OR   PROD_ID=119
OR   PROD_ID=13;

    SELECT   *
    FROM PRODUCTS_TBL
```

```
WHERE PROD_ID<>11235
AND  PROD_ID<>119
AND  PROD_ID<>13;
```

8. Rewrite the queries you wrote in Exercise 7 using the IN operator. Which statement is more efficient? Which one is more readable?

A.
```
SELECT *     FROM PRODUCT_TBL
    WHERE PROD_ID  IN (11235,119,13);
```

```
SELECT *
FROM PRODUCT_TBL
WHERE PROD_ID  IN (11235,119,13);
```

9. Write a query to return all the products that start with the letter *P*. Now write a query to return all products that *do not* start with the letter *P*.

A.
```
SELECT *
FROM PRODUCTS_TBL
                    WHERE PROD_DESC LIKE ('P%');
                    SELECT *
FROM PRODUCTS_TBL
                    WHERE PROD_DESC NOT LIKE ('P%');
```

Hour 9, "Summarizing Data Results from a Query"

Quiz Answers

1. True or False: The AVG function returns an average of all rows from a SELECT column, including any NULL values.

A. False. The NULL values are not considered.

2. True or False: The SUM function adds column totals.

A. False. The SUM function returns a total for a group of rows.

3. True or False: The COUNT(*) function counts all rows in a table.

A. True.

4. Do the following SELECT statements work? If not, what fixes the statements?

a.
```
SELECT COUNT *
FROM EMPLOYEE_PAY_TBL;
```

A. This statement does not work because the left and right parentheses are missing around the asterisk. The correct syntax is

```
SELECT COUNT(*)
FROM EMPLOYEE_PAY_TBL;
```

    b. `SELECT COUNT(EMP_ID), SALARY`
        `FROM EMPLOYEE_PAY_TBL`
        `GROUP BY SALARY;`

A. Yes, this statement works.

    c. `SELECT MIN(BONUS), MAX(SALARY)`
        `FROM EMPLOYEE_PAY_TBL`
        `WHERE SALARY > 20000;`

A. Yes, this statement works.

    d. `SELECT COUNT(DISTINCT PROD_ID) FROM PRODUCTS_TBL;`

A. Yes, this statement works.

    e. `SELECT AVG(LAST_NAME) FROM EMPLOYEE_TBL;`

A. No, this statement does not work because LAST_NAME needs to be a numeric value.

    f. `SELECT AVG(PAGER) FROM EMPLOYEE_TBL;`

A. Yes, this statement works with the current set of data in the database.

Exercise Answers

1. Use EMPLOYEE_PAY_TBL to construct SQL statements to solve the following exercises:

    a. What is the average salary?

A. The average salary is $30,000.00. The SQL statement to return the data is

```
SELECT AVG(SALARY)
FROM EMPLOYEE_PAY_TBL;
```

    b. What is the maximum bonus?

A. The maximum bonus is $2000.00. The SQL statement to return the data is

```
SELECT MAX(BONUS)
FROM EMPLOYEE_PAY_TBL;
```

c. What are the total salaries?

A. The sum of all the salaries is $90,000.00. The SQL statement to return the data is

```
SELECT SUM(SALARY)
FROM EMPLOYEE_PAY_TBL;
```

d. What is the minimum pay rate?

A. The minimum pay rate is $11.00 an hour. The SQL statement to return the data is

```
SELECT MIN(PAY_RATE)
FROM EMPLOYEE_PAY_TBL;
```

e. How many rows are in the table?

A. The total row count of the table is six. The SQL statement to return the data is

```
SELECT COUNT(*)
FROM EMPLOYEE_PAY_TBL;
```

2. Write a query to determine how many employees are in the company whose last names begin with a G.

A. We should get two employees using the following syntax:

```
SELECT COUNT(*)
FROM EMPLOYEE_TBL
WHERE LAST_NAME LIKE 'G%';
```

3. Write a query to determine the total dollar amount for all the orders in the system. Rewrite the query to determine the total dollar amount if we set the price of each item as $10.00.

A.
```
SELECT SUM(COST*QTY)
FROM ORDERS_TBL,PRODUCTS_TBL
WHERE ORDERS_TBL.PROD_ID=PRODUCTS_TBL.PROD_ID;
SELECT SUM(QTY) * 10
FROM ORDERS_TBL;
```

4. Write two sets of queries to find the first employee name and last employee name when they are listed in alphabetical order.

A. `SELECT MIN(LAST_NAME) AS LAST_NAME FROM EMPLOYEE_TBL;`

```
SELECT MAX(LAST_NAME) AS LAST_NAME
FROM EMPLOYEE_TBL;
```

5. Write a query to perform an AVG function on the employee names. Does the statement work? Determine why it is that you got that result.

   A. `SELECT AVG(LAST_NAME) AS LAST_NAME FROM EMPLOYEE_TBL;`

   It errors out because it is not a numeric value.

Hour 10, "Sorting and Grouping Data"

Quiz Answers

1. Will the following SQL statements work?

   a.
   ```
   SELECT SUM(SALARY), EMP_ID
   FROM EMPLOYEE_PAY_TBL
   GROUP BY 1 AND 2;
   ```

   A. No, this statement will not work. The and in the GROUP BY clause does not belong there, and you cannot use an integer in the GROUP BY clause. The correct syntax is
   ```
   SELECT SUM(SALARY), EMP_ID
   FROM EMPLOYEE_PAY_TBL
   GROUP BY SALARY, EMP_ID;
   ```

   b.
   ```
   SELECT EMP_ID, MAX(SALARY)
   FROM EMPLOYEE_PAY_TBL
   GROUP BY SALARY, EMP_ID;
   ```

   A. Yes, this statement will work.

   c.
   ```
   SELECT EMP_ID, COUNT(SALARY)
   FROM EMPLOYEE_PAY_TBL
   ORDER BY EMP_ID
   GROUP BY SALARY;
   ```

   A. No, this statement will not work. The ORDER BY clause and the GROUP BY clause are not in the correct sequence. Also, the EMP_ID column is required in the GROUP BY clause. The correct syntax is
   ```
   SELECT EMP_ID, COUNT(SALARY)
   FROM EMPLOYEE_PAY_TBL
   GROUP BY EMP_ID
   ORDER BY EMP_ID;
   ```

     d.
```
SELECT YEAR(DATE_HIRE) AS YEAR_HIRED,SUM(SALARY)
FROM EMPLOYEE_PAY_TBL
GROUP BY 1
HAVING SUM(SALARY)>20000;
```

      A. Yes, this statement will work.

2. True or false: You must also use the GROUP BY clause when using the HAVING clause.

     A. False. The HAVING clause can be used without a GROUP BY clause.

3. True or false: The following SQL statement returns a total of the salaries by groups:

```
SELECT SUM(SALARY)
FROM EMPLOYEE_PAY_TBL;
```

     A. False. The statement cannot return a total of the salaries by groups because there is no GROUP BY clause.

4. True or false: The columns selected must appear in the GROUP BY clause in the same order.

     A. False. The order of the columns in the SELECT clause can be in a different order in the GROUP BY clause.

5. True or false: The HAVING clause tells the GROUP BY which groups to include.

     A. True.

Exercise Answers

1. No answer required.

2. No answer required.

3. No answer required.

4. Modify the query in Exercise 3 by ordering the results in descending order, from highest count to lowest.

     A.
```
SELECT CITY, COUNT(*)FROM EMPLOYEE_TBL
GROUP BY CITY
ORDER BY 2 DESC;
```

5. Write a query to list the average pay rate by position from the EMPLOYEE_PAY_TBL table.

> **A.** ```
> SELECT POSITION, AVG(PAY_RATE)
> FROM EMPLOYEE_PAY_TBL
> GROUP BY POSITION;
> ```

6. Write a query to list the average salary by position from the EMPLOYEE_PAY_TBL table where the average salary is greater than 20000.

> **A.** ```
> SELECT POSITION, AVG(SALARY)
> FROM EMPLOYEE_PAY_TBL
> GROUP BY POSITION
> HAVING AVG(SALARY)>20000;
> ```

Hour 11, "Restructuring the Appearance of Data"

Quiz Answers

1. Match the descriptions with the possible functions.

> **A.**

Description	Function
a. Used to select a portion of a character string	SUBSTR
b. Used to trim characters from either the right or left of a string	LTRIM/RTRIM
c. Used to change all letters to lowercase	LOWER
d. Used to find the length of a string	LENGTH
e. Used to combine strings	||

2. True or false: Using functions in a SELECT statement to restructure the appearance of data in output also affects the way the data is stored in the database.

> **A.** False.

3. True or false: The outermost function is always resolved first when functions are embedded within other functions in a query.

   A. False. The innermost function is always resolved first when embedding functions within one another.

Exercise Answers

1. No answer required.

2. No answer required.

3. Write an SQL statement that lists employee email addresses. Email is not a stored column. The email address for each employee should be as follows:

```
FIRST.LAST @PERPTECH.COM
```

For example, John Smith's email address is
`JOHN.SMITH@PERPTECH.COM`.

   A. `SELECT CONCAT(FIRST_NAME, '.', LAST_NAME, '@PERPTECH.COM')`
   `FROM EMPLOYEE_TBL;`

4. Write an SQL statement that lists each employee's name and phone number in the following formats:

   a. The name should be displayed as SMITH, JOHN.

   b. The employee ID should be displayed as 999-99-9999.

   c. The phone number should be displayed as (999)999-9999.

   A. `SELECT CONCAT(LAST_NAME, ', ', FIRST_NAME),EMP_ID,`
   `CONCAT('(',SUBSTRING(PHONE,1,3),')',SUBSTRING(PHONE,4,3),'-',`
   `SUBSTRING(PHONE,7,4))`
   `FROM EMPLOYEE_TBL;`

Hour 12, "Understanding Dates and Times"

Quiz Answers

1. From where is the system date and time normally derived?

   A. The system date and time are derived from the current date and time of the operating system on the host machine.

2. What are the standard internal elements of a DATETIME value?

    A. YEAR, MONTH, DAY, HOUR, MINUTE, and SECOND.

3. What could be a major factor concerning the representation and comparison of date and time values if your company is an international organization?

    A. The awareness of time zones might be a concern.

4. Can a character string date value be compared to a date value defined as a valid DATETIME data type?

    A. A DATETIME data type cannot be accurately compared to a date value defined as a character string. The character string must first be converted to the DATETIME data type.

5. What would you use in SQL Server, MySQL, and Oracle to get the current date and time?

    A. NOW()

Exercise Answers

1. No answer required.

2. No answer required.

3. No answer required.

4. No answer required.

5. No answer required.

6. On what day of the week was each employee hired?

    A. Use the following statement to find the answer:
    ```
    SELECT EMP_ID, DAYNAME(DATE_HIRE)
    FROM EMPLOYEE_PAY_TBL;
    ```

7. What is today's Julian date (day of year)?

    A. Use the following statement to find the answer:
    ```
    SELECT DAYOFYEAR(CURRENT_DATE);
    ```

8. No answer required.

Hour 13, "Joining Tables in Queries"

Quiz Answers

1. What type of join would you use to return records from one table, regardless of the existence of associated records in the related table?

   A. You would use an outer join.

2. The JOIN conditions are located in what part of the SQL statement?

   A. The JOIN conditions are located in the WHERE clause.

3. What type of JOIN do you use to evaluate equality among rows of related tables?

   A. You would use an equijoin.

4. What happens if you select from two different tables but fail to join the tables?

   A. You receive a Cartesian product by not joining the tables (this is also called a cross join).

5. Use the following tables:

```
ORDERS_TBL
ORD_NUM       VARCHAR2(10)   NOT NULL      primary key
CUST_ID       VARCHAR2(10)   NOT NULL
PROD_ID       VARCHAR2(10)   NOT NULL
QTY           INTEGER        NOT NULL
ORD_DATE      DATE


PRODUCTS_TBL
PROD_ID       VARCHAR2(10)   NOT NULL      primary key
PROD_DESC     VARCHAR2(40)   NOT NULL
COST          DECIMAL(,2)    NOT NULL
```

   Is the following syntax correct for using an outer join?

```
SELECT C.CUST_ID, C.CUST_NAME, O.ORD_NUM
FROM CUSTOMER_TBL C, ORDERS_TBL O
WHERE C.CUST_ID(+) = O.CUST_ID(+)
```

   A. No, the syntax is not correct. The (+) operator should only follow the O.CUST_ID column in the WHERE clause. The correct syntax is

```
SELECT C.CUST_ID, C.CUST_NAME, O.ORD_NUM
FROM CUSTOMER_TBL C, ORDERS_TBL O
WHERE C.CUST_ID = O.CUST_ID(+)
```

What would the query look like if you used the verbose JOIN syntax?

```
SELECT C.CUST_ID, C.CUST_NAME, O.ORD_NUM
FROM CUSTOMER_TBL C LEFT OUTER JOIN ORDERS_TBL O
ON C.CUST_ID = O.CUST_ID
```

Exercise Answers

1. No answer required.

2. No answer required.

3. Rewrite the SQL query from Exercise 2 using the INNER JOIN syntax.

   A.
   ```
   SELECT E.LAST_NAME, E.FIRST_NAME, EP.DATE_HIRE
   FROM EMPLOYEE_TBL E  INNER JOIN
   EMPLOYEE_PAY_TBL EP ON
   E.EMP_ID = EP.EMP_ID;
   ```

4. Write an SQL statement to return the EMP_ID, LAST_NAME, and FIRST_NAME columns from EMPLOYEE_TBL and SALARY and BONUS columns from EMPLOYEE_PAY_TBL. Use both types of join techniques. Once that's completed, use the queries to determine what the average employee salary per city is.

   A.
   ```
   SELECT E.EMP_ID, E.LAST_NAME, E.FIRST_NAME, EP.SALARY, EP.BONUS
   FROM EMPLOYEE_TBL E,
        EMPLOYEE_PAY_TBL EP
   WHERE E.EMP_ID = EP.EMP_ID;

   SELECT E.EMP_ID, E.LAST_NAME, E.FIRST_NAME, EP.SALARY, EP.BONUS
   FROM EMPLOYEE_TBL E INNER JOIN
   EMPLOYEE_PAY_TBL EP
   ON E.EMP_ID = EP.EMP_ID;

   SELECT E.CITY, AVG(EP.SALARY) AVG_SALARY
   FROM EMPLOYEE_TBL E,
        EMPLOYEE_PAY_TBL EP
   WHERE E.EMP_ID = EP.EMP_ID
   GROUP BY E.CITY;

   SELECT E.CITY, AVG(EP.SALARY) AVG_SALARY
   FROM EMPLOYEE_TBL E INNER JOIN
   EMPLOYEE_PAY_TBL EP
   ON E.EMP_ID = EP.EMP_ID
   GROUP BY E.CITY;
   ```

5. No answer required.

Hour 14, "Using Subqueries to Define Unknown Data"

Quiz Answers

1. What is the function of a subquery when used with a SELECT statement?

   A. The main function of a subquery when used with a SELECT statement is to return data that the main query can use to resolve the query.

2. Can you update more than one column when using the UPDATE statement in conjunction with a subquery?

   A. Yes, you can update more than one column using the same UPDATE and subquery statement.

3. Do the following have the correct syntax? If not, what is the correct syntax?

   a.
   ```
   SELECT CUST_ID, CUST_NAME
         FROM CUSTOMER_TBL
         WHERE CUST_ID =
                     (SELECT CUST_ID
                      FROM ORDERS_TBL
                      WHERE ORD_NUM = '16C17');
   ```

   A. Yes, this syntax is correct.

   b.
   ```
   SELECT EMP_ID, SALARY
         FROM EMPLOYEE_PAY_TBL
         WHERE SALARY BETWEEN '20000'
                     AND (SELECT SALARY
                          FROM EMPLOYEE_PAY_TBL
                          WHERE SALARY = '40000');
   ```

   A. No. You cannot use the BETWEEN operator in this format.

   c.
   ```
   UPDATE PRODUCTS_TBL
         SET COST = 1.15
         WHERE PROD_ID =
                     (SELECT PROD_ID
                      FROM ORDERS_TBL
                      WHERE ORD_NUM = '32A132');
   ```

   A. Yes, this syntax is correct.

4. What would happen if you ran the following statement?

```
DELETE FROM EMPLOYEE_TBL
WHERE EMP_ID IN
              (SELECT EMP_ID
               FROM EMPLOYEE_PAY_TBL);
```

A. All rows that you retrieved from the EMPLOYEE_PAY_TBL would be deleted from the EMPLOYEE_TBL. A WHERE clause in the subquery is highly advised.

Exercise Answers

1. No answer required.

2. Using a subquery, write an SQL statement to update CUSTOMER_TBL. Find the customer with the order number 23E934, contained in the field ORD_NUM, and change the customer name to DAVIDS MARKET.

```
    A. UPDATE CUSTOMER_TBL
        SET CUST_NAME = 'DAVIDS MARKET'
        WHERE CUST_ID =
                    (SELECT CUST_ID
                     FROM ORDERS_TBL
                     WHERE ORD_NUM = '23E934');
```

3. Using a subquery, write a query that returns the names of all employees who have a pay rate greater than JOHN DOE, whose employee identification number is 343559876.

```
    A. SELECT E.LAST_NAME, E.FIRST_NAME, E.MIDDLE_NAME
        FROM EMPLOYEE_TBL E,
            EMPLOYEE_PAY_TBL P
        WHERE P.PAY_RATE > (SELECT PAY_RATE
                            FROM EMPLOYEE_PAY_TBL
                            WHERE EMP_ID = '343559876');
```

4. Using a subquery, write a query that lists all products that cost more than the average cost of all products.

```
    A. SELECT PROD_DESC
        FROM PRODUCTS_TBL
        WHERE COST > (SELECT AVG(COST)
                      FROM PRODUCTS_TBL);
```

Hour 15, "Combining Multiple Queries into One"

Quiz Answers

Refer to the syntax covered in this hour for the following quiz questions when referring to the INTERSECT and EXCEPT operators. Remember that MySQL does not currently support these two operators.

1. Is the syntax correct for the following compound queries? If not, what would correct the syntax? Use EMPLOYEE_TBL and EMPLOYEE_PAY_TBL as follows:

```
EMPLOYEE_TBL
EMP_ID          VARCHAR(9)      NOT NULL,
LAST_NAME       VARCHAR(15)     NOT NULL,
FIRST_NAME      VARCHAR(15)     NOT NULL,
MIDDLE_NAME     VARCHAR(15),
ADDRESS         VARCHAR(30)     NOT NULL,
CITY            VARCHAR(15)     NOT NULL,
STATE           VARCHAR(2)      NOT NULL,
ZIP             INTEGER(5)      NOT NULL,
PHONE           VARCHAR(10),
PAGER           VARCHAR(10),


EMPLOYEE_PAY_TBL
EMP_ID              VARCHAR(9)      NOT NULL,    primary key
POSITION            VARCHAR(15)     NOT NULL,
DATE_HIRE           DATETIME,
PAY_RATE            DECIMAL(4,2)    NOT NULL,
DATE_LASTRAISE      DATE,
SALARY              DECIMAL(8,2),
BONUS               DECIMAL(6,2),
```

   a. SELECT EMP_ID, LAST_NAME, FIRST_NAME
      FROM EMPLOYEE_TBL
      UNION
      SELECT EMP_ID, POSITION, DATE_HIRE
      FROM EMPLOYEE_PAY_TBL;

   A. This compound query does not work because the data types do not match. The EMP_ID columns match, but the LAST_NAME and FIRST_NAME data types do not match the POSITION and DATE_HIRE data types.

   b. SELECT EMP_ID FROM EMPLOYEE_TBL
      UNION ALL
      SELECT EMP_ID FROM EMPLOYEE_PAY_TBL
      ORDER BY EMP_ID;

A. Yes, the statement is correct.

    c.
```
SELECT EMP_ID FROM EMPLOYEE_PAY_TBL
INTERSECT
SELECT EMP_ID FROM EMPLOYEE_TBL
ORDER BY 1;
```

A. Yes, this compound query works.

2. Match the correct operator to the following statements:

Statement	Operator
a. Show duplicates	UNION ALL
b. Return only rows from the first query that match those in the second query	INTERSECT
c. Return no duplicates	UNION
d. Return only rows from the first query not returned by the second	EXCEPT

Exercise Answers

Refer to the syntax covered in this hour for the following exercises. You might have to write your queries by hand because MySQL does not support some of the operators covered in this hour. When you are finished, compare your results to ours.

Use CUSTOMER_TBL and ORDERS_TBL as listed:

```
CUSTOMER_TBL
CUST_IN        VARCHAR(10)    NOT NULL    primary key
CUST_NAME      VARCHAR(30)    NOT NULL,
CUST_ADDRESS   VARCHAR(20)    NOT NULL,
CUST_CITY      VARCHAR(15)    NOT NULL,
CUST_STATE     VARCHAR(2)     NOT NULL,
CUST_ZIP       INTEGER(5)     NOT NULL,
CUST_PHONE     INTEGER(10),
CUST_FAX       INTEGER(10)


ORDERS_TBL
ORD_NUM        VARCHAR(10)    NOT NULL    primary key
CUST_ID        VARCHAR(10)    NOT NULL,
PROD_ID        VARCHAR(10)    NOT NULL,
QTY            INTEGER(6)     NOT NULL,
ORD_DATE       DATETIME
```

1. Write a compound query to find the customers who have placed an order.

   A. `SELECT CUST_ID FROM CUSTOMER_TBL`
   `INTERSECT`
   `SELECT CUST_ID FROM ORDERS_TBL;`

2. Write a compound query to find the customers who have not placed an order.

   A. `SELECT CUST_ID FROM CUSTOMER_TBL`
   `EXCEPT`
   `SELECT CUST_ID FROM ORDERS_TBL;`

Hour 16, "Using Indexes to Improve Performance"

Quiz Answers

1. What are some major disadvantages of using indexes?

   A. Major disadvantages of an index include slowing batch jobs, storage space on the disk, and maintenance upkeep on the index.

2. Why is the order of columns in a composite important?

   A. Because query performance is improved by putting the column with the most restrictive values first.

3. Should a column with a large percentage of NULL values be indexed?

   A. No. A column with a large percentage of NULL values should not be indexed because the speed of accessing these rows degrades when the value of a large percentage of rows is the same.

4. Is the main purpose of an index to stop duplicate values in a table?

   A. No. The main purpose of an index is to enhance data retrieval speed, although a unique index stops duplicate values in a table.

5. True or false: The main reason for a composite index is for aggregate function usage in an index.

   A. False. The main reason for composite indexes is for two or more columns in the same table to be indexed.

6. What does cardinality refer to? What is considered a column of high-cardinality?

   A. Cardinality refers to the uniqueness of the data within a column. The SSN column is an example of such a column.

Exercise Answers

1. For the following situations, decide whether an index should be used and, if so, what type of index should be used.

   a. Several columns, but a rather small table.

   A. Being a very small table, no index is needed.

   b. Medium-sized table; no duplicates should be allowed.

   A. A unique index could be used.

   c. Several columns, very large table, several columns used as filters in the WHERE clause.

   A. A composite index on the columns used as filters in the WHERE clause should be the choice.

   d. Large table, many columns, a lot of data manipulation.

   A. A choice of a single-column or composite index should be considered, depending on filtering, ordering, and grouping. For the large amount of data manipulation, the index could be dropped and re-created after the INSERT, UPDATE, or DELETE jobs were done.

2. No answer required.

3. Create a statement to alter the index you just created to make it unique. What do you need to do to create a unique index on the SALARY column? Write the SQL statements that you need to run them in the sequence.

   A.
   ```
   DROP INDEX EP_POSITON ON EMPLOYEE_PAY_TBL;
          CREATE UNIQUE INDEX EP_POSITION
          ON EMPLOYEE_TBL(POSITION);
   ```

4. Study the tables used in this book. What are some good candidates for indexed columns based on how a user might search for data?

    A. `EMPLOYEE_TBL.LAST_NAME`
`EMPLOYEE_TBL.FIRST_NAME`
`EMPLOYEE_TBL.EMP_ID`
`EMPLOYEE_PAY_TBL.EMP_ID`
`EMPLOYEE_PAY_TBL.POSITION`
`CUSTOMER_TBL.CUST_ID`
`CUSTOMER_TBL.CUST_NAME`
`ORDERS_TBL.ORD_NUM`
`ORDERS_TBL.CUST_ID`
`ORDERS_TBL.PROD_ID`
`ORDERS_TBL.ORD_DATE`
`PRODUCTS_TBL.PROD_ID`
`PRODUCTS_TBL.PROD_DESC`

5. Create a multicolumn index on `ORDERS_TBL`. Include the following columns: `CUST_ID`, `PROD_ID`, and `ORD_DATE`.

    A. `CREATE INDEX ORD_IDX ON ORDERS_TBL (CUST_ID, PROD_ID, ORD_DATE);`

6. Answers will vary.

Hour 17, "Improving Database Performance"

Quiz Answers

1. Would the use of a unique index on a small table be of any benefit?

    A. The index might not be of any use for performance issues, but the unique index would keep referential integrity intact. Referential integrity is discussed in Hour 3, "Managing Database Objects."

2. What happens when the optimizer chooses not to use an index on a table when a query has been executed?

    A. A full table scan occurs.

3. Should the most restrictive clause(s) be placed before the join condition(s) or after the join conditions in the WHERE clause?

A. The most restrictive clause(s) should be evaluated before the join condition(s) because join conditions normally return a large number of rows.

Exercise Answers

1. Rewrite the following SQL statements to improve their performance. Use `EMPLOYEE_TBL` and `EMPLOYEE_PAY_TBL` as described here:

```
EMPLOYEE_TBL
EMP_ID          VARCHAR(9)      NOT NULL      Primary key
LAST_NAME       VARCHAR(15)     NOT NULL,
FIRST_NAME      VARCHAR(15)     NOT NULL,
MIDDLE_NAME     VARCHAR(15),
ADDRESS         VARCHAR(30)     NOT NULL,
CITY            VARCHAR(15)     NOT NULL,
STATE           VARCHAR(2)      NOT NULL,
ZIP             INTEGER(5)      NOT NULL,
PHONE           VARCHAR(10),
PAGER           VARCHAR(10),
EMPLOYEE_PAY_TBL
EMP_ID           VARCHAR(9)      NOT NULL   primary key
POSITION         VARCHAR(15)     NOT NULL,
DATE_HIRE        DATETIME,
PAY_RATE         DECIMAL(4,2)    NOT NULL,
DATE_LAST_RAISE  DATETIME,
SALARY           DECIMAL(8,2),
BONUS            DECIMAL(8,2),
```

a.
```
SELECT EMP_ID, LAST_NAME, FIRST_NAME,
       PHONE
FROM EMPLOYEE_TBL
WHERE SUBSTRING(PHONE, 1, 3) = '317' OR
      SUBSTRING(PHONE, 1, 3) = '812' OR
      SUBSTRING(PHONE, 1, 3) = '765';
```

A.
```
SELECT EMP_ID, LAST_NAME, FIRST_NAME,
       PHONE
  FROM EMPLOYEE_TBL
  WHERE SUBSTRING(PHONE, 1, 3) IN ('317', '812', '765');
```

From our experience, it is better to convert multiple OR conditions to an IN list.

b.
```
SELECT LAST_NAME, FIRST_NAME
FROM EMPLOYEE_TBL
WHERE LAST_NAME LIKE '%ALL%';
```

A. SELECT LAST_NAME, FIRST_NAME
FROM EMPLOYEE_TBL
WHERE LAST_NAME LIKE 'WAL%';

You cannot take advantage of an index if you do not include the first character in a condition's value.

c. SELECT E.EMP_ID, E.LAST_NAME, E.FIRST_NAME,
EP.SALARY
FROM EMPLOYEE_TBL E,
EMPLOYEE_PAY_TBL EP
WHERE LAST_NAME LIKE 'S%'
AND E.EMP_ID = EP.EMP_ID;

A. SELECT E.EMP_ID, E.LAST_NAME, E.FIRST_NAME,
EP.SALARY
FROM EMPLOYEE_TBL E,
EMPLOYEE_PAY_TBL EP
WHERE E.EMP_ID = EP.EMP_ID
AND LAST_NAME LIKE 'S%';

2. Add another table called EMPLOYEE_PAYHIST_TBL that contains a large amount of pay history data. Use the table that follows to write the series of SQL statements to address the following problems.

```
EMPLOYEE_PAYHIST_TBL
PAYHIST_ID        VARCHAR(9)     NOT NULL      primary key,
EMP_ID            VARCHAR(9)     NOT NULL,
START_DATE        DATETIME       NOT NULL,
END_DATE          DATETIME,
PAY_RATE          DECIMAL(4,2)   NOT NULL,
SALARY            DECIMAL(8,2)   NOT NULL,
BONUS             DECIMAL(8,2)   NOT NULL,
CONSTRAINT EMP_FK FOREIGN KEY (EMP_ID)
REFERENCES EMPLOYEE_TBL (EMP_ID)
```

What steps did you take to ensure that the queries you wrote perform well?

a. Find the SUM of the salaried versus nonsalaried employees by the year in which their pay started.

A. SELECT START_YEAR,SUM(SALARIED) AS SALARIED,SUM(HOURLY) AS HOURLY
FROM
(SELECT YEAR(E.START_DATE) AS START_YEAR,COUNT(E.EMP_ID) AS SALARIED,0 AS HOURLY
FROM EMPLOYEE_PAYHIST_TBL E INNER JOIN
(SELECT MIN(START_DATE) START_DATE,EMP_ID
FROM EMPLOYEE_PAYHIST_TBL
GROUP BY EMP_ID) F ON E.EMP_ID=F.EMP_ID AND

```
E.START_DATE=F.START_DATE
    WHERE E.SALARY > 0.00
    GROUP BY YEAR(E.START_DATE)
    UNION
SELECT YEAR(E.START_DATE) AS START_YEAR,0 AS SALARIED,
    COUNT(E.EMP_ID)   AS HOURLY
    FROM EMPLOYEE_PAYHIST_TBL E INNER JOIN
    ( SELECT MIN(START_DATE) START_DATE,EMP_ID
    FROM EMPLOYEE_PAYHIST_TBL
    GROUP BY EMP_ID) F ON E.EMP_ID=F.EMP_ID AND
E.START_DATE=F.START_DATE
    WHERE E.PAY_RATE > 0.00
    GROUP BY YEAR(E.START_DATE)
    ) A
    GROUP BY START_YEAR
    ORDER BY START_YEAR
```

b. Find the difference in the yearly pay of salaried employees versus nonsalaried employees by the year in which their pay started. Consider the nonsalaried employees to be working full time during the year (PAY_RATE * 52 * 40).

A.
```
SELECT START_YEAR,SALARIED AS SALARIED,HOURLY AS HOURLY,
    (SALARIED - HOURLY) AS PAY_DIFFERENCE
    FROM
    (SELECT YEAR(E.START_DATE) AS START_YEAR,AVG(E.SALARY) AS
SALARIED,
    0 AS HOURLY
    FROM EMPLOYEE_PAYHIST_TBL E INNER JOIN
    ( SELECT MIN(START_DATE) START_DATE,EMP_ID
    FROM EMPLOYEE_PAYHIST_TBL
    GROUP BY EMP_ID) F ON E.EMP_ID=F.EMP_ID AND
E.START_DATE=F.START_DATE
    WHERE E.SALARY > 0.00
    GROUP BY YEAR(E.START_DATE)
    UNION
SELECT YEAR(E.START_DATE) AS START_YEAR,0 AS SALARIED,
    AVG(E.PAY_RATE * 52 * 40 ) AS HOURLY
    FROM EMPLOYEE_PAYHIST_TBL E INNER JOIN
    ( SELECT MIN(START_DATE) START_DATE,EMP_ID
     FROM EMPLOYEE_PAYHIST_TBL
    GROUP BY EMP_ID) F ON E.EMP_ID=F.EMP_ID AND
E.START_DATE=F.START_DATE
    WHERE E.PAY_RATE > 0.00
    GROUP BY YEAR(E.START_DATE)
    ) A
    GROUP BY START_YEAR
    ORDER BY START_YEAR
```

c. Find the difference in what employees make now versus what they made when they started with the company. Again, consider the nonsalaried employees to be full-time. Also consider that the employees' current pay is reflected in the EMPLOYEE_PAY_TBL as well as the EMPLOYEE_PAYHIST_TBL. In the pay history table, the current pay is reflected as a row with the END_DATE for pay equal to NULL.

A.
```
SELECT CURRENTPAY.EMP_ID,STARTING_ANNUAL_PAY,CURRENT_
ANNUAL_PAY,
CURRENT_ANNUAL_PAY - STARTING_ANNUAL_PAY AS PAY_DIFFERENCE
FROM
(SELECT EMP_ID,(SALARY + (PAY_RATE * 52 * 40)) AS
CURRENT_ANNUAL_PAY
  FROM EMPLOYEE_PAYHIST_TBL
  WHERE END_DATE IS NULL) CURRENTPAY
INNER JOIN
(SELECT E.EMP_ID,(SALARY + (PAY_RATE * 52 * 40)) AS
STARTING_ANNUAL_PAY
  FROM EMPLOYEE_PAYHIST_TBL E
  ( SELECT MIN(START_DATE) START_DATE,EMP_ID
          FROM EMPLOYEE_PAYHIST_TBL
          GROUP BY EMP_ID) F ON E.EMP_ID=F.EMP_ID AND
E.START_DATE=F.START_DATE
  ) STARTINGPAY ON
  CURRENTPAY.EMP_ID = STARTINGPAY.EMP_ID
```

Hour 18, "Managing Database Users"

Quiz Answers

1. What command establishes a session?

   A. The CONNECT TO statement establishes this.

2. Which option drops a schema that still contains database objects?

   A. The CASCADE option allows the schema to be dropped if there are still objects under that schema.

3. Which command in MySQL creates a schema?

   A. The CREATE SCHEMA command creates a schema.

4. Which statement removes a database privilege?

   A. The REVOKE statement removes database privileges.

5. What command creates a grouping or collection of tables, views, and privileges?

   A. The CREATE SCHEMA statement.

6. What is the difference in SQL Server between a login account and a database user account?

    A. The login account grants access to the SQL Server instance to log in and access resources. The database user account is what gains access to the database and is assigned rights.

Exercise Answers

1. Describe how you would create a new user 'John' in your learnsql database.

    A. `USE LEARNSQL:`
       `CREATE USER JOHN`

2. How would you grant access to the EMPLOYEE_TBL to your new user 'John'?

    A. `GRANT SELECT ON TABLE EMPLOYEE_TBL TO JOHN;`

3. Describe how you would assign permissions to all objects within the learnsql database to 'John'.

    A. `GRANT SELECT ON TABLE * TO JOHN;`

4. Describe how you would revoke the previous privileges from 'John' and then remove his account.

    A. `DROP USER JOHN CASCADE;`

Hour 19, "Managing Database Security"

Quiz Answers

1. What option must a user have to grant another user privileges to an object not owned by the user?

    A. `GRANT OPTION`

2. When privileges are granted to PUBLIC, do all database users acquire the privileges, or only specified users?

    A. All users of the database are granted the privileges.

3. What privilege is required to look at data in a specific table?

    A. The SELECT privilege.

4. What type of privilege is SELECT?

    A. An object-level privilege.

5. What option revokes a user's privilege to an object as well as the other users that they might have granted privileges to by use of the GRANT option?

>   **A.** The CASCADE option is used with the REVOKE statement to remove other users' access that was granted by the affected user.

Exercise Answers

1. No answer required.

2. No answer required.

3. No answer required.

4. No answer required.

Hour 20, "Creating and Using Views and Synonyms"

Quiz Answers

1. Can you delete a row of data from a view that you created from multiple tables?

>   **A.** No. You can only use the DELETE, INSERT, and UPDATE commands on views you create from a single table.

2. When creating a table, the owner is automatically granted the appropriate privileges on that table. Is this true when creating a view?

>   **A.** Yes. The owner of a view is automatically granted the appropriate privileges on the view.

3. Which clause orders data when creating a view?

>   **A.** The GROUP BY clause functions in a view much as the ORDER BY clause (or GROUP BY clause) does in a regular query.

4. Which option can you use when creating a view from a view to check integrity constraints?

>   **A.** You can use the WITH CHECK OPTION.

5. You try to drop a view and receive an error because of one or more underlying views. What must you do to drop the view?

   A. Re-execute your DROP statement with the CASCADE option. This allows the DROP statement to succeed by also dropping all underlying views.

Exercise Answers

1. Write a statement to create a view based on the total contents of EMPLOYEE_TBL.

   A. CREATE VIEW EMP_VIEW AS
      SELECT * FROM EMPLOYEE_TBL;

2. Write a statement that creates a summarized view containing the average pay rate and average salary for each city in EMPLOYEE_TBL.

   A. CREATE VIEW AVG_PAY_VIEW AS
      SELECT E.CITY, AVG(P.PAY_RATE), AVG(P.SALARY)
      FROM EMPLOYEE_PAY_TBL P,
      EMPLOYEE_TBL E
      WHERE P.EMP_ID = E.EMP_ID
      GROUP BY E.CITY;

3. Create another view for the same summarized data except use the view you created in Exercise 1 instead of the base EMPLOYEE_TBL. Compare the two results.

   A. CREATE VIEW AVG_PAY_ALT_VIEW AS
      SELECT E.CITY, AVG(P.PAY_RATE), AVG(P.SALARY)
      FROM EMPLOYEE_PAY_TBL P,
      EMP_VIEW E
      WHERE P.EMP_ID = E.EMP_ID
      GROUP BY E.CITY;

4. Use the view in Exercise 2 to create a table called EMPLOYEE_PAY_SUMMARIZED. Verify that the view and the table contain the same data.

   A. SELECT * INTO EMPLOYEE_PAY_SUMMARIZED FROM AVG_PAY_VIEW;

5. Write statements that drop the three views that you created in Exercises 1, 2, and 3.

   A. DROP VIEW EMP_VIEW;
      DROP VIEW AVG_PAY_VIEW;
      DROP VIEW AVG_PAY_ALT_VIEW;

Hour 21, "Working with the System Catalog"

Quiz Answers

1. In some implementations, the system catalog is also known as what?

    A. The system catalog is also known as the data dictionary.

2. Can a regular user update the system catalog?

    A. Not directly; however, when a user creates an object such as a table, the system catalog is automatically updated.

3. Which Microsoft SQL Server system table retrieves information about views that exist in the database?

    A. SYSVIEWS is used.

4. Who owns the system catalog?

    A. The owner of the system catalog is often a privileged database user account called SYS or SYSTEM. The owner of the database can also own the system catalog, but a particular schema in the database does not ordinarily own it.

5. What is the difference between the Oracle system objects ALL_TABLES and DBA_TABLES?

    A. ALL_TABLES shows all tables that are accessible by a particular user, whereas DBA_TABLES shows all tables that exist in the database.

6. Who makes modifications to the system tables?

    A. The database server makes these modifications.

Exercise Answers

1. No answer required.

2. No answer required.

3. No answer required.

Hour 22, "Advanced SQL Topics"

Quiz Answers

1. Can a trigger be altered?

   A. No, the trigger must be replaced or re-created.

2. When a cursor is closed, can you reuse the name?

   A. This is implementation specific. In some implementations, the closing of the cursor enables you to reuse the name and even free the memory, whereas for other implementations you must use the DEALLOCATE statement before you can reuse the name.

3. Which command retrieves the results after a cursor has been opened?

   A. The FETCH command does this.

4. Are triggers executed before or after an INSERT, DELETE, or UPDATE statement?

   A. Triggers can be executed before or after an INSERT, DELETE, or UPDATE statement. Many different types of triggers can be created.

5. Which MySQL function retrieves information from an XML fragment?

   A. EXTRACTVALUE is used.

6. Why do Oracle and MySQL not support the DEALLOCATE syntax for cursors?

   A. They do not support the statement because they automatically deallocate the cursor resources when the cursor is closed.

7. Why is a cursor not considered a set-based operation?

   A. Cursors are not considered set-based operations because they operate on only one row at a time by fetching a row from memory and performing some action with it.

Exercise Answers

1. No answer required.

2. Write a SELECT statement that generates the SQL code to count all rows in each of your tables. (Hint: It is similar to Exercise 1.)

   A. SELECT CONCAT('SELECT COUNT(*) FROM ',TABLE_NAME,';') FROM TABLES;

3. Write a series of SQL commands to create a cursor that prints each customer name and the customer's total sales. Ensure that the cursor is properly closed and deallocated based on which implementation you are using.

   A. An example using SQL Server might look similar to this:

```
BEGIN
        DECLARE @custname VARCHAR(30);
        DECLARE @purchases decimal(6,2);
        DECLARE customercursor CURSOR FOR SELECT
        C.CUST_NAME,SUM(P.COST*O.QTY) as SALES
        FROM CUSTOMER_TBL C
        INNER JOIN ORDERS_TBL O ON C.CUST_ID=O.CUST_ID
        INNER JOIN PRODUCTS_TBL P ON O.PROD_ID=P.PROD_ID
        GROUP BY C.CUST_NAME;
        OPEN customercursor;
        FETCH NEXT FROM customercursor INTO @custname,@purchases
        WHILE (@@FETCH_STATUS<>-1)
                BEGIN
                    IF (@@FETCH_STATUS<>-2)
                    BEGIN
                        PRINT @custname + ': $' + CAST(@purchases AS
VARCHAR(20))
                    END
        FETCH NEXT FROM customercursor INTO @custname,@purchases
        END
        CLOSE customercursor
        DEALLOCATE customercursor
END;
```

Hour 23, "Extending SQL to the Enterprise, the Internet, and the Intranet"

Quiz Answers

1. Can a database on a server be accessed from another server?

   A. Yes, by using a middleware product. This is called accessing a remote database.

2. What can a company use to disseminate information to its own employees?

   A. An intranet.

3. Products that allow connections to databases are called what?

   A. Middleware.

4. Can SQL be embedded into Internet programming languages?

   A. Yes. SQL can be embedded in Internet programming languages, such as Java.

5. How is a remote database accessed through a web application?

   A. Via a web server.

Exercise Answers

1. Answers will vary.

2. No answer required.

Hour 24, "Extensions to Standard SQL"

Quiz Answers

1. Is SQL a procedural or nonprocedural language?

   A. SQL is nonprocedural, meaning that the database decides how to execute the SQL statement. The extensions discussed in this hour were procedural.

2. What are the three basic operations of a cursor, outside of declaring the cursor?

   A. OPEN, FETCH, and CLOSE.

3. Procedural or nonprocedural: With which does the database engine decide how to evaluate and execute SQL statements?

   A. Nonprocedural.

Exercise Answers

1. No answer required.

CREATE TABLE Statements for Book Examples

This appendix is useful because it not only lists the CREATE TABLE statements used in the examples, but also gives you some of the syntax differences among the various database platforms. You can use these statements to create your own tables for performing hands-on exercises.

MySQL

EMPLOYEE_TBL

```
CREATE TABLE EMPLOYEE_TBL
(
EMP_ID              VARCHAR(9)        NOT NULL,
LAST_NAME           VARCHAR(15)       NOT NULL,
FIRST_NAME          VARCHAR(15)       NOT NULL,
MIDDLE_NAME         VARCHAR(15),
ADDRESS             VARCHAR(30)       NOT NULL,
CITY                VARCHAR(15)       NOT NULL,
STATE               CHAR(2)           NOT NULL,
ZIP                 INTEGER(5)        NOT NULL,
PHONE               CHAR(10),
PAGER               CHAR(10),
CONSTRAINT EMP_PK PRIMARY KEY (EMP_ID)
);
```

EMPLOYEE_PAY_TBL

```
CREATE TABLE EMPLOYEE_PAY_TBL
(
EMP_ID              VARCHAR(9)        NOT NULL    primary key,
POSITION            VARCHAR(15)       NOT NULL,
DATE_HIRE           DATE,
PAY_RATE            DECIMAL(4,2),
DATE_LAST_RAISE     DATE,
SALARY              DECIMAL(8,2),
BONUS               DECIMAL(6,2),
CONSTRAINT EMP_FK FOREIGN KEY (EMP_ID) REFERENCES EMPLOYEE_TBL (EMP_ID)
);
```

CUSTOMER_TBL

```
CREATE TABLE CUSTOMER_TBL
(
CUST_ID              VARCHAR(10)    NOT NULL      primary key,
CUST_NAME            VARCHAR(30)    NOT NULL,
CUST_ADDRESS         VARCHAR(20)    NOT NULL,
CUST_CITY            VARCHAR(15)    NOT NULL,
CUST_STATE           CHAR(2)        NOT NULL,
CUST_ZIP             INTEGER(5)     NOT NULL,
CUST_PHONE           CHAR(10),
CUST_FAX             INTEGER(10)
);
```

ORDERS_TBL

```
CREATE TABLE ORDERS_TBL
(
ORD_NUM              VARCHAR(10)    NOT NULL      primary key,
CUST_ID              VARCHAR(10)    NOT NULL,
PROD_ID              VARCHAR(10)    NOT NULL,
QTY                  INTEGER(6)     NOT NULL,
ORD_DATE             DATE
);
```

PRODUCTS_TBL

```
CREATE TABLE PRODUCTS_TBL
(
PROD_ID        VARCHAR(10)    NOT NULL        primary key,
PROD_DESC      VARCHAR(40)    NOT NULL,
COST           DECIMAL(6,2)   NOT NULL
);
```

Oracle and SQL Server

EMPLOYEE_TBL

```
CREATE TABLE EMPLOYEE_TBL
(
EMP_ID              VARCHAR(9)      NOT NULL,
LAST_NAME           VARCHAR(15)     NOT NULL,
FIRST_NAME          VARCHAR(15)     NOT NULL,
MIDDLE_NAME         VARCHAR(15),
ADDRESS             VARCHAR(30)     NOT NULL,
CITY                VARCHAR(15)     NOT NULL,
STATE               CHAR(2)         NOT NULL,
```

```
ZIP                 INTEGER         NOT NULL,
PHONE               CHAR(10),
PAGER               CHAR(10),
CONSTRAINT EMP_PK PRIMARY KEY (EMP_ID)
);
```

EMPLOYEE_PAY_TBL

```
CREATE TABLE EMPLOYEE_PAY_TBL
(
EMP_ID              VARCHAR(9)      NOT NULL    primary key,
POSITION            VARCHAR(15)     NOT NULL,
DATE_HIRE           DATE,
PAY_RATE            DECIMAL(4,2),
DATE_LAST_RAISE     DATE,
SALARY              DECIMAL(8,2),
BONUS               DECIMAL(6,2),
CONSTRAINT EMP_FK FOREIGN KEY  (EMP_ID) REFERENCES EMPLOYEE_TBL (EMP_ID)
);
```

CUSTOMER_TBL

```
CREATE TABLE CUSTOMER_TBL
(
CUST_ID             VARCHAR(10)     NOT NULL        primary key,
CUST_NAME           VARCHAR(30)     NOT NULL,
CUST_ADDRESS        VARCHAR(20)     NOT NULL,
CUST_CITY           VARCHAR(15)     NOT NULL,
CUST_STATE          CHAR(2)         NOT NULL,
CUST_ZIP            INTEGER         NOT NULL,
CUST_PHONE          CHAR(10),
CUST_FAX            VARCHAR(10)
);
```

ORDERS_TBL

```
CREATE TABLE ORDERS_TBL
(
ORD_NUM             VARCHAR(10)     NOT NULL        primary key,
CUST_ID             VARCHAR(10)     NOT NULL,
PROD_ID             VARCHAR(10)     NOT NULL,
QTY                 INTEGER         NOT NULL,
ORD_DATE            DATE
);
```

PRODUCTS_TBL

```
CREATE TABLE PRODUCTS_TBL
(
PROD_ID        VARCHAR(10)    NOT NULL      primary key,
PROD_DESC      VARCHAR(40)    NOT NULL,
COST           DECIMAL(6,2)   NOT NULL
);
```

APPENDIX E

INSERT Statements for Data in Book Examples

This appendix contains the INSERT statements that were used to populate the tables that are listed in Appendix D, "CREATE TABLE Statements for Book Examples." These INSERT statements can populate the tables after you create them.

MySQL and SQL Server

EMPLOYEE_TBL

```
INSERT INTO EMPLOYEE_TBL VALUES
('311549902', 'STEPHENS', 'TINA', 'DAWN','RR 3 BOX 17A', 'GREENWOOD',
'IN', '47890', '3178784465',NULL);

INSERT INTO EMPLOYEE_TBL VALUES
('442346889', 'PLEW', 'LINDA', 'CAROL', '3301 BEACON', 'INDIANAPOLIS',
'IN', '46224', '3172978990', NULL);

INSERT INTO EMPLOYEE_TBL VALUES
('213764555', 'GLASS', 'BRANDON', 'SCOTT', '1710 MAIN ST', 'WHITELAND',
'IN', '47885', '3178984321', '3175709980');

INSERT INTO EMPLOYEE_TBL VALUES
('313782439', 'GLASS', 'JACOB', NULL, '3789 WHITE RIVER BLVD',
'INDIANAPOLIS', 'IN', '45734', '3175457676','8887345678');

INSERT INTO EMPLOYEE_TBL VALUES
('220984332', 'WALLACE', 'MARIAH', NULL, '7889 KEYSTONE AVE',
'INDIANAPOLIS', 'IN', '46741', '3173325986', NULL);

INSERT INTO EMPLOYEE_TBL VALUES
('443679012', 'SPURGEON', 'TIFFANY', NULL, '5 GEORGE COURT',
'INDIANAPOLIS', 'IN', '46234', '3175679007', NULL);
```

EMPLOYEE_PAY_TBL

```
INSERT INTO EMPLOYEE_PAY_TBL VALUES
('311549902', 'MARKETING', '1999-05-23',NULL,'2009-05-01','40000', NULL);

INSERT INTO EMPLOYEE_PAY_TBL VALUES
('442346889', 'TEAM LEADER', '2000-06-17', '14.75', '2009-06-01', NULL,
NULL);

INSERT INTO EMPLOYEE_PAY_TBL VALUES
('213764555', 'SALES MANAGER', '2004-08-14',NULL, '2009-08-01', '30000',
'2000');

INSERT INTO EMPLOYEE_PAY_TBL VALUES
('313782439', 'SALESMAN', '2007-06-28',NULL, NULL, '20000', '1000');

INSERT INTO EMPLOYEE_PAY_TBL VALUES
('220984332', 'SHIPPER', '2006-07-22', '11.00', '1999-07-01', NULL, NULL);

INSERT INTO EMPLOYEE_PAY_TBL VALUES
('443679012', 'SHIPPER', '2001-01-14', '15.00', '1999-01-01', NULL, NULL);
```

CUSTOMER_TBL

```
INSERT INTO CUSTOMER_TBL VALUES
('232', 'LESLIE GLEASON', '798 HARDAWAY DR', 'INDIANAPOLIS',
'IN', '47856', '3175457690', NULL);

INSERT INTO CUSTOMER_TBL VALUES
('109', 'NANCY BUNKER', 'APT A 4556 WATERWAY', 'BROAD RIPPLE',
'IN', '47950', '3174262323', NULL);

INSERT INTO CUSTOMER_TBL VALUES
('345', 'ANGELA DOBKO', 'RR3 BOX 76', 'LEBANON', 'IN', '49967',
'7658970090', NULL);

INSERT INTO CUSTOMER_TBL VALUES
('090', 'WENDY WOLF', '3345 GATEWAY DR', 'INDIANAPOLIS', 'IN',
'46224', '3172913421', NULL);

INSERT INTO CUSTOMER_TBL VALUES
('12', 'MARYS GIFT SHOP', '435 MAIN ST', 'DANVILLE', 'IL', '47978',
'3178567221', '3178523434');

INSERT INTO CUSTOMER_TBL VALUES
('432', 'SCOTTYS MARKET', 'RR2 BOX 173', 'BROWNSBURG', 'IN',
'45687', '3178529835', '3178529836');

INSERT INTO CUSTOMER_TBL VALUES
('333', 'JASONS AND DALLAS GOODIES', 'LAFAYETTE SQ MALL',
'INDIANAPOLIS', 'IN', '46222', '3172978886', '3172978887');
```

```
INSERT INTO CUSTOMER_TBL VALUES
('21', 'MORGANS CANDIES AND TREATS', '5657 W TENTH ST',
'INDIANAPOLIS', 'IN', '46234', '3172714398', NULL);

INSERT INTO CUSTOMER_TBL VALUES
('43', 'SCHYLERS NOVELTIES', '17 MAPLE ST', 'LEBANON', 'IN',
'48990', '3174346758', NULL);

INSERT INTO CUSTOMER_TBL VALUES
('287', 'GAVINS PLACE', '9880 ROCKVILLE RD', 'INDIANAPOLIS',
'IN', '46244', '3172719991', '3172719992');

INSERT INTO CUSTOMER_TBL VALUES
('288', 'HOLLYS GAMEARAMA', '567 US 31 SOUTH', 'WHITELAND',
'IN', '49980', '3178879023', NULL);

INSERT INTO CUSTOMER_TBL VALUES
('590', 'HEATHERS FEATHERS AND THINGS', '4090 N SHADELAND AVE',
'INDIANAPOLIS', 'IN', '43278', '3175456768', NULL);

INSERT INTO CUSTOMER_TBL VALUES
('610', 'REGANS HOBBIES INC', '451 GREEN ST', 'PLAINFIELD', 'IN',
'46818', '3178393441', '3178399090');

INSERT INTO CUSTOMER_TBL VALUES
('560', 'ANDYS CANDIES', 'RR 1 BOX 34', 'NASHVILLE', 'IN',
'48756', '8123239871', NULL);

INSERT INTO CUSTOMER_TBL VALUES
('221', 'RYANS STUFF', '2337 S SHELBY ST', 'INDIANAPOLIS', 'IN',
'47834', '3175634402', NULL);
```

ORDERS_TBL

```
INSERT INTO ORDERS_TBL VALUES
('56A901', '232', '11235', '1', '2009-10-22');

INSERT INTO ORDERS_TBL VALUES
('56A917', '12', '907', '100', '2009-09-30');

INSERT INTO ORDERS_TBL VALUES
('32A132', '43', '222', '25', '2009-10-10');

INSERT INTO ORDERS_TBL VALUES
('16C17', '090', '222', '2', '2009-10-17');

INSERT INTO ORDERS_TBL VALUES
('18D778', '287', '90', '10', '2009-10-17');

INSERT INTO ORDERS_TBL VALUES
('23E934', '432', '13', '20', '2009-10-15');
```

PRODUCTS_TBL

```
INSERT INTO PRODUCTS_TBL VALUES
('11235', 'WITCH COSTUME', '29.99');

INSERT INTO PRODUCTS_TBL VALUES
('222', 'PLASTIC PUMPKIN 18 INCH', '7.75');

INSERT INTO PRODUCTS_TBL VALUES
('13', 'FALSE PARAFFIN TEETH', '1.10');

INSERT INTO PRODUCTS_TBL VALUES
('90', 'LIGHTED LANTERNS', '14.50');

INSERT INTO PRODUCTS_TBL VALUES
('15', 'ASSORTED COSTUMES', '10.00');

INSERT INTO PRODUCTS_TBL VALUES
('9', 'CANDY CORN', '1.35');

INSERT INTO PRODUCTS_TBL VALUES
('6', 'PUMPKIN CANDY', '1.45');

INSERT INTO PRODUCTS_TBL VALUES
('87', 'PLASTIC SPIDERS', '1.05');

INSERT INTO PRODUCTS_TBL VALUES
('119', 'ASSORTED MASKS', '4.95');
```

Oracle

EMPLOYEE_TBL

```
INSERT INTO EMPLOYEE_TBL VALUES
('311549902', 'STEPHENS', 'TINA', 'DAWN','RR 3 BOX 17A', 'GREENWOOD',
'IN', '47890', '3178784465',NULL);

INSERT INTO EMPLOYEE_TBL VALUES
('442346889', 'PLEW', 'LINDA', 'CAROL', '3301 BEACON', 'INDIANAPOLIS',
'IN', '46224', '3172978990', NULL);

INSERT INTO EMPLOYEE_TBL VALUES
('213764555', 'GLASS', 'BRANDON', 'SCOTT', '1710 MAIN ST', 'WHITELAND',
'IN', '47885', '3178984321', '3175709980');

INSERT INTO EMPLOYEE_TBL VALUES
('313782439', 'GLASS', 'JACOB', NULL, '3789 WHITE RIVER BLVD',
'INDIANAPOLIS', 'IN', '45734', '3175457676','8887345678');
```

```
INSERT INTO EMPLOYEE_TBL VALUES
('220984332', 'WALLACE', 'MARIAH', NULL, '7889 KEYSTONE AVE',
'INDIANAPOLIS', 'IN', '46741', '3173325986', NULL);

INSERT INTO EMPLOYEE_TBL VALUES
('443679012', 'SPURGEON', 'TIFFANY',  NULL, '5 GEORGE COURT',
'INDIANAPOLIS', 'IN', '46234', '3175679007', NULL);
```

EMPLOYEE_PAY_TBL

```
INSERT INTO EMPLOYEE_PAY_TBL VALUES
('311549902', 'MARKETING', TO_DATE('1999-05-23','YYYY-MM-
DD'),NULL,TO_DATE('2009-05-01','YYYY-MM-DD'),'40000', NULL);

INSERT INTO EMPLOYEE_PAY_TBL VALUES
('442346889', 'TEAM LEADER', TO_DATE('2000-06-17','YYYY-MM-DD'), '14.75',
TO_DATE('2009-06-01','YYYY-MM-DD'),  NULL, NULL);

INSERT INTO EMPLOYEE_PAY_TBL VALUES
('213764555', 'SALES MANAGER', TO_DATE('2004-08-14','YYYY-MM-DD'),NULL,
TO_DATE('2009-08-01','YYYY-MM-DD'),  '30000', '2000');

INSERT INTO EMPLOYEE_PAY_TBL VALUES
('313782439', 'SALESMAN', TO_DATE('2007-06-28','YYYY-MM-DD'), NULL, NULL,
'20000', '1000');

INSERT INTO EMPLOYEE_PAY_TBL VALUES
('220984332', 'SHIPPER', TO_DATE('2006-07-22','YYYY-MM-DD'),  '11.00',
'2009-07-01', NULL, NULL);

INSERT INTO EMPLOYEE_PAY_TBL VALUES
('443679012', 'SHIPPER', TO_DATE('2001-01-14','YYYY-MM-DD'),  '15.00',
'2009-01-01', NULL, NULL);
```

CUSTOMER_TBL

```
INSERT INTO CUSTOMER_TBL VALUES
('232', 'LESLIE GLEASON', '798 HARDAWAY DR', 'INDIANAPOLIS',
'IN', '47856', '3175457690', NULL);

INSERT INTO CUSTOMER_TBL VALUES
('109', 'NANCY BUNKER', 'APT A 4556 WATERWAY', 'BROAD RIPPLE',
'IN', '47950', '3174262323', NULL);

INSERT INTO CUSTOMER_TBL VALUES
('345', 'ANGELA DOBKO', 'RR3 BOX 76', 'LEBANON', 'IN', '49967',
'7658970090', NULL);

INSERT INTO CUSTOMER_TBL VALUES
('090', 'WENDY WOLF', '3345 GATEWAY DR', 'INDIANAPOLIS', 'IN',
'46224', '3172913421', NULL);
```

```
INSERT INTO CUSTOMER_TBL VALUES
('12', 'MARYS GIFT SHOP', '435 MAIN ST', 'DANVILLE', 'IL', '47978',
'3178567221', '3178523434');

INSERT INTO CUSTOMER_TBL VALUES
('432', 'SCOTTYS MARKET', 'RR2 BOX 173', 'BROWNSBURG', 'IN',
'45687', '3178529835', '3178529836');

INSERT INTO CUSTOMER_TBL VALUES
('333', 'JASONS AND DALLAS GOODIES', 'LAFAYETTE SQ MALL',
'INDIANAPOLIS', 'IN', '46222', '3172978886', '3172978887');

INSERT INTO CUSTOMER_TBL VALUES
('21', 'MORGANS CANDIES AND TREATS', '5657 W TENTH ST',
'INDIANAPOLIS', 'IN', '46234', '3172714398', NULL);

INSERT INTO CUSTOMER_TBL VALUES
('43', 'SCHYLERS NOVELTIES', '17 MAPLE ST', 'LEBANON', 'IN',
'48990', '3174346758', NULL);

INSERT INTO CUSTOMER_TBL VALUES
('287', 'GAVINS PLACE', '9880 ROCKVILLE RD', 'INDIANAPOLIS',
'IN', '46244', '3172719991', '3172719992');

INSERT INTO CUSTOMER_TBL VALUES
('288', 'HOLLYS GAMEARAMA', '567 US 31 SOUTH', 'WHITELAND',
'IN', '49980', '3178879023', NULL);

INSERT INTO CUSTOMER_TBL VALUES
('590', 'HEATHERS FEATHERS AND THINGS', '4090 N SHADELAND AVE',
'INDIANAPOLIS', 'IN', '43278', '3175456768', NULL);

INSERT INTO CUSTOMER_TBL VALUES
('610', 'REGANS HOBBIES INC', '451 GREEN ST', 'PLAINFIELD', 'IN',
'46818', '3178393441', '3178399090');

INSERT INTO CUSTOMER_TBL VALUES
('560', 'ANDYS CANDIES', 'RR 1 BOX 34', 'NASHVILLE', 'IN',
'48756', '8123239871', NULL);

INSERT INTO CUSTOMER_TBL VALUES
('221', 'RYANS STUFF', '2337 S SHELBY ST', 'INDIANAPOLIS', 'IN',
'47834', '3175634402', NULL);
```

ORDERS_TBL

```
INSERT INTO ORDERS_TBL VALUES
('56A901', '232', '11235', '1', TO_DATE('2009-10-22','YYYY-MM-DD'));

INSERT INTO ORDERS_TBL VALUES
('56A917', '12', '907', '100', TO_DATE('2009-09-30','YYYY-MM-DD'));
```

```
INSERT INTO ORDERS_TBL VALUES
('32A132', '43', '222', '25', TO_DATE('2009-10-10','YYYY-MM-DD'));

INSERT INTO ORDERS_TBL VALUES
('16C17', '090', '222', '2', TO_DATE('2009-10-17','YYYY-MM-DD'));

INSERT INTO ORDERS_TBL VALUES
('18D778', '287', '90', '10', TO_DATE('2009-10-17','YYYY-MM-DD'));

INSERT INTO ORDERS_TBL VALUES
('23E934', '432', '13', '20', TO_DATE('2009-10-15','YYYY-MM-DD'));
```

PRODUCTS_TBL

```
INSERT INTO PRODUCTS_TBL VALUES
('11235', 'WITCH COSTUME', '29.99');

INSERT INTO PRODUCTS_TBL VALUES
('222', 'PLASTIC PUMPKIN 18 INCH', '7.75');

INSERT INTO PRODUCTS_TBL VALUES
('13', 'FALSE PARAFFIN TEETH', '1.10');

INSERT INTO PRODUCTS_TBL VALUES
('90', 'LIGHTED LANTERNS', '14.50');

INSERT INTO PRODUCTS_TBL VALUES
('15', 'ASSORTED COSTUMES', '10.00');

INSERT INTO PRODUCTS_TBL VALUES
('9', 'CANDY CORN', '1.35');

INSERT INTO PRODUCTS_TBL VALUES
('6', 'PUMPKIN CANDY', '1.45');

INSERT INTO PRODUCTS_TBL VALUES
('87', 'PLASTIC SPIDERS', '1.05');

INSERT INTO PRODUCTS_TBL VALUES
('119', 'ASSORTED MASKS', '4.95');
```

Glossary

alias   Another name or term for a table or column.

ANSI   American National Standards Institute. This institute is responsible for issuing standards for a variety of topics. This is where the SQL standard is published.

application   A set of menus, forms, reports, and code that performs a business function and typically uses a database.

buffer   An area in memory for editing or execution of SQL.

Cartesian product   The result of not joining tables in the WHERE clause of an SQL statement. When tables in a query are not joined, every row in one table is paired with every row in all other tables.

client   The client is typically a PC, but it can be server that is dependent on another computer for data, services, or processing. A client application enables a client machine to communicate with a server.

column   A part of a table that has a name and a specific data type.

COMMIT   Makes changes to data permanent.

composite index   An index that is composed of two or more columns.

condition   Search criteria in a query's WHERE clause that evaluates to TRUE or FALSE.

constant   A value that does not change.

constraint   Restrictions on data that are enforced at the data level.

cursor   A work area in memory that uses SQL statements to typically perform row-based operations against a set of data.

data dictionary   Another name for the system catalog. *See* system catalog.

data type   Defines data as a type, such as number, date, or character.

database   A collection of data that is typically organized into sets of tables.

DBA   Database administrator. An individual who manages a database.

DDL   Data Definition Language. The part of the SQL syntax that specifically deals with defining database objects such as tables, views, and functions.

default   A value used when no specification has been made.

distinct   Unique; used in the SELECT clause to return unique values.

DML   Data Manipulation Language. The part of the SQL syntax that specifically deals with manipulating data, such as that used in update statements.

domain   An object that is associated with a data type to which constraints may be attached; similar to a user-defined type.

DQL   Data Query Language. The part of the SQL syntax that specifically deals with querying data using the SELECT statement.

end user   Users whose jobs require them to query or manipulate data in the database. The end user is the individual for which the database exists.

field   Another name for a column in a table. *See* column.

foreign key   One or more columns whose values are based on the primary key column values in another table.

full table scan   The search of a table from a query without the use of an index.

function   An operation that is predefined and can be used in an SQL statement to manipulate data.

GUI   Graphical user interface. This is what an application interface is typically referred to when it provides graphical elements for the user to interact with.

host   The computer on which a database is located.

index   Pointers to table data that make access to a table more efficient.

JDBC   Java Database Connectivity. Software that allows a Java program to communicate with a database to process data.

join   Combines data from different tables by linking columns. Used in the WHERE clause of an SQL statement.

key   A column or columns that identify rows of a table.

normalization   Designing a database to reduce redundancy by breaking large tables into smaller, more manageable ones.

NULL value   A value that is unknown.

objects   Elements in a database, such as triggers, tables, views, and procedures.

ODBC   Open Database Connectivity. Software that allows for standard communication with a database. ODBC is typically used for inter-database communication between different implementations and for communication between a client application and a database.

operator A reserved word or symbol that performs an operation, such as addition or subtraction.

optimizer Internal mechanism of the database (consists of rules and code) that decides how to execute an SQL statement and return an answer.

parameter A value or range of values to resolve a part of an SQL statement or program.

primary key A specified table column that uniquely identifies rows of the table.

privilege Specific permissions that are granted to users to perform a specific action in the database.

procedure A set of instructions that are saved for repeated calling and execution.

public A database user account that represents all database users.

query An SQL statement that retrieves data from a database.

record Another name for a row in a table. *See* row.

referential integrity Ensures the existence of every value of a column from a parent that is referenced in another table. This ensures that the data in your database is consistent. Referential integrity is normally used between two tables, but in some tables it can be used so that a table references itself. A self-referenced table is referred to as a *recursive relationship*. In databases, this is often referred to as a foreign key relationship.

relational database A database that is organized into tables that consist of rows, which contain the same sets of data items, where tables in the database are related to one another through common keys.

role A database object that is associated with a group of system or object privileges, used to simplify security management.

ROLLBACK A command that undoes all transactions since the last COMMIT or SAVEPOINT command was issued.

row Sets of records in a table.

savepoint A specified point in a transaction to which you can roll back or undo changes.

schema A set of related objects in a database owned by a single database user.

security The process of ensuring that data in a database is fully protected at all times.

SQL Structured Query Language designed for use with databases and used to manage the data within those systems.

stored procedure SQL code that is stored in a database and ready to execute.

subquery A SELECT statement embedded within another SQL statement.

synonym Another name given to a table or view.

syntax for SQL   A set of rules that shows mandatory and optional parts of an SQL statement's construction.

system catalog   Collection of tables or views that contain information about the database.

table   The basic logical storage unit for data in a relational database.

transaction   One or more SQL statements that are executed as a single unit.

trigger   A stored procedure that executes upon specified events in a database, such as before or after an update of a table.

user-defined type   A data type that is defined by a user, which can be used to define table columns.

variable   A value that does not remain constant.

view   A database object that is created from one or more tables and can be used the same as a table. A view is a virtual table that has no storage requirements of its own.

APPENDIX G

Bonus Exercises

The exercises in this appendix are bonus exercises that are specific to MySQL. We provide an explanation or question and then provide sample MySQL-based SQL code to execute. Remember that the SQL code can vary from implementation to implementation, so some of these statements need to be adjusted depending on what system you are working on. Study the question, code, and results carefully to improve your knowledge of SQL.

1. Create a new database for bonus exercises and name it BONUS.

   ```
   CREATE DATABASE BONUS;
   ```

2. Point MySQL to your new database.

   ```
   USE BONUS;
   ```

3. Create a table to keep track of basketball teams.

   ```
   CREATE TABLE TEAMS
   ( TEAM_ID        INTEGER(2)    NOT NULL,
     NAME           VARCHAR(20)   NOT NULL );
   ```

4. Create a table to keep track of basketball players.

   ```
   CREATE TABLE PLAYERS
   ( PLAYER_ID      INTEGER(2)    NOT NULL,
     LAST           VARCHAR(20)   NOT NULL,
     FIRST          VARCHAR(20)   NOT NULL,
     TEAM_ID        INTEGER(2)    NULL,
     NUMBER         INTEGER(2)    NOT NULL );
   ```

5. Create a table to keep track of players' personal information.

   ```
   CREATE TABLE PLAYER_DATA
   ( PLAYER_ID      INTEGER(2)     NOT NULL,
     HEIGHT         DECIMAL(4,2)   NOT NULL,
     WEIGHT         DECIMAL(5,2)   NOT NULL );
   ```

6. Create a table to keep track of games played.

   ```
   CREATE TABLE GAMES
   ( GAME_ID          INTEGER(2)     NOT NULL,
     GAME_DT          DATETIME       NOT NULL,
   ```

```
    HOME_TEAM_ID       INTEGER(2)     NOT NULL,
    GUEST_TEAM_ID      INTEGER(3)     NOT NULL );
```

7. Create a table to keep track of each team's score for each game.

```
CREATE TABLE SCORES
( GAME_ID      INTEGER(2)     NOT NULL,
  TEAM_ID      INTEGER(2)     NOT NULL,
  SCORE        INTEGER(3)     NOT NULL,
  WIN_LOSE     VARCHAR(4)     NOT NULL );
```

8. View all the tables that you created.

```
SHOW TABLES;
```

9. Create records for the basketball teams.

```
INSERT INTO TEAMS VALUES ('1','STRING MUSIC');
INSERT INTO TEAMS VALUES ('2','HACKERS');
INSERT INTO TEAMS VALUES ('3','SHARP SHOOTERS');
INSERT INTO TEAMS VALUES ('4','HAMMER TIME');
```

10. Create records for the players.

```
INSERT INTO PLAYERS VALUES ('1','SMITH','JOHN','1','12');
INSERT INTO PLAYERS VALUES ('2','BOBBIT','BILLY','1','2');
INSERT INTO PLAYERS VALUES ('3','HURTA','WIL','2','32');
INSERT INTO PLAYERS VALUES ('4','OUCHY','TIM','2','22');
INSERT INTO PLAYERS VALUES ('5','BYRD','ERIC','3','6');
INSERT INTO PLAYERS VALUES ('6','JORDAN','RYAN','3','23');
INSERT INTO PLAYERS VALUES ('7','HAMMER','WALLY','4','21');
INSERT INTO PLAYERS VALUES ('8','HAMMER','RON','4','44');
INSERT INTO PLAYERS VALUES ('11','KNOTGOOD','AL',NULL,'0');
```

11. Create records for the players' personal data.

```
INSERT INTO PLAYER_DATA VALUES ('1','71','180');
INSERT INTO PLAYER_DATA VALUES ('2','58','195');
INSERT INTO PLAYER_DATA VALUES ('3','72','200');
INSERT INTO PLAYER_DATA VALUES ('4','74','170');
INSERT INTO PLAYER_DATA VALUES ('5','71','182');
INSERT INTO PLAYER_DATA VALUES ('6','72','289');
INSERT INTO PLAYER_DATA VALUES ('7','79','250');
INSERT INTO PLAYER_DATA VALUES ('8','73','193');
INSERT INTO PLAYER_DATA VALUES ('11','85','310');
```

12. Create records in the GAMES table based on games that have been scheduled.

```
INSERT INTO GAMES VALUES ('1','2002-05-01','1','2');
INSERT INTO GAMES VALUES ('2','2002-05-02','3','4');
INSERT INTO GAMES VALUES ('3','2002-05-03','1','3');
INSERT INTO GAMES VALUES ('4','2002-05-05','2','4');
INSERT INTO GAMES VALUES ('5','2002-05-05','1','2');
INSERT INTO GAMES VALUES ('6','2002-05-09','3','4');
```

```
INSERT INTO GAMES VALUES ('7','2002-05-10','2','3');
INSERT INTO GAMES VALUES ('8','2002-05-11','1','4');
INSERT INTO GAMES VALUES ('9','2002-05-12','2','3');
INSERT INTO GAMES VALUES ('10','2002-05-15','1','4');
```

13. Create records in the SCORES table based on games that have been played.

```
INSERT INTO SCORES VALUES ('1','1','66','LOSE');
INSERT INTO SCORES VALUES ('2','3','78','WIN');
INSERT INTO SCORES VALUES ('3','1','45','LOSE');
INSERT INTO SCORES VALUES ('4','2','56','LOSE');
INSERT INTO SCORES VALUES ('5','1','100','WIN');
INSERT INTO SCORES VALUES ('6','3','67','LOSE');
INSERT INTO SCORES VALUES ('7','2','57','LOSE');
INSERT INTO SCORES VALUES ('8','1','98','WIN');
INSERT INTO SCORES VALUES ('9','2','56','LOSE');
INSERT INTO SCORES VALUES ('10','1','46','LOSE');

INSERT INTO SCORES VALUES ('1','2','75','WIN');
INSERT INTO SCORES VALUES ('2','4','46','LOSE');
INSERT INTO SCORES VALUES ('3','3','87','WIN');
INSERT INTO SCORES VALUES ('4','4','99','WIN');
INSERT INTO SCORES VALUES ('5','2','88','LOSE');
INSERT INTO SCORES VALUES ('6','4','77','WIN');
INSERT INTO SCORES VALUES ('7','3','87','WIN');
INSERT INTO SCORES VALUES ('8','4','56','LOSE');
INSERT INTO SCORES VALUES ('9','3','87','WIN');
INSERT INTO SCORES VALUES ('10','4','78','WIN')
```

14. Determine the average height of all players.

```
SELECT AVG(HEIGHT) FROM PLAYER_DATA;
```

15. Determine the average weight of all players.

```
SELECT AVG(WEIGHT) FROM PLAYER_DATA;
```

16. Create a list of player information as follows:

```
NAME=LAST NUMBER=N HEIGHT=N WEIGHT=N
SELECT CONCAT('NAME=',P1.LAST,' NUMBER=',P1.NUMBER,'
HEIGHT=',P2.HEIGHT,' WEIGHT=',P2.WEIGHT)
FROM PLAYERS P1,
     PLAYER_DATA P2
WHERE P1.PLAYER_ID = P2.PLAYER_ID;
```

17. Create a team roster that looks like the following:

```
    TEAM NAME        LAST, FIRST    NUMBER
SELECT T.NAME, CONCAT(P.LAST,', ',P.FIRST), P.NUMBER
FROM TEAMS T,
     PLAYERS P
WHERE T.TEAM_ID = P.TEAM_ID;
```

18. Determine which team has scored the most points of all games.

```
SELECT T.NAME, SUM(S.SCORE)
FROM TEAMS T,
     SCORES S
WHERE T.TEAM_ID = S.TEAM_ID
GROUP BY T.NAME
ORDER BY 2 DESC;
```

19. Determine the most points scored in a single game by one team.

```
SELECT MAX(SCORE)
FROM SCORES;
```

20. Determine the most points scored collectively by both teams in a single game.

```
SELECT GAME_ID, SUM(SCORE)
FROM SCORES
GROUP BY GAME_ID
ORDER BY 2 DESC;
```

21. Determine if there are any players who are not assigned to a team.

```
SELECT LAST, FIRST, TEAM_ID
FROM PLAYERS
WHERE TEAM_ID IS NULL;
```

22. Determine the number of teams.

```
SELECT COUNT(*) FROM TEAMS;
```

23. Determine the number of players.

```
SELECT COUNT(*) FROM PLAYERS;
```

24. Determine how many games were played on May 5, 2002.

```
SELECT COUNT(*) FROM GAMES
WHERE GAME_DT = '2002-05-05';
```

25. Determine the tallest player.

```
SELECT P.LAST, P.FIRST, PD.HEIGHT
FROM PLAYERS P,
     PLAYER_DATA PD
WHERE P.PLAYER_ID = PD.PLAYER_ID
ORDER BY 3 DESC;
OR
SELECT MAX(HEIGHT) FROM PLAYER_DATA;
SELECT P.LAST, P.FIRST, PD.HEIGHT
FROM PLAYERS P,
     PLAYER_DATA PD
WHERE HEIGHT = 85;
```

26. Remove Ron Hammer's record from the database, and replace him with Al Knotgood.

```
SELECT PLAYER_ID
FROM PLAYERS
WHERE LAST = 'HAMMER'
  AND FIRST = 'RON';
DELETE FROM PLAYERS WHERE PLAYER_ID = '8';
DELETE FROM PLAYER_DATA WHERE PLAYER_ID = '8';
SELECT PLAYER_ID
FROM PLAYERS
WHERE LAST = 'KNOTGOOD'
  AND FIRST = 'AL';
UPDATE PLAYERS
SET TEAM_ID = '4'
WHERE PLAYER_ID = '11';
```

27. Determine Al Knotgood's new teammate.

```
SELECT TEAMMATE.LAST, TEAMMATE.FIRST
FROM PLAYERS TEAMMATE,
     PLAYERS P
WHERE P.TEAM_ID = TEAMMATE.TEAM_ID
  AND P.LAST = 'KNOTGOOD'
  AND P.FIRST = 'AL';
```

28. Generate a list of all games and game dates. Also, list home and guest teams for each game.

```
SELECT G.GAME_ID, HT.NAME, GT.NAME
FROM GAMES G,
     TEAMS HT,
     TEAMS GT
WHERE HT.TEAM_ID = G.HOME_TEAM_ID
  AND GT.TEAM_ID = G.GUEST_TEAM_ID;
```

29. Create indexes for all names in the database. Names are often indexed because you frequently search by name.

```
CREATE INDEX TEAM_IDX
ON TEAMS (NAME);
CREATE INDEX PLAYERS_IDX
ON PLAYERS (LAST, FIRST);
```

30. Determine which team has the most wins.

```
SELECT T.NAME, COUNT(S.WIN_LOSE)
FROM TEAMS T,
     SCORES S
WHERE T.TEAM_ID = S.TEAM_ID
  AND S.WIN_LOSE = 'WIN'
GROUP BY T.NAME
ORDER BY 2 DESC;
```

31. Determine which team has the most losses.

```
SELECT T.NAME, COUNT(S.WIN_LOSE)
FROM TEAMS T,
     SCORES S
WHERE T.TEAM_ID = S.TEAM_ID
  AND S.WIN_LOSE = 'LOSE'
GROUP BY T.NAME
ORDER BY 2 DESC;
```

32. Determine which team has the highest average score per game.

```
SELECT T.NAME, AVG(S.SCORE)
FROM TEAMS T,
     SCORES S
WHERE T.TEAM_ID = S.TEAM_ID
GROUP BY T.NAME
ORDER BY 2 DESC;
```

33. Generate a report that shows each team's record. Sort the report by teams with the most wins and then by teams with the fewest losses.

```
SELECT T.NAME, SUM(REPLACE(S.WIN_LOSE,'WIN',1)) WINS,
       SUM(REPLACE(S.WIN_LOSE,'LOSE',1)) LOSSES
FROM TEAMS T,
     SCORES S
WHERE T.TEAM_ID = S.TEAM_ID
GROUP BY T.NAME
ORDER BY 2 DESC, 3;
```

34. Determine the final score of each game.

```
SELECT G.GAME_ID,
       HOME_TEAMS.NAME "HOME TEAM", HOME_SCORES.SCORE,
       GUEST_TEAMS.NAME "GUEST TEAM", GUEST_SCORES.SCORE
FROM GAMES G,
     TEAMS HOME_TEAMS,
     TEAMS GUEST_TEAMS,
     SCORES HOME_SCORES,
     SCORES GUEST_SCORES
WHERE G.HOME_TEAM_ID = HOME_TEAMS.TEAM_ID
  AND G.GUEST_TEAM_ID = GUEST_TEAMS.TEAM_ID
  AND HOME_SCORES.GAME_ID = G.GAME_ID
  AND GUEST_SCORES.GAME_ID = G.GAME_ID
  AND HOME_SCORES.TEAM_ID = G.HOME_TEAM_ID
  AND GUEST_SCORES.TEAM_ID = G.GUEST_TEAM_ID
                        ORDER BY G.GAME_ID;
```

Index

Sams Teach Yourself

When you only have time
for the answers™

Whatever your need and whatever your time frame, there's a Sams **Teach Yourself** book for you. With a Sams **Teach Yourself** book as your guide, you can quickly get up to speed on just about any new product or technology—in the absolute shortest period of time possible. Guaranteed.

Learning how to do new things with your computer shouldn't be tedious or time-consuming. Sams **Teach Yourself** makes learning anything quick, easy, and even a little bit fun.

SharePoint Foundation 2010 in 24 Hours

Mike Walsh
ISBN-13: 9780672333163

C++ in 24 Hours, Fifth Edition

Jesse Liberty
Rogers Cadenhead

ISBN-13: 9780672333316

the ADO.NET Entity Framework in 24 Hours

Paul Kimmel

ISBN-13: 9780672330537

iPhone Application Development in 24 Hours, Second Edition

John Ray

ISBN-13: 9780672332203

Windows Workflow Foundation in 24 Hours

Robert Eisenberg

ISBN-13: 9780321486998

FIFTH EDITION
Includes Coverage of
Oracle and
Microsoft SQL
Implementations

Sams Teach Yourself
SQL
in 24 Hours

SAMS

FREE Online Edition

Your purchase of **Sams Teach Yourself SQL in 24 Hours** includes access to a free online edition for 45 days through the Safari Books Online subscription service. Nearly every Sams book is available online through Safari Books Online, along with more than 5,000 other technical books and videos from publishers such as Addison-Wesley Professional, Cisco Press, Exam Cram, IBM Press, O'Reilly, Prentice Hall, and Que.

SAFARI BOOKS ONLINE allows you to search for a specific answer, cut and paste code, download chapters, and stay current with emerging technologies.

Activate your FREE Online Edition at www.informit.com/safarifree

> **STEP 1:** Enter the coupon code: RJJHQVH.

> **STEP 2:** New Safari users, complete the brief registration form.
> Safari subscribers, just log in.

If you have difficulty registering on Safari or accessing the online edition, please e-mail customer-service@safaribooksonline.com

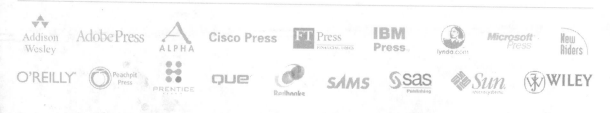